INSIGHTS AND PARALLELS

Problems and Issues of American Social History

EDITED BY

William L. O'Neill

BURGESS PUBLISHING COMPANY • MINNEAPOLIS, MINNESOTA

Printed in the United States of America
Library of Congress Card Number 72-94039
SBN 8087-1510-0

1 2 3 4 5 6 7 8 9 0

Contents

WILLIAM L. O'NEILL

The Study of Social History

ALTHOUGH PEOPLE HAVE BEEN writing what in effect was social history for a long time, it is only recently that it has become thought of as a separate branch of the discipline. There is still no general agreement on what constitutes social history. As a rule, historians tend to define it negatively, that is to say, what is not diplomatic, political, intellectual, cultural, or economic is social. One of the aims of this volume is to reverse the process, to offer specimens of social history and thus define it by example. Six essays, probably even sixty, are too few to show the full range and diversity of American social history. The essays in this book were chosen not because they deal with every important topic but because they concern subjects of great interest today and because their authors are talented scholars dealing either with new fields of inquiry or bringing fresh approaches to old ones.

Though topical these essays do not suggest solutions to current problems. Historians disagree on whether their discipline will ever contribute to decision-making in the way some social sciences do. But most historians are agreed that with the tools available at present we can never be certain our knowledge of the past is good enough to make projections into the future. History is, therefore, not a social science yet. All the same, historians believe, though not always for the same reasons, that the study of history is functional. Some think it useful chiefly as a mental discipline, that by studying history the reasoning powers are improved. Others think it useful for what it tells us about behavior. If one knows a great deal about, say, ancient Romans, then one knows something about human nature that will enable a person to cope better with the living. Most historians feel that social problems cannot be solved without knowing the history behind them. There is no proof of this, but it is deeply believed anyway, especially by social historians who are likely to be more preoccupied with current issues than most of their colleagues are.

These essays all show how historical research can illuminate troublesome social questions. They also demonstrate how persistent these troubles are and how difficult it is to find in the past answers to them. Laymen are fond of saying "history shows," but historians know that history can prove anything depending on who writes it and for what purposes it is written. Many social historians want to find material that will help social reformers today. The more sophisticated realize that honest research often turns up things one does not want to find, but that in the long run they may prove useful too. This is one of the crucial differences between scholarship and ideology. Though scholarship can be used ideologically, it is most successful when done openmindedly. We frequently need to know what we don't want to know. In this book some essays do just that and consequently are likely to be more controversial than others, which is a good reason for reading them. On the other hand, that some of the essays appear less arguable is no reason to slight them. Controversy for its own sake is as foolish as the fear of controversy. Serious historians work in different ways and for different purposes, as this collection hopes to show.

Robert Twombly's essay is an example of what some call "history from the bottom up." By this is meant the effort to show how ordinary people lived and thought. Black history has usually focused on outstanding individuals, partly so as to be uplifting, partly because it is very hard to find much about average people regardless of race. But as Twombly proves, being oppressed and largely illiterate does not keep people from thinking and acting and leaving behind records of their struggle.

Twombly's essay reminds us again how deeply rooted in the past our racial difficulties are, and how durable certain responses have proved to be. Slavery was maintained with the help of stereotypes that would last long after the peculiar institution itself was destroyed. Colonials saw blacks as childlike, ignorant, dependent, irresponsible, and these images would go on blinding Americans to injustice for centuries. Slavery produced violence, as racism and deprivation do now. But the violence committed by slaves was not seen as a consequence of the wrongs done them, only as a function of character. Colonial Americans thought to regulate the behavior slavery caused without dealing with slavery itself. By the same token many today think that police tactics are the best answer to racial problems, even though our ancient experience suggests otherwise.

Twombly shows too that the ingenuity and persistence with which blacks today address their problems are not unique to our time. Colonial blacks, despite overwhelming obstacles, managed to protest their servitude, petition for redress of grievances, and turn the ideology of white men (during the Revolutionary War as now during the Cold War) to their own purposes. And colonial blacks went to court also. Twombly tells us that eighty-two years of court action lay behind emancipation in Massachusetts, an astonishing record that one hopes will not have to be matched in this century. Other parallels will occur to the reader, all showing that while to be a slave was different from being a free black today, it was not all that much different. This essay constitutes, then, one yardstick by which change, or the lack of it, can be measured.

Though Darrett Rutman deals with colonial America too, he approaches it in quite a different way. Rutman employs some of the new methodological techniques now being used in social history. He is one of those who hope to make it much more of a behavioral science than it commonly is. To this end tools and concepts borrowed from sociology, demography, statistics, and other fields are utilized to help answer historical questions. This procedure makes the methods used as interesting (sometimes more interesting) as the results obtained. The facts Rutman discovers are not particularly startling on the whole. It has long been thought that New England towns were more stable and cohesive at first than they later became. What is striking is the theoretical context in which these communities are viewed, the emphasis on vertical and horizontal dimensions, for example. If this way of looking at early communities is valid it obviously has many other applications as well.

Fresh approaches to the study of community are especially welcome because it is one of the most elusive issues in recent American history. Ever since the rise of the city, that is to say since the 1870s or '80s, intellectuals have mourned the decline of communal ties. Reformers have tried to preserve them, radicals have wanted to create new ones. But though the literature on this subject is enormous there is little agreement on what exactly has been lost, still less on what is to be gained, or regained. Small, self-contained villages no longer exist, of course. But it is hardly clear that they represent the best or only kind of community. The entire subject cries out for more sophisticated analysis of the type undertaken here.

Barbara Welter's essay shows that historians not only respond to social problems, they sometimes even anticipate them. She began her study of the woman question well before it was of general interest, and so brings a depth of experience to the history of women that is enjoyed by few others. And she is not afraid to advance a thesis which some will reject for ideological reasons. Although, as Welter points out, the feminization of religion was advantageous to women in many respects, she shows women functioning in stereotyped ways. This will not go down well with some extreme feminists who feel that historians should never depict women except as victims or victors. They think it fine to show how women were oppressed, even better to describe how women overcame adversity, but wrong ever to admit that women did in fact often conform to role models that modern feminists reject. Yet it is just this kind of phenomenon that we most need to examine because it is important to the history of women, and even more perhaps to the general history of American civilization.

One of the most fascinating transformations in our history is the process by which cultural tastes and attributes became sex-linked. In the eighteenth century religion, art, culture, decoration, design and the like were all thought appropriate interests for men. Colonial gentlemen not only designed their homes, but chose the furnishings as well. An intense interest in dress was commonplace. In the nineteenth century things began to change. Art, literature, music, dress, religion, and other cultural modes became largely the province of women, usually as consumers or followers rather than as producers or leaders. This had many consequences. Welter shows it meant that religion became more genteel, and so did culture generally.

Such changes were desirable when they softened harsh doctrines, as in religion, but less so when applied to art where the sentimental and conservative were most favored. Women's status was raised, in one sense, when they came to embody all that was fine and moral. But this also meant that the lower attributes became exclusively masculine. Women could hardly associate with men, tainted as they were by materialism, aggression, and other vices. Relations between the sexes became more strained and distant. Women were thrown more into each other's company. This in turn led to the sororital associations that would become useful later in the struggle for women's rights. By the same token, the division of life into male and female meant, in theory at least, that women were denied access to the world of men, that is to say business, the professions, scholarship, everything that Victorians thought important. Because to feminize an area of life was in effect to trivialize it, the feminization of religion and culture was a decidedly mixed blessing.

David Grimsted also deals with a crucial American institution. Riot is, as H. Rap Brown has reminded us, as American as apple pie. Jacksonian riots, Grimsted makes clear, had features that were unique to the time. Yet they clearly had things in common with the great riots of the 1960s that haunt us still. Like them the Baltimore riot stemmed from injustice. The rioters themselves were young but hardly indigent. Similarly, a study of the 1965 riot in Watts, for example, showed that a large proportion of rioters had incomes well above the poverty level. Because aimed at powerful figures or institutions both riots failed.

Such parallels cannot be pushed too far. Grimsted notes that there are many kinds of riots and historians can help explain them because historians, more than other scholars and social scientists, are especially alive to the discrete and particular. Some historians, it is true, still believe that narration explains all. Others are increasingly eager to make history yield up broad theories and generalizations. Grimsted demonstrates that it is possible, in a sense, to do both, to describe an event and at the same time to connect it with the appropriate theories. This is a valuable work that historians are uncommonly well suited to undertake.

Unlike some of our contributors who sail relatively uncharted seas, Paul Buhle is concerned with a familiar subject, which makes his achievement all the more impressive. The history of American socialism has attracted good scholars for years. In consequence the most important archives have been worked over, major positions staked out, and strong arguments put forward. It is hard under these circumstances to come up with something genuinely new. Yet Buhle has managed to do so. Despite the solid work done earlier, the connection between socialism and immigration has never been handled in an entirely satisfactory manner. This constituted an important defect because the relation was crucial to the failure of socialism in America. We take this failure for granted, as if America was destined from the start to be capitalist. But in fact America is the only major industrial country where socialism never became a powerful force. The socialist parties in the North and West of Europe either became majority parties, or compelled the dominant parties to accept socialist measures in order to retain power. That this did not happen in America, therefore, is a matter of surpassing interest.

American historians, most of whom are not radical, generally take the failure of socialism to be a point in this country's favor. It is often explained as a consequence of the pragmatic, unideological American character. Surely, though, the want of a socialist movement is an important reason why the United States, though first among advanced industrial countries in per capita income, is among the last when it comes to providing social services. And surely one need not fall back on something as elusive as national character when there are concrete social factors ready at hand. Chief among these has to be immigration. Not only was America the only great industrial country where socialism failed utterly, it was the only one to have such an extraordinary mixture of racial and ethnic groups. And it was the only great country to experience a torrential in-migration of aliens at the very moment when socialism was struggling to take root.

The value of Buhle's essay is that it seizes upon these facts and explores them with subtlety and precision. He demonstrates that immigration, together with certain historical events in America and abroad, presented socialists with an insoluble dilemma. They failed not just because, as other historians have argued, they made mistakes, but because there was no way they could have overcome the towering obstacles with which destiny confronted them. In this respect socialists were in an entirely different situation than, say, trade union leaders, who also had some of the same problems. Trade union leaders could afford to wait. They had enough institutional strength to survive many defeats. Time was on their side because the more immigrants became Americanized the more compatible they became with existing trade unionists. Unions did not challenge capitalism's legitimacy, only its failure to properly reward labor. This was a fault that could be remedied without disturbing the system.

But socialists required a deeper commitment that brought few if any immediate benefits. And, as Buhle points out, Americanization worked against them. Buhle does not mean to imply that radicalism is therefore a hopeless undertaking in America, and one should not draw that conclusion for him. But he does show how extraordinarily difficult it is for radicals to function in a country like ours, and how much they are at the mercy of forces and events over which they have no control. This is not meant to invite despair, but is a sobering thought all the same.

Buhle leads us directly to Bertram Wyatt-Brown's essay, which deals with two other kinds of American radicals who also entertained great hopes that were to be dashed by history. Both these essays indicate that the pace of change seems to accelerate as we near the present. Abolition was a visible and important force in American life for perhaps thirty years, socialism for at least twenty. But the New Left was consequential for scarcely more than five years. Most Americans had never heard of it before 1965. By 1970 it was finished. The rate at which history destroys radical movements in modern times is almost terrifying. In the past radical movements grew slowly and even if not ultimately successful left valuable legacies. The men and women schooled in abolition built impressive records in politics and literature. Some became important office holders, others lifelong reformers, feminists, journalists and the like.

The Socialist party was a school also; in fact, a common complaint of organizers was that individual members, their grasp of affairs having been enhanced by party work, became so successful in business and the professions that they lost interest in the party. This was particularly true of Jews. Socialism was partly responsible for the extraordinary rise of New York's Jewry from obscure poverty to significance in little more than a generation. In 1892 three-quarters of the Jews in New York lived on the lower East side, the most congested residential district in the world. By 1916 only 23 per cent remained there. Socialism was not the only reason for this feat, but the party was stronger on the lower East side than in any urban area in the country except Milwaukee. Countless memoirs attest to the party's role as a vital awakening influence. Facts like these account for the argument that in America radical movements succeed through failure. They do not achieve their formal objectives. But they generate ideas and programs that others take up eventually, and they are formative agencies that elevate and extend the consciousness of members, making them more effective members of society. It is too early to know what the subsequent experience of New Leftists will be. Still, the movement was so short-lived, and had such destructive effects on so many that it is hard to be optimistic.

Why is it that abolitionists and socialists were so much more persistent, able to survive repeated defeats and frustrations, not just for years but for decades? Was it because they lived in slower times and so did not expect instant gratification? Or was it because of their early training with its emphasis on discipline, self-denial, and purposeful work? Perhaps no generation born into a society like ours where happiness is regarded not as something to be pursued but as a constant state of being can show the strength abolitionists and socialists displayed. This is not to indict New Leftists personally for lacking character. In fact many showed impressive qualities of mind and spirit. But a culture dominated by the mass media, hence geared to sensation and instantly exploitable events, and directed at an audience whose appetite for novelty can never be appeased, must find it difficult to produce in quantity the heroic virtues great social undertakings require.

Unlike earlier Americans we live in a soft culture, that is to say a more tolerant, flexible, and permissive one – Spiro Agnew and other proponents of Victorian morality notwithstanding. Hence we enjoy many advantages. Few of us would wish to exchange the material comforts and social freedoms of our time for the rigors of early American society. But all gains have their price. The price Americans have paid as a people involves the loss of a certain moral firmness. High-principled Americans in time past, being made of iron so to speak, might break but did not easily bend. We bend freely, but like paper we crumple easily too. This may be a poor metaphor, but such thoughts come to mind when faced with intriguing comparisons of the sort Wyatt-Brown makes, and even when they fail the exercise is always worthwhile. For historians as a group the problem is too little rather than too much intellectual daring. By training and profession we can hardly escape being conservative. That is why we need periodically to break our own rules, to speculate on "what if," for example, or, as here, to analyze and compare movements widely separated in time. To do so freshens the mind, and even when not directly responsible for new ideas helps keep the intellect supple and alive.

All these essays do not illustrate facets of "the new social history," because when we use that term historians usually refer to studies employing demographic and quantitative data. Rutman is the only scholar represented here who is a new social historian in that sense. But all the contributors, however orthodox their methods, are working with new subjects, materials, or ideas. Black history is a relatively new area of inquiry, the history of anonymous people newer still, and practically no one before Twombly has written on the free blacks of colonial Massachusetts. Women's history also has not been studied by professional historians until very recently, and no one else has examined the connection between women's changing roles and the churches as Welter does here. Rutman's handling of community theory and early American communities is unique. Grimsted's inventive application of sociological theory to a specific riot is original too. Buhle has taken standard materials relating to the Socialist party and constructed a novel and persuasive argument out of them. Wyatt-Brown placed much-studied abolitionists alongside nearly unexamined (by historians) New Leftists and, with some help from the social sciences, has written an inventive essay.

What unites these contributions, then, is not the skill that went into making them, though they are all fine examples of the historian's craft, but the original, imaginative thinking that informs them. And, as noted, they all deal with matters of urgent concern to us now. History may never become, as some historians would like it to be, a policy-making discipline like economics or political science. But these essays show it can enrich our thinking and deepen our perspectives just the same. Readers will not find in these articles and documents answers to the problems that vex us most now. But they may find that history can sharpen minds, give them keener edges for the work that lies ahead if America is to resolve its most pressing difficulties. How can anything more be asked of an academic discipline that, in the nature of things, must always rely on incomplete data and elusive concepts?

The curse of our profession is that we can never know anything about history, except the obvious, for certain. Our pride is that we keep on trying. It is in that spirit that we ask the reader to join with us, to the extent his or her interest and ability permits, in one of the most intellectually stimulating and rewarding enterprises available to mankind – the study of history.

ROBERT C. TWOMBLY

Black Resistance to Slavery in Massachusetts

EIGHTEENTH CENTURY OBSERVERS, nineteenth century antiquarians, and twentieth century historians have agreed that slavery in Massachusetts was not as brutal and dehumanizing as in other places. "It was exempt from many of the evils . . . connected with it in the Southern States," a Lexington chronicler wrote in 1868, noting that blacks lived much like other servants, held many religious prerogatives, were allowed to own property, and had access to the courts where they were granted freedom whenever they sued for it. "The mildness with which they were treated," declared the abolitionist historian Emory Washburn, "gave little occasion for dissatisfaction or discontent. . . ." Most citizens of the Bay State, proud of their early prohibition of the institution and their zealous opposition to the Slavocracy, would have agreed with the aristocratic German visitor to Springfield in 1777 who found "the slavery . . . very bearable." If you were free, Cotton Mather assured a group of bondsmen in 1721, "many of you would not *Live* near so well as you do. . . . Your *Servitude* is *Gentle.*"[1]

[1] Charles Hudson, *History of the Town of Lexington* (Boston, 1868), 441; Emory Washburn, *Historical Sketches of the Town of Leicester, Massachusetts, during the First Century from its Settlement* (Boston, 1860), 49; Letter from Baroness Riedesel, 1777, quoted in John H. Lockwood, *Westfield and its Historic Influences* (privately published, 1922), 571-72; Cotton Mather, *Tremanda* (Boston, 1721).

I

The burden of slavery was lightest, of course, on those who were free; people held as chattel had entirely different views of the matter. In 1777, the very year Baroness Riedesel found conditions of bondage so cordial, a group of black petitioners from Boston informed the House of Representatives that "a Life of Slavery, . . . deprived of . . . every thing requisite to render Life even tolerable, is far worse than Non-Existence." (Document 18) The assertion that Massachusetts servitude was comparatively mild may be entirely correct, but it has led historians to dismiss the violence and tension beneath the seemingly placid facade of the peculiar institution in the North. The simple fact is that slaves preferred freedom. In Massachusetts they waged a continuous campaign against their oppression, sometimes in ways acceptable to whites but more often by means considered reprehensible. They also fashioned social and psychological bulwarks against bondage – margins of space for living, as Stanley Elkins has put it – when physical escape was impossible.

Slaves in Massachusetts found few white allies. To be sure, Cotton Mather agonized over black men's souls, Judge Samuel Sewall publicly condemned the institution more than once after 1700, and the Nantucket Quakers declared life servitude "inconsistent with truth" in 1717.[2] But the publisher of the *Boston News-Letter* reflected popular opinion more accurately in 1718 when he took obvious delight in printing a gory description of a black's castration "as a caveat for all Negroes meddling with any White Woman, least they fare with the like Treatment." (Document 1) There was an increase in antislavery activity during the Revolutionary era. But the conventional wisdom was revealed more precisely at the 1773 Harvard commencement forensic debate in which the average black was defined as "a conglomerate of child, idiot, and madman," and in the agreement between Patriot leaders James Warren and John Adams in 1777 to oppose an abolition bill before the Massachusetts House lest it antagonize their Southern allies. Historian George Moore contended correctly in 1866 that "if there was a prevailing public sentiment against slavery in Massachusetts – as has been con-

[2] Obed Macy, *The History of Nantucket: Being a Compendious Account of the First Settlement of the Island by the English, together with the Rise and Progress of the Whale Fishery; and other Historical Facts Relative to said Island and its Inhabitants* (Boston, 1835), 277, 281.

stantly claimed of late – the people of that day, far less demonstrative than their descendants, had an extraordinary way of not showing it."[3]

Massachusetts was never economically dependent upon slavery, but its blacks were numerous enough to attract attention. A French visitor in 1687 was undoubtedly misinformed when he wrote "there is not a House in Boston, however small may be its Means, that has not one or two," but he quite accurately reflected Puritan anxiety over the black presence, the extent of which was frequently exaggerated. Slaves were actually owned, of course, by the most affluent whites – by "the best men in my vicinity," in John Adams's words – the merchants, government officials, Atlantic traders, ministers, and landholders that made up the social and economic elite.[4] Although their numbers in Boston declined at a faster rate than the city's overall population – from 1,374 in 1742 to 848 in 1765 – blacks in the entire colony increased rapidly, from about 2,000 in 1700 to 5,298 in 1765 before leveling off during the Revolution, and they were never less than 1.2 or more than 2.2 per cent of the whole. Like whites they were concentrated in the eastern counties – Suffolk, Middlesex, Essex, Plymouth, Bristol, and Worcester – and outside Boston were most numerous in Salem, Ipswich, Marblehead, Gloucester, and Scituate, each of which had more than a hundred in 1765. Although most blacks were slaves, there were sixty to seventy freemen in Boston as early as 1719, and although most slaves were domestic servants, many men were skilled craftsmen or apprentices in the towns, or worked the fields in rural areas. Blacks were so much a part of life in eastern Massachusetts that after 1704, when the first American newspaper began publication in Boston, hardly an issue failed to mention them.[5]

[3]The 1773 Harvard commencement debate is quoted in Lorenzo J. Greene, *The Negro in Colonial New England* (New York, 1942), 285; John Warren to John Adams, June 22, 1777, and Adams's reply, July 7, 1777, in *Warren-Adams Letters*, I, *Collections of the Massachusetts Historical Society (CMHS)*, 72 (1917), 335; George H. Moore, *Notes on the History of Slavery in Massachusetts* (New York, 1866), 111.

[4]The 1687 visitor was quoted by Nathaniel B. Shurtleff, *A Topographical and Historical Description of Boston* (Boston, 1872), 48; John Adams to Robert J. Evans, June 8, 1819, in Charles F. Adams (ed.), *The Works of John Adams* (Boston, 1856), X, 380.

[5]Population figures are taken from: a 1742 Boston census, *Records of Boston Selectmen, 1736 to 1742* (Boston, 1886), 369; a 1754-55 Massachusetts slave census, *CMHS*, 2nd Ser., III (1844), 95-97; a 1764-65 Massachusetts census, *Columbian Centinel* (Boston), Aug. 17, 1822; and a list of "free people of color" in Boston in 1719, *Proceedings of the American Antiquarian Society*, 44 (Oct. 1934), 257-60.

So it is primarily to the public press that scholars must turn for information on resistance to slavery in early Massachusetts. But they must do so with caution, for newspaper publishers held the same attitudes toward blacks as other citizens – paternalistic at best, hostile at worst. Blacks were usually mentioned in one of five ways: as merchandise for sale, runaways, criminals, rebels in other colonies, and as principals in bizarre episodes. In an age when widespread belief in the supernatural encouraged secular superstition, the fascination of strange events titillated the popular imagination. Publishers included story after story of blacks who fell into wells or through the ice and drowned, vomited up hundred-foot worms, rolled into fires and burned up, or collapsed suddenly in the streets and died. (Document 2) This was standard newspaper fare, and similar incidents involving whites were reported for entertainment and edification, but proportionately not as often. Readers probably retained the impression that blacks were particularly unreliable creatures, careless and somehow more susceptible to the dark and inexplicable forces lurking all around. They were never described as rational mature adults, but as objects of fate, as antisocial deviants, as children to be protected or chastised, and as commodities. Colonial newspapers bear a considerable responsibility for creating and perpetuating racial stereotypes, forcing the student of black history to peel through layers of ignorance, incorrect assumption, and willful distortion to determine for himself the actual significance of proffered information.

II

A case in point is violence, which whites consistently interpreted as carelessness, the errant ways of childlike creatures, or the Devil's work. They never understood – or refused to admit – that physical violence was often retaliation for enslavement, prompted by hatred as well as by the weakness of the flesh. The amount of slave violence against whites is astonishing; it was frequent, always possible, and therefore very much a part of life in colonial Massachusetts, a fact underscored by innumerable newspaper accounts and legislative enactments. Even a comparatively rare form of retaliation, like poisoning, met with uncompromising severity, indicating the profound seriousness with which it was contemplated. Two blacks who planned to kill an entire family in 1735 by putting arsenic in the chocolate were sentenced to sit upon the gallows for an hour with a rope around their necks and to be whipped thirty-nine lashes each. A "Negro wench" who slipped ratsbane into milk for her owner's children was executed in 1751. And in 1755, after poisoning Captain John Codman of Charlestown, Mark was hung and Phillis was burned at the stake, "attended by the greatest Number of Spectators ever known on such an Occasion."[6] At a time when medical knowledge was primitive and when death by strange or unknown causes was an everyday occurrence, many other cases undoubtedly went undetected, but Phillis's fate suggests this form of resistance was especially feared and not unfamiliar.

The arsonist's objective was usually the destruction of property rather than the death of persons. In a celebrated case from 1681, however, in which Black Maria and her associates inadvertently killed a small child when they set fire to two Roxbury houses, her punishment was death by burning at the stake. The severity of the sentence can be attributed to the death, and to public hysteria over a rash of conflagrations set by servants of several races in and around Boston.[7] At least one black was executed during another wave of arson in 1723 which prompted Lieutenant Governor William Dummer to issue a proclamation placing severe penalties on the "villanous and desperate *Negroes*, or other dissolute People" who had "entered into a wicked and horrid Combination to burn and destroy the said Town [of Boston]." Reacting to the public outcry, the Selectmen approved a group of ordinances circumscribing black activity, including carefully regulated movements, a prohibition on gatherings, an evening curfew, and strict instructions to remain indoors during all blazes. (Document 3) But no sooner were several blacks punished under the new provisions than "fires were kindled about Town every day or night," as Benjamin Colman reported to a friend; "the cry of fire terrified us" until the slaves responsible for igniting more than twenty were apprehended, "and so we sleep in peace again. . . ."[8] But not without periodic nightmares: in 1731 a black man was executed

[6] *The Boston Evening-Post*, Sep. 1, 1735; Jan. 21, March 4, April 29, May 20, 1751; Aug. 18, 25, Sep. 22, 1755; *The Boston Weekly News-Letter*, Jan. 17, April 11, 1751; Aug. 21, Sep. 25, 1755.

[7] John Noble, "The Case of Maria in the Court of Assistants in 1681," *Publications of the Colonial Society of Massachusetts*, VI (Jan. 1900), 323-35.

[8] On the 1723 arson outbreak see *The Boston News-Letter*, March 28, April 11, July 4; *The New-England Courant* (Boston), *passim*, April and May, and June 10; and Benjamin Colman to R.H. Wodrow, June 11, 1723 in Niel Caplan (ed.), "Some Unpublished Letters of Benjamin Colman, 1717-1725," *Proceedings of the Massachusetts Historical Society* (PMHS), LXXVII (1965), 131.

for burning down a house on Sunday, and in 1734 another escaped after touching off the jail in which he was languishing. A shop assistant blew up his master's house in 1739 with thirty pounds of gunpowder, and ten years later "a young Negro girl" confessed to destroying three Charlestown barns full of hay. Other accounts of slave arson appeared in the press from time to time, including the 1773 case of a young man who burned a barn, ten horses, a yoke of oxen, twelve tons of hay, and a load of oats because, he said, he was tired of working.[9]

Although assault and murder were common, whites never interpreted them as forms of slave rebellion. But early in their history they did take precautionary measures. "If any negro or mulatto shall smite or strike any English or other Christian person," read a 1705 law, "such negro or mulatto shall be severely whipped at the discretion of the justices." The legislation was timely but ineffectual. Murder and assault fill the pages of the colonial records, beginning at least as early as 1676 when Basto Negro was executed for raping the daughter of Robert Cox, his owner. Shortly thereafter Nicholas from Charlestown stabbed his master after threatening him with a loaded pistol, and John Negro pulled Sarah Phillips of Salem from her horse and attempted "to ravish her." Robert Trayes, a black man from Scituate, shot and killed a white fellow townsman in 1684, and five years later the slave Robin gave John Cheeny of Cambridge "a mortall wound on the head with a stick."[10] In 1745 a Mendon black murdered his mistress with a hatchet, in 1746 a Boston slave was prevented from killing the entire family he lived with only after a protracted struggle with two constables, in 1762 William Clapham's trusted servant planted a tomahawk in his back during a trading expedition to Detroit, and in 1766 the black man Titus beat Ebenezer Downing to death with the butt handle of a whip. In 1747 "a young Molatto Fellow" brandished his gun about the streets before firing at a woman and her daughter standing in a second-story window, and

[9] *The Boston Weekly News-Letter*, Jan. 28, 1731; Aug. 15, 1734; Sep. 6, 1739; Aug. 10, 1749; *The Massachusetts Spy* (Boston), Feb. 25, 1773.

[10] John Noble and John F. Cronin (eds.), *Records of the Court of Assistants of the Colony of the Massachusetts Bay* (Boston, 1901-1928), I, 74, 304-305; Nathaniel B. Shurtleff (ed.), *Records of the Governor and Company of the Massachusetts Bay in New England* (Boston, 1854), V, 117-18; Samuel Eliot Morison (ed.), *Records of the Suffolk County Court, 1671-1680* (2 vols.) in *Publications of the Colonial Society of Massachusetts*, XXIX-XXX (Boston, 1933), II, 884, 1067; Nathaniel B. Shurtleff (ed.), *Records of the Colony of New Plymouth in New England* (Boston, 1855-61), VI, 141-42.

in 1752 four youths including one black were branded on the hand for accidently killing one of the several seamen they had mugged. The newspapers exacerbated fear of violence by reporting additional instances from other colonies, such as the hanging of "two tory Negroes" in New York in 1775 for "engaging to murder their masters who were supporters of liberty [!]"[11]

White observers occasionally remarked that slave violence proved the undesirability of the institution. In 1763, for example, the publisher of the *Boston Evening-Post*, commenting on a Taunton slave who had gouged out his mistress's eye with a hot iron before knocking her down the cellar stairs and axing her to death, noted "the bad Effects of Negroes too freely consorting together." (Document 4) Three years later a writer in the *Boston Gazette*, reflecting on the black who had struck his owner with a hatchet and on another two who had beaten a man after robbing him, was more explicit when he proclaimed sarcastically: "These are the *blessed* Effects of bringing Negro Slaves into the Country! – Scarce one in a hundred proves good for any Thing, and yet the Guinea Trade is continued in Spight of Reason and Humanity." (Document 5) But as these comments indicate, criticism of the institution did not imply sympathy for the slaves, and certainly not endorsement of their attempts to avenge the theft of their persons. Whites usually ignored the cause of violence, or attributed it to something other than the urge for freedom and retribution. "What induced the Fellow to perpetuate this Crime is not known," said the *Massachusetts Gazette* in 1763 of the Taunton eye-gouger, "as he was always treated well, and there had been no Difference with him in the Family." (Document 4) Black offenders were described as "being in an ill Frame," having "a mischievous Disposition," "haueing not the feare of God before youer eyes," or "being instigated by the deuiel." The refusal to confront violence candidly helped perpetuate the notions that blacks were innately untrustworthy, immoral, sinful, and vicious, that they acted irrationally – by Puritan standards a terrible character defect, as Perry Miller has shown – and that they were incapable of tender emotions. Even accounts of organized uprisings aboard slave ships or in other colonies added to misconcep-

[11] *The Boston Weekly News-Letter*, Sep. 20, 1745; March 26, 1747; Nov. 18, 1762; *The Boston Gazette*, Nov. 22, 1762; *The Boston Evening-Post*, Jan. 20, 1746; Nov. 20, 1752; Nov. 15, 1762; *The Massachusetts Gazette* (Boston), Dec. 11, 1766; Sep. 10, 1767; *The New England Chronicle* (Salem), June 1, 1775.

tions by invariably depicting white slaveowners as the innocents and black rebels as murderers and cutthroats. (Document 6)

Had Massachusetts prohibited slavery it might have reduced racial violence, but it chose instead to legislate good behavior. Since black criminality was commonly blamed on "being in Liquor," a 1686 law preventing the purchase and consumption of alcoholic beverages was among the first of many directed toward slaves and other members of the servant class. Repetitious statutes and redundant requests to enforce sobriety dot the record books of the eighteenth century, but to no avail. Recognizing that Saturday night would remain wet despite their efforts, the Boston Selectmen encouraged blacks to dry out in church: in 1732, 1736, 1738, 1741, 1742, and almost as regularly thereafter, they instructed the constables to patrol the main-traveled Boston-Roxbury road on Sunday mornings to inquire of all passersby, especially "Loose vain Persons negroes &c," why they were absent from public worship. The House of Representatives tried to obliterate swearing among slaves (and sailors!) in 1746, and in 1753 and 1756 prohibited anyone – especially "negro servants" – from starting bonfires within ten rods of a building, linking this with a sunset to sunrise ban on pageant shows at which blacks had been known to cause disturbances.[12]

Massachusetts and its towns passed many other laws designed to curb undesirable servant activity. The 1703 "Act to Prevent Disorders in the Night" with its nine o'clock curfew was the first of many aimed at preventing groups of blacks from forming after dark. Slaves were constantly warned against carrying sticks or canes in the street, day or night. At one sitting during the 1723 arson outbreak Boston created a virtually complete code for free and bound Indians, mulattoes, and blacks. (Document 3) Freemen were prohibited from entertaining slaves without masters' permission, from keeping firearms, from selling food and strong drink to the militia (in which they could not serve), from dealing in stolen merchandise, and were required to apprentice all their children between the ages of four and twenty-one to "Some English master." Slaves were subjected to a curfew, prohibited from carrying any sort of weapon, from forming groups of more than two, remaining at the militia grounds after sunset, striking "any of

[12] *Dudley Records* in *PMHS*, 2nd Ser., XIII (1899, 1900), 252, June 18, 1686; *Records of Boston Selectmen, 1716-1736* (Boston, 1885), 223; *1736-1742* (Boston, 1886), 2, 128, 302, 355; *Acts and Resolves of the Province of the Massachusetts Bay*, III, 318-19, 648, 997-98.

his Majesties Subjects," drinking liquor, and being around fires, and were denied other rights and freedoms. Despite the many statutes, resolutions, and penalties, slaves continued to roam the streets at night, cause disturbances, kill whites, set fires, drink, swear, and gather together illegally. The Puritan attempt to insure their own safety by legislating black morality and behavior was decidedly a failure.

Although organized insurrections never materialized in colonial Massachusetts, white fears persisted, prompted by uprisings elsewhere and rumors and conspiracies at home. As early as 1690, a New Jerseyite abolitionist named Isaac Morrill was tried at Ipswich for enticing blacks in the Newbury area to go with him to Canada, there to join with 500 Indians and 300 French for an eventual attack on Haverhill and Amesbury, freeing slaves in the process. Although the scheme did not come off, at least one Massachusetts black was implicated.[13] The flurry of arson in 1723 anticipated the attempt in 1741 by Kate and a male accomplice – who "looked upon every white man as his declared enemy" – to burn down Charlestown, "a malicious and evil intent" that failed except for the firing of one house. During disturbances in November 1747 most people were not as anxious as the House of Representatives, which condemned the "tumultuous riotous assembling of armed Seamen, Servants, Negroes, and others in the Town of *Boston*, tending to the Destruction of all Government and Order." Although the unrest apparently reflected class rather than racial dissatisfaction with wages and prices, black participation was itself a form of protest. Fears were aroused in 1768 when John Wilson, Captain of His Majesty's 59th Regiment, was arrested for allegedly promising slaves their freedom if they would rise up and "cut their masters' throats." The Cambridge constables were ordered to be especially watchful but nothing developed and Wilson, whose indictment was dropped, soon left the colony.[14]

Fear of insurrection seemed to increase during the Revolutionary era, one reason, perhaps, why most Patriots and Tories were antipathetic to abolition. Abigail Adams wrote her husband in September 1774 that "there has been in town a conspiracy of the

[13] Joshua Coffin, *A Sketch of the History of Newbury, Newburyport, and West Newbury* (Boston, 1845), 154; Sidney Perley, "Essex County in the Abolition of Slavery," *Essex-County Historical and Genealogical Register*, I (Jan. 1894), 2.

[14] *The Boston Gazette*, Sep. 28, Oct. 5, 1741; Nov. 7, 1768; *Journals of the House of Representatives of Massachusetts, 1747-1748* (Boston, 1949), 212; *Boston Town Records, 1742 to 1757* (Boston, 1885), 127; *Selectmen's Minutes From 1764 Through 1768* (Boston, 1889), 314.

negroes," adding she did not know what action would be taken since details had been kept secret, so secret, in fact, that corroborating evidence remains undiscovered. Early in 1775, Thomas Nichols, a Natick mulatto, was arrested for "enticing divers Servants . . . to form an unlawful Combination against their Masters," and in neighboring Framingham it was rumored during the Battle of Lexington that blacks were preparing a massacre while the Minutemen were otherwise engaged. But neither uprising took place. In fact, with the exception of the outbreaks of arson in 1681, 1723, and 1741 which may not qualify since only a handful of unarmed blacks were arrested in each case, Massachusetts was free of slave revolts. Nevertheless, whites slept in fear, interpreting individual acts of violence as advance agents of the holocaust. "The Ministerial Tools in London, are regretting, that 20,000 Swiss were not sent over," the Worcester *Massachusetts Spy* declared in August 1775, "to cut the throats of the Americans, in conjunction with the Negroes, who were to be emancipated to slaughter their masters."[15] The Bay Colony was spared black rebels like those in the southern colonies, the West Indies, and aboard slave ships, but their exploits appeared regularly in the press, much to the fear, fascination, and anger of its readers.

An additional manifestation of slave violence, less frightening to whites but highly annoying since it meant economic loss, was suicide. In 1740 the slave of a Boston baker gave himself several cuts in the throat with a penknife but died from additional self-inflicted stab wounds in the belly, after lingering several hours. Asked why he did it he replied that he had grown old and useless and, believing his spirit would return to Africa, said he "had a Mind to go to his own Country again." An unmarried but devoted couple killed themselves in 1746 after learning that the woman was about to be sold away from Boston. (Document 7) Almost ten years later in the Maine province a black man, resenting especially strict punishment, murdered his owner's son. Asked to explain he said he wanted to avoid further "hard usage," but thinking suicide more unlawful and irreligious than murder, decided on the latter course, knowing he would eventually be hanged by the state and while waiting have time to repent. Suicide was uncommon but

[15]Abigail Adams to John Adams, Sep. 22, 1774, quoted in George M. Williams, *History of the Negro Race in America* (1883), I, 226; *The Boston Gazette*, Feb. 27, 1775; Josiah H. Temple, *History of Framingham, Massachusetts Early Known as Danforth's Farms, 1640-1880 with a Genealogical Register* (Framingham, 1887), 275; *The Massachusetts Spy* (Worcester), Aug. 9, 1775.

along with instances of mothers killing their own newborn to keep them from a life of slavery it pricked the consciences of the few who cared.[16]

III

Of the many kinds of resistance that did not involve personal violence or the destruction of property probably the most frequent was running away. Not many newspaper issues went to press after 1704 (when the first American paper, the *Boston News-Letter*, began publication) without notices offering rewards for runaway slaves. (Document 8) Escape was not limited to blacks, of course. The September 10, 1764 issue of the *Boston Gazette*, for example, listed a Spanish Indian, two black slaves who had plotted together, a white and a mulatto apprentice, and a white indentured servant among the week's fugitives. Sometimes blacks fled from particularly cruel treatment, as in the case of Jack from Wethersfield who complained that his owner habitually gave him 100 lashes. Without a specific destination but propelled by the desire for freedom, Jack stole a gun and hid in the woods, supporting himself by begging and theft. On other occasions escapes were organized and itineraries planned. In 1741 five newly arrived slaves in Boston appropriated a long-boat and taking an elderly black presumably with nautical experience set sail for Florida, outside English jurisdiction. (Document 9) The historian Carter G. Woodson discovered Massachusetts slaves who had fled to and intermarried with the Indians, the Mashpee Tribe, for instance, whose population of 327 in 1771 included fourteen blacks.[17]

Scholars are fortunate to have two systematic studies of Massachusetts runaways, one completed in 1944 by Lorenzo J. Greene, the other published in 1962 by Lawrence W. Towner.[18] Greene analyzed sixty-two detailed fugitive slave notices published in

[16] *The Boston Evening-Post* April 7, 1740; Aug. 18, 1755; June 28, 1756; Dec. 5, 1757.

[17] Joseph H. Smith (ed.), *Colonial Justice in Western Massachusetts (1639-1702): The Pynchon Court Record, An Original Judge's Diary of the Administration of Justice in the Springfield Courts in the Massachusetts Bay Colony* (Cambridge, Mass., 1961), 298-99; Carter G. Woodson, "The Relations of Negroes and Indians in Massachusetts," *Journal of Negro History*, V (Jan. 1920), 45-57.

[18] Lorenzo J. Greene, "The New England Negro as Seen in Advertisements for Runaway Slaves," *ibid.*, XXIX (April 1944), 125-46; Lawrence W. Towner, " 'A Fondness for Freedom': Servant Protest in Puritan Society," *The William & Mary Quarterly*, XIX (April 1962), 201-219.

eleven New England newspapers between 1718 and 1784. As might have been expected, half the runaways were from Boston with its large slave population. Young persons were most likely to flee: two-thirds were under twenty-five and five-sixths under thirty-five. Two-thirds left between June and November, when weather was most hospitable and work most arduous; one-half slipped away between August and November – harvest season. Runaways were overwhelmingly male – presumably outside the purview of whites more than females, who were usually domestics – and according to their descriptions tended to be physically strong. One-third carried a bodily defect of some sort – a brand, a scar, a lost or impaired limb – evidence perhaps of mistreatment and therefore special impatience with bondage. Many could read and write English, had taken extra clothing, and had carried off what they could of their owner's possessions.

Greene's data suggests that certain slaves were more anxious to escape than others, that some were better equipped and situated to do so, and that those fleeing understood that certain times were best and certain precautions necessary. Lawrence Towner, approaching the phenomenon from another perspective, researched the files of every Massachusetts newspaper through 1750, and all seventeenth and many eighteenth century court records. His findings reveal that blacks accounted for 223 of 676 known runaways between 1629 and 1750, or one-third of the total, a remarkable percentage for a group that was never more than 2.2 per cent of the population. From 1629 to 1719, 10 per cent of all runaways were black but from 1720 to 1750 the figure rose to well over 40 per cent. The conclusion seems to be that black slaves were more likely to run off than white indentured servants, and that as the years passed and their numbers grew, they did. Indeed, newspapers give the impression that an even higher proportion than usual fled in the months immediately following the Declaration of Independence, applying the logic of that document, it seems, to themselves.[19]

A second form of nonviolent resistance emerged during the Revolutionary era. Between January 6, 1773 and February 10, 1780 blacks petitioned Massachusetts officials for their freedom and other human rights at least eight times, and published three additional documents supporting their claims. (Documents 10-20)

[19] There seemed to be an increase in runaway notices during July and August in *The Boston Gazette* and the *Continental Journal* (Boston).

Several were written by a small group of slaves and freemen, among them Prince Hall, founder of the first Black Masonic Order in America and the Boston African Lodge. Their appeals were ignored, except on March 8, 1774, when the General Court – according to the recollection years later of Samuel Dexter, a member – passed "An Act to prevent importation of negroes, and others, as slaves, into this Province," after reading the June 1773 petition and an accompanying memorial by the same authors.[20] But since the blacks had objected most strenuously to the institution *per se*, the Court may have actually been responding to widespread public antipathy for slave trading, or even to an undercurrent opposed to *any* black presence in the colony. In any case Governor Thomas Hutchinson unexpectedly prorogued the Court on March 9, and the bill never became law.

When they first approached the government, the petitioners were tentative and self-deprecatory, disclaiming any intention of impudence or presumptuousness or of appearing to tell the Court how to conduct its business. They confessed that some of their numbers were "vicious," promised to be obedient as long as God "shall *suffer* us to be holden in Bondage," and said they would always keep His commandments. But on one point the blacks were adamant: every day of their lives, they insisted, was embittered by "this most intollerable Reflection, That, let their Behaviour be what it will, neither they, nor their Children . . . shall ever be able to do, or to possess and enjoy any Thing, no, not even *Life itself*, but in a Manner as the *Beasts that perish.*" (Document 10) Elsewhere they invoked the Golden Rule, praising those whites who had followed it by manumitting their slaves. (Document 11) They were also willing to accept halfway measures. The four authors of the April 20, 1773 letter urged the English to emulate the Spanish who allowed slaves one day a week to earn money toward their purchase price, while the framers of the May 25, 1774 and January 13, 1777 petitions asked simply that their children be set free when they reached the age of twenty-one.

As time passed and their appeals failed to bring results, the blacks, admitting impatience, began to write more graphically of "the cruel conditions of our slavery." They described the impossibility of maintaining family life or of worshipping the Christian

[20]Samuel Dexter to Jeremy Belknap, Feb. 26, 1795, in "Letters and Documents Relating to Slavery in Massachusetts," *CMHS*, 5th Ser., III (1877), 387-88.

God. How could a husband leave his master and cleave to his wife, they asked? How could a wife submit to her husband in all things, as the Bible instructed? How could a child obey his parents or a man his God if the master ordered otherwise? Stolen from Africa, with their children in America stolen from them, they reminded their readers, "we are deprived of every thing that has a tendency to make life even tolerable." (Documents 13, 17) The petitioners usually asked for little more than their freedom, immediately or in the near future, but in one particularly important document from June 1773, after arguing that "we are honestly entitled to some compensation for all our toils and sufferings," they went on to request "some part of the unimproved land, belonging to this province, for a settlement, that each of us may there quietly sit down under his own fig-tree, and enjoy the fruits of his own labour." If, as they expected, this first American advocacy of territorial separation was not adopted, they offered as an alternative "to be transported to our native country within a short time," restating an idea originally advanced the previous April. (Document 13) It is noteworthy that long before blacks could consider integration, the accumulation of political and economic power, or absorption into white institutions as possible remedies for their exploitation in America, some looked first to self-determination in a home of their own.

The black authors made effective use of political ideology from the American struggle with the mother country. After April 1773 they regularly demanded their "natural rights," arguing that their situation among whites was far more deplorable than English treatment of the colonies. "Every principle from which America has acted in the course of her unhappy difficulties with Great-Britain," they wrote in 1777, "pleas stronger than a thousand arguments in favor of your Petitioners," who had few problems demonstrating their bondage to be crueler and more burdensome than the "slavery" claimed by the Patriots. (Document 18) Whites were equally unprepared to face an even more fundamental fact. We are *men*, the blacks declared tirelessly, and men "are all upon an equal footing by nature." Africans were free people, "never conquered by any nation," one writer asserted in February 1774. "We all came from one common father, and HE by the law of nature gave every thing that was made, equally alike, to every man, richly to enjoy." (Document 15) By avowing that *all* men were created equal, by *meaning* all men, and by insisting that everyone possessed certain inalienable rights, these black radicals defended Revolutionary doctrine with greater consistency than the leaders of the independence movement. White ideologues omitted blacks from their theories of the rights of man, but with an impeccable logic untarnished by their manifest self-interest, blacks endorsed the Patriot cause, proving themselves more generous as well as more reasonable.

Another form of nonviolent resistance ultimately brought emancipation. Beginning in 1701 a number of slaves went into court to sue for freedom, a tactic possible in Massachusetts where bondsmen possessed full legal rights except jury service. Although they won almost every case, it took eighty-two years of adjudication to outlaw slavery. In the days before class actions, plaintiffs had to appear as individuals, usually charging owners with reneging on manumission promises. Judges were indisposed to condemn the institution even while freeing its victims. In 1701 the slave Adam accused John Saffin, a Boston merchant and jurist, of violating a contractual obligation to free him, and, after litigation protracted by Saffin's personal and political rivalries, won his case in 1703. In 1735, James of Boston sued his deceased owner's son, who claimed him as part of the inheritance. After threats on his life, James secured a writ of protection from the General Court which, believing his contention that the late owner's misplaced will had provided for his freedom, granted it in 1737. In 1762, Jenny Slew of Ipswich lost her original claim that she had been illegally held in bondage but in 1765 won her appeal plus damages and court costs.[21] The public discussion of political and human rights after the Stamp Act controversy apparently stimulated an increase in freedom suits comparable to the upsurge in petitions. Favorable decisions in *Oliver v. Sale* (1765), *Caesar v. Greenleaf* (1773), the *Cabel Dodge* cases (1774), and the *Elizabeth Freeman* case (1783), among others, created in the opinion of one authority "something of a Massachusetts 'common law' of abolition" culminating in *Commonwealth v. Jennison* (1783) – the final disposition of a suit initiated by the Worcester slave, Quok Walker – which signalled the end of slavery in the Bay State.[22]

[21] Lawrence W. Towner, "The Sewall-Saffin Dialogue on Slavery," *The William & Mary Quarterly*, XXI (1964); Greene, *The Negro in Colonial New England*, 292-97; Moore, *Notes on Slavery*, 112-24.

[22] There has been extensive scholarly debate over the circumstances of abolition in Massachusetts. See William O'Brien, "Did the Jennison Case Outlaw Slavery in Massachusetts?" *The William & Mary Quarterly*, XVII (1960); Arthur Zilversmit, "Quok Walker, Mumbet, and the Abolition of Slavery in Massachusetts," *ibid.*, XXV (1968); John D. Cushing, "The Cushing Court and the Abolition of Slavery in Massachusetts: More Notes on the 'Quok Walker Case,' " *American Journal of Legal History*, V (1961).

IV

Blacks resisted slavery in other ways: by malingering, stealing, destroying property, suing cruel owners in court, or petitioning the legislature for individual acts of manumission. But since many were unable or unwilling to act overtly, a number of more subtle survival techniques evolved, including what Richard C. Wade, studying nineteenth century Southern cities, has called "alley society." Blacks in eighteenth century Boston and other Massachusetts towns were adept at finding ways to enjoy a few hours together in hospitable taverns, private homes, warehouses, and back streets. Aware of this surreptitious activity, whites directed a number of statutes at its elimination, but without success. The need for fraternal interludes was simply too strong to suppress. The oft-repeated curfews and prohibitions on gatherings, which reached their peak in the 1740s and 1750s, were designed "to prevent disorders that are frequently committed by Negroes at night" and to deny them "opportunity of Meeting and conferring together, whereby great Injuries have been done to the Inhabitants. . . ."[23] Whites certainly had reason to fear secret slave assemblies, but they failed to understand that blacks also preferred the pleasure of each other's company and sometimes "conferred together" not to cause disorder or "great injury" but to satisfy the more mundane needs of body and soul.

Although documentation of black social life is sparse – it was, after all, illegal, hidden, and private – evidence of it occasionally surfaced. Newspaper accounts of a warehouse fire on a cold January night in 1738, for example, disclosed that "a parcel of Negroes" had met "to make merry," bringing with them "fowls," bread, sugar, and rum – ingredients, it is supposed, for hot toddies and home-style chicken. The flue clogged during the evening and the roof caught fire, causing the pleasure-seekers to throw their remaining victuals into the harbor, and run. Two years later, a Boston owner searching for his missing slave in Roxbury, entered a noisy tavern late at night to find "about a Dozen black Gentry, He's and She's, in a Room, in a very merry Humour, singing and dancing, having a Violin, and Store of Wine and Punch before them." (Document 19) The Boston Town Meeting complained in 1751 of "Negro and Indian Servants . . . getting into Companies in the Night, for Drinking, Gaming, Stealing, *etc.* and enticing white

[23] *Boston Town Records, 1742 to 1757* (Boston, 1885), 96-97, 193, 315.

Servants to join 'em (of which there has lately been several Instances). . . ." Such activities manifestly eroded labor efficiency, as revealed in a 1734 advertisement in which an owner offered for sale a twenty-one-year-old man who had once been "of a good natural Temper and Disposition" before being led astray by "the Company of a Rascally Club of Negros."[24] Although illegal and dangerous, "alley society" seems to have been an organic component of urban slavery, especially in Boston. There were whites and Indians willing to participate and tavern-keepers eager for the business, but fundamentally black socializing was by and for blacks, an outlet for emotions and a satisfying of needs whose legitimacy Puritan and slaveholding Massachusetts refused to recognize.

The earliest hints of cohesion as well as status differentiation within the black community come not from repressive laws or furtive parties but from newspaper accounts of two Boston funerals in the 1720s. The velvet pall of "Mrs. — Carlington, Consort of Mr. James Carlington, an African, belonging to Robert Auchmuty," the *New-England Courant* reported in 1723, was "supported by six Blacks of the first Rank, and her Funeral attended by two hundred and seventy more of the same colour." Likewise in 1729 when a freeman named Boston died, "a long Train follow'd him to the Grave, it's said about 150 Blacks, and about 50 Whites, several Magistrates, Ministers, Gentlemen, &c." (Documents 20, 21) Assuming reasonable newspaper accuracy, it appears that in both cases the deceased had sufficient social standing to elicit payment of final respects from 10 to 20 per cent of the city's entire black population. This is further substantiated by elegant trappings, by white officials in attendance, by sympathetic press coverage, and may indicate class stratification within the community.[25] Although reasons for elevated rank in the 1720s are unclear, certainly by the 1770s petitioners and freedom suit plaintiffs became the acknowledged spokesmen and most highly regarded blacks in the colony on the basis of individual achievement and advancement of group interests.

Recognition of social prominence at burials seems to have evolved from traditional ceremonies in West Africa where, according to anthropologist Melville J. Herskovits, the deceased "must have a funeral in keeping with his position in the community if he

[24]*The Boston Evening-Post*, Jan. 16, 1738; March 25, 1751; *The Boston Gazette*, June 10, 1734; *The Boston Weekly News-Letter*, Jan. 12, 1738.

[25]*The New-England Courant*, July 22, 1723; *New-England Weekly Journal*, Feb. 24, 1729, reprinted in "Diary of Samuel Sewall," *CMHS*, 5th Ser., VII (1882), 394-95.

is to take his rightful place in the afterworld." Prestige accrued to the family that buried its dead properly, thereby avoiding the recrimination a neglected soul was apt to visit on the survivors. Since West Africans believed familial relationships continued after death with the departed intervening in earthly affairs, persons of standing were often dispatched with dancing, singing, and feasting as a show of good intention and an expression of happy anticipation.[26] To assume the survival in New England of this West African cultural form illuminates the events at a 1797 Salem funeral better than the remarks of a patronizing white observer. All the mourners, according to Reverend William Bentley, "were clean, and they were dressed from common life up to the highest fashion [further indication of an incipient class structure]. . . . They completely aped the manners of the whites and in happiness seemed to surpass them. They did not express so much sorrow at the funeral, as real gratification at appearing so well, a greater sympathy with the living happily than the bereaved."[27]

Transplantation of cultural forms often involves changes in function. In Massachusetts, funerals were among the few public gatherings blacks were allowed to attend, and so they became social events. But anticipating danger even here, whites took precautionary measures to prevent and reform "Disorders at the Funerals of Negroes," as one statute put it, "disorders" presumably referring to singing and dancing. Since these occasions were often well attended, "which practice is of Ill tendency and may be of great Inconveniency to the Town if not prevented," the city fathers declared in 1723, blacks could be buried only on weekdays no later than a half hour before sunset at the nearest cemetery on the most direct route from the place where the body lay. Only one toll from a single bell was allowed, and to ensure white supervision black grave-diggers and officiators were banned. Funerals were virtually the only public function blacks could shape and order to their liking, within the guidelines established by law. The importance they attached to the occasion was emphasized by their repeated attempts in the 1790s to secure permission for one of their own to preside.[28]

[26]Melville J. Herskovits, *The Myth of the Negro Past* (Boston, 1958 ed.), 198; reminiscences by two West African natives in Philip D. Curtin (ed.), *Africa Remembered* (Madison, Wis., 1967), 129, 262.

[27]*The Diary of William Bentley, D.D. Pastor of the East Church Salem, Massachusetts,* 4 vols. (Gloucester, Mass., 1962), II, 235.

[28]*Boston Town Records From 1700 to 1728* (Boston, 1883), 176-77; *Records of Boston Selectmen, 1716 to 1736* (Boston, 1885), 115, 263, 283; *Selectmen's Minutes From 1787 through 1798* (Boston, 1896), 159, 189.

Burial rites were one of several manifestations of African custom in colonial Massachusetts. During the seventeenth and eighteenth centuries, of course, many American blacks were not born here and some, remembering their former lives vividly, clung to the old ways as drowning men to a life raft. "Mr. Mavericks Negro woman came to my chamber window," a visitor to Boston recorded in 1638, "and in her own Countrey language and tune sang very loud and shrill." Claiming to have been a queen at home, she refused to mate with a man chosen for her by her owner. Another situation well over a century later demonstrated the persistence of similar allegiances. A Lynn freeman named Pompey, regarded by all as an African king, was visited for a day each year by slaves from Boston, Salem, and his own town. Children gathered wild flowers to place on his head as a tribute to his station, while he and other elders responded by telling stories from their youth and recalling happier times before slavery.[29]

The annual event known as "Election Day" resembled Pompey's festival. Beginning around 1750 Massachusetts granted its slaves a four day vacation at the end of May. Those along the coast chose a "king" or "governor" and held an inauguration with games, songs, and a banquet. The governor and his appointed officials adjudicated minor disagreements among blacks and even petty complaints brought by whites. He had no power in the larger community but nevertheless commanded the respect of his followers, exercised a modicum of leadership, and to a certain extent was the titular head of the colony's blacks. Although Election Day may have been patterned after the official election which immediately preceded it elsewhere in New England, it was also used to perpetuate traditional folktales and dancing. The chosen government may have been a subtle form of slave control but it was also a rough approximation of the West African political and judicial practice of rule by a chief and council of elders, and may therefore have been an attempt to recreate a bit of home.[30] Other examples of cultural continuity include "Prince Jonar brought from Africa" to Framingham who, though a slave managing someone else's farm, cultivated his own land chosen, he said, because its soil resembled that of his native country. In 1716 Cotton Mather

[29]John Josselyn, *An Account of Two Voyages to New England, Made during the years 1638, 1663* (Boston, 1865 ed.), 26; Alonzo Lewis, *The History of Lynn* (Boston, 1829), 181.

[30]Greene, *The Negro in Colonial New England*, 249-256; Alice Morse Earle, *Customs and Fashions in Old New England* (London, 1893), 226-27; Sidney Perley, "Essex County in the Abolition of Slavery," 26.

wrote a Doctor Woodward at the British Museum that before he had encountered any American or European treatments for small-pox, he had been instructed in preventative innoculation by his servant Onesimus, who had been immunized in Africa.[31] Mather's strong advocacy of innoculation was therefore partly determined by African medical practices. (Document 22)

Throughout the slave period many blacks viewed Africa as a source of inspiration and hope, periodically stating a desire to return. More than any other of her contemporary black authors in Massachusetts, poet Phillis Wheatley accepted white notions of Western cultural superiority but even she began to revise her assessment when she noticed that "divine Light is insensibly chasing away the thick Darkness which broods over the Land of Africa." (Document 16) Others perceived it much more positively. Remembering Africa as a "sunny and happy" place, an old Deerfield woman named Jin had for years saved bits of cloth, glass, crockery, stones, and buttons, anything she could take along, believing like other blacks that her spirit would be transported home after she died. In 1735 the *Boston Evening-Post* noted a Rhode Island couple who "by their Industry and Frugality . . . scrap'd together two or three hundred Pounds, [and] having a Desire to return to their own Country to spend the remainder of their Days, sail'd from *Newport* for *Guinea*. . . ." The petitioners in the 1770s sometimes referred to themselves as Africans, always spoke longingly of home, and twice requested repatriation. We are a "free people," one wrote in 1774, even though America had temporarily placed its "heavy yoke" upon many African sons and daughters. (Documents 12, 13, 15) Many blacks simply did not consider this country a place of liberty and justice for all, a judgment endorsed by the Danvers slave poet Deliverance who wrote: "They stole us from Africa, the home of the free, And brought us in bondage across the blue sea."[32] To most of her color who expressed themselves on the subject – Phillis Wheatley being the principal exception – America was the land of the unfree and the home of the slave. Africa was its antithesis, a bulwark of hope against despair.

[31] Temple, *History of Framingham*, 237; Otho T. Beall, Jr., and Richard H. Shryock, "Cotton Mather: First Significant Figure in American Medicine," *Proceedings of the American Antiquarian Society*, LXIII (April 15, 1963), 138-39.

[32] George Sheldon, "Negro Slavery in Old Deerfield," *The New-England Magazine* (March 1893), 54-55; *The Boston Evening-Post*, Sep. 22, 1735; Anne L. Page, "A Negro Slave in Danvers," *The Massachusetts Magazine*, VII (1914), 137-138.

V

Resistance to slavery in Massachusetts never produced a mass movement or even a good-sized conspiracy. At first glance this is peculiar since there were revolts planned in other urban areas: in New York City in 1712 and 1741, in Richmond in 1800, and in Charleston in 1822. The absence of organized rebellion in the Bay Colony may have resulted from a combination of factors: the demonstrable mildness of the institution compared to its more brutal and dehumanizing forms elsewhere; the Puritans' relentless supervision of servant activity and vigilant prohibitions on gatherings; access to the courts where slaves could testify on their own behalf and sue their owners for cruel treatment;[33] and the small number of blacks, both in absolute terms and in relation to whites. Slaves constituted almost 15 per cent of the New York population during the eighteenth century, one-third of the entire South before 1830, an even higher proportion in Southern cities, but only 5 per cent of Boston in 1765. There were many Southern neighborhoods and plantations where slaves greatly outnumbered whites, but in Massachusetts residential and employment patterns usually kept blacks separated from each other.[34]

Resistance was therefore carried out individually until the independence movement when colony-wide reevaluation of political institutions demonstrated to blacks and whites alike that their demands could only be secured through collective action. Black petitioners spoke for a united community, slave and free. Their predilection for working through established channels – with the pen and not the sword – indicated their assessment of the best way to get results. Petitions and lawsuits were clearly within the Enlightenment tradition, resting on the assumption that reasonable governors would remedy obvious grievances brought by reasonable men. Blacks were perhaps naive to expect so much, but that expectation – also characteristic of the Civil Rights Movement almost two centuries later – was encouraged by official political action, in the one case by Patriot opposition to British "slavery" and in the other by Supreme Court decisions and presidential pronouncements. Working through "the system" in

[33]See Robert C. Twombly and Robert H. Moore, "Black Puritan: The Negro in Seventeenth Century Massachusetts," *The William & Mary Quarterly*, XXIV (April 1967).

[34]Professor Judith Stein of the History Department, City College of New York, made important contributions to the conceptualizations in this last section.

colonial Massachusetts was prompted by a sober appraisal of the possibilities at the time.

Those who ran away from slavery were equally enlightened. Flight generally involved careful planning, and was a rational course of action undertaken in pursuit of life, liberty, happiness, and other "natural rights." Although it brought more tangible results than petitioning, it failed to weaken the institution and, by removing some of the most rebellious, may in fact have strengthened it. On the other hand, peaceful petition was lawful in method, but by aiming to destroy bondage for everyone, it was actually much more revolutionary than running away. Those other individualists who committed desperate existential acts of suicide, assault, or murder were (and are) accused of irrational behavior and vile natures, as though these very characteristics – if they were in fact applicable – were not in part socially determined. The historical records suggest, however, that blacks in colonial Massachusetts directed far more violence toward whites than toward each other, most of it against their own masters, obviously the immediate embodiment of oppression. Black violence was sometimes a spontaneous reaction to particularly cruel treatment and at other times was carefully premeditated, but it is negligent to assume in either case that it was not partially or fully, consciously or unconsciously, an act of retribution. Knowing themselves to be Africans, heirs of a proud heritage and descendants of a free people, some blacks felt no obligation to abide by English law. Their obligation, rather, was to themselves and to their brothers.

FOR FURTHER READING

Bauer, Raymond A., and Alice H. "Day to Day Resistance to Slavery," *The Journal of Negro History*, XXVII (1942).

Cheek, William F., ed. *Black Resistance Before the Civil War.* Beverly Hills, Calif.: Glencoe Press, 1970.

Davis, Angela. "Reflections on the Black Woman's Role in the Community of Slaves," *The Black Scholar*, III (1971).

Greene, Lorenzo J. *The Negro in Colonial New England.* New York: Columbia University Press, 1942.

Harding, Vincent. "Religion and Resistance Among Antebellum Negroes, 1800-1860" in August Meier and Elliot Rudwick, eds. *The Making of Black America,* I. New York: Atheneum, 1969.

Mullin, Gerald. *Flight and Rebellion: Slave Resistance in Eighteenth Century Virginia.* New York: Oxford University Press, 1972.

Towner, Lawrence W. " 'A Fondness for Freedom': Servant Protest in Puritan Society," *William and Mary Quarterly*, XIX (1962).

Twombly, Robert C., and Moore, Robert H. "Black Puritan: The Negro in Seventeenth Century Massachusetts," *The William & Mary Quarterly*, XXIV (1967).

Sources

1

Ruthless Punishment

SOURCE: *The Boston News-Letter*, Feb. 24, 1718, from New London, Connecticut.

By certain Information from a Gentleman we are assured, that some Weeks ago to the Westward of that place, a very remarkable thing fell out, (which we here relate as a caveat for all Negroes meddling with any White Woman, least they fare with the like Treatment,) and it is this, A Negro Man met abroad an English Woman, which he accosted to lye with, stooping down, fearing none behind him, a Man observing his Design, took out his Knife, before the Negro was aware, cut off all his unruly parts Smack and Smooth, the Negro Jumpt up roaring and run for his Life; the Black now an Eunuch and like to recover of his wounds & doubtless cured from any more such Wicked Attempts.

2

A Bizarre Occurrence

SOURCE: *The Boston News-Letter*, Jan. 7, 1717.

On the Lords day Morning the sixth Currant, a strange thing fell out here, One Thomas Smith a Sawyer about four Month ago, bought a Lusty Tall new Negro, fit for his Employ, who often complain'd of something within him, that made a Noise Chip, Chip, Chip; his Master sent for a Doctor, one Sebastian Henry Swetzer a German, who told him he had Worms, whereupon he gave him some Physick on Wednesday: from Thursday till the Lords Day he gave him some Powders, which on the Lords Day had that effect as to cause him to vomit up a long Worm, that measur'd a hundred and twenty eight Foot, which the Negro took to be his Guts; it was almost as big as ones little Finger, its Head was like a Snakes, and would receive a Mans little Finger into its Mouth, it was of a Whitish Colour all full of Joynts, its Tail was long and hard, and with a Miscroscope it seem'd to be hairy; the Negro before voiding the Worm had an extraordinary Stomach.

3

Regulations Governing Indians, Negroes, and Mulattoes

SOURCE: *Boston Records From 1700 to 1728* (Boston, 1883), 173-75.

Pursuant to the Vote & direction of the freeholders & Inhabitants of the Town at their Annuall meeting in March last.

The Select men haue drawn up heads or Articles for the Better Regulating Indians Negros and Molattos within this Town . . .

That if any free Indian Negro or Molatto Shal Receive or Entertain any Indian Negro or Molatto Servant or Slaue into His House yard garden or out house unless Sent there by his master or Employer, Shal forfeit and pay the Sum of Twenty Shillings and be Sent to the House of Correction and there be Severly whiped, And the better to Enforce this order any two free holders may Enter the House of any Such free Indian Negro or Molatto.

That no free Indian Negro or Molatto Shal haue and keep any manner of weapons fire armes, Powder or Ball in his House or the Dependances thereof on forfieture of five pounds & being Severly whipt at the House of Correction.

That no free Indian Negro or Molatto Shal on Training dayes, or any other Publick dayes carry into the Common or Training field Streets or Highwayes any Strong drink Cakes or any other Provision to Sell on Pain of ten pounds and being Sent to the House of Correction and Severly whipt, And any two freeholders Shal haue power to Seize Secure and Dispose of all such Liquors & Provisions for the use and benefit of the Poor.

That every free Indian Negro or Molatto Shal bind out, all their Children at or before they arrive to the age of four years to Some English master, and upon neglect thereof the Select men or Overseers of the Poor Shal be Empowered to bind out all Such Children till the age of Twenty one years.

If any free Indian Negro or Molatto Shal Receive any goods wares Merchandize Money or Provisions from the hands of any Indian Negro or Molatto Servant or Slave or any Stolen goods found in their Houses or Possession upon Conviction Such Indian Negro or Molatto Shall beside making Restitution as by Law already provided be Severly Whipt, And ordered by the Court before whom the Tryal is to depart this Province, And if any Such Shal Return to be taken and Sent to the House of Correction and haue the Discipline of the House and there to Remain and abide during life & keept to hard Labour.

If any Indian, Negro or Molatto bond or free be Convict of Stealing Robbing Pilfering or Breaking into any House Ware house Shop Stable Barn or out house Ship or Vessell He Shal upon Conviction be Transported beyond Sea Remaining in the Comon Goal or House of Correction till Shipt Oft besides making Restitution as the Law Provides.

That no Indian Negro or Molatto Slave or Servant Shal be out of His Masters House or Dependances thereat unless in the Imediat Service of his master, an hour after Sun Sett from the first of march to the first of September nor half an hour after from the Second of September till March nor before Sun Riseing upon Pain of being Sent to the House of Correction and there Severely Whipt.

That no Indian Negro or Molatto Servant or Slave Shall be Suffered to wear or Carry about him any manner of armes or weapons Clubb Stave Cane or knives Except Decriped upon Pain of Severe punishment at the House of Correction.

That if more than Two Indian Negro or Molatto Servants or Slaves be found in the Streets or Highways in or about the Town Idling or Lurking together unless in the Service of their master or Employer. Every one so found Shal be punished at the House of Correction.

That no Indian Negro or Molatto Servant or Slave tho' haueing obtained leave from his Master to go into the Comon or Training field on Training dayes or any other Publick dayes, Shal abide there after Sun Sett upon pain of Sever Whipping at the Hou of Correction.

That if any Indian, Negro, or Molatto Servant or Slave Shal assault Strike Beat wound Bruse or mame any of his Majesties Subjects, He Shal be Severely Punnished at the Discression of the Court before whom Convict and Sent beyond Sea being Confined till his Departure at the Charge of His Master or Owner.

If any Person Shal Sell any Strong Liquor to any Indian Negro, or Molatto Servant or Slave, unless Sent by his master he Shal forfiet & pay ten pounds fine, and Suffer Three months Imprisonment, and if the Person that Sell contrary hereto be a Tavernor Inholder or Retailer He Shal forfeit his Recognizance and be Rendered Ever after incapable of hauing His Licence renewed. The Proof for Conviction to be as in the Case of Selling Strong drink to Indians.

That no Indian Negro or Molatto Bond or free Shal presume to work as a Porter in or about the Town unless first approved by the Select men and Bond given to the Town Treasurer in a Sum not less then fifty Pounds for his fidelity. The forfiture of Such Bonds to be applyed to and for the use of the Poor of the Town And if any appear and are found in Such work Shal be taken up and Sent to the House of Correction, Receive the Discipline of the House & Remain there Six dayes.

That Indian Negro and Molatto Evidences only with Concurring Circomstances Shal be proof Soficient to Convict Indian Negro or Molattos.

That no Indian Negro or Molatto up on the breaking out of fire and the Continuance there of dureing the night Season Shal depart his or his masters House, nor found in the Streets or at or near the place where the fire is upon pain of being forthwith Secured and Sent to the Comon Goal and afterwards whipt at the House of Correction three dayes following before dismist, unless his or his masters House or Estate be on fire or in great hazzard thereof.

That all fines and forfeitures arising by this act be disposed the one halfe to the Poor of the Town the other halfe to the Informer.

4

Brutal Retaliation

SOURCE: *The Boston News-Letter*, June 9, 1763.

A most shocking Murder was committed last Saturday at Taunton, by a Negro Fellow belonging to Dr. McKinstry; – a Sister of the Doctor's getting up early in the Morning to iron Cloaths, the Negro (after making a Fire) got his Master's Horse, and left him at the Door, and finding an Opportunity took up a hot Flat Iron, with which he struck the Woman on the Back of her Head, and stunned her, he repeated the Blow, then dragged her down in the Cellar, and there with an old Ax struck her several Times; he then took the hot Iron and rubb'd over her Face, flicking the Point of it into her Eyes, whereby she was scorch'd considerably; after he had done this, he took the Horse and rode off – The Family soon got up and found the Woman in the above Condition; she continued till the Evening of the next Day, and then died: The Negro was pursued, and taken up at Newport, and confess'd the Fact. – What induced the Fellow to perpetuate this Crime is not known, as he was always treated well, and there had been no Difference with him in the Family.*

*Editor's Note: Commenting on the same occurrence, the *Boston Evening-Post* added on June 13, 1763: "The Boy was an exceedingly good Servant, & remarkable for his obsequious Behaviour, nor was there the least surmise of his bearing Hatred to the deceased, or of the least Occasion for it; tho' since this Affair some Things have come to light which shew the maliciousness of his Mind, and the bad Effects of Negroes too freely consorting together."

5

Doubts About Slavery

SOURCE: *The Boston Gazette*, Aug. 25, 1766, from Portsmouth, N.H.

Last Week, as a Man belonging to New Ipswich, who had taken up two Runaway Negro Men, was returning with them to their Masters; about a Mile from Dover the Villians attacked him, it being in the Evening, and after robbing him of all his Money and Papers, beat him in a cruel Manner, and endeavoured to strangle him; happily they did not find his Knives, which were in one of his Pockets; if they had, 'tis likely they would have cut his Throat. A Man happening to pass by, the Negros jump'd over a Fence and ran away, leaving the unfortunate Person senseless and speechless: – being taken up and carried into a House, he soon recovered and is returned home; and we hear the Negroes are since taken and bro't to their Masters. These are the *blessed* Effects of bringing Negro Slaves into the Country! – Scarce one in a hundred proves good for any Thing, and yet the Guinea Trade is continued in Spight of Reason and Humanity. *Quid Domini sacient, audent cum talia Fures*?

6

A Guerilla Band

SOURCE: *The Boston Weekly News-Letter*, Nov. 8, 1753.

We have Advice from Fish-Kills, in Dutchess County [New York], That a Number of Negroes having lately run away from their Masters in those Parts, had formed themselves into a Gang of about a Dozen, and greatly molested the back Settlements there: That about a Fortnight ago, they came in the Night to a lone House, where there was none but a Man and his Wife, with a Negro Girl in the Kitchen: as they happened to go into the Kitchen first, the Girl immediately cryed out, on which they knock'd her down; the Master thereupon alarm'd, snatch'd up his Gun, and with his Wife escap'd out of the House just as the Negroes entered, and waiting at some Distance, on their coming out fired at them, and shot one mortally, but the rest carried him off after plundering the House. A few days later they came to a Negro who was ploughing alone, and told him, he must steal some Guns and Ammunition for them, and join them; that they had lately lost one of their Gang, wanted some more Arms, and then intended to March off for Canada before Winter: The Fellow promised all they bid him but afterwards told his Master, who thereupon got a Company of the Neighbours to go in quest of the Rogues, but they were not able to discover any of them.

7

Black Lovers Prefer Death to Separation

SOURCE: *The Boston Evening-Post*, Dec. 8, 1746.

Last Thursday Evening a very surprizing Tragedy was acted here, in the following Manner, *viz.* A Negro Fellow at the North End, and a Negro Woman belonging to a Gentleman at the South End of the Town, having contracted an intimate and strict Friendship together, and understanding that the wench was about to be sold into the Country, they resolved to put an End to their lives, rather than be parted; and accordingly, about seven o'Clock, (the Wench being at the House of her countryman) they went up Stairs into the Garret, where the Fellow, as is supposed, cut out the Wench's Throat with a Razor, and then shot himself with a Gun prepar'd for the Purpose. They were both found lying upon the Bed, she with her Head cut almost off, and he with his Head shot all to Pieces.

8

A Runaway Slave Notice

SOURCE: *The Boston News-Letter*, June 18, 1704.

Ran-away from Capt. *Nathanael Cary*, of Charlestown, on *Saturday* the 17th Currant, a well set middle sized *Maddagascar* Negro Woman, called Penelope, about 35 years of Age: With several sorts of Apparel; one whereof is a flowered damask Gown: She speaks English well. Whosever shall take up said Negro Servant, and her Convey to her above-said Master, shall have sufficient Reward.

9

Flight by Sea

SOURCE: *The Boston Evening-Post*, Oct. 5, 1741.

Last Tuesday Night, five Negro or Mulatto Slaves, taken by Capt. *Rouse* in a Spanish Privateer on the Coast of *South-Carolina*, and bro't in and sold to several Persons in this Town, with an old Negro Fellow who has been a Slave here for many Years, took a Ship's long Boat and stood out of the Harbour, with Intent to go to St. *Augustine* or some other *Spanish* Port; but after two or three Days tossing about in our Bay, in which they suffered much Hardship by Reason of contrary Winds, and cold and rainy Weather, in an open and ill rigged Boat, they were met and taken up by a fishing Schooner, and committed to *Plymouth* Goal.

10

First Petition from the Slaves of Massachusetts Bay

SOURCE: *The Appendix: or, some Observations on the expediency of the Petition of the Africans, living in Boston, &c., lately presented to the General Assembly of this Province. To which is annexed, the Petition referred to. Likewise, Thoughts on Slavery with a useful extract from the Massachusetts Spy, of January 28, 1773, by way of an Address to the Members of the Assembly. By a Lover of Constitutional Liberty* (Boston, 1773).

Province of the Massachusetts Bay To His Excellency Thomas Hutchinson, Esq; Governor; To the Honorable His Majesty's Council, and To the Honorable House of Representatives in General Court assembled at Boston, the 6th Day of *January*, 1773.

The humble PETITION of many Slaves, living in the Town of Boston, and other Towns in the Province is this, namely

That your Excellency and Honors, and the Honorable the Representatives would be pleased to take their unhappy State and Condition under your wise and just Consideration.

We desire to bless God, who loves Mankind, who sent his Son to die for their Salvation, and who is no respecter of Persons; that he hath lately put it into the Hearts of Multitudes on both Sides of the Water, to bear our Burthens, some of whom are Men of great Note and Influence; who have pleaded our Cause with Arguments which we hope will have their weight with this Honorable Court.

We presume not to dictate to your Excellency and Honors, being willing to rest our Cause on your Humanity and Justice; yet would beg Leave to say a Word or two on the Subject.

Although some of the Negroes are vicious, (who doubtless may be punished and restrained by the same Laws which are in Force against other of the King's Subjects) there are many others of a quite different Character, and who, if made free, would soon be able as well as willing to bear a Part in the Public Charges; many of them of good natural Parts, are discreet, sober, honest, and industrious; and may it not be said of many, that they are virtuous and religious, although their Condition is in itself so unfriendly to Religion, and every moral Virtue except *Patience*. How many of that Number have there been, and now are in this Province, who have had every Day of their Lives imbittered with this most intollerable Reflection, That, let their Behaviour be what it will, neither they, nor their Children to all Generations, shall ever be able to do, or to possess and enjoy any Thing, no, not even *Life itself*, but in a Manner as the *Beasts that perish.*

We have no Property! We have no Wives! No Children! We have no City! No Country! But we have a Father in Heaven, and we are determined, as far as his Grace shall enable us, and as far as our degraded contemptuous Life will admit, to keep all his Commandments: Especially will we be obedient to our Masters, so long as God in his sovereign Providence shall *suffer* us to be holden in Bondage.

It would be impudent, if not presumptuous in us, to suggest to your Excellency and Honors any Law or Laws proper to be made, in relation to our unhappy State, which, although our greatest Unhappiness, is not our *Fault*; and this gives us great Encouragement to pray and hope for such Relief as is consistent with your Wisdom, Justice, and Goodness.

We think Ourselves very happy, that we may thus address the Great and General Court of this Province, which great and good Court is to us, the best Judge, under God, of what is wise, just and good.

We humbly beg Leave to add but this one Thing more: We pray for such Relief only, which by no Possibility can ever be productive of the least Wrong or Injury to our Masters; but to us will be as Life from the dead.

(signed) FELIX

11

A Plea for Justice

SOURCE: *The Appendix: or, some Observations on the expediency of the Petition of the Africans, living in Boston, &c., lately presented to the General Assembly of this Province. To which is annexed, the Petition referred to. Likewise, Thoughts on Slavery with a useful extract from the Massachusetts Spy, of January 28, 1773, by way of an Address to the Members of the Assembly. By a Lover of Constitutional Liberty* (Boston, 1773).

"Friend, Parent, Neighbour, first will I embrace,
My Country next, and next all human race."

Pope

Wise and good Men in all Ages have celebrated Patriotism as a Virtue of the first Magnitude, and all Men who shine in the List of Fame are renowned for Humanity, or a benevolant Regard to *all* their Fellow Men, this is one of the brightest Jewels in their Crown of Glory; and without this no Man will ever enter the Temple of Fame below, nor the Gates of Heaven above. Animated with this Principle, I would plead Justice in behalf of the most unhappy Part of our Species – the Negroes. This People have been treated in a Manner which disgraces Humanity and the Laws of Heaven; and all the sacred Ties of Nature, Reason, and Conscience have been violated to rob this poor People of the Gifts of God!

Some feeble Efforts have of late been made to justify the black and enormous Crimes above mentioned, but Reason and Conscience mock their vain Attempts, while the Saviour and Judge of the World condemns them and their Cause with this eternal Rule of Righteousness, *Whatsoever ye would that men should do unto you, do ye even so to them.* With this Golden Rule before him, what Christian can countenance the *enslaving* his Fellow Men? By this Practice of *Slave-making*, every Principle of Justice, Humanity, and Righteousness is flagrantly violated; and for such Iniquity we have the utmost Reason to expect that GOD will visit us with his righteous Judgments.

To avert those deserved Judgments, it is hoped the patriotic Legislature of this Province, will in their present Session make a Law to prevent the Importation of any more *Slaves* into this Government: And also adopt some Method to relieve those who are now in *Bondage* in the Province. Unless we *deal justly and love Mercy*, we cannot expect any Thing but the Frowns of that GOD who *loveth Righteousness*.

The word of GOD commands us to give Honor to whom Honor is due, and surely it is not due to any more than to those who relieve the oppressed, and give *Liberty* to them who are in *Bondage*: We desire therefore to mention two honorable Gentlemen who have, from Christian Principles of *Liberty*, given *Freedom* to their *Slaves*, viz. Mr. ROBERT PIERPONT of *Boston*, and Major FULLER of *Newton*. May their noble Example be imitated by all Christians, and the Blessings of Heaven descend on them and on all who do likewise.

The Sons of Africa

12

Slaves Request Reform of the Institution

SOURCE: Letter to the Representative from the town of Thompson, printed as a leaflet. New York Historical Society.

Boston, April 20th, 1773

Sir, The efforts made by the legislative of this province in their last sessions to free themselves from slavery, gave us, who are in that deplorable state, a high degree of satisfaction. We expect great things from men who have made such a noble stand against the designs of their *fellow-men* to enslave them. We cannot but wish and hope Sir, that you will have the same grand object, we mean civil and religious liberty, in view in your next session. The divine spirit of *freedom*, seems to fire every humane breast on this continent, except such as are bribed to assist in executing the execrable plan.

We are very sensible that it would be highly detrimental to our present masters, if we were allowed to demand all that of *right* belongs to us for past services; this we disclaim. Even the *Spaniards*, who have not those sublime ideas of freedom that English men have, are conscious that they have no right to all the services of their fellow-men, we mean the *Africans*, whom they have purchased with their money; therefore they allow them one day in a week to work for themselves, to enable them to earn money to purchase the residue of their time, which they have a right to demand in such portions as they are able to pay for (in due appraizement of their services being first made, which always stands at the purchase money.) We do not pretend to dictate to you Sir, or to the Honorable Assembly, of which you are a member. We acknowledge our obligations to you for what you have already done, but as the people of this province seem to be actuated by the principles of equity and justice, we cannot but expect your house will again take our deplorable case into serious consideration, and give us that ample relief which, *as men,* we have a natural right to.

But since the wise and righteous governor of the universe, has permitted our fellow men to make us slaves, we bow in submission to him, and determine to behave in such a manner as that we have reason to expect the divine approbation of, and assistance in, our peaceable and lawful attempts to gain our freedom.

We are willing to submit to such regulations and laws, as may be made relative to us, until we leave the province, which we determine to do as soon as we can, from our joynt labours procure money to transport ourselves to some part of the Coast of *Africa*, where we propose a settlement. We are very desirous that you should have instructions relative to us, from your town, therefore we pray you to communicate this letter to them, and ask this favor for us.

In behalf of our fellow slaves in this province, and by order of their Committee.

Peter Bestes,
Sambo Freeman,
Felix Holbrook,
Chester Joie

13

A Petition for Freedom or Separation

SOURCE: *The Massachusetts Spy* (Boston), July 29, 1773.

To his Excellency Thomas Hutchinson, Esq; Governor of said province; to the Honourable his MAJESTY'S COUNCIL, and the Honourable HOUSE OF REPRESENTATIVES in General Court assembled, June, A.D. 1773.

The Petition of us the subscribers, in behalf of all those, who by divine permission are held in a state of SLAVERY, within the bowels of a FREE country.

Humbly sheweth,

"THAT your petitioners apprehend, they have in common with other men, a natural right to be free, and without molestation, to enjoy such property, as they may accumulate by their industry, or by any other means not detrimental to their fellow men; and that no person can have any just claim to their services unless by the laws of the land they have forfeited them, or by voluntary compact become servants; neither of which is our case; but we were dragged by the cruel hand of power, some of us from our dearest connections, and others stolen from the bosom of tender parents and brought hither to be enslaved. Thus we are deprived of every thing that has a tendency to make life even tolerable. The endearing ties of husband, wife, parent, child and friend, we are generally strangers to: And whenever any of those connections are formed among us, the pleasures are imbittered by the cruel condition of our slavery. By our deplorable situation we are rendered incapable of shewing obedience to the supreme governor of the universe, by conforming ourselves to the duties, which naturally grow out of such relations. How can a slave perform the duties of husband or parent, wife or child? We are often under the necessity of obeying *man*, not only in omission of, but frequently in opposition to the laws of *God*. So inimical is slavery to religion! As we are hindered by our situation from an observance of the laws of God, so we cannot reap an equal benefit from the laws of the land with other subjects. We are informed, there is no law of this province, whereby our masters can claim our services; mere custom is the tyrant that keeps us in bondage, and deprives us of that use of the law, which he, who happens to have a white skin is intitled to. We are not insensible, that if we should be liberated, and allowed by law to demand pay for our past services, our masters and their families would by that means be greatly damnified, if not ruined: But we claim no rigid justice: Yet as we are honestly entitled to some compensation for all our toils and sufferings; we would therefore, in addition to our prayer, that all of us, excepting such as are now infirm through age, or otherways unable to support themselves, may be liberated and made free-men of this community, and be entitled to all the privileges and immunities of its free and natural born subjects; further humbly ask, that your Excellency and Honours would be pleased to give and grant us some part of the unimproved land, belonging to the province, for a settlement, that each of us may there quietly sit down under his own fig-tree, and enjoy the fruits of his own labour.

"This scheme we apprehend, will remove all rational objections to our freedom; and promises so much good to your oppressed petitioners, as well as future advantage to this province that we cannot but hope, that your Excellency and Honours will give it its due weight and consideration; and that you will accordingly cause an act of this legislative to be passed, enabling all the slaves throughout this province, to demand and obtain their freedom from their masters and mistresses; and at the same time prohibiting any being sent out of the province, previous to the said act's taking place.

"But if your Excellency and Honours cannot in wisdom adopt this plan of relief for us, we humbly and earnestly request, that you would release us from bondage, by causing us to be transported to our native country within a short time; or by such other way or means as to your Excellency and Honours shall seem good and wise upon the whole. And your petitioners, as in duty bound, shall ever pray."

14

Black Petitioners Grow Impatient

SOURCE: *The Massachusetts Spy* (Boston), Sep. 1, 1774.

To the honourable his Majesty's Council and the honourable House of Representatives of the Province of Massachusetts-Bay, in General Court assembled, at Boston, the 20th day of January, 1774.

The many stedfast resolutions made by this large province, to maintain their liberties and privileges, wherewith God hath made them free (without which no man, even the meanest of them can be happy in this life, for what is life without the enjoyment of it?) gives us who are unhappily, and unjustly deprived of that blessing, so great expectations of your taking up our last petition which we laid before your Honours the last sessions; and give us the thousands of poor unhappy Africans their freedom, which we as men, and by nature have a right to demand of your Honours in such a way, and in such a manner as your Honours would expect from such a body of fellowmen, professing the gospel of our Lord and Saviour JESUS CHRIST; we ask nothing for your Honours but what you would desire yourselves, were you in our situation: Nay even the very dumb beasts groan under the heavy load of slavery, and try all manner of ways to get rid of it; much more men who are made after the image of GOD, and have the sense of feelings, cannot but groan under this unjust burden laid upon us, without any colour of justice, but pleasure and custom, and against the wills or consents of our forefathers, or us their children: But since the all-wise GOD hath seen fit to permit it to be so for a number of years past, his will be done, we desire to submit to his will in all things; yet from the first settling of this province it was not so. But yet we can sincerely hope and pray, that GOD would preserve your liberties and privileges as at the beginning, and that peace and love may again be restored between the mother country and the provinces, and that his MAJESTY would hear your prayers, and that you would hear ours, and grant us an answer of peace, that we may rejoice when you rejoice, as well as mourn when you mourn, as we do this day; and as we are not void of fellow-feeling, we conclude we must be men.

15

An African Examines the Laws of God and Man

SOURCE: *The Massachusetts Spy* (Boston), Feb. 10, 1774.

For the MASSACHUSETTS SPY. *Mr. Thomas, You are desired to insert the following in your paper, by your humble servant,* An AFRICAN.

I Rejoice to see that there is in this and the neighboring provinces such a spirit for liberty, for life without it is of little worth. Liberty is one of the greatest blessings the human mind can enjoy. The sweets yours and our fore-fathers have enjoyed, and have fallen asleep therein. But there is a cloud and has been for many years, and it is blackness and darkness itself, but I rejoice that the rays of light faintly break through, and pray that it may shine like the sun in his meridian lustre. Sir, do you apply for your liberty in a right way? You are taxed without your consent, because you are not represented in parliament (I grant that a grievance) and have petitioned for relief and cannot get any. Pray, Sir, what can you impute it to? are the Britons hearts harder than yours? Are not your hearts also hard, when you hold them in slavery who are intitled to liberty, by the law of nature, equal as yourselves? If it be so, pray, Sir, pull the beam out of thine eye, that you may see clearly to pull the mote out off *[sic]* thy brother's eye: And when the eyes of your understanding are opened, then will you see clearly between your case and Great-Britain and that of the Africans. We all came from one common father, and HE by the law of nature gave every thing that was made, equally alike, to every man, richly to enjoy: If so, is it lawful for one nation to enslave another? The law of nature gives no such toleration. I grant for wise reasons,

God suffered the Jews to have servants – But no slaves, but those who had their ears bored to the post by their own consent. I cannot think that one of the sons of Africa, that hath tasted the sweets of freedom, in their own country, and the heavy yoke in this, would submit to have theirs bored to the posts; for the Africans are a free people, born free and were never conquered by any nation. Pray, Sir, what people under heaven have a right to enslave them? None! because it is contrary to the laws of God, and the laws of Great-Britain. But you say we bring them from their own country to make Christians of them: I should rejoice if there was as much pains taken with the Africans as there is with the Indians, by sending missionaries among them, and christianizing them in their own country; – but for the masters of vessels, to fetch them to the West-Indies, and sell them to the greatest villain that appears to purchase him or her, if he will give two bits more than an honest man: So, Sir, christianity is made a cloak to fill their coffers and to screen their villainy. View these poor creatures in this miserable situation, a father fighting for his bosom friend, a mother for a beloved son, a brother for a sister, a friend for a kind companion – I say, to view them in this situation, I should think would make a Heathen blush, and a Christian shudder. And now, Sir, to boast of your liberty when we are all upon an equal footing by nature, for I am convinced that no man has a right to enjoy another man's liberty and property, when it is unlawful to hold that property – I thought men were to be governed by law and reason, but where no law is, the law of reason determines in such cases. Now where conscience is free and unbiassed, it makes the law of Christ its rule – What saith Christ in this case, whatsoever ye would that men should do unto you, do ye even so to them, for this is the law and the prophets. Christ gives his sentiments freely, and then refers us to the law and the prophets. In the law we do not find the word slave; but suppose it was to be found there, it wont appear from thence that the Americans have a warrant from God to make the Africans slaves as the Jews had to hold servants: But as I hinted before, that for wise reasons God suffered the Jews to have servants, and no slaves but such as would willingly be made so, I cannot see by what new invented law they pretend to hold the Africans, without it be custom; a custom to hold any man does not make it lawful for him to be held without there is an express law made to hold that man in the place where he lives. Now I am informed that there is no law in the kingdom of Great-Britain, nor in this province, to hold a man in perpetual slavery. Whatever is contrary to the laws of God and the English constitution must be deemed unlawful; for I always thought the constituted laws of England were drafted from, and founded on the word of God: And if they be, then it follows, that your laws by charter right are founded on the laws of England, for your charter expressly says that you have a right to make laws but not repugnant to the laws of Great-Britain. Now the Americans can't make a law to enslave the Africans without contradicting the laws of God and the laws of Great-Britain.

A Son of AFRICA

16

Poet for the People

At the time of this letter, Phillis Wheatley, a twenty-year-old African-born Boston slave, was an international celebrity, having the year before published *Poems on Various Subjects, Religious and Moral* in London.

SOURCE: *The Boston Weekly News-Letter*, March 24, 1774; *Essex Gazette* (Salem), March 22, 1774; *The Boston Evening-Post, March 21, 1774; The Massachusetts Spy* (Boston), March 24, 1774.

Letter from Phillis Wheatley to Rev. Samson Occam, Feb. 11, 1774: Rev'd and honor'd Sir,

I Have this Day received your obliging kind Epistle, and am greatly satisfied with your Reasons respecting the Negroes, and think highly reasonable what you offer in Vindication of their natural Rights: Those that invade them cannot be insensible that the divine Light is insensibly chasing away the thick Darkness which broods over the Land of Africa; and the Chaos which has resign'd so long, is converting into beautiful Order, and reveals more and more clearly, the glorious Dispensation of civil and religious Liberty, which are so inseparably united, that there is little or no Enjoyment of one without the other: Otherwise, perhaps, the Israelites had been left solicitous for their Freedom from Egyptians Slavery; I don't say they would have been contented without it, by no means, for in every human Breast, God has implanted a Principle, which we call Love of Freedom; it is impatient of Oppression, and pants for Deliverance; and by the Leave of our modern Egyptians I will assert, that the same Principle lives in us. – God Grant Deliverance in his own Way and Time, and get him honour upon all those whose Avarice impels them to countenance and help forward the Calamaties of their fellow Creatures. This I desire not for their Hurt, but to convince them of the strange Absurdity of their Conduct whose Words and Actions are so diametrically opposite. How will the Cry for Liberty, and the reverse Disposition for the exercise of oppressive Power over others agree – I humbly think it does not require the Penetration of a Philosopher to determine –

17

Petitioners Describe the Horrors of Slavery

SOURCE: *Collections of the Massachusetts Historical Society,* 5th Ser., III (Boston, 1877), 432-33.

To his Excellency Thomas Gage Esq. Captain General and Governor in Chief in and over this Province. To the Honourable his Majestys Council and the Honourable House of Representatives in General Court assembled May 25 1774

The Petition of a Grate Number of Blackes of this Province who by divine permission are held in a state of Slavery within the bowels of a free and christian Country

Humbly Shewing

That your Petitioners apprehind we have in common with all other men a naturel right to our freedoms without Being depriv'd of them by our fellow men as we are a freeborn Pepel and have never forfeited this Blessing by aney compact or agreement whatever. But we were unjustly dragged by the cruel hand of power from our dearest frinds and sum of us stolen from the bosoms of our tender Parents and from a Populous Pleasant and plentiful country and Brought hither to be made slaves for Life in a Christian land. Thus we are deprived of every thing that hath a tendency to make life even tolerable, the endearing ties of husband and wife we are strangers to for we are no longer man and wife than our masters or mistresses thinkes proper marred or onmarred. Our children are also taken from us by force and sent maney miles from us wear we seldom or ever see them again there to be made slaves of for Life which sumtimes is vere short by Reson of Being dragged from their mothers Breest Thus our Lives are imbittered to us on these accounts By our deplorable situation we are rendered incapable of shewing our obedience to Almighty God how can a slave perform the duties of a husband to a wife or parent to his child How can a husband leave master to work and cleave to his wife How can the wife submit themselves to there husbands in all things How can the child obey thear parents in all things. There is a great number of us sencear . . . members of the Church of Christ how can the master and the slave be said to fulfil that command Live in love let Brotherly Love contuner and abound Beare yea onenothers Bordenes How can the master be said to Beare my Borden when he Beares me down whith the Have chanes of slavery and operson against my will and how can we fulfill our parte of duty to him whilst in this condition and as we cannot searve our God as we ought whilst in this situation. Nither can we reap an equal benefet from the laws of the Land which doth not justifi but condemns Slavery or if there had bin aney Law to hold us in Bondage we are Humbley of the Opinion ther never was aney to inslave our children for life when Born in a free Countrey. We therefor Bage your Excellency and Honours will give this its deer weight and consideration and that you will accordingly cause an act of the legislative to be pessed that we may obtain our Natural right our freedoms and our children be set at lebety at the yeare of twenty one for whoues sekes more petequeley your Petitioners is in Duty ever to pray.

18

Petitioners Demand Their Natural Rights

SOURCE: Massachusetts Archives, Vol. 212, page 132, the State House, Boston.*

To the Honorable Council & House of Representatives for the State of Massachusetts-Bay, in General Court assembled January 13th 1777 –

The Petition of a great number of Negroes who are detained in a state of Slavery in the Bowels of a free & Christian Country –

Humbly Shewing –

That your Petitioners apprehend that they have, in common with all other Men, a natural & unalienable right to that freedom, which the great Parent of the Universe hath bestowed equally on all Mankind, & which they have never forfeited by any compact or agreement whatever – But they were unjustly dragged, by the cruel hand of Power, from their dearest friends, & some of them even torn from the Embraces of their tender Parents – From a populous, pleasant, & plentiful Country – & in violation of the Laws of Nature & of Nations & in defiance of all the tender feelings of humanity, brought hither to be sold like Beasts of Burthen, & like them condemned to

*Editor's Note: Two additional petitions from the 1780s protested taxation without representation and the continuing Atlantic slave trade. The first, by Paul Cuffe and seven other blacks from the town of Dartmouth, March 14, 1780, is filed at the Massachusetts Historical Society, Boston; the second, written by Prince Hall and dated February 27, 1788, was published in *The Massachusetts Spy* (Worcester), April 24, 1788.

Slavery for life – Among a people professing the mild Religion of Jesus – A people not insensitive of the sweets of national freedom – Nor without Spirits to resent the unjust endeavours of others, to reduce them to a State of Bondage & Subjection – Your Honors need not to be informed that a Life of Slavery, like that of your petitioners, deprived of every social privelege, of every thing requisite to render Life even tolerable, is far worse than Non-Existence – In imitation of the laudable example of the good People of these States, your Petitioners have long & patiently waited the event of Petition after Petition, by them presented to the Legislative Body of this State, & can not but with grief reflect that their success has been but too similar – They can not but express their astonishment, that it has never been considered, that every principle from which America has acted in the course of her unhappy difficulties with Great-Britain, pleas stronger than a thousand arguments in favor of your Petitioners – They therefore humbly beseech your Honors, to give this Petition its due weight & consideration, & cause an Act of the legislature to be passed whereby they may be restored to the enjoyment of that freedom which is the natural right of all men – & their Children (who were born in this land of Liberty) may not be held as slaves after they arrive at the age of twenty-one years – So may the Inhabitants of this State (no longer chargeable with the inconsistency of acting, themselves, the part which they condemn & oppose in others) be prospered in their present glorious struggle for Liberty, & have those blessings secured to them by Heaven, of which benevolent minds can not wish to deprive their fellow Men. –

And your Petitioners, as in duty bound, shall ever pray –

(signed) Lancaster Hill
X Peter Bess
Bryter Hensen
Prince Hall
Job Lock

and the marks (X) of
Jack Pierpont
Nero Suniss
Newport Sumner

19

"Nocturnal Frolicks"

SOURCE: *The Boston Evening-Post,* Jan. 14, 1740.

Last Friday Night a Gentleman of this Town went over to *Roxbury* to look for his Negro Woman, who had been gone from him a few Days; and hearing a Noise in the Tavern, he went in, (past Nine o'Clock) and found about a Dozen black Gentry, He's and She's, in a Room, in a very merry Humour, singing and dancing, having a Violin, and Store of Wine and Punch before them. They all belonged to Gentlemen in this Town; and 'tis much to be wondered at, how they can be absent from their respective Families without their Masters Knowledge: And 'tis yet more to be wondered at, if they obtain their Masters leave to attend these Nocturnal Frolicks, which must needs be very expensive, and 'tis well known that their own Revenues are very small. Whether it be convenient that publick Houses should give Entertainment to our Slaves, at all, but especially at the Time of Night above-mentioned, we leave to the Consideration of our Betters.

20

A Consort's Funeral

SOURCE: *The New-England Courant* (Boston), July 22, 1723.

On Wednesday morning last dyed here Mrs. -----Carlington, Consort of Mr. James Carlington, an African, belonging to Robert Auchmuty Esq. Her Corpse was carryed in a Coach to her Mother's House, at the North End of the Town, on Wednesday Night; and on Thursday Night she was magnificently interr'd at the North Burying Place, the (Velvet) Pall being supported by six Blacks of the first Rank, and her Funeral attended by two hundred and seventy more of the same Colour.

21

A Freeman's Funeral

SOURCE: *New-England Weekly Journal,* Feb. 24, 1729, reprinted in "Diary of Samuel Sewall," *Collections of the Massachusetts Historical Society,* 5th Ser., VII (1882), 394-95.

On the 14th died here a Negro Freeman named Boston in an advanced Age; and on the 17th, was very decently Buried. A long Train follow'd him to the Grave, it's said about 150 Blacks, and about 50 Whites, several Magistrates, Ministers, Gentlemen &c. He having borne the Character of a sober, virtuous Liver, and of a very trusty honest and faithful Servant to all that employ'd him, and having acquir'd to himself the general Love and Esteem of his Neighbours by a Readiness to do any good offices in his power for every one; his Funeral was attended with uncommon Respects and his Death much lamented.

22

Inoculation Against Smallpox

SOURCE: Otho T. Beall, Jr., and Richard H. Shryock, "Cotton Mather: First Significant Figure in American Medicine," *Proceedings of the American Antiquarian Society,* LXIII (April 15, 1953), pp. 138-9.

Letter of Cotton Mather to Dr. Woodward, July 12, 1716:

. . . many months before I mett with any Intimations of treating the Small-Pox, with the Method of Inoculation, any where in Europe; I had from a Servant of my own, an Account of its being practised in Africa. Inquiring of my Negro-man Onesimus, who is a pretty Intelligent Fellow, Whether he ever had the Small-Pox; he answered, both, Yes, and No; and then told me, that he had undergone an Operation, which had given him something of the Small-Pox, & would forever praeserve him from it; adding, That it was often used among the Guramantese . . . and his Description of it, made it the same, that afterwards I found related unto you by your Timonious.

DARRETT B. RUTMAN

The Social Web: A Prospectus for the Study of the Early American Community

IN JANUARY 1640, in the church at Boston in the Massachusetts Bay colony, Mistress Temperance Sweet stood dejectedly before the congregation as Pastor John Wilson admonished her "in the name of the Lord and with the consent of the church." Mistress Sweet had been maintaining an unofficial and illegal public house, inviting into her home a "disorderly company and ministering unto them wine and strong waters unto drunkenness, and that not without some iniquity both in the measure and price."

Almost half a century later, in another church – Piankatank Church, Middlesex County, Virginia – one Mistress Jones stood not dejectedly but angrily before the churchwarden. Mistress Jones was the housekeeper of the Honorable Colonel Christopher Wormeley and the mother of two illegitimate children. This Sabbath morning she had, for whatever her reasons, changed her seat in the church, choosing a place "above her degree." Churchwarden Matthew Kemp had admonished her presumption, asked her to move back, been answered with "hard words," but persisted and eventually succeeded in "displacing" the angry woman. A month later the leading parishioners, through their vestry, tendered thanks to Mr. Kemp "for his diligence in his duty," pronounced "that they approve of what was . . . done" and averred that they would "stand by him not only in this but in all actions of the like nature."[1]

The cases of Mistress Sweet and Mistress Jones are widely separated in time and place. But in both one sees the force of a community being exercised against what community members discerned as transgressions against common values and a common way.

I

"Community" – what does the word mean?

Such a question is not generally asked by the historian. For the historian has, generically, been guided by the language of the people of the past he is studying. Community is a word common in the ideological rhetoric of the seventeenth century, particularly (in the American context) in the rhetoric of those we call "Puritan." The Puritans, as they arrived in New England, settled not in a scattered fashion, on farms here and there, but in relatively tight-knit towns. And American historians have tended to link the rhetoric and settlement pattern to effect an implicit definition of community as the ideal Puritan town. They have waxed eloquent over the community orientation of the New Englanders and used that community orientation as a touch-phrase to distinguish New England from other regions where – in the absence of both Puritan rhetoric and a town-based settlement pattern – community is discerned as much diminished or totally absent.[2]

[1] First Church of Boston, Records and Baptisms, 1630-1687, manuscript copy in the Massachusetts Historical Society Library, Boston, under date of January 8, 1639/40; C.G. Chamberlayne, ed., *The Vestry Book of Christ Church Parish, Middlesex County, Virginia: 1663-1767* (Richmond, Va., 1927) 63. All quotations in the text have been modernized. Successive versions of this paper have been offered at the Brandeis University Conference on the New England Town in the Seventeenth and Eighteenth Centuries: Patterns of Behavior and Change, February 1970; the Southern Historical Association, November 1970; and before student-faculty groups at the University of New Hampshire, the University of Maryland, and the University of Rhode Island. Each airing has been followed by revision and amendment. The author's research has been considerably furthered by support received from the Central University Research Fund and Computation Center of the University of New Hampshire, and by the labors of his research assistants, Fleurange Jacques, Ellen Ramsey, and, undertaking programming, Edward G. Fisher.

[2] *cf.* Michael Zuckerman, *Peaceable Kingdoms: New England Towns in the Eighteenth Century* (New York, 1970) on the one hand and, on the other, David Bertelson, *The Lazy South* (New York, 1967) and Morris Talpalar, *The Sociology of Colonial Virginia* (New York, 1960). Note also Page Smith, *As a City Upon a Hill: The*

Yet the question is pertinent. The remnants of the past – documents, maps, physical remains – are few; they were the work of men and women of far different outlook and were prepared for far different purposes than the outlook and purposes of the historians perusing them. To a new breed of historians, less interested in the past for its own sake and interested more in the past as a laboratory for the study of human behavior over time, the fallacy of allowing the dim shadow of the past to structure the study of past behavior has become obvious.[3] For such historians the study of communal behavior must begin with the abstract question: What is a community?

Moreover, the question is pertinent to those who would effect reforms in contemporary America by reviving what they discern as a lost sense of community. For notably there is a school of enthusiasts today which diagnoses the social ailment of the land as a severe deficiency of community life and would set about to cure the malady by recreating communities large and small – preferably small.[4] One can suggest that historians and reformers are related, for implicit in the diagnosis and proposed cure of the latter is a view of the American past stretching through the nineteenth century, when the depersonalizing city rose in contrast to the singularly virtuous small town, to the colonial years and the New England town, looming majestically in its simplicity, harmony, and unity. White clapboard houses rimming a green common, a church spire overtopping the trees – the picture evokes the image of the early New Englanders gathering on Sabbath day for services, on militia-day for training, and on town meeting day to determine for themselves the everyday affairs of their lives. Here, truly, was the epitome of community in American life! By contrast, the American colonists beyond New England, particularly in the South, lived hard, lonely lives on scattered farms and plantations, without community. The epitome

---

Town in American History (New York, 1966) where community is epitomized as the town, and the town, in terms of the nation, is considered an export from New England. That the present author, all too recently, held to the same dichotomy – see his *American Puritanism: Faith and Practice* (Philadelphia, 1970), 47 – is evidence only that scholars are merely students, continually learning.

[3] A good critique of classic historiography and argument for a new approach is Robert F. Berkhofer, Jr., *A Behavioral Approach to Historical Analysis* (New York, 1969).

[4] See e.g., Maurice R. Stein, *The Eclipse of Community: An Interpretation of American Studies* (Princeton, 1960) and the best-selling Charles A. Reich, *The Greening of America* (New York, 1970), 7.

of community – the New England town, a product of the historian's pen – serves as an implicit model for the enthusiasts; the contrasting South solidifies the simplistic dichotomy on which they base diagnosis and cure: One lives meaningfully within community and meaninglessly without. The fact of model and dichotomy would seem to require an understanding of community in a historical perspective and in particular of the early American community. And understanding must begin with a definition of what is to be understood. The question poses itself again: Community – what does the word mean?

II

Anthropologists and sociologists – not historians – have grappled with, and argued about, the definition of community. For them, human society, certainly in evolution and perhaps in present fact, is founded upon, first, the family, and second, collective or communal activity by groups of families.[5] To study the latter, some among them have sought out specific places in which communal activity is readily observable, describing in a lengthy series of "community studies" places, people, and activities. And their very approach has tended to define the subject matter. "Some consensus exists," writes one, "concerning at least three elements in the definition of community."

> One, community is a social unit of which space is an integral part; community is a place, a relatively small one. Two, community indicates a configuration as to way of life, both as to how people do things and what they want – their institutions and collective goals. A third notion is that of collective action. Persons in a community should not only be able to, but frequently do act together in the common concerns of life.[6]

[5] William J. Gore, "An Overview of Social Science Perspectives Toward the Small Community" in William J. Gore and Leroy C. Hodapp, eds., *Change in the Small Community: An Interdisciplinary Survey* (New York, 1967), 13ff. The extent of sociological work alone is indicated in the 142 pages of Raymond Payne and Wilfrid C. Bailey, comps., *The Community: A Classified, Annotated Bibliography* (Athens, Ga., 1967). See also the bibliography in Conrad M. Arensberg and Solon T. Kimball, *Culture and Community* (New York, 1965).

[6] Harold R. Kaufman, "Toward an Interactional Conception of Community," in Roland L. Warren, ed., *Perspectives on the American Community* (Chicago, 1966), 89. (Originally published in *Social Forces*, XXXVIII [1959], 9-17.) See also George A. Hillery, Jr., "Definitions of Community: Areas of Agreement," *Rural Sociology*, XX (1955), 111-123; his "The Folk Village: A Comparative Analysis," *Rural Sociology*, XXVI (1961), 337-358; and his *Communal Organizations: A Study of Local Societies* (Chicago, 1968).

Others in these sister disciplines have concerned themselves less with single places and more with the collectivity of places which make up large social units – the multitudes of communities which make up cities, regions, states, nations, even *Homo sapiens* as a world-girdling society. In the way of scholars, such have not always dealt nicely with their predecessors and colleagues. Sociologists and anthropologists dealing with single places, writes one critic, have "fallen into the pattern of treating the community as if it were a desert island culture, almost completely cut off from the surrounding world." "We do not," he wails, "have an adequate theoretical framework for analysing the relations of the community to the surrounding society and culture."[7] To rectify the deficiency such scholars have introduced the notion of dimension into the definition of community. The community is a place, true; persons within the community are marked by a common way of life and act together in common concerns; but what is common within the locality is only the *horizontal* dimension of the community. Invariably, particular persons within the locality have individual or collective associations of particular kinds outside the community and these extra-communal associations constitute a *vertical* dimension.[8] The essentials of any community, therefore –

[7] Roland L. Warren, "Toward a Reformulation of Community Theory," in Robert Mills French, ed., *The Community: A Comparative Perspective* (Itasca, Ill., 1969), 42. (Originally published in *Human Organization,* XV [1956], 8-11.) See also Julian H. Steward, "Area Research: Theory and Practice," Social Science Research Council, *Bulletin,* LXIII (1950), 22-23. The classic introduction to community – R.M. MacIver, *Community: A Sociological Study* (New York, 1931) – stressed communal interaction, but few followed his lead until the early 1950s, and most community studies still ignore the question. Some of the most exciting contemporary social history revolves around the study of the New England town, e.g., John Demos, *A Little Commonwealth: Family Life in Plymouth Colony* (New York, 1970); Charles S. Grant, *Democracy in the Connecticut Frontier Town of Kent* (New York, 1961); Philip J. Greven, Jr., *Four Generations: Population, Land, and Family in Colonial Andover, Massachusetts* (Ithaca, N.Y., 1970); Kenneth A. Lockridge, *A New England Town: The First Hundred Years* (New York, 1970); Sumner Chilton Powell, *Puritan Village: The Formation of a New England Town* (Middletown, Conn., 1963); Darrett B. Rutman, *Winthrop's Boston: Portrait of a Puritan Town* (Chapel Hill, N.C., 1965). And the town has become a popular dissertation topic, e.g., Bruce P. Stark's 1970 University of Connecticut dissertation on Lebanon, Connecticut. To an extent these works are based upon that of English and French historians such as Louis Henry, Etienne Gautier, Pierre Goubert, Pierre Deyon, W.G. Hoskins, E.A. Wrigley, and Peter Laslett. But in none of the studies is the community the specific subject, only the locale, be it a New England town, an English parish, or a French village. And it would seem that such historians are making the same mistake that sociologists and anthropologists have made, that is, dealing with their locales as "desert islands" and ignoring the position of their locales within a web of locales making up larger social units – i.e., the vertical dimension.

[8] See again Warren, "Toward a Reformulation of Community Theory," 42ff; his

from a medieval (or early American) village, to a modern suburb or an inner city street-corner society – are to be defined in terms of the space it occupies, the way of life accepted as common by its inhabitants, the collective actions chosen or forced by conditions upon those inhabitants, and the external associations which, by way of particular persons, link the community to the larger social units.

We need not follow the sociologists and anthropologists as they refine – some would say rarify – this definition, nor need we allow them to entangle us in their disputes: Does, for example, the definition set adequate heuristic boundaries for the study of *all* human communities, from the primitive hunting band which seems deficient in place to our modern suburbs which seem deficient in common life and activity? Is it not too all-inclusive a definition in that a prison or insane asylum can be conceived of as a community?

But we do need to recognize – and recognize clearly – that the definition is not that of a unique entity. It does not, for example, prescribe the exact balance between the vertical and horizontal dimensions but allows an infinite number of points between a theoretical (but never actual) community completely self-contained and self-concerned, absolutely definable in terms of its horizontal dimension, and the equally theoretic opposite extreme of a community completely outer-concerned, absolutely definable in terms of its vertical dimension. Neither does it prescribe the exact form or structure of the community. It does not stipulate, for example, that all communities assume the form of a tight-knit, concentric village; therefore people living on scattered farms are devoid of community. In brief, the definition offers – as reality invariably suggests – a multiplicity of community types.

If we allow this definition to guide our exploration of early American communities, we abandon immediately the simplistic dichotomy which assigns the New England villager to community life and those elsewhere, living in scattered fashion, to a community-less existence. Indeed, the compact village and the dispersed, open-country amalgamation of farm families are equally communities, long recognized as specific types among the myriad

---

The Community in America (Chicago, 1963), chap. 8; and Robert Redfield, *Peasant Society and Culture* (Chicago, 1956), chap. II. Other social scientists – e.g., Steward, "Area Research" – reverse the terminology to define the vertical dimension in terms of the locale and the horizontal dimension in terms of the inter-communal web.

of types by students of community.[9] One finds both in the England of the late sixteenth and early seventeenth centuries – an open-country amalgamation of single farmsteads and tiny hamlets or neighborhoods tending to pervade the north and west of the island kingdom, the compact village pervading the south and east. This English division itself was merely a reflection of a European-wide division associated with (if not following from) diverse agricultural practices – areas devoted more to livestock and less to grain having tended toward dispersal while areas devoted more to grain and less to livestock tended toward compaction.[10] And a familiarity with both types was inevitably carried to America as part of the cultural baggage upon which the first settlers drew as they restructured their lives in the new world.[11]

III

Space – the occupancy of a given area, whatever the form of that occupancy – is an essential element of our definition of community. But other things are definable in terms of space as well, units of government, for example, and therein lies a great deal of confusion. A Virginia county or a New England town was (and is) a unit of government legally defined with reference to specific boundaries. But those living within such boundaries did not *necessarily* constitute communities. The elements of our definition are interrelated and space is determined by the outer limits of the common way of life recognized by the inhabitants and of the common actions they take. The community, therefore, can be said to bound itself by virtue of its recognition of itself. How then does the outsider, intent on studying the community, find its boundaries? Sociologists and anthropologists have, at times, simply asked the inhabitants to what community they

[9] Arensberg and Kimball, *Culture and Community,* chap. iv; Walter L. Slocum, *Agricultural Sociology: A Study of Sociological Aspects of American Farm Life* (New York, 1962), 113; Walter A. Terpenning, *Village and Open Country Neighborhoods* (New York, 1931), *passim.*

[10] Joan Thirsk, "The Farming Regions of England," in H.P.R. Finberg, ed., *The Agrarian History of England and Wales,* IV, *1500-1640* (Cambridge, Eng., 1967), 5ff; Arensberg and Kimball, *Culture and Community,* 89-90.

[11] Space and above all the paucity of depth studies of single communities and their limitation in the main to New England's towns requires a limitation here to a consideration of early New England and early Virginia. Very largely I am drawing upon the town studies cited in note 7 above and my own studies of the New Hampshire towns on the one hand, and of Virginia counties, particularly Middlesex, on the other.

belong.[12] The historian cannot resort to this for the inhabitants of his past communities stand mute. He has, instead, to *infer* the boundaries of the communities he studies.

Such inference with regard to the very earliest New England towns is easily made. New England's Puritan leaders – lay and ministerial – arrived in America with a rigid view of the ideal society, one accenting the obligations of the individual to the common good.[13] The ideal was not uniquely theirs as Puritans. Indeed, in the England of the moment any who thought about society – the literate, the educated, the ministers, playwrights and poets, the merchants and men of government – idealized it as an organic and ordered whole, a single hierarchical entity, God-ordained, in which each individual contentedly occupied a particular niche, sublimating his own aspirations and desire to the well-being of the whole. "Every degree of people, in their vocations, calling, and office, hath appointed to them their duty and order" – so postulated *The Book of Homilies* of 1562; "Some are in high degree, some in low; some kings and princes, some inferiors and subjects; priests and laymen, masters and servants, fathers and children, husbands and wives, rich and poor; and every one have need of other."[14] A high churchman some sixty years later warned that "if any man be so addicted to his private, that he neglect the common state, he is void of the sense of piety, and wisheth peace and happiness to himself in vain."

> For whoever he be, he must live in the body of the Commonwealth . . . and if [its] joints be out, and in trouble, how can he hope to live in "peace"? This is just as much as if the exterior parts of the body should think they might live healthful, though the stomach be full of sick and swollen humors.[15]

Degree, order, obedience, subordination of self to the social good, but also the physical proximity of one member of society to another were exalted – indeed, the ideal was far more reflective of the English village community of the moment than of the open-country community. In 1625, for example, the same high

[12] E.g., Irvin T. Sanders and Douglas Ensminger, *Alabama Rural Communities: A Study of Chilton County* ("Bulletin Published Quarterly by Alabama College," XXXIII, No. 1A; Montevallo, Ala., 1940), 19ff.

[13] What follows summarizes Rutman, *American Puritanism,* chap. 3.

[14] "An Exhortation to Obedience," *The Book of Homilies* (1562) in Society for the Propagation of the Christian Church, *Certain Sermons or Homilies* (London, 1890), 109. See also E.M.W. Tillyard, *The Elizabethan World Picture* (New York, 1943).

[15] *The Works of the Most Reverend Father in God, William Laud, D.D. Sometime Lord Arch-bishop of Canterbury* (Oxford, 1847-60), I, 28-29.

churchman took as his text Psalm 122 ("Jerusalem is builded as a city that is compact together") to speak of society as "like 'a city at unity in itself,' that is, for the inhabitants. For the beauty and artificial joining of the houses is expressed but as a type of this unity; when men dwell as near in affection as their houses stand in place."[16]

New England's leaders, however, coming to the new world with the intention of building religious *and social* perfection, accented the ideal and sought to make of it a reality. John Winthrop, leader of the 1630 migration to Massachusetts Bay, reflected as much when he, together with other leaders, made plans for a single, compact settlement to hold his thousand-odd emigrants, and when, in a lay-sermon delivered to the settlers at sea before their arrival, he told them:

> We must entertain each other in brotherly affection. We must be willing to abridge ourselves of our superfluities for the supply of others' necessities. We must uphold a familiar commerce together in all meekness, gentleness, patience, and liberality. We must delight in each other, make others' conditions our own, rejoice together, mourn together, labor and suffer together, always having before our eyes our commission and community in the work, our community as members of the same body.[17]

Accident, not design, scattered this first major group to land in the Bay area. The initial intention of the leaders to have a single settlement was frustrated by, among other things, an epidemic countered only by dispersing into small clusters which quickly and naturally took the form of the English village community – the type from which most of these first settlers seem to have come.[18] But thereafter all of the authority of the leading laymen, all of the rhetorical vehemence of the Puritan ministers, was thrown on the side of the renascent villages.

Sermons regularly bespoke the communal ideal: degree, order, obedience, subordination of self, proximity. Land was granted by the central government largely to groups committed to settle as a single social unit. A brief-lived law of the 1630s required all to build their houses within a half-mile of the meetinghouse. The village, incorporated as the town, was made a primary unit of

[16] *Ibid.*, 63-65.

[17] "A Modell of Christian Charity," Massachusetts Historical Society, *Winthrop Papers* ([Boston], 1929-47), II, 294. See also Rutman, *Winthrop's Boston,* chap. I and Appendix I.

[18] Carl Bridenbaugh, *Vexed and Troubled Englishmen: 1590-1642* (New York, 1968), 465.

social action, as in 1642 when the Massachusetts General Court, "taking into consideration the great neglect of many parents and masters in training up their children in learning and labor, and other employments which may be profitable to the commonwealth" ordered that the town selectmen "shall henceforth stand charged with the care and redress of this evil."[19] Above all, the town was made the primary unit of the religious structure. Each town, ideally, had its church, and each church, as congregationalism formalized from Puritanism, was theoretically an entity in itself, a locus of exclusive identity for the townsmen. With the rhetoric and the laws of the leadership reinforcing the natural inclination of the settlers to restructure their lives about the familiar village community, town and community, at least momentarily, became one. The first townsmen of Dedham, in the explicit terms of their town covenant, exemplify the conjunction:

> We whose names are hereunto subscribed do, in the fear and reverence of our Almighty God, mutually and severally promise amongst ourselves and each other to profess and practise one truth according to that most perfect rule the foundation whereof is everlasting love.

So ran the preface, while in the body the townsmen promised "peaceable conversation" and "the mutual encouragement unto all temporal comforts in all things," the resolution, among themselves, of all disputes, their submission to all "orders and constitutions" which they might make in common "as well for loving and comfortable society in our said town as also for the prosperous and thriving condition of our said fellowship," and to exclude all those in future who would not similarly promise.[20] Clearly the Dedhamites recognized their town as an area of common life and common action, and the historian, studying this early New England community, can safely infer its boundaries from the boundaries of the town.

Such inference can *only* be made safely for New England's earliest years, however. It is less safely made the farther in time one proceeds from the founding years. True, the rhetoric of community remained, and of the coextensiveness of the boundaries of the town and the limits of common life and common action. Historian Michael Zuckerman, in a study of Massachusetts

[19] Nathaniel B. Shurtleff, ed., *Records of the Governor and Company of the Massachusetts Bay in New England* (Boston, 1853-54), II, 6.

[20] *Early Records of the Town of Dedham* (Dedham, Mass., 1886-1936), III, 2-3.

towns in the eighteenth century, has indicated as much.[21] But beneath the facade of the rhetoric a process vital to the student of communities was underway.

Notably, the earliest towns *qua* communities occupied only small portions of the extensive territories of the towns as legal entities. Dedham's first hundred families, for example, clustered in the northeast corner of a tract some twenty miles long by an average of eight miles wide; Boston, in the 1630s, included isolated tracts almost encircling Boston Harbor; Dover, one of the earliest towns in what would become New Hampshire, encompassed over eighty-three square miles, its first inhabitants clinging together on a small peninsula between two of the many rivers feeding the "great bay" of New Hampshire; Plymouth, the Pilgrims' original community, at mid-seventeenth century embraced, as a town, an area of roughly 144 square miles.[22] Within only a few years of the founding of any early town, the original, tight-knit settlement, constrained in a corner of the town's broad grant, tended to degenerate as families began moving outward onto the land, occupying quasi-isolated farms or clustering loosely in scattered neighborhoods or peripheral villages. The recognition of the area of common life and common action – the community's recognition of itself – was clearly strained in the process. Thus Plymouth's leaders wrote to Boston's in 1639 seeking advice as to "the holding of farms of which there is no less frequent use with yourselves than with us." The farms, they wrote, were "needful for the comfort and well being" of the community, but in separating men from each other and from the church, were they not also an evil? And Plymouth's William Bradford complained that "there was no longer any holding them together, but now they must of necessity go to their great lots [i.e., their farms]. . . .

[21] Zuckerman, *Peaceable Kingdoms, passim.*

[22] See the map of Dedham in Lockridge, *A New England Town,* x; of Boston in Rutman, *Winthrop's Boston,* 71; *idem* on Plymouth in *Husbandmen of Plymouth: Farms and Villages in the Old Colony, 1620-1692* (Boston, 1967), 23-24. Dover's original size is found (as part of the author's continuing study of the New Hampshire towns) by combining the area of the towns breaking away from Dover and the remnant Dover size, using Eliphalet and Phineas Merrill, comps., *Gazetteer of the State of New Hampshire* (Exeter, N.H., 1817); John Farmer and Jacob B. Moore, comps., *A Gazetteer of the State of New Hampshire* (Concord, N.H., 1823); and the documents and notes in Nathaniel Bouton, et al., eds., *Documents and Records Relating to the Province [Towns and State] of New Hampshire, 1623-1800* (Concord, N.H., etc., 1867-1943), IX, XI-XIII, XXIV-XXVI. A similar survey of the Connecticut towns conforms, the mean area of the ten towns of the first decade (1630-1640), for example, being slightly over 97 square miles.

by which means they were scattered all over the Bay quickly and the town in which they lived compactly till now was left very thin and in a short time almost desolate."[23] Far-flung Boston neighborhoods came to share more with their nearer-neighbors than with their fellow-townsmen across the harbor, even church membership. Neighborhoods, without leaving the legal entity of their parent towns, gradually came to recognize a shared communality distinct from that of the towns, as the Oyster River neighborhood of New Hampshire's Dover seems to have done in 1669 when it sought the town's approval for a separate church and minister of its own; by early eighteenth-century it would recognize itself – and be recognized – as a distinct "parish."[24] More often than not, the strained recognition of communality led ultimately to a complete break. Town boundaries were readjusted to shift neighborhoods from one town to another, or neighborhoods were established as independent towns. Dedham, for example, spawned twelve towns, Dover five. The conjunction of the community recognizing itself as such and of the town as a legal entity was perhaps reachieved by this ultimate step. But in the confusion of the ongoing process, the observing historian intent on locating the community had best be wary. When is a gradually separating neighborhood a community in and of itself, apart from its parent community but sharing the legal entity of the town? When is a neighborhood legally within one town in actuality a part of a community centered in another? The inference as to the town/community conjunction in the case of any particular New England town once the founding years are past is not at all sure, but uneasy and tentative.

For any time period, to infer the boundaries of Virginia's communities is neither easy nor safe. True, the English idealization of society arrived in the south, as it arrived in New England. Sir Thomas Dale, Virginia's stern marshal and, sporadically between 1611 and 1616, acting governor, reflected it in his building (in 1611) of Henrico, a fortified and centralized village up-river from Jamestown. He reflected it again in a prayer he appended to the colony's first law code in 1612:

[23] John Reyner and William Brewster for the church in Plymouth to the church in Boston, August 5, 1639, Cotton Papers, Prince Collection, Boston Public Library; William Bradford, *Of Plymouth Plantation,* Samuel Eliot Morison, ed., (New York, 1953), 253.

[24] Rutman, *Winthrop's Boston,* 93ff; Bouton, et al., eds., *Documents and Records Relating to . . . New Hampshire,* XXIV, 102ff. Lockridge, *A New England Town,* 93ff well covers the disintegration of Dedham.

> O Lord we pray thee fortify us. . . . Let them mock such as help to build up the walls of Jerusalem . . . but let not the rod of the wicked fall upon the lot of the righteous. . . . O Lord we earnestly beseech thee to receive us into thy favor and protection. Defend us from the delusion of the devil, the malice of the heathen, the invasions of our enemies, and mutinies and dissensions of our own people. *Knit our hearts altogether in faith and fear of thee, and love one to another.*[25]

But neither the vehemence of the preachers (they were initially few and not particularly Puritan)[26] nor the single-minded idealism of the leaders was present, as it was in New England. Relatively unsupported by law or rhetoric, the ideal could not guide the developing situation. Initial settlement largely by single men seeking the main chance (as against New England's families intent on restructuring the entirety of their lives, including their English communities),[27] the distribution of land on the basis of the number of laborers imported, and the appearance of a tobacco culture which put a premium upon both labor and land – all combined, in the absence of the strong assertion of the ideal, to disperse the Virginians into loosely clustered farms from the very beginning. The dispersal provoked periodic complaints from observers, one of whom – an English parson – wrote of the Virginians "scatteringly seated upon the sides of rivers" and "at such distances from each other" as to deprive themselves of "Christian neighborhood, or brotherly admonition, of holy examples of religious persons, of the comfort of theirs, and their ministers' administrations in sickness and distresses, of the benefit of Christian and civil conferences and commerce."[28] But the good parson was inveighing against the scarcity and scattering of ministers and the absence of the English communal ideal, not necessarily against the absence of communities as we have defined them.

[25] *For the Colony in Virginiea Britannia. Lawes Divine, Morall and Martiall, &c.* (London, 1612), in Peter Force, comp., *Tracts and Other Papers Relating Principally to the . . . Colonies . . .* (Washington, 1836-47), III, Tract II, 67-68. Italics inserted.

[26] Rutman, *American Puritanism,* 49-51 – in 1650 there were thirty-seven ministers in Massachusetts alone, one per 415 people; in Virginia there were only six ministers, one per 3,239 persons.

[27] Cf. chaps. XI and XII of Bridenbaugh, *Vexed and Troubled Englishmen* or the number of family groupings indicated in the various shipping lists printed in (e.g.) John Camden Hotten, ed., *The Original Lists of Persons of Quality . . . Who Went from Great Britain to the American Plantation, 1600-1700* (New York, 1880).

[28] R[oger] G[reen] *Virginia's Cure: Or An Advisive Narrative Concerning Virginia* (London, 1662), in Force, comp., *Tracts . . . Relating Principally to the . . . Colonies,* III, Tract XV, 4-6.

Virginia's families (for women *did* eventually arrive, and men took wives and begat children), even while living more distant from one another than in New England,[29] established relationships, recognized in each other a measure of common life, and accepted the obligations of common actions. Virginia's government seems to have recognized, albeit unconsciously, the basic communal structure emerging when, in the 1620s, it named "commanders" – combination militia and civil officers – for each of a number of vague, shadowy areas, Mr. John Utie, for example, commissioned commander for "all between Martin's Hundred and Archers' Creek."[30] In the 1630s counties were established as the basic unit of local government. And the counties reflected to some extent a felt-unity among the inhabitants of the particular regions; the inhabitants by vote, or commissions consisting of a few leading inhabitants, had a say as to the boundaries. But any single county, then or thereafter, was a complex of loose farm neighborhoods. The regular division of counties, the establishment of new counties from old, and the readjustment of county boundaries, indicate the same process of shifting communal recognition as in the later New

[29] The distinctive spatial patterns of later New England towns and Virginia counties can, however, be overstated. The significant differences were that in Virginia (at least Tidewater Virginia) villages per se were lacking until well into the eighteenth century, individual holdings were, on the average, larger, and the distances between houses, even in population clusters, consequently greater, as were the distances between such clusters. But except for the absence in Virginia of New England's relatively abiding and (in the American context) peculiar communal ideal, the differences sum up to a matter of degree rather than kind. The innate similarity can be sensed in density figures. Dover, N.H., in 1715, had an area of 83 square miles, a population of about 1,560 in all neighborhoods, a density of 19 per square mile; a petition of 1722 noted "the circumstances and situation of settlements of the inhabitants of said town lying and being in such manner as . . . the houses being so scattered over the whole township that in no one place six houses are within call." (Bouton, et al., *Documents and Records Relating to . . . New Hampshire,* IX, 156.) Middlesex County, Virginia had a population of about 1,950 in the 1680s – some twenty years after settlement in the area – living in loose but identifiable farm neighborhoods, an area of 175 square miles, and a density of about 11 per square mile; by 1715, the population had risen to about 2,800, density to 16 per square mile. The description of Dover is by no means unique – see the descriptions of Lynn, Massachusetts and Hampton, New Hampshire in Carl Bridenbaugh, ed., *Gentleman's Progress: The Itinerarium of Dr. Alexander Hamilton, 1744* (Chapel Hill, N.C., 1948), 117-18, 123, 127. Few historians have sensed the dispersal of the New Englanders. George Francis Dow did (see his *Every Day Life in the Massachusetts Bay Colony* [Boston, 1935], 118-19); Lockridge does for later Dedham; Charles E. Clark, *The Eastern Frontier: The Settlement of Northern New England, 1610-1763* (New York, 1970), chap. XIII sees it as an eighteenth century phenomenon. A view of Plymouth Colony (see Rutman, *Husbandmen of Plymouth,* chap. I) moves it back into the early and mid-seventeenth century.

[30] H.R. McIlwaine, ed., *Minutes of the Council and General Court of Colonial Virginia, 1622-1632, 1670-1676* (Richmond, Va., 1924), 192-93.

England towns.[31] As with regard to the later towns, therefore, we can only tentatively and uneasily infer the conjunction of county and community in any particular case.

This tentative and inferential acceptance of the conjunction, in terms of space, of particular communities and legal entities – towns and counties – must keep us aware that we are dealing with fluid situations, that communities as self-recognizing areas of common life and action could and did redefine themselves. But we can proceed by accepting as a generalization the coextensiveness of communities and legal entities in early America. For one thing, the fact that legal entities were units of local government, and, as we shall see, institutionalized a whole range of common actions, always reinforced the spatial conjunction; the redefinition of a community apart from the legal entity occurred in spite of a natural tendency to keep the two congruent. For another, the acceptance of the generalization does not bar us from accepting as well the notion that there were exceptions, even many and crucial exceptions. It does, however, allow us to generalize the common life and actions of the inhabitants of communities as they are reflected in the most readily available evidence, the remnant records of towns and counties.[32]

IV

From the standpoint of the individual the recognized area of common life and activity – his community – spread concentrically outward from the family. For everywhere along the Anglo-American coast the family was basic. And, with few exceptions, the families individually and severally devoted themselves to the soil, to farms. The differing products of the farms – grains and livestock in New England, grains, livestock and tobacco in Virginia – need not concern us for the moment. The family basis of the community was true regardless.[33]

[31] Robert Beverley, *The History and Present State of Virginia,* Louis B. Wright, ed. (Chapel Hill, N.C., 1947), 243 is suggestive, as are Philip Alexander Bruce, *Institutional History of Virginia in the Seventeenth Century* (New York, 1910), II, 295ff and the early chapters of Albert Ogden Porter, *County Government in Virginia: A Legislative History, 1607-1904* (New York, 1947).

[32] Such generalizations as are offered in the following can only be suggestive given the limited number of depth studies available.

[33] On contemporary European attitudes see Philippe Aries, *Centuries of Childhood: A Social History of Family Life,* Robert Baldick, trans. (New York, 1962); on New England attitudes, Demos, *A Little Commonwealth* particularly, but also Edmund S. Morgan, *The Puritan Family: Religion and Domestic Relations in Seventeenth-Century*

Within the family, individuals were born or, in the case of orphans and servants, placed by law and custom, there to be educated – socialized is the modern word – to the ways of the community. Maturity was indicated by departure from the family, marriage, and the founding of new families. But maturing children did not tend to stray far. Geographic mobility was, in the main, limited. Marriages, for example, were most often intra-communal; a study of some 8,000 marriages in ten New Hampshire towns during the eighteenth century indicates that approximately 80 per cent of all young men and women found partners within their communities.[34] Sons – all but one usually, and he staying on to care for aging parents and eventually assuming the parents' farm – were more often than not settled by parents on farms in their near vicinity, creating geographic kinship clusters. So too was social mobility limited, for families tended to define for the children their status within the community. Marriages were more often across social-economic levels than up or down, and positions of power and authority within communities tended to be dominated by relatively few families. Fathers prominent in the community introduced their sons early to the community's business – "the children of illustrious families," wrote John Adams of Massachusetts, "have generally greater advantages of education and earlier opportunities to be acquainted with public characters and informed of public affairs than those of meaner ones" – and such fathers sponsored their sons as young men in their efforts for public office.[35] Above all, however, families were the principal agencies of cooperation within communities.

To some extent this last is to point to commonplace traditions

New England (New York, 1966). Morgan's *Virginians at Home: Family Life in the Eighteenth Century* (Williamsburg, Va., 1952) is a limited study of gentry families and has yet to be supplemented by a more general and sophisticated work. See Bernard Bailyn, *Education in the Forming of American Society* (Chapel Hill, N.C., 1960), [part I] on the educative role of the family.

[34] Drawing from a seminar study by Raymond B. Wilbur conducted at the University of New Hampshire. A sample of Middlesex marriage, 1703-1704 conforms: 85 per cent of the marriage partners identifiable as Middlesex residents found their spouses within the boundaries of the county; moreover, 82 per cent of the marriages were between persons identified as being within the same social group (Greater Gentry, Gentry, Generality, Transient Renters and Servants).

[35] Adams quoted in Robert Zemsky, *Merchants, Farmers, and River Gods: An Essay on Eighteenth-Century American Politics* (Boston, 1971), 75-76. In Middlesex sixteen family names accounted for 58 per cent of the eighty-four active vestrymen during the years 1663-1729; families dominated the County Court to a similar degree. On patrilocal clustering see particularly Greven, *Four Generations.*

of early farm life, barn raisings and harvest parties, and to cooperation between the nucleated parts of families. Brothers collaborated in the advancement of their individual families, for example, or one member of a family cared for another fallen into adversity, as Marvill Moseley of Middlesex, Virginia, was expected to care for an orphaned brother-in-law, providing him with two years' schooling and an apprenticeship to a ship captain.[36] But more was involved.

Families were patriarchal; fathers ruled, and sons, daughters, wives, servants – all – were subsumed in and, to all beyond the family, represented by the father. It was as heads of families that men held office or otherwise participated in the institutions of the community, most notably the church and local government, and through these self-same fathers the institutions called upon families for cooperation in the interest of the community.[37] In the most rudimentary form, it was a direct call for service, as in early Boston when the town's families were called upon to "bestow fourteen days work, by equal proportion" upon fortifications, or in Middlesex, Virginia when, in 1686, every head of family was required to send "one third part" of the persons "in his or their family or charge" to work upon the roads.[38] More commonly, however, the expenses of community work were apportioned among the community's families in the form of taxes or tithes to be paid by fathers on behalf of their families. In this way the families collectively provided for themselves what individually they could not: highways and bridges, church and public buildings, whatever extra-familial education (i.e., formal schools) the community deemed needful; the care of those indigent and orphans who had no family help available.

Through the communal institutions, too, the fathers regulated relationships between families, stipulating in laws and ordinances the common terms of inter-family relationships, from the location of boundaries between properties (regularly "perambulated") and the height and heft of fences, to the standard weights and measures to be used in transactions. They adjudicated or arbitrated differences that arose. And they maintained the moral

[36] Middlesex County, Virginia, Order Book No. 1, 1673-1680, p. 34.

[37] Notably those drawing up tax and land lists, even early censuses, were generally content to list only the family head, either the father or, occasionally, the widow.

[38] "Boston Town Records [1634-1660/61]," City of Boston, *Report of the Record Commissioners,* II (Boston, 1877), 208; Chamberlayne, ed., *Vestry Book of Christ Church Parish, Middlesex,* 52-53.

boundaries of the community, defining right conduct by summoning and publicly degrading the wrongdoer. The admonishment in Boston's church of Mistress Sweet and in Middlesex's of Mistress Jones, the conviction in a Boston court of Daniel Fairfield for the abuse of "the tender body" of Dorcas Humphrey and his being ordered to wear "an hempen rope about his neck" at all times in public, the presentment, conviction, and fining of Middlesex's John Furrell for " profaning the Lord's Day and absenting himself from the church, condemning divine service in the holy institution" – in all of these the intention was not solely the correction of the malefactor but also the community's edification.[39]

In such familially based communities, moreover, relationships were typically familiar and face-to-face. In a relatively immobile age one covered no more than twenty miles from one's home with a hard and full day's travel. Few traveled more than a day. But one regularly came together with one's fellows of the community, all gathering as participants at funerals and weddings, town meeting day in New England, court day in Virginia, Sabbath church services, and militia training everywhere. Indeed, church and public buildings were both real and symbolic loci of the communities, implicitly recognized as such by the care devoted to their placement, construction, and maintenance. On the church, court, or townhouse door public and personal notices were displayed, while in and about the edifices men and women periodically mingled. Even "the sacredness" of the New England Sabbath "did not prevent discreet conversation on purely secular topics," while in Virginia secularity was open, the time before the service given over to "letters of business, reading advertisements, consulting about the price of tobacco, grain, etc. and settling either the lineage, age, or qualities of favorite horses," that after service to "strolling round the church among the crowd."[40] Position and reputation were familiar to all, and gossip a thread linking all together. There was no need, for example, for the

[39]For the case of Mistress Sweet see First Church of Boston, Records and Baptisms, 1630-1687, manuscript copy in the Massachusetts Historical Society Library, Boston, under date of January 8, 1639/40; for Jones see Chamberlayne, ed., *Vestry Book of Christ Church Parish, Middlesex,* 63; for Fairfield see Shurtleff, ed.,*Records . . . of the Massachusetts Bay,* II, 12-13, 61, II, 273; for that of Furrell, Middlesex County, Virginia, Order Book No. 1, 1673-80, pp. 82-83. See also Kai T. Erikson, *Wayward Puritans: A Study in the Sociology of Deviance* (New York, 1966).

[40]Dow, *Life in the Massachusetts Bay*, 119; Hunter Dickinson Farish, ed., *The Journal and Letters of Philip Vickers Fithian: A Plantation Tutor of the Old Dominion, 1773-1774* (Williamsburg, Va., 1957), 167.

Middlesex vestrymen to investigate the morals of Mary Hutson, servant to Mrs. Frances Sheppard; her three bastard children were common knowledge, as was the fact that Joseph Smith "peremptorily owns himself father of the latter of the said three," and the vestrymen had only to take note of the common talk to present the erring couple to the county court for punishment. And in Scituate, Massachusetts, it was enough for the justices to take note of Daniel Turner, Joseph Studley, and Peter Worthylake "for their abusive frequenting the ordinaries . . . spending their time there, and expending their estates, so as they are become very poor"; their penchant for hard liquor, and their persons, were well enough known, and the court had simply to order the town's tavernkeepers "to take effectual course" that the three "be not entertained so frequently."[41]

Conversely, if the community knew its own, it also readily recognized the stranger. The simple traveler, particularly one well dressed and obviously a gentleman, was greeted and congenially entertained for the news and novelty he offered. But should the stranger be without obvious means he was more an object of suspicion than novelty, to be prodded on his way unless quickly attached to a family as sojourner or servant, or unless some head-of-family stood surety both for his good behavior and that he would not become a financial burden on the community.[42]

To stress the essential familial and familiar basis of community life is not, however, to deny differences between communities. The ages of communities varied, and with the simple passage of time any single community passed from a rude wilderness broken by occasional clearings into a complex patchwork of fields and houses; to contemplate many communities at once is to contemplate communities at various points in this transition, all different in this one aspect, although not necessarily different in their familial and familiar organization. Similarly, the simple passage of

[41] Chamberlayne, ed., *Vestry Book of Christ Church Parish, Middlesex*, 49; Edwin Powers, *Crime and Punishment in Early Massachusetts; 1620-1692, A Documentary History* (Boston, 1966), 377.

[42] See e.g., Josiah Henry Benton, *Warning Out in New England* (Boston, 1911) and Marcus Wilson Jernegan, *Laboring and Dependent Classes in Colonial America, 1607-1783* (Chicago, 1931), 180ff, 192ff, but compare with Edmund and Dorothy Smith Berkeley, eds., *The Reverend John Clayton: A Parson with a Scientific Mind, His Scientific Writings and Other Related Papers* (Charlottesville, Va., 1965), 3; Beverley, *History and Present State of Virginia,* 312; and the reception given prominent travelers in, for example, Bridenbaugh, ed., *Gentlemen's Progress, passim* and Gilbert Chinard, ed., *A Huguenot Exile in Virginia or Voyages of a Frenchman . . . with a description of Virginia & Maryland* (New York, 1934), *passim.*

time tended to strain the economic base of early communities. Family fecundity and whatever in-migration occurred steadily enlarged the populations, but being for the most part agricultural, communities could support only so many people. Within two generations – roughly sixty-six years – in any specific area a maximum density was reached, perhaps passed; fathers were strained to provide nearby land for their sons. Within three generations a few of the sons and grandsons tended to gravitate outward. Undoubtedly the contemplation, eventually the fact, of a departure from known surroundings produced personal and family tensions, and the level of tension varied between communities. But the basic configuration of the communities was untouched. Family clusters did not disappear from the older communities. Neither was a new mobility substituted for an old immobility and familialism and familiarity generally lost. Those who stayed behind were still locked in a familial and familiar web; those who went ultimately found land and founded families, reencapsulating themselves in a familial and familiar situation. Between communities the basic distinction was simply that some were old and regularly lost excess sons and daughters, although remaining constant in population; others were new and steadily grew.[43]

Location varied, too, and with location the crops to which the families devoted their energies varied, both within and between regions. Traditions varied even in such a young society – indigenous traditions between New England and Virginia, for example, and national traditions between people of different national origins as, in the eighteenth century, varying nationalities were added to the essentially English population of the seventeenth century. Such variations certainly affected life-styles,

[43]Kenneth A. Lockridge, "The Population of Dedham, Massachusetts, 1636-1736," *Economic History Review,* Ser. 2, XIX (1966), 318-44 and "Land, Population and the Evolution of New England Society, 1630-1790," *Past and Present*, XXXIX (1968), 62-80; Greven, *Four Generations,* Part III. An analysis of 198 New Hampshire towns and forty Virginia counties shows a clear and significant curvilinear correlation between age – the years elapsed from settlement in the area – and population. Similarly, age and growth rates correlate significantly. Between 1767 and 1790 New Hampshire towns of age 3 and under were growing at a rate of 10.46 per cent per year; 4 to 33 years at a rate of 6.1 per cent; 34-66 at a rate of 1.95 per cent; and over 67 at a rate of .03 per cent. Of the last group of towns 44.4 per cent were losing population, as against none of the first group and but 8.3 of the second. The seminar study of intra- and inter-communal marriages cited in note 34 shows a tendency for inter-communal marriages to increase with time, indicative of marriageable youths seeking partners beyond the immediate community. A study of sex-ratios by age of the New Hampshire towns conforms.

sometimes subtly, sometimes blatantly. To consider all such variations is beyond the scope of this essay, however. Indeed, a great deal of work on many specific communities must be done before generalizations can be attempted, although one suggests that variations associated with location and tradition will be on the familial and familiar theme – a common theme in pre-modern western Europe – rather than departures from the theme. But one area of variation must be tentatively explored here, for it is inherent in our definition of community: Variations in the different balances between the vertical and horizontal dimensions achieved by different communities. One can suggest that variations of this sort will in the long run prove to be the most significant.

V

To speak of the familial and familiar basis of communities is to speak of their horizontal dimension, of the community in and of itself without reference to an outside world. But no early American community existed in isolation. All were, to one degree or another, linked vertically to each other to form a larger social web.[44]

We can sense the nature of this vertical linkage by journeying, in the mind, to the simplest of early American communities. Internally, it is a web of cooperating families; in the main, the families look inward toward the community itself, their activities and their contemplations confined, localized. But here and there among the families are some whose activities and thoughts exceed the community – the individual owning land in more than one community, for example, or the storekeeper who takes in the surplus agricultural commodities raised by his neighbors, passes the surplus into channels of commerce, receiving back articles which the community cannot produce for itself and selling such goods to his neighbors. There is the minister, on the one hand shepherd of his local flock, on the other drawn irresistibly into association with his compeers throughout the area, formally and informally meeting with them at regular intervals, as subject to the

[44] Lockridge, *A New England Town,* concentrating on the horizontal dimension of Dedham in the earliest period, gives the impression of absolute isolation, neglecting both the theoretic improbability of such isolation and broad clues such as Edward Johnson's description of the Dedhamites carrying their "garden fruits" into Boston "to supply the markets of the most populous town." J. Franklin Jameson, ed., *Johnson's Wonder-Working Providence, 1628-1651* (New York, 1910), 179.

guidance, even discipline, of the association as he is to the needs of the community. There are those who, by virtue of their offices, are part of an elaborate political web stretching from the lowly poundkeeper obliged to enforce the colony laws relative to stray animals, through the leadership in the colonial capital, to the officers of the Crown in London. Such men were obviously embedded in the familial and familiar life of the community. But beyond the community their associations were born not of ties of family or familiarity but of the specific common interests of the larger association; their obligations were not those demanded by blood or communal affiliation but voluntarily assumed by implicit or explicit contract. Such men served purposes in the life of the community – indeed, were essential to it. But their activities were not confined to the purposes of the community, for they served the purposes of their extra-communal associations as well. In a word, such men lived dual lives.

Anthropologist Robert Redfield has described the existence of such men as ministers, storekeepers, and public servants within our community as "an interpenetration of two opposite kinds of living, thinking, and feeling," as the coexistence of "an isolated, homogenous, sacred, and personal community" and a "heterogenous, secular, and impersonal" associationalism.[45] It was not (and is not, for the interpenetration is a continual fact of social existence)[46] a peaceful coexistence. The homogenous and personal community – a broader version of the familial and familiar – tended (and tends) toward conservatism and resistance in the face of changes pressed by heterogenous and impersonal associations pursuing particular goals.[47] In both New England and Virginia, for example, communities resisted changes pressed upon

[45] Robert Redfield, *The Little Community: Viewpoints for the Study of a Human Whole* (Chicago, 1955), 147.

[46] Arthur J. Vidich and Joseph Bensman, *Small Town in Mass Society: Class, Power and Religion in a Rural Community* (Rev. edn.: Princeton, 1968) well exemplifies this.

[47] The spokesman for the latter, sociologist Roland Warren writes, "is task oriented, focusing on the particular task to be accomplished . . . is likely to be highly specialized, and an expert in his own special field . . . likely, in other words, to 'know better than the community does what the community really needs.' Thus, he is paternalistic . . . He cannot encourage the community to consider all the possible alternatives . . . He is 'selling' a particular program. He thus tends to lean toward the ethical absolutist side, toward the side which knows what is right and wants that right to prevail." (Warren, "Toward a Reformulation of Community Theory," 45-46.) The community, on the other hand, accepts such spokesmen ambivalently. To paraphrase Vidick and Bensman, *Small Town in Mass Society,* 101: Such spokesmen have respect because of their power or wealth, and because their norms have the legitimacy of acceptance in wide areas of the larger society. Yet the very dominance of the larger society causes resentments since,

them in the interest of commerce.[48] In both, too, ministers provoked disputes as they attempted to implement in their specific communities matters of doctrine or polity arrived at by extra-communal associations of ministers. Thus in New England in the 1660s ministerial associations espoused a new doctrine regarding church membership – that of the Half-way Covenant – but individual ministers bringing the doctrine to their communities met opposition and, in persisting, provoked bitter controversies.[49] In Virginia in 1690 an assemblage of ministers established ecclesiastic courts within the various "precincts" of the colony, superseding existent local and lay autonomy in matters of morality and church discipline; Virginia's communities were stronger than the ministerial association, however, and the courts were quashed as soon as they attempted to exercise jurisdiction.[50] Such controversies throw into bold relief the innate opposition of the horizontal and vertical dimensions of communities. (And, conversely, an understanding of the horizontal and vertical dimensioning of communities rationalizes controversies too often put forth as irrational.)[51] But more important for our purposes is

---

in the light of this dominance, the life of the immediate community is devalued. These assessments seem as applicable in the seventeenth and eighteenth centuries as they do in the twentieth.

[48] See e.g. Bernard Bailyn, *The New England Merchants in the Seventeenth Century* (Cambridge, Mass., 1955) on the Childites (pp. 106-107); Thomas J. Wertenbaker, *Virginia under the Stuarts, 1607-1688* (Princeton, 1914), 232ff, and Wesley Frank Craven, *The Southern Colonies in the Seventeenth Century, 1607-1689* ([Baton Rouge, La.], 1949), 398f, on the Virginia tobacco riots of 1682.

[49] Robert G. Pope, *The Half-Way Covenant: Church Membership in Puritan New England* (Princeton, 1969) *passim.* See also Robert F. Scholz, " 'The Reverend Elders': Faith, Fellowship, and Politics in the Ministerial Community of Massachusetts Bay," and Paul R. Lucas, "Valley of Discord: The Struggle for Power in the Puritan Churches of the Connecticut Valley, 1636-1720," both unpublished doctoral dissertations, University of Minnesota, 1966, 1970, and Scholz, "Clerical Consociation in Massachusetts Bay: Reassessing the New England Way and Its Origins," *William and Mary Quarterly,* Ser. 3, XXIX (1972), 391-414.

[50] George Maclaren Brydon, *Virginia's Mother Church and the Political Conditions under Which It Grew* (Richmond, Va., and Philadelphia, 1947-52), I, 281ff; Henry Hartwell, James Blair, Edward Chilton, *The Present State of Virginia, and the College,* Hunter Dickinson Farish, ed. (Williamsburg, Va., 1940), 68-69-72-73; John P. Kennedy and H.R. McIlwaine, eds., *Journals of the House of Burgesses of Virginia: [1619-1776]* (Richmond, Va., 1905-15), II *(1659-1695),* 366-67. Much the same situation existed in Maryland. See Elizabeth L. Grundner, "The Ministerial Mind and the Failure of Maryland's Established Church," unpublished M.A. thesis, University of Minnesota, 1967.

[51] Similarly controversies between historians become comprehensible. Zuckerman, *Peaceable Kingdoms,* appears to argue for the near-independence of the towns of Massachusetts in the late eighteenth century, bringing down upon himself the wrath of

the fact that the degree of influence of these opposites varied from community to community both within and between the regions of early America.

Historians have, until quite recently, contented themselves with crude and rough categorizations of colonial communities. They have referred to communities as "frontier" or "established" – an overly simplistic expression of the variations flowing from age. They have categorized by geography: coastal towns vis-à-vis inland towns in New England, Tidewater vis-à-vis Piedmont in Virginia, again in New England upland vis-à-vis valley towns. But perhaps a categorization according to the balance of the vertical and horizontal dimensions would be more pertinent.

The state of our knowledge is such that such a categorical scheme can be suggested for New England. At one extreme we can conceive of the subsistence agricultural community – subsistence in the sense that the inhabitants consumed most of what they grew, sending out of the community only the barest minimum (and even then sometimes depriving themselves of consumables) in order to pay for the few absolute essentials which they could not produce for themselves.[52] The subsistence nature of the economy minimized commercial ties, while the paucity of the economy minimized a whole range of external associations. Capital could not be amassed for extra-communal investment (nor was the impoverished community promising to investors from the outside). It was, moreover, improbable that a man could achieve the social and political visibility required by the larger society for anything higher than purely local social or political position. In a word, all ties to the greater world were minimal; the familial and

L. Kinvin Wroth, whose work on the legal structure has indicated the position of the towns as legally subordinate to the colony's courts. (Wroth, "Possible Kingdoms: The New England Town from the Perspective of Legal History," *American Journal of Legal History*, XV [1971], 318-30.) In reality, Zuckerman is, like Lockridge (note 44), concentrating on the horizontal dimension to the exclusion of the vertical; Wroth on one aspect of the vertical to the exclusion of the horizontal. An understanding of the dimensions of the community does, however, suggest the inadequacy of Zuckerman's categorization of disputes. Disputes can be categorized as purely horizontal (between parts of the community and disruptive of the community) and as horizontal vs. vertical (between the community and spokesmen for the outside, ergo supportive of the community), with the latter fully capable of transformation into the former as spokesmen for the vertical win converts to their positions.

[52] James T. Lemon, "Household Consumption in Eighteenth-Century America and Its Relationship to Production and Trade: The Situation Among Farmers in Southeastern Pennsylvania," *Agricultural History*, XLI (1967), 59-70 suggests a technique to arrive at a ratio between local consumption and export.

familiar web forming the horizontal community was barely penetrated by the vertical; the community was isolated not so much by geography (although that could be the case as well) but by virtue of the thinness of the tie to the web of communities. At this level of communal life, time, to the observing historian, seems halted, dispute and change imperceptible; men tilled their fields, begat families, and conducted their public affairs in what some delight in calling "immemorial ways."

The subsistence agricultural community is at one extreme of our categorical scheme. At the other extreme is the community which, by virtue of the complexity of the roles it played as the primary economic, social, and political center in a wide web of communities seems all encompassed by its vertical dimension, more a web of associations than of families. Boston, the seat of government of Massachusetts, the commercial entrepôt for all New England, and virtually its intellectual capital, is a prime example. Falling between these extremes is what historian Jackson T. Main has called the commercial agricultural community in contrast to the subsistence community, the former having produced and exported a true surplus with which the community purchased more than absolute necessities, indeed, even luxuries.[53] The contrast lies not in the production of a surplus, however, but in the effect of that surplus upon the social fabric – the surplus required stronger economic ties to the larger society and allowed the possibility of capital accumulation, investment from the outside, social and economic visibility, ergo the possibility of extra-communal social and political position. No longer was the penetration of the vertical dimension minimal, as it was in the subsistence community; but neither was it maximized as it was in the primary center.

Clearly the three categories postulated – ranging from the subsistence agricultural community, through the commercial agricultural community, to the primary commercial, political, and social center – lie in ordinal relationship to each other, defining a scale ranging from minimal to maximum vertical penetration. We can conceive of other categories lying upon such a scale. New England's commercial structure involved not merely port merchants and village storekeepers but a range of secondary and tertiary merchants as well, men intermediate between the villages

[53] Jackson Turner Main, *The Social Structure of Revolutionary America* (Princeton, 1965), chap. I.

and the ports, gathering produce from a number of villages and forwarding it toward the sea, all the while wholesaling merchandise as it passed from the sea to the villages. The government of Massachusetts, moreover, from the very early period, encompassed counties as judicial and administrative units, and with counties, county seats. We can conceive of the combination of commercial agriculture, county government, and secondary merchants in any given community as having augmented the vertical dimension of that community and consequently elevating the community on our scale to a point above the simple commercial agricultural town but below the point of extreme vertical penetration found in the primary center. Indeed, historian Edward M. Cook has discerned two such calibrated levels below the level of the primary: a secondary county center and a tertiary rural center.[54]

Such a categorical scheme offers a promising approach to New England's communities. Historians are sensing innate differences between communities of roughly the same age. Cook, for example, has suggested that the political and social structure of the towns in the eighteenth century varied from relatively unstratified and equalitarian to relatively stratified and elitist. Robert Zemsky has suggested that political positions among town representatives to the General Court of Massachusetts (and of the communities which sent such representatives) varied systematically, suggesting a relationship between political position and the town's placement in an awkward categorical scheme involving both function (was the town a seaport or not?) and geographic location. Even the rate at which young people sought mates in towns other than their

[54]Cook's work is in progress but parts have been delivered in papers: "Local Leadership and the Typology of New England Towns, 1700-1785," *Political Science Quarterly,* LXXXVI (1971); "Toward a Typology of the New England Towns in the Eighteenth Century," paper delivered before the New England Historical Association, Amherst, Mass., April 1971. The work of James T. Lemon and Gary B. Nash is suggestive on the general subject, although Lemon's *The Best Poor Man's Country: A Geographical Study of Early Southeastern Pennsylvania* (Baltimore, 1972) is consistently wrongheaded in the definition and application of the concept "community." See Lemon and Nash, "The Distribution of Wealth in Eighteenth-Century America: A Century of Change in Chester County, Pennsylvania, 1693-1802," *Journal of Social History,* II (1968), 1-24; Lemon, "Urbanization and the Development of Eighteenth-Century Southeastern Pennsylvania and Adjacent Delaware," *William and Mary Quarterly,* Ser. 3, XXIV (1967), 501-42. See too Margaret E. Martin, *Merchants and Trade of the Connecticut River Valley, 1750-1820* ("Smith College Studies in History," XXIV, Nos. 1-4; Northampton, Mass., 1938-39) and descriptions by travelers of New England towns, notably those of Ezra Stiles in manuscript, Yale University, and Timothy Dwight's *Travels in New England and New York* (Cambridge, Mass., 1969).

own varied.[55] Studies of single communities tend to indicate differences of still other kinds, including a range in key demographic indices, in the pattern of family relationships, the degree of occupational diversity, and the consequent degree of freedom men have to choose among occupations.[56] The suggestion here is that such differences were essentially associated with the degree of interpenetration between the vertical and horizontal dimensions, that, for example, Cook's social stratification and political elitism were, in the eighteenth century, most characteristic of primary centers where interpenetration was greatest and least characteristic of the subsistence agricultural communities where interpenetration was minimal.[57]

But the consideration of communities in terms of the degree of interpenetration of the two dimensions is not to be confined to New England. One can approach communities elsewhere in the same way. In Virginia, the area which would become Middlesex was first entered by prominent men, most of whom were already settled in established communities in other parts of the colony, with ready access to land grants by virtue of a favored economic, social, or political position in the colony as a whole – in other words, by men more vertically than horizontally oriented. The familial and familiar dimension of the community formed only with the passage of time and the entry into the locale of lesser

[55] Drawing upon the work of Cook and Wilbur cited above in notes 34 and 54; Zemsky, *Merchants, Farmers, and River Gods,* appendices. Van Beck Hall, *Politics Without Parties: Massachusetts, 1780-1791* (Pittsburgh, 1972), has applied a well-developed three-part categorization of the Massachusetts towns to the politics of the Confederation period.

[56] See, for example, Daniel Scott Smith, "The Demographic History of Colonial New England," *Journal of Economic History,* XXXII (1972), 172; and compare Philip J. Greven, Jr., "Family Structure in Seventeenth-Century Andover, Massachusetts," *William and Mary Quarterly,* Ser. 3, XXIII (1966), 234-56 and his "Old Patterns in the New World: The Distribution of Land in Seventeenth-Century Andover," *Essex Institute Historical Collections,* CI (1965), 133-48 on the one hand and John Demos, "Notes on Life in Plymouth Colony" and "Families in Colonial Bristol, Rhode Island: An Exercise in Historical Demography," *William and Mary Quarterly,* Ser. 3, XXII (1965), 264-86 and XXV (1968), 40-57 on the other with respect to family patterns; Allan Kulikoff, "The Progress of Inequality in Revolutionary Boston," *William and Mary Quarterly,* Ser. 3, XXVIII (1971), 375-412, and Rutman, *Husbandmen of Plymouth* on occupational diversity.

[57] If we consider that interpenetration is even greater today, it would follow that stratification would be greater. One can argue that such is indeed the case, that political and economic power is indeed more concentrated in the few, even that wealth is more concentrated if we enter as subjects for our stratification not merely individuals but corporations.

men and families.[58] Even then, however, the horizontal dimension could not dominate the new community. On the one hand, the familial and familiar web was, in the seventeenth century, regularly strained by the necessity of accommodating from the outside large numbers of white indentured servants, hired overseers, and renters whose relationships within the community were essentially contractual and transient; only with the substitution of the white servant by the black in the eighteenth century – the black irrevocably immobile and linked to a particular family by his very status as chattel, property – did the strain ease. On the other hand, the economic structure was such as to exaggerate the vertical dimension, for early Middlesex was a commercial agricultural community, its dependence upon tobacco creating a dependence upon the system (and the men) linking it to the tobacco warehouses of England. Moreover, Virginia's political, ecclesiastical, and land systems were keyed to a central authority to a far greater extent than those of New England and, therefore, more susceptible to the pressures of the great world and less to the small world of the community. County justices, for example, were ultimately selected by the central authority in contrast to the New England community's election of its selectmen; land in Virginia was largely obtained apart from the community, from the central government. In such a community it is not at all unfathomable that preeminence among men was defined to a significant degree in terms of the vertical dimension, or that preeminent men were as attuned to affairs in the world beyond the community as they were to the community itself; indeed, the most preeminent – the Wormeley family – lived far more in the context of their equals in the broader world than in the context of the small community.[59]

Middlesex was but one of Virginia's many communities. What of others? What of categories of Virginia's communities? We can conceive of some marked by a lesser degree of interpenetration – Main has found subsistence areas of Virginia as well as of New England, and these would be linked less firmly to the economic

[58] Bernard Bailyn, "Politics and Social Structure in Virginia," in James Morton Smith, ed., *Seventeenth-Century America: Essays in Colonial History* (Chapel Hill, N.C., 1959), 90-115 implicitly suggests this as a general phenomenon in seventeenth-century Virginia.

[59] In this lies the connection between Virginia's eighteenth-century county community and what has been implicitly described as a cross-county (i.e., vertical) elite community (or association). See, for example, Jackson T. Main, "The One Hundred," *William and Mary Quarterly*, Ser. 3, XI (1954), 354-84 and Charles S. Sydnor, *Gentlemen Freeholders: Political Practices in Washington's Virginia* (Chapel Hill, N.C., 1952), chap. 5.

web than Middlesex. And we can conceive of Virginia communities potentially marked by a higher degree of penetration – the towns of the eighteenth century, Williamsburg (the rising political center), Norfork (rising to meet particular commercial needs).[60] But what of the comparative range of categories? One can suggest that given the dependence of the local community upon the central authority, no early Virginia county could conceivably display the low level of interpenetration (and consequently high level of horizontal or communal orientation) found in at least some New England towns. But if the range of interpenetration is constrained, is the range of other social variables – stratification, for example – equally constrained, a phenomenon to be expected if indeed interpenetration and stratification are associated? And if the range of stratification is constrained – if no Virginia community displays a significant departure from a high level of interpenetration and stratification found in Middlesex – does this not help us understand a peculiar phenomenon of Virginia's political structure, the diffusion of its leadership through many communities in contrast to the concentration of Massachusetts' leadership in and immediately about the highly stratified primary centers?[61]

At this point, however, the state of our knowledge fails us. We do not know enough to go beyond highly tentative suggestions. We can discern only that by virtue of the common approach to communities in New England and Virginia – considering them from the common standpoint of the varying degrees of interpenetration – we have been led to essential questions relative to the entirety of the social fabric.

VI

The study of life at the level of communities can be a keen analytic tool. Studied singularly and from the standpoint of the

[60] See James H. Soltow, *The Economic Role of Williamsburg* (Williamsburg, Va., 1965); Carl Bridenbaugh, *Seat of Empire: The Political Role of Eighteenth-Century Williamsburg* (Williamsburg, Va., 1950); John W. Reps, *Tidewater Towns: City Planning in Colonial Virginia and Maryland* (Charlottesville, Va., 1971).

[61] Cf. the appendices of Zemsky, *Merchants, Farmers, and River Gods* and Jack P. Greene, *The Quest for Power: The Lower Houses of Assembly in the Southern Royal Colonies, 1689-1776* (Chapel Hill, N.C., 1963). Stratification among Middlesex landowners alone was, in the early eighteenth century, at and above the high levels described for Boston by James A. Henretta, "Economic Development and Social Structure in Colonial Boston," *William and Mary Quarterly*, Ser. 3, XXII (1965), 75-92 and Kulikoff, "Progress of Inequality in Revolutionary Boston."

internal web of individuals and families – the way in which early American historians have generally been studying communities for the past decade – one can catch a glimpse of the routine of life that underlay and, as a backdrop, colored the great events of the past: the ways of childhood, marriage, family life, of work and worship, of recreation, even procreation, of neighbors and neighborhoods. And from these glimpses we can even infer the character and temperament which not only colored but also radically affected the great events.[62] When, to the study of the internal web we add that of the external web – the vertical dimension linking the single community to the larger society – we have the opportunity of ordering the variations between communities and glimpsing the essential structure of the whole society, of the place of individuals, families, neighborhoods, and communities within the larger social web. But even beyond that, a consideration of the vertical dimension of communities *over time* gives us ready entry into the dialectic of the past.

In the seventeenth and eighteenth centuries, change was relatively slow paced and went on in the context of the general predominance of the horizontal dimension of life. We have used the terms maximum and minimum to describe the degree of interpenetration of the two dimensions. But this has been in the interest of contrasting extremes in the specific time (the colonial years) and place (the Anglo-American coast). In terms of the larger context of American history, the impact of the vertical dimension anywhere in early America was far from maximum. Government was small, social agencies few, economic diversity limited. Men's lives were largely lived in the familial and familiar web, even where the linkages to the larger society were most concentrated. Indeed, the dominance of the horizontal was such that men could define even their associations very largely in terms of the familial and familiar. Vertical linkages were themselves frequently familial, the particular family ties of one man offering opportunities to enter extra-communal economic or political associations denied another;[63] the mind-set of the time – the values and attitudes by which men conceived the world about them – tended largely to exaggerate the familial and familiar, the homogenous and personal,

[62] As does Demos in *A Little Commonwealth.*

[63] Bailyn, *New England Merchants* is an excellent description of familial opportunities and economic associations; Sydnor, *Gentlemen Freeholders* and Greene, *Quest for Power* of familial opportunities and political associations.

even while, in particular communities, relationships were more and more heterogenous and impersonal.[64]

Nevertheless, communities changed, and change is never the product of capricious fate or an elusive *zeitgeist* but of social processes capable of analysis. That analysis – of the impact upon the local society of a community's transition into a port, of growth and emerging complexity in a farm community, or decline and emerging simplicity – seems best made in terms of the changing balance between dimensions. The point is most quickly made by casting forward from the relatively slow-paced seventeenth- and eighteenth-century America (although change can certainly be highlighted for those early years).[65] Virginia's Middlesex in the early nineteenth century, for example, would become a rural backwater. The decline can be clearly associated with the exhaustion of her soil; from a commercial agricultural community the county slid to the level of subsistence agriculture.[66] But unless we are content with an agronomical analysis we must attempt to trace out the social process at work. The depletion of the soil led some preeminent families to depart while all fell in economic position. Capital departed. The political and social visibility of the community's major families dimmed and the community tended toward social and political isolation; few individuals were attuned to the great world, and a provincial and local cast of mind predominated. Men no longer exported a surplus and imported luxuries to any extent, and the economic tie to the larger web weakened. In brief: The horizontal dimension of the community became more and more important, the vertical less. On the other hand, in New England some communities in the nineteenth century were transformed as subsistence agriculture gave way to textile mills. The economies of the towns quickened. Occupational diversity appeared – where before all men were farmers, men now had something of a choice between the farm and the mill. "Immemorial ways" changed. But again, the essential nature of the transformation can be traced in the changing balance

[64] If, however, one follows Sydney V. James, "Colonial Rhode Island and the Beginnings of the Liberal Rationalized State," Melvin Richter, ed., *Essays in Theory and History: An Approach to the Social Sciences* (Cambridge, Mass., 1970), 165-185, one can sense a rationalization of heterogenous and impersonal relationships.

[65] As it is in Lockridge, *A New England Town* and Rutman, *Winthrop's Boston,* or in contrasting Henretta, "Economic Development and Social Structure in Colonial Boston" and Kulikoff, "Progress of Inequality in Revolutionary Boston."

[66] See Avery O. Craven's classic *Soil Exhaustion as a Factor in the Agricultural History of Virginia and Maryland, 1606-1860* (Urbana, 1926), *passim.*

between communal dimensions, the mills in effect introducing a pervasive dependence upon the external web and exaggerating the influence of the vertical dimension in the life of the community.[67]

To go a step beyond the particulars of Middlesex and the mill towns, one can suggest that a consideration of the external web of communities in terms of their horizontal and vertical dimensions leads to a fundamental point in American history. The mill towns preluded the future, for the economic transformation of the nineteenth century – from industrialization and urbanization to the phenomena of mechanized agriculture and "store bought" clothes – together with the bureaucratization (in terms of both public and private agencies) and the mass communication so characteristic of the twentieth, can be seen as a steady augmentation of the vertical dimension of life. Far more than anything else, this pervasive vertical dimension separates us from our Early American past.

FOR FURTHER READING

Bumsted, J.M. and Lemon, J.T. "New Approaches in Early American Studies: The Local Community in New England." *Histoire Sociale/Social History, A Canadian Review,* II (1968), 98-112.

French, Robert Mills, ed., *The Community: A Comparative Perspective.* Itasca, Ill.: F.E. Peacock, 1969.

Greven, Philip J., Jr., *Four Generations: Population, Land, and Family in Colonial Andover, Massachusetts.* Ithaca, N.Y.: Cornell University Press, 1970.

____. "Historical Demography and Colonial America." *William and Mary Quarterly,* 3rd Ser., XXIV (1967), 438-454.

Hillery, George A., Jr. *Communal Organizations: A Study of Local Societies.* Chicago: University of Chicago Press, 1968.

Lockridge, Kenneth A., *A New England Town, The First Hundred Years: Dedham, Massachusetts, 1636-1736.* New York: W.W. Norton, 1970.

MacIver, Robert M. *Community: A Sociological Study.* London: Macmillan, 1917.

Redfield, Robert. *The Little Community.* Chicago: University of Chicago Press, 1955.

Rutman, Darrett B. *Winthrop's Boston: Portrait of a Puritan Town, 1630-1649.* Chapel Hill: University of North Carolina Press, 1965.

[67] Harold Fisher Wilson, *The Hill Country of Northern New England: Its Social and Economic History in the Nineteenth and Twentieth Centuries* (Montpelier, Vt., 1947) is suggestive, as is Stephan Thernstrom, *Poverty and Progress: Social Mobility in a Nineteenth Century City* (Cambridge, Mass., 1964) although Thernstrom deals with the transformation of a commercial-oriented port.

Soltow, James J. *The Economic Role of Williamsburg*. Williamsburg, Va.: Colonial Williamsburg, 1965.

Warren, Roland L., ed. *Perspectives on the American Community*. Chicago: Rand McNally, 1966.

Sources

1

Community Theory

Social history involves a fusion of abstract thought concerning the nature of society, and historical research. Without the first, there is no direction to the second; without the second, the study ceases to be history. To date, sociologists and anthropologists rather than historians have contributed most to the theory of community. Working in the present, they have assiduously observed the structures of diverse communities in industrial and nonindustrial, literate and nonliterate cultures, deriving theory from their empirical observations. The resultant theoretical literature is large – Roland L. Warren, ed., *Perspectives on the American Community* (1966) and Robert Mills French, ed., *The Community: A Comparative Perspective* (1969) offer convenient entries via selective readings. The particular selection presented in part here, although relatively old (1956) has been chosen first because it succinctly expresses the essential notions of the dual dimension of communities and of the existence of the single community in a larger social field; second, because of the explicit dialectic or process suggested, from horizontal dominance to vertical dominance. Inevitably concerned with time and change, the historian can both use this concept as an organizing principle to describe the changing community and, by attempting to apply the concept to communities over time, test the viability of the concept.

SOURCE: Roland L. Warren, "Toward a Reformulation of Community Theory." Reproduced by the permission of the Society for Applied Anthropology from Vol. 15, No. 2, Yr. 1956,

Human Organization. Footnotes and subheads have been deleted. (Roland L. Warren is Professor of Sociology at Brandeis University and author of *The Community in America* [1963].)

Few students of the community are satisfied with current theoretical approaches to this perplexing social group. . . . The inadequacy of [existent] theories stems not only from their inability to deal coherently with the many aspects of community living which have been newly explored since these theories were first formulated (one thinks of recent work in stratification and informal group analysis, for example); the inadequacy is caused also by developments in community living which have become more markedly apparent in recent decades and which none of these formulations was adequate to accommodate in a systematic framework. These developments have been variously described as: the transition from Gemeinschaft to Gesellschaft, from sacred to secular, from folk culture to mass culture, from primary group association to secondary group association, from sympathetic contacts to categorical contacts, from locality groups to interest groups, from simple organization to complex.

However these polarities and processes are described, they cause some social scientists to wonder whether the very concept of community is not already a nonfunctional survival from earlier days, while others feel impelled to admonish the world that the community is going to hell because I don't know the name of the man across the street in apartment 4B.

This paper does not propose to sketch out a completely comprehensive theory of the community. But it will attempt to relate some concepts which in a modest fashion – on the level of Merton's "middle range," perhaps – may prove more adequate to cope with the data of the modern scene where interest is eclipsing locality as a central focus of association, where we know less and less about the man in apartment 4B, and yet where, far from disintegrating or vanishing, the interrelated cluster of people and facilities which we call a community is more delicately interdependent and more functionally vital than ever before.

The community is not dying out as an effective locality group. Rather, it is changing structure and function to accommodate modern developments. This change is in the direction of greater specialization which our times embody.

The structural-functional changes in the community can be analyzed in terms of a horizontal axis and a vertical axis. The *horizontal axis* emphasizes locality. It involves the relationship of individual to individual or of group to group within the locality. It is illustrated by a group of citizens coming together to form a neighborhood association, and by the local community chest or welfare council. . . . The *vertical axis* emphasizes specialized interest. It involves the relationship of the individual to a local interest group and of that local interest group to a regional, state, or national organization. It is illustrated by the relation of John Smith to his local Red Cross chapter and the relation of that Red Cross chapter to the regional and national Red Cross. . . .

This conceptual framework of a vertical axis of orientation and a horizontal axis is admittedly abstract, yet I believe we shall see that it is useful as we go along. Using these two terms we can see that the progressive reorganization (rather than deterioration) of community living mentioned earlier is in such a direction that the horizontal axis becomes increasingly less important, the vertical axis increasingly more important. This is much more than to say that there has been a shift from locality grouping toward interest grouping. For the shift involves the whole structure of the community as a system of interdependent parts; it involves the types of problems which communities are pressed to solve, the types of associational life the people lead, and the types of leadership roles which are appropriate.

What occurs seems to be that as communities grow, or as they perdure through time under modern conditions, there is a greater specialization of effort within the community, a reflection of the overall process of a progressive division of labor. This process is especially familiar to all of us in the gradual differentiation of older family functions and their assumption by such social agencies as the school, the church, governmental bodies, and commercial enterprises. Community development thus manifests a progressive differentiation of function and structure. As this process occurs, a more intricate network of interdependent, specialized parts forms the increasingly complex system and with this progressive fragmentation of function, the problem of community coherence arises. Can the increasingly specialized parts be kept in coordination? Can the increasingly specialized interest groups work together for common community goals?

If the analysis so far is sound, then the major weakness of conventional community theory becomes apparent. Conventional community theory is set up to emphasize the horizontal axis, the factor of locality, the factor of common interests, common life, common associations, common institutions based on locality. And, it is just this factor which is becoming progressively weaker as time goes on.

It is perhaps for this reason that community sociologists have so characteristically fallen into the pattern of treating the community as if it were a desert island culture, almost completely cut off from the surrounding world. We do not have an adequate theoretical framework for analyzing the relations of the community to the surrounding society and culture, even though we realize that this is a great lack. "There are few studies," Steward points out, "which attempt to show how the larger society affects the community under investigation; and there are no studies which undertake to conceptualize fully and in detail the relationship between the community and the larger whole." We do not have an adequate framework for such a conceptualization because our rudimentary community theory is adequate to a rural, sacred, primary-group-oriented, pre-industrial society, but is inadequate to accommodate the very changes which are transforming the nature of American communities in our time.

As a system becomes more complex, there arises greater need for coordination. As a school, or a church, for example, takes on many specialized functions, there is greater administrative need for holding all these differentiated functions together in an efficiently operating system. As the schools, churches, social agencies, business establishments, and other community facilities multiply and differentiate, there is need for keeping these facilities in some sort of adequate coordination with respect to each other. This coordinating function can be performed within the community, along the horizontal axis, through the community welfare council or various types of local planning agencies, or the coordination function can be performed on a supercommunity level; that is, along the vertical axis. Thus, the national organization of the labor union, the Red Cross, the Methodist Church, or a state department of education, can lay down rules and procedures for the structure and function governing its particular community association or agency, thus fitting the community organization into the vertical system of local members, local units, district, regional, state, and national organization, and, in this way, the efforts can be coordinated along the vertical axis of common interest.

Putting the vertical coordination another way, supercommunity units, like state voluntary organizations or state and federal government departments, develop patterns for their local units in communities. For example, the size of the new post office door in Alfred, New York was determined by a national policy of the United States Post Office Department. Similar decisions are made by the formal leadership structure of a Masonic Lodge, a Catholic Church, or the program set-up of a grange meeting. Thus, on this vertical axis, coordination of the local unit with the state or national unit becomes the important focus, guaranteeing that the total effort of the overall organization with respect to its special area of interest and operation will be brought to bear in coordinated fashion.

In addition, there is the problem of local coordination with other agencies of different types on the community level. Here, such questions are relevant as: How good a citizen of your community is the local heart or polio organization, or the local branch of a veterans' organization, or the local factory, or the local public welfare department, granted that each is pursuing its own interest as best it can?

The conflict between vertical and horizontal axes of orientation is nowhere more readily apparent in our communities today than in the two competing systems of fund raising for health and welfare. I am referring, of course, to the all-inclusive community chest campaign, on the one hand, and the special fund-raising campaigns, particularly of the various health groups, on the other. Here is the horizontal orientation of agencies getting together for fund raising on a locality basis, and the vertical orientation of state and national organizations reaching into the local community through their individualized, task-oriented branches, to carry on fund-raising activities in little relation to what this adds up to on the local community level. Thus the local community quota for the problem-oriented health association is calculated with respect to the state and national program of the specialized organization, rather than in relation to the respective needs and services of other problem-oriented associations in the local community. We begin to gain perspective on this competition in fund raising once we realize that they are but a part of the overall division of community activities into horizontal and vertical components, with the vertical components gradually increasing as communities become more differentiated. . . .

We have all seen the important role in community differentiation played by the problem-area specialist. This is the man from the state education department, or from the mental hygiene department or from this or that national voluntary agency. His orientation is vertical, in that he is relating the state or national program to the local community unit. He is task oriented, focusing on the particular task to be accomplished – the new clinic, the new social service, etc. – he is likely to be highly specialized, and an expert in his own special field, having had experience with many, many communities in his particular subject. He is thus likely to have many of the answers before he reaches the community. He is likely, in other words, to "know better than the community does what the community really needs." Thus, he is paternalistic. He may be democratically oriented with respect to group self-determination, but by the very nature of his role he cannot encourage the community to consider all the possible alternatives for community improvement. He is "selling" a particular program. He thus tends to lean toward the ethical absolutist side, toward the side which knows what is right and wants that right to prevail. If he is successful in activating his program, that is, in inducing the new school consolidation or in establishing the new clinic, the impact of his work is bound to be disruptive, as the power structure, balance of agency functions, and other nice relationships are disturbed by the institutional innovation. His loyal group who have helped put across the improvement may have also created antagonisms in the process. . . . The results of the task-oriented activity of the problem-area specialist have been to produce disalignments which have structural, functional, and emotional aspects. It has become more difficult to keep this structurally differentiated community "together," to keep effective horizontal relationships of parts while vertical changes go on apace.

It is in this situation that the horizontally oriented permissive community organizer, the nonspecialist, the "process man," whose chief concern is with what happens to the interrelated parts of the community in planning, coordinating, and changing, comes into the picture. He is permissive and equalitarian, rather than paternalistic. His orientation is horizontal, toward the relationship of the parts of the community to each other. His chief focus is on process, on what happens to interacting people and groups in the community, rather than on the accomplishment of this or that specific task. In this respect, since he places greater weight on the rightness of whatever decision the community makes in a democratic, permissive context, he tends toward ethical relativism, being less sure that he knows in advance what is "right" and being less willing to impose his "right," as he sees it, on others. The overall impact of his function is tension reducing. He tries to help ease tensions resulting from uneven developments and from the hostility engendered by the pulls and tugs to which the community is subjected by problem-area specialists and their local related vertical interest groups. . . .

Thus we begin to see the community as a social system which undergoes stresses and strains but whose overall longtime process is one of increasing differentiation of function and structure, and whose chief orientation of interest and association is shifting from the horizontal to the vertical as defined above. We also begin to get a picture of the dynamics of induced community change, in which the problem-area specialist and his vertically oriented interest group achieve accomplishments which in turn make for greater differentiation of function and also create tensions within the community. Complementing this function is that of the permissive community organizer with his horizontal focus of interest and his typical leadership functions of tension reduction and coordination among the parts of the system. . . .

What we see, if the above analysis is sound, is a perpetual process of new achievement and consolidation, coupled with a process of tension induction and reduction, and we have seen that in this multiple process there are roles in our communities both for the man whose eye is on the task of accomplishment, and for the man whose eye is on the relationships existing among people . . .

2

England, 1562: A Homily Exhorting Obedience

Two different types of historical materials are basic to research by the social historian, that which reflects the articulated social ideals of the past, and that which reflects social action. To concentrate exclusively on the first assumes that men inevitably act according to the expressed ideas of their society – an assumption obviously false. To concentrate exclusively on the latter is to assume that social actions and ideational expressions of a society are unrelated – again, obviously false. The following selections (two through seven) are of the former sort. The first is from a homily exhorting obedience prepared by a general convocation of the clergy of England and issued on the authority of the King's Council to be read periodically in all the churches of the realm. For the most part such homilies reflected generally accepted propositions, the mind-set of the time, rather than debatable points on which men divided. We can, therefore, conceive of the sense of hierarchy and order in the selection as a general attitude of the time.

SOURCE: "An Exhortation to Obedience," *The Book of Homilies* (1562) in The Society for the Propagation of the Christian Church, *Certain Sermons or Homilies* (London, 1890), p. 109.

. . . Almighty God hath created and appointed all things, in heaven, earth, and waters, in a most excellent and perfect order. In heaven he hath appointed distinct (or several) orders, and states of archangels and angels. In earth, he hath assigned and appointed kings and princes, with other governors under them, all in good and necessary order. The water above is kept, and raineth down in due time and season. The sun, moon, stars, rainbow, thunder, lightning, clouds, and all birds of the air, do keep their order. The earth, trees, seeds, plants, herbs, corn, grass and all manner of beasts, keep themselves in their order. All the parts of the whole year, as winter, summer, months, nights and days, continue in their order. All kinds of fishes in the sea, rivers and waters, with all fountains and springs, yea the seas themselves, keep their comely course and order. And man himself also hath all his parts both within and without, as soul, heart, mind, memory, understanding, reason, speech, with all and singular corporal members of his body, in a profitable, necessary, and pleasant order. Every degree of people, in their vocation, calling, and office, hath appointed to them their duty and order. Some are in high degree, some in low; some kings and princes, some inferiors and subjects; priests and laymen, masters and servants, fathers and children, husbands and wives, rich and poor; and every one have need of other. . . .

3

England, 1621, 1625: Two Sermons of William Laud

William Laud, Bishop of St. Davids at the time he delivered the two sermons quoted – the first before the King, the second at the opening of Parliament – was a rising star in the English church and a leading exponent of emerging Anglicanism. In 1628 he would be named Bishop of London, in 1633 Archbishop of Canterbury; in 1645, during the English Civil War, he would be executed. The sentiments in the quoted passages can be found in the more-often quoted sermons of his Puritan opponents as well, but they are here taken from Laud to make the point that such sentiments were not Anglican or Puritan but generally English.

SOURCE: *The Works of the Most Reverend Father in God, William Laud, D.D. Sometime Lord Arch-bishop of Canterbury,* I (Oxford, 1847), pp. 28-29, 63-66.

. . . if any man be so addicted to his private, that he neglect the common State, he is void of the sense of piety, and wisheth peace and happiness to himself in vain. For whoever he be, he must live in the body of the Commonwealth, and in the body of the Church; and if their joints be out, and in trouble, how can he hope to live in "peace?" This is just as much as if the exterior parts of the body should think they might live healthful, though the stomach be full of sick and swollen humors. . . .

• • • • •

. . . My text is nothing but a most deserved praise of Jerusalem. And not of the particular material Jerusalem alone, but of any State, of any Church, that is as Jerusalem then was, and that doth as Jerusalem then did. . . . The first commendation of Jerusalem is from the unity and concord that is in it. It is like a city that is "compacted together;" that is, for the buildings; no desolation in the midst of it, saith Saint Basil. It is like "a city at unity in itself;" – that is, for the inhabitants. For the beauty and artificial joining of the houses is expressed but as a type of this unity; when men dwell as near in affection as their houses stand in place.

It is a great ornament of a city, that the buildings be fair, that they stand not scattering, as if they were afraid of each other. But wheresoever it is so, the city is beholding to unity for it. Let the citizens break their unity once, they will spend so much in quarrels that they cannot build the city. No other times but when the inhabitants are at peace can build; nor no other time can keep them from waste.

But what? hath God care of "houses?" Out of question not, but for the "inhabitants" that dwell therein. "He that taketh the simple out of the dust, and lifts the poor out of the mire," loves not man for his house, nor no city for the buildings. Jerusalem will not let me wander for an instance: for here, so long as the inhabitants served God, and were at unity, what city like Jerusalem? "The city of the great King" – "the glory (joy) of the whole earth." But when they fell from God to idols, from unity to heart-burnings among themselves, what then became of Jerusalem? What? why just that which our Saviour foretold, "that one stone should not be left upon another that should not be thrown down," not one, neither of temple nor city. And so it came to pass before Adrian left it. If any man therefore will have his house stand, he hath no way but this; to labour that Jerusalem, the city, may serve God in unity. . . .

4

New England, 1630: John Winthrop to the Settlers Aboard the *Arbella*

The largest single group of settlers to New England – some 1,000 men, women, and children in eleven ships – sailed in 1630, ultimately to settle a number of towns on and around Boston Harbor. John Winthrop, a lay Puritan, was the acknowledged leader of the venture. At sea he wrote and presumably delivered to those aboard ship with him the lay sermon from which the following is taken.

SOURCE: Reprinted with permission from "A Modell of Christian Charity," *Winthrop Papers,* II (Boston: Massachusetts Historical Society, 1931), pp. 282-95.

. . . It rests now to make some application of this discourse by the present designe which gave the occasion of the writeing of it. Herein are 4 things to be propounded: first the persons, 2ly the worke; 3ly, the end, 4ly, the meanes.

I. For the persons, wee are a Company professing our selves fellow members of Christ, In which respect onely though wee were absent from eache other many miles, and had our imploymentes as farre distant, yet wee ought to account our selves knitt together by [a] bond of love, and live in the exercise of it, if wee would have comforte of our being in Christ. . . .

2ly. for the worke wee have in hand, it is by a mutuall consent through a special overruleing providence, and a more then an ordinary approbation of the Churches of Christ to seeke out a place of Cohabitation and Consorteshipp under a due forme of Government both civill and ecclesiasticall. In such cases as this the care of the publique must oversway all private respects, by which not onely conscience, but meare Civill pollicy doth binde us; for it is a true rule that perticuler estates cannott subsist in the ruine of the publique.

3ly. The end is to improve our lives to doe more service to the Lord the comforte and encrease of the body of christe whereof wee are members that our selves and posterity may be the better preserved from the Common corrupcions of this evill world to serve the Lord and worke out our Salvacion under the power and purity of his holy Ordinances.

4ly. for the meanes whereby this must bee effected, they are 2fold, a

Conformity with the worke and end wee aime at, these wee see are extraordinary, therefore wee must not content our selves with usuall ordinary meanes whatsoever wee did or ought to have done when we lived in England, the same must wee doe and more allsoe where we go: That which the most in theire Churches mainetaine as a truthe in profession onely, wee must bring into familiar and constant practise, as in this duty of love wee must love brotherly without dissimulation, wee must love one another with a pure hearte fervently wee must beare one anothers burthens, wee must not looke onely on our owne things, but allsoe on the things of our brethren, neither must wee think that the lord will beare with such faileings at our hands as he dothe from those among whom we have lived. . . .

Thus stands the cause betweene God and us, wee are entered into Covenant with him for this worke, wee have taken out a Commission, the Lord hath given us leave to drawe our owne Articles wee have professed to enterprise these accions upon these and these ends, wee have hereupon besought him of favour and blessing: Now if the Lord shall please to heare us, and bring us in peace to the place wee desire, then hath hee ratified this Covenant and sealed our Commission, [and] will expect a strickt performance of the Articles contained in it but if wee shall neglect the observacion of these Articles which are the ends wee have propounded, and dissembling with our God, shall fall to embrace this present world and prosecute our carnall intencions, seekeing greate things for our selves and our posterity, the Lord will surely breake out in wrathe against us be revenged of such a perjured people and make us knowe the price of the breache of such a Covenant.

Now the onely way to avoyde this shipwracke and to provide for our posterity is to followe the Counsell of Micah, to doe Justly, to love mercy, to walke humbly with our God, for this end, wee must be knitt together in this worke as one man, wee must entertaine each other in brotherly Affeccion, wee must be willing to abridge our selves of our superfluities, for the supply of others necessities, wee must uphold a familiar Commerce together in all meekenes, gentlenes, patience and liberallity, wee must delight in eache other, make others Condicions our owne, rejoyce together, mourne together, labour, and suffer together, allwayes haveing before our eyes our Commission and Community in the worke, our Community as members of the same body, soe shall wee keepe the unitie of the spirit in the bond of peace . . . that men shall say of succeeding plantacions: the lord make it like that of New England. . . .

5

New England, 1642: Edward Johnson on "The Manner of Planting Towns and Churches"

Edward Johnson was one of those who arrived in 1630. He settled for a while in Charlestown, then moved on as one of the founders of Woburn, Massachusetts, in 1642. For thirty-two years he was a leader in that town. About 1650 he began to write *The Wonder-Working Providence of Sion's Savior in New England,* a history in which, to a modern writer, one catches "the very spirit of New England thought."

SOURCE: Reprinted from J. Franklin Jameson, ed., *Johnson's Wonder-working Providence, 1628-1651* (New York: Barnes and Noble, 1910), pp. 212-16.

There was a Town and Church erected called Wooburn, this present year, but because all the action of this wandering people meet with great variety of censures, the Author will in this Town and Church set down the manner how this people have populated their Towns, and gathered their Churches . . . to begin, this town, as all others, had its bounds fixed by the General Court, to the contenese [contents] of four miles square, (beginning at the end of Charles Town bounds). The grant is to seven men of good and honest report, upon condition, that within two year they erect houses for habitation thereon, and so go on to make a Town thereof, upon the Act of Court; these seven men have power to give and grant out lands unto any persons who are willing to take up their dwellings within the said precinct, and to be admitted to al common priviledges of the said Town, giving them such an ample portion, both of Medow and Upland, as their present and future stock of cattel and hands were like to improve, with eye had to others that might after come to populate the said Town; this they did without any respect of persons, yet such as were exorbitant, and of a turbulent spirit, unfit for a civil society, they would reject, till they come to mend their manners; such came not to enjoy any freehold. These seven men ordered and disposed of the streets of the Town, as might be best for improvement of the Land, and yet civil and religious society maintained; to which end those that had land nearest the place for Sabbath Assembly, had a lesser quantity at home and more farther off to improve for corn, of all kinds; they refused not men for their poverty, but according to their ability were helpful to the poorest sort, in building their houses, and distributed to them land accordingly; the poorest had six or seven acres of Medow, and twenty five of Upland, or thereabouts. Thus was this Town populated, to the number of sixty families, or thereabout, and after this manner are the Towns of New England peopled. The scituation of this Town is . . . very full of pleasant springs, and great variety of very good water, which the Summers heat causeth to be more cooler, and the Winters cold maketh more warmer; their Medows are not large, but lye in divers places to particular dwellings, the like doth their Springs; their Land is very fruitful in many places, although they have no great quantity of plain land in any one place . . . their meeting-house stands in a small Plain where four streets meet; the people are very laborious, if not exceeding some of them.

Now to declare how this people proceeded in religious matters, and so consequently all the Churches of Christ planted in New-England, when they came once to hopes of being such a competent number of people, as might be able to maintain a minister, they then surely seated themselves, and not before, it being as unnatural for a right N.E. man to live without an able Ministery as for a Smith to work his iron without a fire; therefore this people that went about placing down a Town, began the foundation-stone, with earnest seeking of the Lord's assistance, by humbling of their souls before him in daies of prayer, and imploring his aid in so weighty a work, then they addressed themselves to attend counsel of the most Orthodox and ablest Christians, and more especially of such as the Lord had already placed in the Ministery, not rashly running together themselves into a Church, before they had hopes of attaining an Officer to preach the Word and administer the Seals unto them, choosing rather to continue in fellowship with some other Church for their Christian watch over them, till the Lord would be pleased to provide: They, after some search meet with a young man named Mr. Thomas Carter, then belonging to the Church of Christ at Water-Town, a reverend godly man, apt to teach the sound and wholesome truths of Christ; having attained their desires, in hopes of his coming unto them, were they once joyned in Church-estate, he exercising his gifts of preaching and prayer among them in the mean-time. . . . After this they make ready for the work, and the 24. of the 6. moneth 1642, they assemble together in the morning about eight of the clock; After the reverend Mr. Syms had continued in preaching and prayer about the space of four or five houres, the persons that were to joyn in Covenant, openly and professedly before the Congregation, and messengers of divers Neighbour Churches . . . [as also magistrates of the civil government, these last] . . . to countenance the people of God in so pious a work, that under them they may live a quiet and peaceable life, in all godliness and honesty . . . the persons stood forth and first confessed what the Lord had done for their poor souls, by the work of his Spirit in the preaching of his Word, and Providences, one by one; and that all might know their faith in Christ was bottomed upon him, as he is revealed in his Word, and that from their own knowledg, they also declare the same according to that measure of understanding the Lord had given them the Elders, or any other messengers there present question with them, for the better understanding of them in any points they doubt of, which being done, and all satisfied, they in the name of the Churches to which they do belong, hold out the right hand of fellowship unto them, they declaring their Covenant, in words expressed in writing to this purpose.

THE CHURCH-COVENANT

We that do assemble our selves this day before God and his people, in an unfeigned desire to be accepted of him as a Church . . . from the bottom of our hearts agree together through his grace to give up our selves, first unto the Lord Jesus as our only King, Priest and Prophet, wholly to be subject unto him in all things, and therewith one unto another, as in a Church-Body to walk together in all the Ordinances of the Gospel, and in all such mutual love and offices thereof, as toward one another in the Lord. . . .

6

Virginia, 1612: Sir Thomas Dale's Prayer

Sir Thomas Dale was one of three professional soldiers hired by the Virginia Company of London to take the leadership of the failing settlement at Jamestown. Dale arrived in 1611 as acting governor and marshal. Almost immediately he compiled the colony's existent laws and orders, added orders of his own, and sent the compilation to England to be printed. Attached to the compilation was a lengthy prayer – from which the following is taken – which was to be read aloud twice a day.

SOURCE: *For the Colony in Virginiea Britannia. Lawes Divine, Morall and Martiall, &c.* (1612), in Peter Force, comp., *Tracts and Other Papers, Relating Principally to the . . . Colonies in North America,* III (Washington, 1844), Tract II, pp. 63-68.

. . . . Lord, sanctifie our spirits, & give us holy harts that so we may be thy instrumẽts in this most glorious work: lord inspire our souls with thy grace, kindle in us zeale of thy glory: fill our harts with thy feare, & our tongues with thy praise, furnish us all from the highest to the lowest with all gifts & graces needful not onely for our salvation, but for the discharge of our duties in our severall places, adorne us with the garments of justice, mercy, love, pitie, faithfulnesse, humility, & all vertues, & teach us to abhor al vice, that our lights may so shine before these heathen, that they may see our good works, & so be brought to glorifie thee, our heavenly Father. And seeing Lord [that] we professe our selves thy servants, & are about thy worke, Lord blesse us, arme us against difficulties, strength us against all base thoughts & temptations, that may make us looke backe againe. And seeing [that] by thy motion & work in our harts, we have left our warme nests at home, & put our lives into our hands principally to honour thy name, & advance the kingdome of thy son, Lord give us leave to commit our lives into thy hands. . . . And whereas we have by undertaking this plantatiõ, undergone the reproofs of the base world, insomuch as many of our owne brethren laugh us to scorne, O Lord we pray thee fortifie us against this temptation: let *Sanballat*; & *Tobias*, Papists & players, & such other *Amonits* & *Horonits* the scum & dregs of the earth, let the[m] mocke such as helpe to build up the wals of Jerusalem, and they that be filthy, let the[m] be filthy still, & let such swine still wallow in their mire, but let not ye rod of the wicked fal upon the lot of the righteous.

. . . And seeing this work must needs expose us to many miseries, & dangers of soule & bodie, by land & sea, O Lord we earnestly beseech thee to receive us into thy favour & protection, defend us from the delusion of the divel, the malice of the heathẽ[n], the invasions of our enemies, & mutinies & dissentions of our owne people, knit our hearts altogether in faith & feare of thee, & love one to another, give us patience, wisedome & constancy to goe on through all difficulties & temptations, til this blessed work be accomplished. . . .

7

Virginia, 1662: Her Disease and Cure

Roger Green's *Virginia's Cure: Or An Advisive Narrative Concerning Virginia* . . . was prepared by an Anglican clergyman in 1661 after his return from a sojourn in Virginia, presented to the Bishop of London who was presumed to have authority over the Virginia churches, and, in 1662, published. It was part of a campaign to obtain reforms in the Virginia churches, including a bishop resident in the colony. The effort, sporadically pursued by various churchmen until the American Revolution, failed.

SOURCE: Peter Force, comp., *Tracts and Other Papers, Relating Principally to the . . . Colonies in North America,* III (Washington, 1844), Tract XV, pp. 3-11.

. . . [Virginia] is divided into several Counties, and those Counties contain in all about Fifty Parishes, the Families whereof are dispersedly and scatteringly seated upon the sides of Rivers. . . . The Families of such Parishes being seated after this manner, at such distances from each other, many of them are very remote from the House of God, though placed in the middest of them. Many Parishes as yet want both churches and Gleabes, and I think not above a fifth part of them are supplyed with Ministers, where there are Ministers the People meet together Weekly, but once upon the Lords day, and sometimes not at all, being hindred by Extremities of Wind and Weather: and divers of the more remote Families being discouraged, by the length or tediousnesse of the way, through extremities of heat in Summer, frost and

Snow in Winter, and tempestuous weather in both, do very seldome repair thither. ... Long experience hath ascertained, and the before described manner of their Planting makes it evident, that whilest our Planters in *Virginia* continue as at this day, dispersedly and remotely planted from the House of God, they will continue to rob God in a very great measure of his publick Worship and Service in his House of Prayer. Which is the same Sin the Jews were Cursed for, and must needs put them under the same Curse of God.

But though this be the saddest Consequent of their dispersed manner of Planting themselves (for what Misery can be greater than to live under the Curse of God?) yet this hath a very sad Train of Attendants which are likewise consequents of their scatter'd Planting. For, hence is the great want of Christian Neighbourhood, or brotherly admonition, of holy Examples of religious persons, of the Comfort of theirs, and their Ministers Administrations in Sicknesse, and Distresses, of the Benefit of Christian and Civil Conference and Commerce. . . . It were easie to adde to these a heap of evill consequents of their scattered Planting, which hinder their Temporal, as well as Spirituall happinesse. But I forbear, it being a task unsuitable for my Profession [as a minister], and for that I know the Remedy to be the same for both, and the removing the one will be the removing of the other. . . .

The onely way of remedy for *Virginia's* disease (without which all other help will only palliate, not cure) must be by procuring Towns to be built, and inhabited in their several Counties. ... For hereby her Planters will be convenienced to give God the honour due unto his Name, by attending constantly in full Congregations upon his publick Worship and Service, they will enjoy the benefits of Christian Offices, of frequent civil commerce and Society, which begets mutual confidence, trust and friendship, the best groundwork for raising Companies of the best qualified, and most able persons to combine in Designs, most advantagious to their own and the publick Weal; they will enjoy the benefits of vertuous Examples, of publick Catechizing and Instructing their Children and Servants in the Principles and Duties of the Christian Religion . . . whereby not only Children and Servants, but Parents and Masters who are ignorant, may (without being ashamed) be enlightned with true saving knowledge, and their Children in Schools of Learning may grow up to be serviceable both in Church and State. . . .

8

The Sociology of Community: Space Plymouth, Massachusetts, 1632

To trace the articulation of community ideals as we have done in selections two through seven leads clearly to the proposition that while sixteenth- and seventeenth-century English notions of community were brought to both New England and Virginia, they persisted only to the north and were lost in the south. Yet articulated ideals as to community are not to be confused with the social reality of men and women occupying a given space, recognizing a common life, and acting in common concerns. In other words, we have not yet touched upon the community as defined in theory, only upon the community as idealized at a past moment in time. The remaining selections seek the social reality in a variety of materials and through a variety of devices. In selections eight, nine, and ten it becomes clear that the peopling of Anglo-America was a process of successive community formulations. Selection eight, by Plymouth's frequent governor during the earliest decades, describes the scattering of Plymouth's original tight-knit town and the reencapsulation of those scattering into new churches and towns.

SOURCE: Reprinted with permission from William Bradford, *Of Plymouth Plantation, 1620-1647,* Samuel Eliot Morison, ed., New York: Alfred A. Knopf, Inc., 1953, pp. 252-54.

. . . The people of the Plantation began to grow in their outward estates, by reason of the flowing of many people into the country, especially into the Bay of the Massachusetts. By which means corn and cattle rose to a great price, by which many were much enriched and commodities grew plentiful. And yet in other regards this benefit turned to their hurt, and this accession of strength to their weakness. For now as their stocks increased and the increase vendible, there was no longer any holding them together, but now they must of necessity go to their great lots. They could not otherwise keep their cattle, and having oxen grown they must have land for plowing and tillage. And no man now thought he could live except he had cattle and a great deal of ground to keep them, all striving to increase their stocks. By which means they were scattered all over the Bay quickly and the town in which they lived compactly till now was left very thin and in a short time almost desolate.

And if this had been all, it had been less, though too much; but the church must also be divided, and those that had lived so long together in Christian and comfortable fellowship must now part and suffer many divisions. First, those that lived on their lots on the other side of the Bay, called Duxbury, they could not long bring their wives and children to the public worship and church meetings here, but with such burthen as, growing to some competent number, they sued to be dismissed and become a body of themselves. And so they were dismissed about this time, though very unwillingly. . . . To prevent any further scattering from this place and weakening of the same, it was thought best to give out some good farms to special persons that would promise to live at Plymouth, and likely to be helpful to the church or commonwealth, and so tie the lands to Plymouth as farms for the same; and there they might keep their cattle and tillage by some servants and retain their dwellings here. . . . But alas, this remedy proved worse than the disease; for within a few years those that had thus got footing there rent themselves away, partly by force and partly wearing the rest with importunity and pleas of necessity, so as they must either suffer them to go or live in continual opposition and contention. And others still, as they conceived themselves straitened or to want accommodation broke away under one pretence or another, thinking their own conceived necessity and the example of others a warrant sufficient for them. . . .

9

Middlesex, Virginia, 1657

In the very earliest documents relative to Middlesex County, Virginia one finds the same concern for defining the spatial boundaries of a new community as was found in Plymouth. The area was originally included in the single parish and county of Lancaster, being the unpopulated area of that county falling south of the Rappahannock River. Settlement began in the early 1650s, but at opposite ends of what would become the county. In 1657, at the urging of those at one end, the area was divided into two parishes, but those at the other end did not agree that the parish boundaries were aptly drawn and petitioned for a revision which was granted. By 1666 the two areas had grown together and the two parishes could unite. When the county was established in 1669 county and parish bounds became coterminous.

SOURCE: Lancaster County, Virginia, MS Orders, Etc., 1655-1666, Virginia State Library, Richmond, p. 35.

Whereas at a Court helde for this Countie May the 27th 1657 upon the peticon of the inh[ab]itants of the upp[er] pte of the Southside of this County the sd Southside of the sd Countie was devided into two parishes this day a peticon being prsented to this Court from the inh[ab]itants of the lower pte of the sd Southside complayninge that the saide order was obtayned wthout their knowledge & Consent & contrary to the acte of Assembly for layeing out of parishes it is hereby ordered that the sd order of May the 27th 1657 for the devideing of the sd Southside into two parishes be made voide and of none effect and for the future establishment thereof it is hereby ordered that the sd Southside bee devided into two parishes & the bounds of the sd two parishes to bee as followeth (vizt.) to beginn at the plantacon late of Capt. Brocus upon Rappahannocke river, includinge the said plantacon of Capt Brocus into the upp[er] parishe, and from thence to runn upon a direct line to the plantacon of Thomas harwood upon Pianketancke rivr includeinge the sd Thomas harwoods plantacon into the lowr p[ar]ishe, and that the sd upp[er] p[ar]ishe bee called or knowne by the name of Lancaster p[ar]ishe and the lower by the name of Pianketancke p[ar]ishe.

10

Hawke, New Hampshire, 1760

The process discerned in Plymouth was still continuing well into the eighteenth century. Like Middlesex, Hawke was originally settled (1735) as part of another community, Kingston. In 1760 fifty-eight heads of families presented a petition and map – the latter an interesting contrast to the idealized view of the New England town – to the central government of the province asking for separate parish status; the petition was acted upon favorably. Hawke, now Danville, was subsequently incorporated as a town.

SOURCE: Nathaniel Bouton et al., eds., *Documents and Records Relating to the Province [Towns and State] of New Hampshire, 1623-1800* (Concord, etc., 1867-1943), IX, pp. 450-51. Fifty-eight signatures deleted. Map from XXIV, following p. 678.

HAWKE (NOW DANVILLE), N.H.
1760

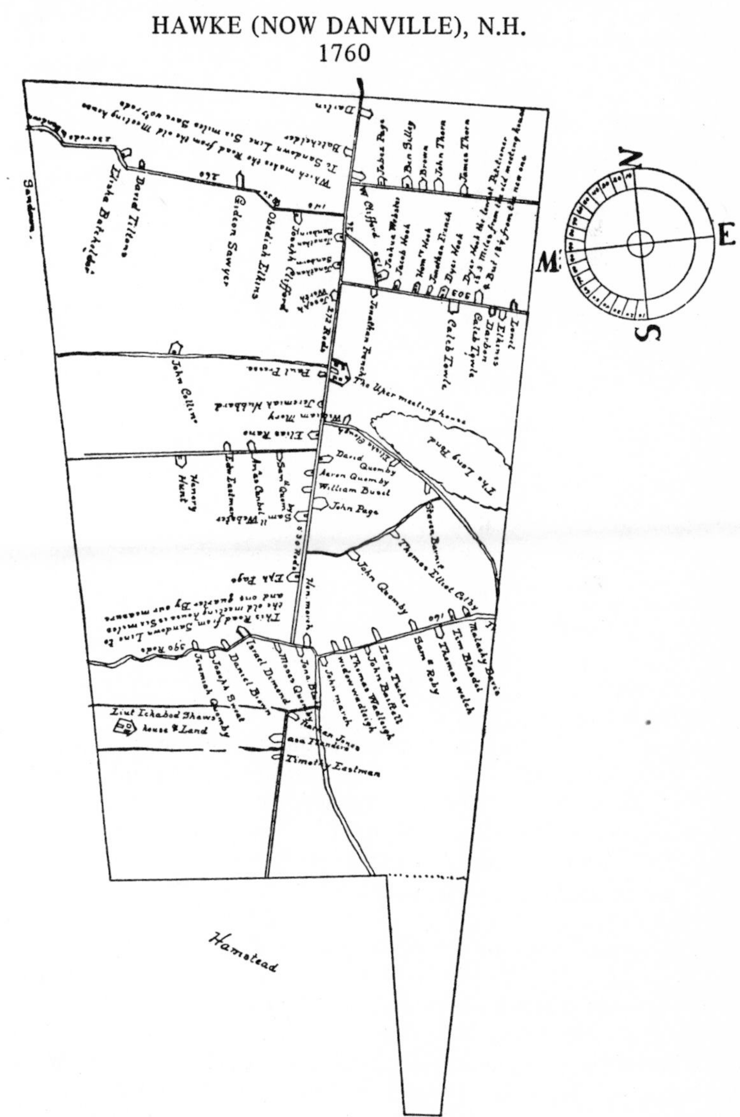

The Petition of Sundry of the Inhabitants of that Part of Kingston . . . adjoining on the Parish of Sandown, Humbly Shews,

That whereas Providence hath placed us at a great Distance from any place of stated public Worship in Town & so rendered our Attendance thereon very difficult & our Families often impracticable: We have built a meeting House among us to accomodate ourselves & Families, That we & they might more conveniently attend the public Worship of God & with more ease & comfort enjoy the Word & ordinances necessary for Salvation, And being disirious at our own cost & charge to maintain the Worship of God among us, We petitioned The Town to Set us off to be a Parish Separate from them, But they (as we apprehend) not regarding our difficult Circumstances have unreasonably denied our Request: Wherefore We humbly pray that we may be sett off & incorporated into a Parish distinct from them . . . And that we may be discharged from paying to the ministry & the School in the other part of the Town & enjoy the Powers and Priviledges of other Parishes.

And your Petitioners as in Duty bound shall ever Pray, &c.

11

The Area of Common Life Middlesex Marriages, 1703-1704

Mass prosopography is a prime tool of community study: All pertinent records of the locale are culled and every item of information regarding every individual is extracted and gathered in what are, in effect, dossiers or short biographies for each. These, in turn, are resorted to for the answers to specific questions. In the present case, the question asked is: Do the legal boundaries of Middlesex County tend to reflect the boundaries of social action in terms of marriages? A time-specific sample of marriages was chosen – all marriages in the county in the years 1703 and 1704; the marriage records themselves are merely lists of names, but prosopography enables the historian to identify the residence of most of the marriage partners. The analysis itself takes the form of a simple tabulation of percentages. The results can be extended over time by the device of undertaking the analysis for a series of years.

SOURCE: *The Parish Register of Christ Church, Middlesex County, Va. From 1653 to 1812* (Richmond, 1897), pp. 63ff.

For space reasons, only the first few entries for 1703 are given here.

Hugh Finley & Mary Picket were Married Jan ye 8th 1703.
Thomas Kingsley & Mary Ockoldham were Married April ye 14th 1703.
Robert Biggs & Mary Armistead were Married
William Chelton & Margaret Wheatherstone were married May ye 18th 1703.
Mr. John Lomax & Mrs. Elizabeth Wormley were Married June ye 1st 1703.
Theophilus Staunton & Mary Percifull were Married June ye 2nd
William Harfoot & Mary Caree were Married July ye 14th 1703.
William Barber & Mary Gray were Married July ye 22nd 1703.
Gabriel Roberts & Sarah Bendall were Married July ye 26th.
Mr. William Churchill & Mrs. Elizabeth Wormley were Married Octobr ye 5th.
. . .

● ● ● ● ●

MIDDLESEX, VIRGINIA
MARRIAGE PARTNERS 1703-1704 BY RESIDENCE*

	Number	Percentage
Resident of Mddsx marrying resident	58	74
Resident marrying nonresident	6	8
Nonresident marrying nonresident	10	13
Residence unknown	4	5
Total	78	100

*Residence is defined as four years or more in an established location.

Note that the third category includes couples coming into Middlesex to avail themselves of a minister when their own locale was without a minister or, as in nearby Petsworth Parish during this period, parishioners were at odds with their minister.

12

The Pattern of Common Life
Stratification in Middlesex, 1704

To the extent that a man's economic and political position reflected his general position in the internal hierarchy of his society, the nature of the hierarchical structure can be measured and assessed. One way to do this is offered by extant tax and property lists, in this case the roll of properties subject to quitrents in Middlesex in 1704. The roll itself is merely a list of property holders and the land they hold subject to quitrents. And not all inhabitants are included – none without property is enrolled, for example. But the list can be made to depict a general view of the stratification of landholding by plotting the per cent of land held by given percentages of property owners. The plot and a generalized statistic indicating the extent of the departure from an absolute equality of landholding – i.e., everyone owning the same amount, ergo no stratification – can be compared to that of other communities. And the individuals making up the percentage groups in terms of property can be compared to the individuals making up percentage groups in a similar plotting of another variable, political office, for example, to see if economic and, in this example, political stratification equate.

SOURCE: "A Perfect Role of the Land in Middlesex County Anno Dom. 1704," *Virginia Magazine of History and Biography*, XXXIII (1925), pp. 47-50. Reprinted with permission of the Virginia Historical Society. Again, only the first few entries are given in order to conserve space. For an explanation of the statistical device see Charles M. Dollar and Richard J. Jensen, *Historian's Guide to Statistics: Quantitative Analysis and Historical Research* (New York, 1971), 121ff.

A PERFECT ROLE OF THE LAND
IN MIDDLESEX COUNTY
ANNO DOM. 1704

	Acres
Richard Atwood	100
Richard Allen	150
Tho Blewford	100
Mr. Blaiss	300
John Bristow	140
Robt. Blackley	100
Coll. Corbin	2260
Coll. Carter	1150
John Cheedle	50 . . .

• • • • •

STRATIFICATION OF PROPERTY HOLDING AMONG
MIDDLESEX COUNTY, VIRGINIA PROPERTY HOLDERS
1704

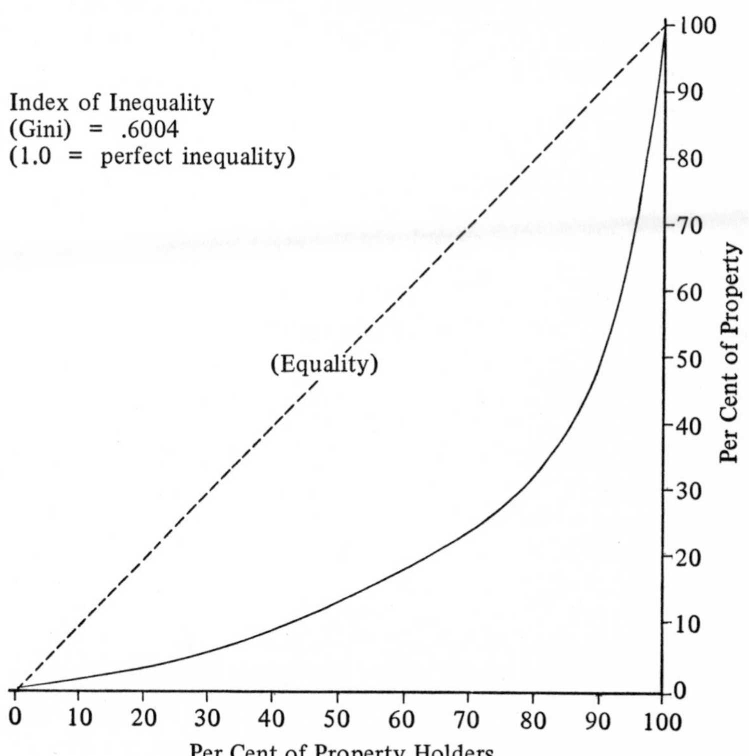

13

Centers of Common Life
Virginia, 1684

Communal life is structured both formally and informally about one or more centers of activity. Obvious centers in the early American community were the church and local government. Selections thirteen, fourteen, and fifteen indicate something of the organization of those centers in a New England town, a Virginia county, and the broad scope of common life centered in them.

SOURCE: C.G. Chamberlayne, ed., *The Vestry Book of Christ Church Parish, Middlesex County, Virginia, 1663-1767* (Richmond, 1927), 44 ff; Middlesex County, Virginia, MS Order Book No. 2, 1680-1694, Richmond, pp. 179 ff. Reprinted with permission from Virginia State Library.

Att a Vestry held ye 4th of Novembr 1684 at the House of Mr Richard Robinson for Christ Church parish In Middlesex County

Mr Duell Pead Minister
The Honorble Ralph Wormeley Esqr

Collo Chr Wormeley
Mr Richd Perrot Senr
Capt Walter Whittaker
Mr Robert Smith
Mr Abrã Weekes
Collo Cuthbert Potter
Mr Nicholas Cock

Mr. Matthew Kemp
Mr John Man
Mr Oswald Cary
Mr John Wortham
Mr William Churchhill
Mr William Daniell
Mr Richd Robinson

lb. Tob[acc]o

It is ordered by this present Vestry that Duell Pead Minister be paid for his Officiating as Minister in This P[ar]ish this present Yeare the Sum̃e of 16000

. . .

It is Ordered that Mr. William Churchhill Church Warden for

Reparations done to ye Lower Chappell According to his accompt be paid	2758
It is Ordered that Mr. John Wortham Churchwarden be paid for Posting of the Stable at ye Grt Church according to his accot	250
It is Ordered that Mr. Robert Price Ch warden be paid for Reparations done to the Uper Chapll according to his accot	100
It is ordered that Dor Stapleton be paid for his Physick Trouble and paines Taken about a poore Sick & Diseased Man Termed Henry Fricston, of late Deseased	1000
It is Ordered that Major Robert Beverley be paid for Keeping of one Thomas Watson, a poore decripped Man a whole yeare	1000
It is Ordered that Mr. John Nicholls be paid for Richd Watts a poore Aged Sick Weake Man being past his Labor and now upon the parish	1000
It is Ordered that Jone Deverdale be pd for Keeping a bastrd Child of Dorothy Suttons Servt to Collo Wormeley, half a Yeare	500

. . . .

It is Ordered that Capt Walter Whittaker High Sherriff Doe Collect the parish Levey at 51 1/2 p pole 634 Tythables in all.

• • • • •

Att a Courte held for ye County of Mddsx Novemr ye 3d 168[4]

Present

Capt: Walter Whitaker mr. Matt Kemp
Coll Cuthbert Potter mr: Oswld Cary
prsent Mr: Richd. Perrot Senr:

. . . .

Ordered that Janie Leucas Servant to Capt: Whitaker be freed her time of Servitude being out in may last & that She [be] paid for the time and paid her corne and Cloathes.

Edward ffletcher & William Hews Sworne in Court to prove Willm. Harrison Servant to Capt: Whitaker, for hogg stealing Ordered that William Harrison . . . Serve his Master Two yeares after his Indented time for hogg stealeing

prsent

Mr. Abraham Weekes
Mr. William Daniell

Itt is the opinion of this Court That John Davis Molitto Servt: to Capt: Walter Whitaker is a Slave & to serve accordingly: Ordered that ye estate of mr: Humphry Jones, Deced be Inventorid and appraised the appraisers appoynted are mr: Robert Price mr. Francis Weeks mr: William Cheyny & mr. Tho: Haslewood or any three of them. . . .

Mrs: Mary Seager makes choyce of her Husband mr. Randolph Seager to be Joyned with her in ye Executorship of ye estate of mr: Humphrey Jones Deced

Order is granted to Arthur Meutice against ye estate of mr. Humphry Jones decd for Twelve Hundred & Ninety pound of Tobaccoe & caske it being for a Chirurgeons accompt. . . .

Martha Butcher in open Court makes choyce of Capt: Walter Whitaker for her guardian

prsent

Ralph Wormely Esqr:
Coll Christopr: Wormely

. . . .

John Beeching bringing an accon to this Court agt: mr. Oswald Carey for his ffredome by an Indenture but not being able to prove it in Court It is Ordered by this Court that he returne to his master & serve according to Custome of ye Country

Ordered That Charles Roan doth forthwith deliver unto Richard Willis Two Cattle which ye said Willis bought of Richd. Benger if they are to be found. . . .

Ordered That Thomas Carrington & Cornelius Mowar Servants to Richd. Robinson be by the Sherriffe taken into his Custody & Carried to ye publicke place at ye Whippeing post & theire Whipt with Twenty lashes, well layd on theire bare backes it being for hogg stealing & that they receive ye Same every court untill they have Satisfied the Law. . . .

Thomas Lake & John ffranckham Sworne in Court in a difference between mr. Deuell Pead & Robert Gillham

The Suite . . . in an accon of trespasse is referrd to ye next Court. . . .

The difference betwixt mr: Deuell Pead plaintiffe and Eliza: Moreland defendt: is referrd to ye next Court at ye defendts. requests: in an accon of Defamacon

The diferrence betwixt mr: Duell Pead & Eliza: Moreland in an accon of Debt is refferd to ye next Court at ye defendts: request

Mr: Philip May did produce a Comision from his Excellencie Lord: Effingham [the governor of the colony] for pleading in ye County Courts which is Allowed of. . . .

The Same Court Continues ye 4th: day of November 1684. . . .

[Payments to be made by the court:]

	[Pounds tobacco]
mr William Churchill [for] a wolfes head	0100
mr: Nicholas Cocke for a wolfes head	0100

Henry Nicholls Junr: for a wolfes head	0100
Benjamin Clarke for a wolfes head	0100
Henr: Thacker for a wolfes head	0100
To mr: Matt Kempe for 2 Inquests	0266
To mr: Abram Weeks for an Inquest	0133
To mr: Oswald Carey for an Inquest	0133
To mr: William Churchill for [a copy of] ye lawes of Virginia	0150
To Richard Robinson for the Court house and accomodacions	5000
To Robert Williams for Levie overcharged last yeare	0085
To the Burgesses theire accompt	15290
To the Clarke of the Assembly Assigned to mr: Abra Weekes	0400
To mr: Richard Robinson for Extraordinary paines as Clark	2000
To mr: Petty Subsherriffe	01200
To Richard Robinson for Extraordinary Trouble in Layeing the Levie	0500
... To [paying the] publicke [i.e. colony] Levie	25662

... Ordered that the Sherriffe of this Countie mr Robert Smith Levie of each Titheable person in this County Eighty Seven pound and a halfe of Tobaccoe for defraying the publicke [i.e., colony] & Countie Charge

14

New England, 1766

SOURCE: *Records of the Town of Braintree, 1640-1793* (Randolph, Mass., 1886), pp. 407 ff.

... The freeholders and other inhabitants of the town of Braintree qualified to vote in town affairs being assembled [March 3rd, 1766] at the meeting-house in the middle precinct of said town for the choice of town officers and the transacting other affairs ... chose Samuel Niles, Esq., Moderator.

Elisha Niles chosen clerk & also treasurer for the town.

Constables. Chosen Mr. Joseph Cleverly, Ensign Thomas Thayer and Benjamin Spear Jr.

Wardens. Mr. Robert Williams, Jonathan Bass 2d, Balch Cowen, John Vinton, Capt. Peter Thayer, Ensign Jonathan Wild. ...

Selectmen chosen: Mr. Norton Quincy, John Adams, Esq., Deacon James Penniman, Ebeezer Thayer, Esq., Mr. Benjamin Porter. . . .

[Other officers chosen: constables, tithingmen, fence viewers, fire wardens, surveyors of lumber, sealers of leather, cullers of staves, sealer of shingles, hog-reeves, surveyors of highways.]

Voted. The highways within said town be repaired the ensuing year by a tax laid on the inhabitants and freeholders in the same proportion as the last years.

Separately, voted, Ebenezer Miller, Esq., Samuel Niles, Esq., and Capt. Thomas Wales, a committee to lease out the town's land and to give and take security in the name and behalf of the town, said committee to determine respecting planting said land the next term.

The affair respecting the fish referred to the adjournment of this meeting. . . .

1766 March 17. . . .

Voted, that no owner of any mill or dam across or upon Monotaquot or Moor's Farm Rivers (so-called) nor any other person upon any pretence whatsoever shall draw up or shut down any gate or make any weir or any obstruction whatsoever that may obstruct the passage of the fish called ale-wives up said rivers or any branch of said rivers for the space of thirty days to begin from and after the last day of April the ensuing year without leave of the committee of the town appointed for that purpose, upon the penalty of twenty shillings for each and every such offence, to be sued for and recovered in any court proper to try the same, or before any justice of the peace in the county of Suffolk. . . .

Also voted, that no person be permitted to fish for ale-wives in any part of said rivers within the said term of thirty days, excepting on Tuesdays and Fridays, and every person or persons presuming to fish on any other days for every such offence shall forfeit and pay twenty shillings to be sued for as aforesaid. . . .

Also, voted the above votes respecting the fish be presented to the Court of General Sessions of the Peace for their approbation and confirmation for the year ensuing as a by-law, according to the law of this province in such cases made and provided. . . .

The selectmen offered a report to the town respecting ways laid out as follows, viz.:

Braintree, Febry. 28th. 1766

We, the subscribers, selectmen of the town of Braintree, being requested by sundry of the inhabitants of said town, on the day above said, went and viewed a way lately obtained by a number of the inhabitants of this town, of Samuel Belcher on the southerly side of the westerly part of his home place next Mr. Sawen's land, of which way they have a deed of said Mr. Belcher, of one rod and half wide. They desire it may be a town way to help them mend said way, there being no other charge arising therefrom; which motion we look upon reasonable and recommend to the town for their acceptance. . . .

The above report was voted accepted.

15

Virginia, 1774

SOURCE: Hunter Dickinson Farish, ed., *The Journal and Letters of Philip Vickers Fithian: A Plantation Tutor of the Old Dominion, 1773-1774* (Williamsburg, 1957), p. 167 – copyright by Colonial Williamsburg, Inc.

. . . [There are, in Virginia] the three grand divisions of time at the Church on Sundays, Viz. before Service giving & receiving letters of business, reading Advertisements, consulting about the price of Tobacco, Grain &c. & settling either the lineage, Age, or qualities of favourite Horses 2. In the Church at Service, prayrs read over in haste, a Sermon seldom under & never over twenty minutes, but always made up of sound morality, or deep studied Metaphysicks 3. After Service is over three quarters of an hour spent in strolling round the Church among the Crowd, in which time you will be invited by several different Gentlemen home with them to dinner. . . .

16

The Vertical Dimension
Robert Keayne, Boston Merchant

Here and there in these selections the tie between the community and the larger society has shown itself – the onlookers at the gathering of the Woburn Church in selection five, for example; in selection fourteen, the necessity for Braintree to obtain approval of its fish ordinance from a higher body and to collect fines from violators by suing in a province court; the necessity for Middlesex, in selection thirteen, to raise a levy for the colony government. The innate competition between the vertical and horizontal dimensions appears in selection seven – the program-oriented ministerial specialist (to use the theoretical language of the first selection) arguing for fundamental changes in society in the interest of his program. The present and the following selection are indicative of the link between the community and the broad economic web of the society and the inherent competition between the two dimensions. Robert Keayne was a merchant in Boston in the earliest decades; censured in 1639 by church and state for overcharging for his goods, he brooded long and, in drawing up his will, attempted to justify himself. Robert Carter was a prominent Virginia planter living in Lancaster County – just north of Middlesex; the varied, extra-communal interests of a Virginia gentleman are indicated in his letter to one Mr. William Dawkins.

SOURCE: "The Last Will and Testament of Me, Robert Keayne . . . (1653)," City of Boston, *Report of the Record Commissioners*, X (Boston, 1886), 1-53.

. . . I dare not say nor did I ever thinke (as farr as I can call to minde) that the Censure [by the colony government and Boston church] was just & righteous. . . . Was the price of a Bridle, not for takeing but only asking, 2s for [that] wch cost here 20d such a haynous sine which have since beene comonly sould & are still for 2s 6d & 3s or more, though worse in kinde, the selling of 2 or 3 dozine of great gold buttons for 2s 10d p dozine that cost 2s 2d ready money in London & bought at the best hand (such a haynous sine) as I shewed to many by my Invoyce. . . . The buttons [were] not payd for when the complaynt was made, nor I thinke not yet; neither did the complaint come from him that bought & owed them nor with his knowledge or consent as he hath since affirmed, but meerly from the spleene & envy of another, whome it did nothing concerne Was this so great an offence; Indeed that it might be made so some out of there ignorance would needs say they were coper & not worth 9d p dozine but these were weake grounds to passe heavie censures upon, was the selling of 6d. nayles for 8d p lb. & 8d nayles for 10d. p lb. such a crying & oppressing sine though as I remember it was above two yeares before he that bought them payd me for them (& not payd for if I forgot not) when he made that quarreling exception & unrighteous complaint in the Court against me . . . as if I had altered & corrupted my booke in adding more to the prize than I had set downe for them at first delivery, wch if I had set down 8d for that after 2 yeares forbearance, wch I would have sould for 7d if he had payd me prsently, I thinke it had beene a more honest act in me then it was in him that promissed or at least prtended to pay me prsently that he might git them at a lower prize then a man could well live upon. . . .

17

Robert Carter, Virginia Planter

SOURCE: Louis B. Wright, ed., *Letters of Robert Carter, 1720-1727: The Commercial Interests of a Virginia Gentleman* (San Marino, Calif., 1940), pp. 91-92. Reprinted with permission of the Henry E. Huntington Library and Art Gallery, San Marino, California.

Rappahannock, Mar. 25th, 1721

I wrote to you from Williamsburg an answer to yours relating to some lands that were offered to you [for] sale in Stafford County . . . belonging to some persons in England that are heirs to one Ashton. Since [then] I have made inquiry into these lands and am informed 'tis a seat worth buying. John Fitzhugh since his arrival hither hath reported he hath bought them for two hundred pound but had left the deeds behind him to be executed after he came away, which makes me think it is nothing but pretense. If you'll give yourself the trouble to inquire into the title, if the claiming persons can make me a good sale, I should not care if I were the purchaser. Whoever can buy a good title to it for two hundred and fifty pound I believe it may be well worth the money. . . .

We begin to look hard for the London ships. The Spaniards of St. Augustin[e] continue to play the rogue; a vessel lately arrived hither went thither with goods. The master and six of the men were taken out of the ship, and their goods; the remaining part of the crew, to prevent the ship's being made a prize, ran away with her. A vessel from Barbados reports that six pirates were fitting at St. Domingo. . . . 'Tis [not] to be doubted some of them will infest our coast this spring, but sure there will be some care taken of us for the security of our trade. I want salt; if you can find a way to send me 3 or 400 bushels 'twill be very welcome.

18

Communities in the Aggregate

The selections thus far have been illustrative of single communities, although the arrangement has been such as to allow some comparison between communities in New England and Virginia. But the highest level of community study – and the most difficult – involves the aggregation and categorization of many communities. The existence of census figures from a number of years allows aggregation for narrow purposes, and such can be a beginning to broader studies. In the present case, the recorded population of the individual New Hampshire towns in 1767 and 1790 were used to compute a percentage yearly rate of growth and the results categorized according to the number of years elapsed since the first settlement in the area of the town. The censuses themselves are, in comparison with modern censuses, crude and inexact. To the eye they are but lists of towns with populations broken down into various categories – e.g., "unmarried men from 16 to 60," "married men from 16 to 60," "boys from 16 years and under," "females unmarried," etc. The 1790 Federal Census adds an enumeration by family heads and is consequently superior to the pre-independence tallies. For space purposes a sample of the census data is omitted and only the tabulation presented.

SOURCE: Nathaniel Bouton et al., eds., *Documents and Records Relating to the Province [Towns and State] of New Hampshire, 1623-1800* (Concord, etc., 1867-1943), VIII, pp. 166-71, and Department of Commerce and Labor, Bureau of the Census, *Heads of Families at the First Census of the United States Taken in the Year 1790: New Hampshire* (Washington, 1907), pp. 9-10. The computation technique has been adopted from George W. Barclay, *Techniques of Population Analysis* (New York, 1958), 28 ff.

POPULATION GROWTH OF NEW HAMPSHIRE TOWNS BY AGE OF TOWN, 1767-1790

Towns of Age	Number	Per Cent Losing Population	Annual Rate of Pop. Growth (per cent)	Annual Rate of Density Increase (per cent)
3 & less	12	0	10.46	10.48
4-33	36	8.3	6.1	6.41
34-66	25	20.0	1.95	2.37
67+	18	44.4	.03	.08

DAVID GRIMSTED

Democratic Rioting: A Case Study of the Baltimore Bank Mob of 1835

In a year that featured widespread rioting in most parts of the United States, the Baltimore Bank of Maryland riot of 1835 was a particularly dramatic incident. Before it was over, the authorities had killed five persons and wounded some twenty others. The rioters had severely injured several members of a citizen's guard and sacked six homes belonging to Baltimore's wealthiest and most prominent leaders including the mayor, and had damaged several other houses. For one day almost every civil official fled the city, leaving it wholly to the mercy of the mob which destroyed property without opposition, frequently cheered on by large numbers of citizens. The President of the United States, Andrew Jackson, sent troops to restore order, but they arrived only after an eighty-three-year-old veteran of the War of 1812 organized a heavily armed citizen's patrol to keep the peace. Eight rioters were convicted in December 1835, and the next spring the Maryland legislature took over $100,000 from Baltimore's harbor funds to compensate the riot's victims for their losses.

THE PROBLEM

Behind these events lurked many of the deepest problems of

Jacksonian society, which was experiencing the disruptions of both rapid economic change and a newly belligerent sense of democracy. The riot was tied to speculative banking resulting from the main political controversy of the 1830s, Andrew Jackson's attack on the United States Bank. More directly, it grew from a gross, if legal, financial swindle in which Baltimore's entire press and power structure tacitly sanctioned what amounted to a stealing from the poor to aid the rich. The leading beneficiaries of this fraud were Reverdy Johnson, destined to become a United States Senator and Attorney General, and his friends; they were abetted by many of Baltimore's leading citizens, including Roger B. Taney, Attorney General under Andrew Jackson and soon to be Chief Justice of the United States Supreme Court. The riot also developed out of Jacksonian attitudes toward law and popular control. In this instance, Jacksonian rhetoric about the evils of speculators and stock-jobbers and about power justly residing in the hands of the people encouraged violence against those whose financial misdeeds were deemed so gross that the perpetrators no longer deserved social protection. Tacitly the rioters argued that the legal system was not sacred if, as in this case, the law was used not to punish but to protect the guilty. Also implicit in the riot was the major democratic dilemma of how order was to be kept and minorities were to be protected in a democracy. Did democratic authorities have the right to act against citizens perpetrating violence in the name of social justice and the people's will? Did they have the right to set up permanent authorities such as a professional police force to impose order on the people? All these questions, essential to the basic nature of democratic and capitalistic society, were embedded in the Baltimore riot and the many other riots that erupted in 1835.

The drama of the Bank Riot of 1835 and the important individuals and significant issues it involved seemingly should have attracted some historical attention, but such has not been the case. Historians of Baltimore have written of the riot as a kind of curio; historians of the United States have ignored it along with most of the hundreds of other antebellum riots. The reasons for this neglect have less to do with a tendency to ignore the more sordid aspects of American life than with a lack of connection between these events and general American development. Most historians have accepted for the Jacksonian period what one has called "the myth of peaceful progress" (or lack of progress), because these violent incidents contributed nothing in an obvious way to the nation's development. The memory of those Jacksonian riots still widely recalled was kept alive by powerful groups such as Catholics, Mormons, and abolitionists who were their victims. Hence the whole problem has seemed one too simply of religious or proslavery bigotry, and most instances of Jacksonian riot have been left in the hands of local antiquarians who have passed on the tales in much the form in which they received them from early newspapers.

Widespread rioting in the United States in the 1960s increased the interest in the history of social violence but even before this development certain European historians, particularly George Rudé and Eric Hobsbawm, had suggested that instances of riot could be used tellingly in historical studies. They urged a theory of riot that stressed its socially purposive quality and made clear the value of riot as indication of the hopes and fears of lower social classes, which traditional history had often ignored. Their approach also showed how historical evidence could be used in relation to specific questions about the riotous mob and its society. In short, Rudé and Hobsbawm sketched both a method and a reason for studying riots intensively.

The contribution of Rudé and Hobsbawm to human understanding was a modest triumph of the kind historians sometimes make. A commitment to plumbing events in a specific context often keeps historians from developing theories which are as encompassing or stimulating as those worked out in other fields. Theorists like Karl Marx or Sigmund Freud gained intellectual prominence from the genius with which they pursued the pervasive influence of their chosen key to all mythologies. The historian, like most people, is apt to be impressed, but to mumble, particularly in regard to his own area of interest: "Well, of course, the economic factor is very important, the sexual component very interesting, but what about all the other things of importance or interest to my topic? Maybe everything could be subsumed under one theory or the other, but why should it be, unless one is a true believer rather than a true seeker?" Most historians look suspiciously at their colleagues – Hegel, Marx, Spengler, Toynbee – who have attempted to impose a unified pattern on history because these men's desire for a grand design has often forced them to simplify or caricature the specific events used to illustrate their pattern.

The intellectual figures from whom historians Hobsbawm and Rudé wrested the study of crowd behavior were sociological theorists, whose commitment to a "science" of the subject led them not to close investigation of the facts of particular riots but to the construction of theories or typologies that would be "inclusive" and allegedly "testable," although no one ever got around to testing them in a serious way. The most influential of these sociologists was the man who in 1895 first set forth a theory of crowd behavior, Gustav Le Bon. His arguments contained some obvious flaws. Man acting singly acts rationally, he insisted, while irrationalism prevails in groups, where men revert to more instinctual forms of behavior – "primitive," "bestial," "child-like," "feminine" were his favorite adjectives for group conduct. Many of his explanatory devices can hardly be taken seriously – Mediterranean crowds are the most volatile, he tells us, because "they are the most feminine of all" – and he neglected all the irrational aspects of individual behavior as well as those of purposiveness in collective action. He also failed to distinguish between types of crowd behavior; riotous mobs, parliaments or juries, and all behavior in mass society were for him identically irrational. Le Bon's assessment of the crowd was not wholly negative; he recognized elements of heroism, generosity and even grandeur in crowd behavior. But his focus on impulsive irrationality gave a negative tone to his general picture. His contribution to the study of crowd behavior lay less in his explanations than in his description of certain changes that seemed to take place in the individual who became part of a riotous crowd. The freedom that grows from the "anonymity" within the crowd, the "sense of omnipotence" that comes from being part of it, and a potential for doing things in a crowd at variance with the individual's normal behavior remain provocative descriptive aspects of Le Bon's work.

Sociologists had long disputed parts of Le Bon's theory, particularly aspects of his "irrationality" thesis, and had developed distinctions between types of crowds. Yet as late as 1953 a standard survey of the sociological literature on crowd behavior reported, "As yet no one has questioned the irrationality of the riot or the lynch mob." A year earlier Eric Hobsbawm published his initial study of the Luddite riots, and since then the scholarly investigation of riot by both historians and sociologists has radically changed, partly in response to the new theories, partly in response to new riots.

While sociologists tend to disregard the details of specific cases in their search for general laws or inclusive structures, historians are often wary of moving beyond their particular case to its implications for general thought. There are reasons for this: Two instances are never identical and the cultural and temporal context is bound, the historian feels, to create differences in the quality and meaning of specific examples in any category of event. Yet historical causation has its defects as well, partly because language requires that man have some notion of riot in general and not just some facts about the Baltimore Bank Mob of 1835. The historian who too steadfastly "sticks to his subject" often prevents others from seeing the broad implications of his discoveries and even blinds himself to the many assumptions undergirding his account. A series of able monographs on English riots which preceded the studies by Rudé and Hobsbawm failed to receive the broad attention they deserved in part because their implications for riot theory were left inchoate. If sociologists are right in their assumption that acceptable theories of human behavior must be inclusive of all instances, all essential aspects of riot must be present in the Bank mob of 1835. While retaining a certain skepticism about the sociological-transcendental conviction that the universe may be encompassed in a theory or a flower, it is worthwhile to consider what the Baltimore riot implies about Jacksonian rioting, and about the general nature of riotous activity in a democratic society.

The narrowness of subject focus in the historian's vision creates no certainty in his conclusions. Reconstructing the milieu and meaning of the simplest historical event always encompasses broad assumptions and deep perplexity, about which the most cautious historian can hardly make the reader fully aware. The best way for the student to glimpse the problems of written history, and its creativity both in a positive and negative sense, is to read through the documents on this riot making some notes about certain basic questions. Precisely who rioted? Why did the riot occur at that particular time? Was it spontaneous or planned? If it was planned, who instigated it and who led the mob? What were the causes of the riot, social and psychological? Was the rioters' behavior best explained in terms of Le Bon's irrationality or Rudé and Hobsbawm's social purposiveness grown of social injustice? Was the riot socially justified or desirable? What were its results? What are its implications about the character of Jacksonian society and the nature of riot in a democracy? The evidence in the documentary section contains only a small part of what could be used, but the selection suggests the various types of sources available with their often conflicting clues and interpretations. The movement from this evidence to an understanding of the Bank mob to an understanding of Jacksonian riot to an understanding of riot in general involves great leaps of uncertainty at each step, but such is the elusive course of historical or human knowledge. The historian is a detective reconciled to never surely getting his man because he wishes to know not simply who-done-it, but why it was done and what its significance was. To such questions there are no certain answers, but only ones that are relatively coherent, convincing, complex, intelligently probing.

A DESCRIPTIVE HISTORY

The weather was unusually balmy for a Maryland August, but it wasn't primarily the pleasant evenings between August 3 and 7, 1835 that attracted large numbers of Baltimoreans to Monument Square. The conversation was generally about the continuing problems over the Bank of Maryland, which had closed its doors seventeen months earlier. A lot of poor people had had their small savings in the Bank of Maryland and they had not been able to get them back because of the refusal of its trustees to settle the Bank's accounts. Particularly maddening was the general belief that the Bank's former president, Evan Poultney, was telling the truth when he said that the Bank had enough assets to pay all creditors at least ninety cents on every dollar, and maybe full value. Poultney had just published a second pamphlet, this time explicitly charging what many people had long suspected: that the rich people who had borrowed money from the Bank of Maryland didn't want accounts settled because the longer the business dragged on the more chance they had to buy up credits on the bank at a quarter of their value or even less, and thus make huge profits from their indebtedness and poor people's desperation. Of course, it was hard to be sure who was lying; everybody said old John B. Morris, one of the trustees who refused to settle, was honest and kindly. But the Poultneys and their personal and financial relations, the Ellicotts, were Quakers too, and Evan Poultney was a generous man. At least he had pledged his personal fortune to pay the creditors, while the people he accused of being the real culprits were looking prosperous these days. Right here on Monument Square was Reverdy Johnson's new home – mansion, you could call it – and it was hard to make enough money to pay for something like that in the law business, even if you were as sharp as Johnson. And Hugh McElderry and David M. Perine, two others whom Poultney said were "secret partners" in the bank, had also just finished building new mansions. At any rate, thousands had lost heavily in the Bank, while others suddenly had a lot of money to spend. It looked like what President Jackson had warned about: speculators and stock-jobbers waxing fat on money taken from honest, hardworking folk.

Other topics of conversation circulated among the crowd. That young blade, Joseph Bossière was back in town for his trial. A few weeks earlier a man from Washington, whose ward was in a Baltimore girls' school, had followed her to Bossière's house. He concluded that Bossière had debauched the girl, and there was a rumor that the head of the school had acted as procuress. Bossière was going to trial for assault and battery for throwing the guardian out, but that was the least of his crimes. There ought to be something that could be done about men who ruined innocent girls. Maybe those people in other parts of the country were right when they didn't wait for the law to take its course, but hired "Judge Lynch" to get things done. Those people in Mississippi certainly had a right to stop that plot where gangsters, abolitionists, and slaves were planning to kill all white men so that the blacks could make the women their concubines and escape to Mexico while the white plotters took the loot. It was hard to tell what those abolitionists were up to; nothing but trouble ever since they started using the mails last month to send their literature to the South. No good could come of sending antislavery papers among slaves; people said that Nat Turner a few years back got his ideas about killing whites from William Lloyd Garrison's *Liberator.* Besides, slavery was no business of the North, and Southerners had the right to do what had to be done to protect their families and their property.

When it wasn't the abolitionists causing trouble these days, it was the gamblers. Early in July the people in Vicksburg, Mississippi, had hung five gamblers and driven others away, and since then a lot of citizens had acted to rid their towns of the "card and dice gentry." Of course, a lot of people said that the Vicksburg lynching really started as a brawl between groups of toughs, drunk at a Fourth of July picnic, and that the law could handle gamblers. The Mayor of Cincinnati had said he wouldn't tolerate an antigambling mob in his town because the laws were sufficient. Maybe he was right, but the law didn't seem to do much. Like in the Bank of Maryland case. . . .

Maybe those handbills urging Judge Lynch to take care of Reverdy Johnson and his friends were a little extreme. No one had the right to drive a citizen out of town, but still, if the charges were true, tarring and feathering would be no more than the crooks deserved. Of course, the law was the law, but it seemed to be the rich man's law when clever lawyers like Reverdy Johnson and John Glenn got hold of it. After all, legal cases that Johnson, as attorney to the trustees, had brought against the Poultneys and Ellicotts had provided the excuse for not settling the Bank's affairs. The courts and trustees said the public couldn't inspect the books until these cases were finished, and none of the trials had even begun yet. If the Poultneys had absconded with funds, why not open the books to prove it? The one accountant who had gone through the Bank's financial records had said that there was no basis for the criminal charges, that Poultney was right about the assets of the Bank, and that the charge of fraud against Poultney was fabricated, possibly by Reverdy Johnson, who had been Poultney's attorney at the time the Bank failed. Yet what good could violence do? In fact it might upset the creditors' legal hopes of getting John B. Morris and Richard Gill officially removed as trustees and the Bank's books opened. The court's decision was expected any day now. Johnson and Glenn, too, were preparing a reply to Poultney's latest pamphlet and perhaps they'd have something to say for themselves in that. A lot of young men, especially the volunteer fireboys, wouldn't mind a frolic at the expense of Johnson and his sort; a lot of other people wouldn't much mind if it happened. But better wait and see what developed. A name like "Mob Town," which had been used for Baltimore after a riot in 1812, would do the city no good. A couple of people had been killed then, and no one wanted that now.

At ten or eleven in the evenings people drifted home from Monument Square to rest for another working day.

Growing public anger against Johnson and his associates worried Jacksonian Mayor Jesse Hunt. On Thursday the crowd had been angrier than before, and a few "boys" in the crowd had thrown some stones at Johnson's house. Hunt talked to them from Johnson's steps, and they dispersed quietly, but Hunt decided a public meeting of leading citizens might discourage violence. The meeting went mostly as planned; resolutions decried any resort to violence and offered a reward for any information about people circulating inflammatory handbills. The one problem was a volunteer resolution calling on the trustees to open the Bank's books. The acclamation with which this resolve was accepted made clear the extent of popular concern, and the resolution's acceptance might later be used to justify violence if the trustees once again refused to comply. Hunt's own position was uncomfortable. He had himself been a "nominal" director of the Bank of Maryland. Few doubted that he had had little knowledge of its financial situation, but there was a rumor that after the failure Hunt had bought a widow's credits on the Bank at depreciated value to pay off a small personal loan. Later he'd paid her full value, but such second-thought virtue seemed a little politically calculated. Hunt too prided himself on being a working man, and, although he employed some twenty men in his saddler's shop, much of his political support lay in the Jacksonian rank and file where General Jackson's warnings about "monied aristocrats" struck deepest. Hunt desperately wanted to keep the peace, but in some ways he was poorly situated to resist effectively rising popular anger.

He did what he could on Friday evening when the crowd in Monument Square was larger than ever. The leading attorneys for the Bank's creditors, Walter Jones and William Preston, were on hand to deprecate violence as a danger to pending legal action. Hunt was there, too, and, although jeered as a former Bank director, he made clear his commitment to protecting Johnson's home. The crowd was boisterous so that some of the speakers could hardly be heard, but it remained good-natured and peaceable. A few stones were again thrown, this time breaking a few windows, but the crowd quietly dispersed about ten, neither pacified nor yet ready for violence.

The law-and-order forces suffered several setbacks on Saturday. Early that week Johnson and Glenn's second pamphlet appeared; in it they repeated their charges against Poultney but without presenting any new evidence in support of their increasingly unconvincing position. Another development late in the week was the news that the Bank of Tennessee, the largest institutional creditor of the Bank of Maryland, had sold its $260,000 worth of credits for some $60,000. The purchaser was another Baltimore Quaker businessman, W.H. Freeman, whose own bank had failed and who owed the Bank of Maryland $50,000. Thus for an additional $10,000 Freeman bought credits worth over $200,000.

Two announcements on Saturday further fueled popular sentiment. The trustees John B. Morris and Richard Gill announced once again that they wouldn't mind opening the books but couldn't because these were now impounded by the Harford County Court. It was also announced that the creditors' legal attempt to have the trustees removed was once again postponed, this time because of the illness of the presiding judge. Saturday was also payday, the day on which working men stopped off for a few drinks on their way home.

No information exists about the planning of mob activity for that night, except that Jesse Massy of the Patapso Fire Company borrowed from a free black a drum which was later to lead the march against John Glenn's house. But expectation of violence was so general that Mayor Hunt called another meeting of leading citizens, this time not to pass resolutions but to organize defense. The meeting agreed that a citizens' guard was the one hope of avoiding destruction, but there was debate about how that guard should be armed. A few people wanted to carry guns, but the Mayor questioned the right of democratic authorities to fire on the people, and argued that carrying firearms might trigger violence. The decision was to arm the guard with clubs – later the volunteers were to be dubbed "Mayor Hunt's rolling pin brigade" – and to use guns only as a last resort. Part of the guard was to be mounted.

The crowd on Saturday evening became riotous shortly after dark and began throwing bricks and paving stones at the guard. The guard bravely repelled repeated surges toward Johnson's house, the most serious one by a charge of the mounted members into the crowd. Numerous arrests were made but many arrestees were rescued by the crowd while being taken to jail. The guard was not sufficiently numerous or well armed to convince the rioters of serious danger to themselves if they continued to attack. The sight of fellow citizens being arrested and, even more, being attacked by mounted horsemen for acting in what most people considered a just cause increased animosity toward the authorities. When one guardsman fell from his horse, a rioter grabbed his sword and was about to run him through when cooler heads in the crowd restrained him. Sometime during the night Joseph Bossière gave himself up to the crowd to protect his sister's house where he was staying. No one reported what was done to him, but he might have been the man the mob partially tarred and beat through the streets.

Bricks and paving stones continued to fly at the guard, some of whose leaders decided at this juncture that the use of firearms was essential. A city judge granted permission, and a single volley was fired into the crowd. The five deaths in the riot came from this firing; most of the victims were reportedly bystanders, and one of them, a hatter named Potts, had been active in trying to keep the peace. The crowd retired from in front of Johnson's house carrying their dead and wounded, but already a part of the mob had attacked the less well-guarded home of John Glenn and begun to destroy its facade and burn its furniture. Rumor of the guard's approach there caused the mob to flee, and by 2:00 or 3:00 A.M. Sunday Baltimore's streets were again quiet.

It was an uneasy quiet. No one had any illusion that the trouble was over, and Mayor Hunt called on the militia for help. Militia leader and Jacksonian Congressman Benjamin C. Howard said later that he tried to get out his troops but that only two or three appeared. Perhaps Howard didn't try very hard; the rumor spread Sunday that the mob had marked the leaders of the guard on Saturday for retaliation. Popular sentiment seemed behind the rioters more firmly than ever, and anger ran deep about the shootings. Before noon some rioters were back at work sacking John Glenn's house and, when no one opposed them, their numbers swelled. All afternoon Glenn's rich furnishings fueled a fire in front of his house, and his excellent wine cellar slacked the thirst of rioters. During the morning members of the guard had been leaving town with what personal goods they could conveniently carry, and Sunday afternoon Mayor Hunt had notices posted saying that the guard's use of firearms had been "against my advice and without my concent." After peace was restored, Hunt explained that he did not mean to imply the firing was unauthorized, but the notice read as though the mayor were repudiating the peace-keeping authorities he himself had organized. When the guard left town, they left it essentially in the hands of the mob. Sunday afternoon cautious Baltimoreans stayed at home, but more curious citizens strolled around Glenn's house watching, and sometimes cheering on, the fifty to two hundred people engaged in active destruction. Late in the afternoon the sacking of the homes of Reverdy Johnson and John B. Morris began, continuing into the evening. Some of the mob by this time were quite drunk; a fireboy, Peter Harman, while exhorting the mob to keep up the good work, was briefly knocked unconscious when a fellow laborer dropped a plank on his head from a second story window, and Samuel Reed almost fell out a window while drunkenly haranguing the crowd. But there was a good deal of decorum, too. No houses were burnt so there would be no danger to adjoining property, and furnishings were destroyed only where the fire would not spread. A good many things were stolen; later that evening one rioter told a bystander he had taken a pile of Hugh McElderry's sheets which he estimated to be of the precise value of his losses in the Bank of Maryland. But aside from the alcohol which was drunk the mob insisted that most goods be destroyed rather than taken. The crowd of observers was large and the destruction was carried out with good humor. Cheering was especially loud as Reverdy Johnson's law books were burnt. Farmer Henry Brown came into Baltimore from the country when he heard the people were rising up against the "monied aristocrats" and arrived in time to help sack John B. Morris's house. The farmer was already very drunk by the time his friend Jeremiah Tittle saw Brown and told him that Morris was really the poor man's friend. Brown said that he wouldn't have hurt the house had he known that but went on railing against the "damned aristocrats." The crowd at one time came onto the steps of Evan Poultney's house. Poultney came out and said he would offer no resistance, but that his property was already pledged to the creditors. One person in the crowd yelled that they wished no harm to "honest men," and the crowd moved on, leaving a couple of men to wipe the mud from Poultney's steps.

As night came on most of the crowd drifted home. The main targets of popular anger – speculators Johnson and Glenn and trustee Morris – had been punished, and uneasiness grew among citizens about what had been done and even more about what might still be done. At the same time groups consisting of one or two hundred rioters, many of whom had been drinking heavily, were determined to attack other offenders, and small groups spent much of the night damaging the homes of "secret partners" Hugh McElderry and Evan T. Ellicott and of Mayor Hunt and three members of the guard particularly blamed for the previous night's shooting. At this point Leon Dyer, son of a Jewish meatpacker in Baltimore, and, in a secondary way, Benjamin Lynch, half-brother of one of the victimized leaders of the guard, exerted some leadership over the crowd. Both argued later that their efforts were to cooperate with the crowd enough to dissuade them from more serious violence.

Uncertainty about how far the mob might safely go was

seemingly shared by the rioters themselves, who showed frequent willingness to be swayed from destruction. They desisted when the contractor of David M. Perine's new home told them that he had not yet given the keys to Perine and hence would be financially liable for all damage. They left Dr. Hintze's house when the doctor's mother called from the window that the house was hers and not her son's. They were almost dissuaded from doing damage at Evan T. Ellicott's home because it was technically owned by Ellicott's mother-in-law, pictured as the widow of an Irish patriot. The mob by a single vote elected not to burn McElderry's lumber yard, on the grounds that the fire might destroy adjacent property. (The minority argued that such danger would be small if fire engines were kept on hand.) The crowd initially decided not to harm Hunt's, but came back two hours later and then did extensive damage. Most active at Hunt's was James Spencer, who had had his "knuckles shot off" in the shooting on Saturday night.

At dawn Monday a few rioters were still in the streets. For a while they played a fife and drum in front of John Glenn's house, where earlier Leon Dyer had been boarding up the windows and jokingly telling bystanders that he intended to send Glenn a bill for his carpenter services. The mob seemingly intended to take further action; some leading citizens received notes saying their financial activities were being investigated, and rumor had it that fifty or sixty more persons were to be tried by "Judge Lynch." Some rioters were euphoric about their success. Fireboy Peter Harman claimed that now he was mayor, and went around appointing his friends to office. But public sentiment was changing. A public meeting was called at noon. General Samuel Smith rode through town in a carriage sporting an American flag to the meeting and argued eloquently that a total determination to resist violence was needed. The crowd agreed and Smith promptly organized heavily armed patrols to keep the peace. By the time President Jackson sent federal troops the situation was under full control. Some mob supporters issued a proclamation urging the peace be kept to give the culprits a chance to rectify their errors, and a meeting of Tenth Ward Citizens led by Jacksonian politician Samuel Mass passed resolutions in favor of nonviolence but also warning Reverdy Johnson that he would be lynched if he had the effrontery to return to Baltimore. But this was all bluster. No more violence occurred although two weeks after the riot the numerous patrols made Baltimore look still like "an armed camp."

Mayor Hunt, embarrassed by his proclamation of Sunday,

resigned, and General Smith, with the support of both parties and all newspapers, became the law-and-order candidate to replace him. A segment of the citizens, seemingly mostly Jacksonians, tried to get someone to oppose him. Hunt temporarily agreed to run but then was talked out of it, and at the last moment the anti-Smith forces turned to Moses Davis, seemingly a town drunk, as their candidate. Davis polled over one-fifth of the votes, and the voting was light despite efforts to induce a large turnout for Smith to redeem Baltimore's reputation.

In December and January some twenty-three men were tried for riot and eight were convicted; all were pardoned by the Whig governor the next June. In the spring of 1836 the Maryland legislature passed an indemnity bill generously compensating the riot victims with money taken from the city's harbor funds. Reverdy Johnson lobbied for the bill skillfully, but he needed help from his friend, Roger B. Taney, who got his friend, President Andrew Jackson, to write a letter in support of the bill. Johnson was also busy prosecuting the Poultneys and Ellicotts for the next year and a half. He lost all his criminal cases against them and most of the civil suits. But he continued to prosecute the civil cases until his victims, now bankrupt, accepted meaningless adverse judgments rather than continue the cases. Little money was recovered, but Johnson trumpeted these decisions as vindication of himself and the policy of the trustees. In 1838, over four years after the Bank of Maryland stopped operation, trustees John B. Morris and Richard Gill settled accounts. All debts were paid in full, plus a dividend of 10¢ on the dollar. Presumably the money had always been available, but long before settlement almost all poor people whose savings had been in the bank were forced to sell their credits to speculators at a fraction of their worth.

SOME INTERPRETATIONS

Any description of an event implicitly encompasses interpretation of it, but it is perhaps desirable to ask some of the basic questions about the nature and meaning of the Baltimore bank mob more specifically.

Was the behavior of the mob irrational in Le Bon's sense of the term? Answers to this kind of question have traditionally centered on two separate issues: Were the victims chosen on some reasonable basis, and was the action of the mob against them circumspect and moderate?

The first issue requires an evaluation of the mob's financial judgment in its choice of victims and of the economic realities in the Bank of Maryland case. No one has denied that those who lost money in the Bank had reason to be angry, but traditionally the mob's choice of scapegoats has seemed a wholly irrational attack on the largely innocent that specifically avoided injuring the culpable former President of the Bank, Evan Poultney. The French traveller Michael Chevalier published this interpretation in 1837, and most historians of Baltimore have repeated it, partly out of unwillingness to believe that leading Baltimoreans were legal swindlers deserving popular chastisement. Historians like Archibald Hawkins, who have noticed the oddity of a mob's forming seventeen months after the alleged triggering cause, have stressed factors like moralistic anger over the Bossière affair.

A simpler explanation alone accounts for what is known and also supports the reasonableness of the mob: the riot was motivated not by the Bank's failure, but by the interminable delay in settling its affairs after it was put in trusteeship. The financial maneuverings in the Bank of Maryland were complex, but the outline is clear. The Bank under Evan Poultney attracted deposits from those of modest means by offering interest on them, and was run in a speculative way. The fatal part of its speculation was the buying up of 90 per cent of its own stock at inflated values by Poultney and the five secret partners and their large purchase of Tennessee Bonds on the expectation of quick profits. Crisis came with the financial recessions of October 1833 and March 1834. In the first of these, acting Secretary of the Treasury Roger B. Taney bailed the Bank out of immediate trouble through a draft-loan on government funds intended to go indirectly to the Bank of Maryland. By next March the secret partners had shed their connection with the Bank, and Taney refused to send further aid. Poultney, believing that the Bank would not be able to pay its debts if it continued operation, suspended payments. Two trustees, acting under the legal counsel of Reverdy Johnson, refused to settle accounts, issued reports suggesting huge imbalances against the Bank, and began legal proceedings against the Poultneys and Ellicotts for fraud. The case against Evan Poultney was based largely on a note he had signed at the urging of his legal counsel, Reverdy Johnson; the indictments came at the urging of trustee and City Attorney Richard Gill from a grand jury headed by secret partner Hugh McElderry. By July of 1834 it was widely believed that settlement was being held up to benefit speculators;

in January 1835 the first accountant's report confirmed Poultney's contentions, and the trustees responded by denying the accountant further access to the books. The final settling of the Bank's affairs offered proof of the correctness of the mob's financial opinions. Compared to, say, most subsequent historians, the mob was not only rational but financially astute.

The mob's actions were well suited to the object of its righteous wrath. Judging from the handbills, the rioters wanted to tar and feather the secret partners and the trustees. Since these men absented themselves from town, the mob settled on destroying their property, with anger particularly focused on the newly built mansions supposedly paid for with their ill-gotten speculative gains. All action was against those involved in the financial plot or those held responsible for the deaths on Saturday. The mob was extraordinarily fastidious in its concern that the property of the innocent not be damaged. The rioters avoided firing houses because the flames might spread, but instead removed furnishings to the streets for burning and kept fire engines on hand to prevent any possible extension of the blaze. Looting was also uncommon. Some things were stolen but the tendency was to destroy rather than take, and often the mob insisted on this. In short, the rioters selected their victims rationally and were moderate and restrained in their actions.

Do aspects of social rationality in a mob necessarily deny the reality of emotional and psychological release that Le Bon emphasized? That there were valid social reasons for the riot does not necessarily mean that the riot grew only from these. One advantage of studying this riot is that the handbills, the "Junius" letters, and the trial records are so richly suggestive of the emotive realities of the riot, an aspect often neglected in written sources. The handbills give a sense of the fury behind the mob, the tendency to see the situation in the simplest moral terms with rioters being wholly righteous and their victims the source of all social evils. The longest handbill suggests vividly how all things that bothered democratic man – economic uncertainties, rapid change, the deviousness of the law, intellectual and class pretensions, even fears about the stability of family life – were welded together in the fury directed against the bank speculators. In the mind of the handbill writer, Bossière's alleged seduction was an aspect of the Bank of Maryland fraud, and presumably all problems would be solved if a few people – in this case five men and three etceteras – were driven out of town. The tone of the handbills is similar to what "Junius" describes as the mood which overcame the crowd on Saturday when the guard prevented them from sacking Johnson's house: "Every countenance was flushed with the spirit of destruction – reason had thrown down the reigns and ungovernable fury had taken them up."

Other emotions came to the fore on Sunday when the mob was unopposed. Here a spirit of enjoyment and release prevailed as the mob drank and destroyed in high spirits. Riotous actions were neither vicious nor unrestrained, but clearly there was an element of exaltation in the possession of unlimited power represented by untrammeled pillaging and destruction. Crowds cheered on the rioters, and the fury that justified the riot was transformed into pleasurable camaraderie. Many societies have an institutionalized "Saturnalia," a time each year or at the death of a ruler when ordinary laws were discarded and, under a mock king, people were permitted to break usual taboos and regulations without fear of punishment. In democracy perhaps riot informally filled this same function for people who were constantly told that power was theirs while they lived under a system intended to deny power, in the sense of immediate control over others, to everyone. Rioters drinking Glenn's wine and calling it "American blood," James Spencer inviting the crowd to a tea party as he threw Mayor Hunt's china into the streets, or Peter Harman proclaiming himself mayor and appointing his friends to municipal office – all were acting out social and political fantasies that society, ostensibly egalitarian and ruled by the people, prohibited. One witness, a carpenter who admitted to being with the rioters, described this feeling well. A court reporter recorded him as explaining that he was only "a little warm" with drink: "Might have been insane – a great many passions make a man insane beside liquor – excited to see so much property destroyed."

What were the results of the riot? One consideration in judging the rationality of human action is whether or not the results accord with the desires of the participants. Sometimes riots call attention to previously neglected social ills, but they often do much more to create sympathy and strength for their victims. The Baltimore riot aided the restoration to social preeminence of its victims, who came to be viewed less as beneficiaries of legal fraud than as injured citizens, whose vindication was connected with the cleansing of Baltimore's reputation. All of the mob's victims were compensated fully and probably generously for their losses, Mayor Hunt by a public subscription and the rest by an indirect tax levied by the state on the city of Baltimore. Not only did the riot not appreciably aid the bank sufferers, but the attorneys for the creditors were probably right in their conviction that the riot could not have promoted the cause presumably motivating the mob. The riot also led to the resignation of Mayor Jesse Hunt, the favorite of the lower-echelon democracy, and his replacement by law-and-order – and Whig – candidate, Samuel Smith. The situation illustrated a general truth about the effectiveness of riot in the Jacksonian period: in terms of the rioter's own desires, mobs were commonly successful only when directed at people with little social, political, or economic power in the community. They usually failed in all but the most immediate sense when groups of some prominence or social strength were attacked.

Was the riot spontaneous or planned? The Bank Riot was certainly not perfectly spontaneous. For over a week handbills had incited to riot, and an awareness of probable violence was general by Saturday. People commonly believed that there was some organizational structure behind the mob. This may have been partly a conspiratorial fantasy, but the handbills and letters both before and during the riots lend credence to the probability of some behind-the-scenes manipulation. On the other hand, the riot clearly was imbedded in general popular outrage against the profiteers, and no evidence was introduced at the trial to prove any conspiracy. Nor is it likely that anyone could have fully planned and controlled the course of the riot. David Perine left a note in his manuscript collection intimating that Poultney organized the mob to distract attention from his pending trial and to destroy the documents collected by Johnson and Glenn to substantiate their case. The second part of Perine's assertation is certainly false, since the Johnson-Glenn pamphlet appeared a few days prior to the riot. The whole charge fits much better as part of the conspiracy to exonerate the financial culprits than as probable explanation for the riot. Part of the difficulty in this question lies in the excessive contrast in the conventional juxtaposition of spontaneity and conspiracy: seldom do riots occur without some prior urging and awareness of their possibility, but seldom are they so wholly the product of manipulation and control as to justify conspiratorial explanation.

Who led the riot? The question of conspiracy is related to the question of leadership in the riot. Certainly someone or some group wrote the handbills inciting to riot and those notices of warning that appeared on Monday, but there is no evidence suggesting who was responsible. During the destruction late Sunday night the trial records make plain that Leon Dyer exerted considerable influence on the mob. There is no positive proof discrediting his explanation that he was active only to steer rioters away from destruction, but the riot testimony cumulatively makes it improbable that his involvement was only philanthropic. Somewhat similar is the secondary leadership role of convicted rioter Benjamin Lynch who, like Dyer, claimed that he was active to dissuade the mob from violence and more specifically to protect his half-brother who had been active in the citizens' guard Saturday night. Whatever the truth of this explanation, Lynch was active with the mob in a part of town distant from his half-brother's store. The most plausible explanation of Lynch's role, and in a more important way of Dyer's, is that they, as people who had some influence on and responsibility for the mob's action, were acutely conscious of the need to keep damage within the bounds of community tolerance. The statement attributed to Lynch – "Gentlemen, we have gone far enough, if we go further we shall lose the sympathies of the people" – offers the most coherent explanation of their conduct.

Almost nothing is known about Lynch, except that he was a young carpenter and the son of a small merchant. Dyer was the son of a German Jew who founded Baltimore's first Hebrew Congregation and was an early meatpacker. After the riot, Dyer pursued a romantic career in New Orleans, Mexico, and San Francisco. Most interestingly, he apparently had close ties with the more plebian wing of the Jacksonian party. Roger B. Taney, miffed at the discourtesy of Baltimore's Jacksonian representatives in not calling on him when he went to Annapolis to lobby for the riot indemnity bill, expressed surprise that these men, like Baltimore's Jacksonian editor, should follow the political guidance of Leon Dyer. Another possible leader of the mob was a cooper, Jacksonian politician Samuel Mass. Archibald Hawkins, in the best history of the riot, but one written long after its occurrence, identified Mass as "Red Jacket." Hawkins might have confused Mass's resolution against Johnson after the riot with more active leadership in the mob, although Hawkin's facts are generally accurate. Leaders of most mobs were sensible and powerful enough to avoid serious legal implication, so these tentative clues about the roles played by Dyer and Mass are intriguing. If these men were leaders, it would suggest that the mob grew in part from the lower-class wing of the Jacksonian party, among men who took rhetoric about stock-jobbers and speculators stealing from the people much more to heart than did respectable Jacksonians such as Taney and Congressman Benjamin Chew Howard.

Who were the rioters? The natural supposition would be that they were people who had suffered losses because of the failure to settle the Bank of Maryland's affairs. Some of them were, judging from comments made by individual rioters that they were getting their $100 or $200 worth of fun in destroying property or that they were stealing bed sheets worth precisely the amount of their losses. But creditor attorney William Preston was probably right when he informed the mayor that those likely to be rioting were not creditors. The riot trials suggest some general traits of the rioters. Twenty-two men were identified by name in the trials who seem to have been rioting actively at one point or another, including most of those judged guilty, a few who were acquitted, and three witnesses or people mentioned by witnesses. Of these, fourteen can be identified by profession, and of these all but three were mechanics (working men with some particular skill or craft). One was a farmer, one a small merchant and the other – who perhaps had done no more than take home a part of one of John Glenn's carpets – was a recently immigrated Irish laborer. Aside from the Irishman and the farmer, the rioters were residents of Baltimore, many of them for all their lives.

Ages of defendants were not given, but in at least six cases mention was specifically made of the rioter's youth or his being an apprentice. Seemingly most of the rioters were in their late teens or early twenties. Five of them had connections with local fire companies, which were manned usually by people in this age group. Many of the rioters were drinking heavily at the time, two of them were described as having problems with alcoholism, and one had a history of serious mental derangement. The evidence, if sketchy, is better than that available for most riots and corresponds with the outlines of the situation in other cases. Rioters were not, as Reverdy Johnson asserted, "the dregs and refuse of society"; rather they tended to be young men, employed and moderately respectable. They were most often still unmarried and susceptible to the attraction of peer group activity. Their belonging to fire companies, the socially purposive nineteenth-century equivalents of the twentieth-century urban gang, suggests the same thing. Riots also attracted a handful of alcoholics, mentally disturbed people, or those with criminal proclivities, but seldom did such persons constitute their main element.

What does the Bank Riot suggest about Jacksonian society? The riot clearly grew partly out of the financial dislocations of the period, some of which were stimulated by Jackson's attack on the national bank. Poultney's over-circulation of bank notes coincided with the United States Bank's loss of that secure position which had allowed it to check such practices. One of the principal speculations of the "secret partners" was to buy up stock in the Union Bank which they knew was to be designated a "pet bank." The financial problems of the Bank of Maryland really began when the Union Bank's stock failed to rise in value after it became a government depository. Jackson's attack on "the monster" United States Bank actually encouraged the viciously speculative financial practices Jackson wished to control.

The mob's willingness to use violence against the speculators certainly owed something to Jackson's antibank rhetoric which suggested that the people were being preyed upon by vague "stock-jobbers" whose influence he associated with the national bank. The possible leadership of Dyer and Mass in the riot would suggest that this had great importance; certainly Henry Brown came to town to riot when he heard that the people were rising against "the monied aristocracy." Even more important may have been Jackson's influence both in popularizing the idea that in a democracy power belonged directly to the people and in symbolizing certain attitudes about the relation of the individual to the state which lay close to the heart of the American political ideal. Historians have long associated Jacksonianism with the rise of democracy and the common man, an idea that has merit even though most of the legal changes in voting occurred before Jackson's presidency and the size of the electorate increased only after it. What Jackson represented was the triumph of psychological democracy, the average man's sense of his ability and right to rule without deference to or guidance from his social and intellectual betters. The Jacksonian promise of popular control created a new vitality in democratic and demagogic procedures, but was also frustrating because the promise of power to individual citizens inevitably far exceeded its reality.

Jackson bolstered democratic man's self-confidence even more by his example than by his political theory. Jackson's lack of formal education and manner allowed intense popular identification with him. He himself deplored the rioting that became frequent in his second term, but it seems probable that his actions and personality also stimulated it. One of the basic tenets of

American government was that the individual was to take precedence over the state, that the state's primary responsibility was to secure to the individual his right to the private pursuit of happiness. This created some tension in American attitudes toward the law, which was the means through which state power most touched the lives of citizens. Legal control was practically necessary, extensively used, generally well administered, and irksome: expensive, uncertain, in the hands of a legal aristocracy, and inevitably deciding things on the basis of established rules rather than an ideal of perfect justice. Able work by judicial conservatives improved legal learning and the legal system to the point where attacks on it were doomed, but distaste remained. The United States in the 1830s was a government of laws not men, but democratic man was not altogether happy about it.

The legal system, and even more strongly social conventions, bound Americans who were told they should be free, but their favorite popular myths centered on men – Natty Bumppo, Huck Finn, western heroes – who because they lived above social requirements and according to an elevated personal code offered not a threat to society but its surest protection. Andrew Jackson, more than any other American politican, came to represent this anarchic hero, the man who followed his own sure vision of right regardless of popular clamor over the bank, or judicial decisions in favor of the Cherokees, or technical requirements about bank deposits. Jackson's example suggested that for him the popular will was superior to legal technicalities, and Americans vicariously enjoyed his freedom because they had confidence in the integrity of his individual code. But his example offered, quite unintentionally, justification of resort to extralegal violence when the legal system proved unwilling or unable to respond to what was viewed as serious wrongdoing.

The political situation in the summer of 1835 further encouraged riotous outbreaks. During the year there were some thirty-seven riots, most of them concentrated in late summer and fall. The most obvious reason for this outburst of rioting was increased abolitionist activity, particularly the sending of antislavery literature south. The South responded with fear and fury, and much of the rioting of the year was over alleged slave insurrections in the South or against abolitionists and blacks in the North. A kind of contagion of violence also encouraged riots wholly unconnected with the racial-slavery question. The tendency to riot was also fostered by the presidential election in the summer of 1835. Martin Van Buren, already campaigning to be elected President as Jackson's successor, was politically weak in the South, and his leading opponent at this time, Hugh Lawson White of Tennessee, had great strength there. Hence the two parties vied with one another in trying to appease the South, and the partisan press of the nation proved totally unwilling to condemn riots aimed at abolitionists, blacks, or alleged insurrectionists. This tacit tolerance for pro-slavery riots made ambiguous the position of people who strongly condemned other types of riot, and helped create a general climate of tolerance for mobs.

What does the Bank of Maryland riot suggest about the nature of riot in a democracy? The Baltimore mob suggests that democratic rioting has roots in social protest, but that this involves neither revolutionary intent nor any clear reform policies. In a riot situation problems were commonly viewed in such immediate and personal terms that violence seldom contributed to the solution of social problems in the Jacksonian period. As in the Baltimore riot, the tendency was to focus anger so wholly on persons that legal and institutional causes were neglected. Commonly anger was also directed not against those in social power, but against those who were less influential than the rioters. The Baltimore mob attacked their social betters, but more commonly minorities such as Catholics, nativists, Mormons, Englishmen, and especially blacks were the victims. Perhaps particularly in a democracy, where peaceful channels for protest and influence exist, riot most often is socially conservative and oppressive rather than institutionally progressive.

Riot poses deep problems for a democracy because it reflects some of its highest ideals and strongest tendencies, and yet threatens the protection the nation owes to all citizens, especially the weak and unpopular. Democracy implies that the citizen is to have preeminence over the state, that all men have a responsibility for social justice, and that obedience to law is an obligation secondary to obedience to conscience. Along with this ideological grounding for riot, democracy fosters certain psychological needs that riot meets. The mob situation allows democratic man the immediate possession of power that the system both promises and denies him and also permits escape from the uncertainties of a mobile society by briefly permitting a perfect sense that his will and the social will are one. For a democratic government to react harshly to riot is to endanger people who acted out of their own sense of justice ostensibly for the general good; to react mildly is to make the state an accomplice in what is done by refusing legal protection to the unpopular. Mayor Hunt's uncertainty about using arms against the mob reflects a constant dilemma for democratic officials.

The social dangers of riot to the weak and unpopular and to society in general were well brought out in the best law-and-order speech of the Jacksonian period. Young Abraham Lincoln in 1837 spoke in response to the wide scale rioting of the mid-1830s. He mentioned the hanging of gamblers in Vicksburg, Mississippi, the burning of a Catholic convent in Massachusetts, and the burning to death of a Negro murderer in St. Louis. He didn't mention the recent death of abolitionist editor Elijah Lovejoy at the hands of a mob attacking his press in Alton, Illinois, but Lincoln and his audience doubtless had it in mind, too:

> When men take it in their heads today, to hang gamblers, or burn murderers, they should recollect, that, in the confusion usually attending such transactions, they will be as likely to hang or burn some one, who is neither a gambler nor a murderer as one who is; and that, acting upon the example they set, the mob of tomorrow, may, and probably will, hang or burn some of them, by the very same mistake. And not only so; the innocent, those who have ever set their faces against violations of law in every shape, alike with the guilty, fall victims to the ravages of mob law; and thus it goes on, step by step, till all the walls erected for the defence of the persons and property of individuals, are trodden down, and disregarded.

Such tendencies could lead, Lincoln argued, to vicious anarchy, against which there was only one sure protection.

> Let reverence for the laws, be breathed by every American mother, to the lisping babe, that prattles on her lap – let it be taught in schools, in seminaries, and in colleges; – let it be written in Primmers, spelling books, and in Almanacs; – let it be preached from the pulpit, proclaimed in legislative halls, and enforced in courts of justice. And, in short, let it become the political religion of the nation; and let the old and the young, the rich and the poor, the grave and the gay, of all sexes and tongues, and colors and conditions, sacrifice unceasingly upon its alters.

There were important truths in the dangers Lincoln outlined; there was danger as well in the extent to which he carried these truths. Riot does endanger individuals and groups – and sometimes those most truly deserving of protection – but it also counteracts the danger of totalitarian acceptance of the state's power and serves as a safety valve for some of the tensions endemic to democratic society.

FOR FURTHER READING

James L. Cutler, *Lynch-Law* (New York: Longmans, Green & Co., 1905) remains the best general survey of social violence in nineteenth-century United States. Many of the articles in *Violence in America: Historical and Comparative Perspectives* (New York: F.A. Praeger, 1969), edited by Hugh Davis Graham and Ted Robert Gurr are important, especially Richard Maxwell Brown's "The American Vigilante Tradition." Richard Hofstadter and Michael Wallace edited *Violence in America* (New York: Alfred A. Knopf, 1970), a good collection of brief primary accounts of American social violence; Hofstadter's lengthy introduction is provocative. Leonard Richards, *"Gentlemen of Property and Standing": Anti-Abolition Mobs in Jacksonian America* (New York: Oxford University Press, 1970) interprets one type of mob, and Laurence Veysey, *Law and Resistance: American Attitudes Toward Authority* (New York: Harper Torchbook, 1970) presents documents exploring the intellectual roots of American attitudes toward law. An excellent article by Pauline Maier, "Popular Uprisings and Civil Authority in Eighteenth Century America" *William and Mary Quarterly,* 3rd ser., 27 (1970), 3-35 explores the nature of riot in an earlier period. David Grimsted "Rioting in its Jacksonian Setting," *American Historical Review* (April, 1972) discusses some of the ideas in this essay in a somewhat broader context.

The classic study of crowd behavior was written in 1895 by Gustav Le Bon: *The Crowd: A Study of the Popular Mind*, ed. Robert K. Merton (New York: Viking Press, 1960). The best summary of sociological modifications and questioning of Le Bon's theory is an article by Stanley Milgram and Hans Toch "Collective Behavior: Crowds and Social Movements" in Gardner Lindzey and Elliot Aronson, *Handbook of Social Psychology,* 2nd ed. (Reading, Mass.: Addison-Wesley, 1968) 4:542-84. The ablest of recent attempts to formulate a sociological model of violence is that of Ted R. Gurr in *Why Men Rebel* (Princeton: Princeton University Press, 1970). Historical studies of the European crowd which have suggested new approaches are: Eric J. Hobsbawm, "The Machine Breakers," *Past and Present* (1952), 57-70, and *Primitive Rebels: Studies in Archaic Forms of Social Movements in the Nineteenth and Twentieth Centuries* (Manchester: Manchester University Press, 1959); George Rudé, *The Crowd in the French Revolution* (Oxford: Clarendon Press, 1959) and *The Crowd in History: A Study of Popular Disturbances in France and England, 1730-1848* (New York: John Wiley & Sons, 1964); and Hobsbawm and Rudé, *Captain Swing* (New York: Partheon Books, 1968).

Some important books suggesting interpretations of the psychological origins of human violence are: Jacob Bronowski, *The Face of Violence* (New York: George Braziller, 1955); Elias Canetti, *Crowds and Power* (New York: Viking Press, 1963); Konrad Lorenz, *On Aggression* (New York: Bantam, 1967); and Hans Toch, *Violent Men: An Inquiry into the Psychology of Violence* (Chicago: Aldine Publishing Co., 1969).

Sources

1

Town Meeting Report, Baltimore, 1835

SOURCE: *Niles' Weekly Register* 48 (Aug. 15, 1835), 413-19. (All of the documents in this section were also printed in the Baltimore *Gazette, American, Republican,* and *Chronicle.*)

TOWN MEETING

At an unusually large and very respectable meeting of the citizens of Baltimore, convened by the mayor for the purpose of taking into consideration matters connected with the peace of the city. . . . The committee, reported the following, which were adopted:

1st. Resolved, That this meeting regards with the most profound regret and disapprobation, the recent attempts to create disturbance in our city.

2d. Resolved, That the spirit of violence which has been exhibited of late in different parts of the United States, is calculated to injure our country in the esteem of other nations – to annihilate her weight in the social system – and to excite the most serious alarm in the friends of free institutions.

3d. Resolved, That while popular excesses are, under despotic governments, sometimes justified, by the inveteracy of evils to which no other corrective can be applied, they are inexcusable in free states where the people, being the sources of authority and dispensers of power, can easily remedy any defect in their legal systems.

4th. Resolved, That universal obedience to the laws is the only guaranty of republican liberty.

5th. Resolved, That we should especially deplore any demonstration of a contrary spirit in Baltimore, whose reviving prosperity it would seriously impair, while it would degrade her from her high moral stand among American cities.

6th. Resolved, That, in the opinion of this meeting, it is the duty of every friend of good order to co-operate with the civil authorities, in all such measures as may be deemed necessary for the maintenance of the public peace and the reputation of the city.

7th. Resolved, That it is recommended to the mayor to offer suitable rewards for the detection of persons who may be guilty of disseminating papers instigating the rash and the unthinking to a breach of the public peace.

8th. Resolved, That parents, guardians and masters, are respectfully requested to restrain those under their control from frequenting nightly assemblages.

On motion of James H. Thomas, esq. it was

Resolved, That, in the opinion of this meeting, it would promote the peace of the city, if the present trustees would relinquish the trust held by them, and transfer over to the creditors of the bank of Maryland the books and papers connected therewith.

The meeting then adjourned.

2

Statement of the Attorneys for the Creditors, August 8, 1835

SOURCE: *Niles' Weekly Register* 48 (Aug. 15, 1835), 413-19.

To the creditors of the bank of Maryland.

The committee of creditors of the bank of Maryland, desirous of promoting social order, and evincing their entire disapprobation of any measure tending to weaken a proper obedience and respect for the laws of the land, conceive it to be their duty to publish, for the information of those concerned, the following letter from general Walter Jones, of Washington city, which as it will be seen, is perfectly concurred in by the other counsel in the case. By order of the committee,

GEO. W. ANDREWS, secretary.

Baltimore, August 8, 1835.

GENTLEMEN: . . .

As to the abstract propriety, or the practical effect, of any popular movement, or any manifestation of public indignation against persons suspected of standing in the way of justice in this case, I shall only say, on the present occasion, that no such procedure can by any possibility, advance or benefit the cause; the only purpose that can by any possibility, be answered by such procedure, is mere vengeance on obnoxious individuals: they may be buried in the ruins of their houses, and yet the creditors remain just as they were. . . . I do say that any irregular movement of its professing friends, to outstrip the orders of the law, in asserting or vindicating the justice of the cause will have a direct tendency to injure its substantial interests in the only quarter from which the creditors can ever hope to obtain redress. I am, gentlemen, your obedient servant.

W. JONES

As counsel for the creditors of the bank of Maryland, we concur in the statements and views above expressed by Mr. Jones.

CHARLES F. MAYER.
WM. P. PRESTON.
HENRY STUMP.

3

Statements of Mayor Jesse Hunt, August 9 and 10, 1835

SOURCE: *Niles' Weekly Register* 48 (Aug. 15, 1835), 413-19.

Mayor's office, Baltimore, Aug. 9, 1835

Once more I appeal to my fellow citizens, to stay the progress of violence, and prevent a repetition of the lamentable events of last night. Called by your free suffrages to the mayoralty of your city, and charged by you with the preservation of its order, I have throughout my whole official career, and up to the present moment, labored, unceasingly to promote that object, by the FORCE OF REASON and THE UNARMED HAND OF LAW. I have deeply deplored the disregard with which my earnest appeals have been met, and the resort to deadly weapons, AGAINST MY JUDGMENT AND ADVICE, has been unfortunately taken.

It remains for the prudent, the pacific, the lovers of good order, those who would not expose the property of the city to pillage, to arouse before it is too late, and restore to us our recent boasted tranquility, and its accompanying happiness and prosperity. . . .

Mayor's office, Baltimore, Aug. 10th.

Having stated in a publication of yesterday, in reference to the melancholy occurrences of the past nights, that fire arms were resorted to against my judgment and advice, and having learned with extreme pain that the language used by me has induced some persons to suppose that the use of fire arms was entirely unauthorised by any competent power, I deem it an imperative act of justice, at the first moment of being informed of the interpretation which I supposed this part of my publication of yesterday might bear, distinctly to state that the persons who used fire arms were fully authorised so to do, but again repeat that the order was not issued by me.

4

Card Exonerating Leon Dyer, August 10, 1835

SOURCE: *Niles' Weekly Register* 48 (Aug. 15, 1835), 413-19.

A CARD

I think it necessary to publish the following certificate, to correct certain misrepresentations which have been circulated in regard to my conduct.

LEON DYER

Being present last evening, (Sunday, 9th August, 1835) at the house said to be owned by Hugh McElderry, in Calvert street, adjoining that occupied by Mr. Carter A. Hall, at the moment when a crowd of persons assembled, as was understood, for the purpose of demolishing said house, we take pleasure in saying, that through the instrumentality and exertion made use of by Mr.

Leon Dyer, the collection of persons were made satisfied that the house did not belong to Mr. McElderry, and that the course intended to be pursued was desisted from, and the crowd dispersed or went off. We further declare as our opinion, that it was at the imminent peril of life that Mr. Dyer stepped forward, and through his sole persuasion violence was prevented.

A.L. MOORE,
W. COWLES,
GEORGE NEILSON,
C.A. HALL,
W. BROMWELL,
SAMUEL K. GEORGE.

5

Mob Handbill

SOURCE: [David M.] Perine Papers (M.S. 645), Maryland Historical Society, Baltimore, Md. (David M. Perine added the following note to the handbills he saved: "The principal object of the party creating the mob was first to divert public attention from themselves, . . . and to prevent the publication which was then about to be issued by Messrs. Johnson and Glenn.")

CIRCULAR
To be shown to all your acquaintances.

Have the people of Baltimore any spirit, or are they a parcel of cowards. The widows and orphans have been robbed by Glenn, Johnson, and Evan T. Ellicot. The courts of justice offer no relief. What is to be done –

Tar & feathers will forever disgrace them.

Let it be done – who will be the brave men that will lead on to justice. Whose heart does not bleed for the Ruined Widows & Orphans.

There is not 300 men in Baltimore but what will willingly see these swindlers tarred and feathered.

6

Mob Handbill—A Call to Arms

SOURCE: Vertical File, Maryland Historical Society, Baltimore, Md.

Arm! Arm! – and defend your rights – my countrymen – citizens of this republic, and of this city, will you suffer your firesides to be molested – will you suffer your beds to be poluted – will you suffer your pockets to be riffled and your wives and children beggared – orphans rob of their all and cast upon the cold charities of the world – I ask one and all – you will certainly answer NO – then arouse and rally around that free and unbiassed judge Lynch, who will be placed upon the seat of justice and the people enmasse will be the members of the Bar and these lions of the law shall be made to know that the people will rise in their majesty and redress their own grievances – How have the people of this city been treated when their claims have been presented at the Court of Justice; have not the whole bar and the judges linked in a combination together and brow-beaten these very people out of their just rights, with a full determination to swindle and rob the industrious and poor part of the community out of their hard earnings – yes, my fellow citizens, this is the Solemn truth – so help me God. . . . And by whom has it been done, by designing lawyers and lazy greedy peculators, who have labored to initiate themselves into the favour of the people, for the very sole purpose of robbing them of their hard earnings – these smiling villains nearly all of them are building palaces, and riding in their carriages with the very money taken from the poor labourer, orphans and honest hard working mechanics – these savings were intended for the frosty winter of age – want staring your poor heart broken wives in the face – your little children clinging around their mother crying mother, mother a piece of bread, – bread mother, – mother bread – I say mother bread – O! mother give me some bread, – while these protected villains are roling in luxury and ease, laughing to scorn the people they have just robbed – these very villains stroll the streets with a bold and impudent assurance, and pass for honest men – not satisfied with robbing you of your money, but treat you as vassals to their noble lordships to gratify their venery desires, hire pimps and procuresses to go to pollute your wives and prostitute your daughters – Gracious God! is this our fair famed Baltimore – is our moral city come to this – has man descended so much below his fellow man – No! – Then we have a remedy, my fellow citizens – Judge Lynch will be notified that he is to be at our head, and will take his place upon the bench – his maxims are virtue, honesty and good decent behaviour – his remedies are simple Tar and Feathers, effigys, gallowses and extermination from our much injured city – the victims that fall under this new law, I hope will be Johnson, Morris, Glenn, McElderry, Freeman, and that dirty fellow Bossier etc etc etc –

Let the Warhoop be given – from the corner of every street, let the horn sound – let the mob move from street to street until our number be strong and powerful – no half way measures – be firmly united, and act like men – like free men – arouse and claim your rights – Liberty, Equality, Justice or Death!!!

Look well to this. How easy it would be for John B. Morris, R.W. Gill, or R. Johnson who hold the books of the Bank of Maryland to place them in Johnson or Morris's house and fire it for the purpose of destroying the Books, leaving the people without any evidence, and by that means pocket the whole of the people's money, and make themselves still richer –

Print this, publish it, and by all means promulgate it to the whole City. –

7

Mob Handbill – A Warning

SOURCE: [Brantz] Mayer Papers (M.S. 1574), Maryland Historical Society, Baltimore, Md.

August 12

Mr. [Charles F] Mayer –

Your house was to have been attacked on Monday night but we will wait until we see what will be done with Freeman's books.

One of the Mob

8

Mob Handbill — A Plea for Further Popular Investigation

SOURCE: Printed in *Niles' Weekly Register* 48 (Aug. 15, 1835), 417.

Fellow citizens – let us pause!

Last night we have nobly shown what robbers are to expect at the hands of Baltimoreans, but let us stop now and give them a chance once more to make restitution, and if they can to justify themselves.

For this purpose, let US in general town meeting, on Wednesday next (to give all concerned time to appear) of which hour and place will be published in the daily papers, appoint five respectable citizens, and THEY five more, to examine all the affairs of the bank of Maryland, and on their verdict let their innocence or guilt rest. IF innocent we have done them WRONG – if GUILTY, and they do not make restitution to the widow and orphan to the FULL EXTENT of their means, let us visit them with the just indignation of an injured community. But fellow citizens you are beseeched not to proceed further at present, out of respect to your characters as good men, but to afford, in mercy to the guilty, once more a chance to turn from the evil of their ways. It will be doing as we would be done by. More need not be said.

ONE OF THE PEOPLE.

9

A Newspaper Account of the Attack on the Homes

SOURCE: Baltimore *Patriot,* August 10, 1835.

Our task to day is one of a most painful nature. It devolves upon us to record the scenes and outrages which have taken place in the city. . . .

At about seven o'clock on Saturday night, the mayor, having previously called together a considerable number of citizens, it was agreed to station some hundreds of citizens, each provided with a staff or insignia of office, to guard every avenue leading to Reverdy Johnson's house in Monument square. About thirty of this guard were mounted on horses. By dark, multitudes of people had assembled. The principal point of concentration, at this time, was in Baltimore street at the intersection of North Calvert, which leads to the square. Here the crowd made frequent rushes upon the guard. Brickbats and stones were showered upon the guard like hail, and ultimately by the guard returned. A number of the latter were severely bruised and wounded. They however kept their posts. A large portion of the rioters, finding it impossible to get access to Johnson's house, started off to the house of John Glenn, in North Charles street, which was not guarded, and commenced throwing stones and missiles at the windows and front door. The house was of brick, strongly built, and the door was barricaded in anticipation of an attack. For a brief space of time the assailants were diverted from their assaults upon the house by a number of the mounted guard rushing down and firing upon them. The assailants, however, soon renewed their attacks upon the house, and after a continued effort of near half an hour, it was taken possession of, and all the furniture it contained was broken up, and thrown into the street, and utterly destroyed.

The work of demolition was renewed sometime during yesterday, by numbers of young men and boys, who got in and continued through the afternoon to break up the wood work, and to beat down the jams of the outer wall. A portion of the front wall of the second and third story has been thrown down, and the house exhibits the appearance of a wreck.

The guard stationed in different parts of the city, finding themselves so severely attacked, armed with muskets. At about one o'clock on Sunday morning, a company of some twenty-five, or perhaps thirty armed citizens, marched against the rioters, in Charles street. They were received with a shower of stones, and in return fired into the crowd they opposed. They loaded and fired, we understand, there, several times. The police and guard also fired upon their assailants at their several stations, a number of times. It is supposed that in all there were eight or ten persons killed and dangerously wounded. A much larger number were less severely wounded. It is impossible to ascertain at this time, how many, and who, have been killed. Some of the mortally wounded have since died.

Last night, (Sunday) at dark, the attack was renewed upon Reverdy Johnson's house. *There was now no opposition.* It was supposed, that several thousand people were spectators of the scene. The house was soon entered, and its furniture, a very extensive law library, and all its contents, were cast forth, and a bonfire made of them in front of the house. The whole interior of the house was torn out and cast upon the burning pile. The marble portico in front, and a great portion of the front wall, were torn down by about 11 o'clock. Previous to this, however, an attack was commenced upon the house of John B. Morris, in South street, one of the trustees of the bank of Maryland. His dwelling was entered and cleared – and the furniture and other contents piled up in the street and burnt. In the course of the proceedings, the house took fire inside, as R. Johnson's was also near doing, from the bonfire near it. In both instances, the engines were brought promptly to the spot, and the fire put out, so that the neighboring dwellings would not suffer.

From John B. Morris' house they proceeded to that of the mayor of the city, Jesse Hunt, esq. broke it open, took out the furniture and burnt it before the door. They also destroyed the furniture of Evan T. Ellicott, and much injured his dwelling, in Pratt street. They proceeded to the new house of Hugh McElderry, in North Calvert street, now finishing, broke the front windows, entered the door, and began to destroy the house, when the builder appeared and stated that as it was not finished, the key had not been given up, and that all the injury it might sustain would fall upon him, and thus complete his ruin. Upon this assurance, they desisted and retired. They were directors, it will be recollected, of the bank of Maryland.

They also attacked capt. Willey's hardware store, in Franklin street, and commenced destroying its contents, but desisted at the urgent solicitations of Mr. Lynch, who assured them that he and not Mr. W. was the owner, and that capt. Willey had left town.

The house of Dr. Hintze was assailed; but his lady making her appearance, and declaring that the property was her own, she having received it from her father's estate – they listened to her appeal and departed without doing any injury.

Capt. Benzinger's house was also attacked, and all his furniture destroyed. This, as well as the attack on capt. Willey and Dr. Hintz, was because of their opposition to the rioters; and, we are told, that more than 30 others were marked, on the same account. Among them the sheriff.

10

On Violence

SOURCE: Baltimore *American,* August 8 and 12, 1835.

August 8: Violence can only hurt the creditors' cause by destroying in every case all public sympathy. In all societies there exist constant feelings of injustice, real or imaginary, but freemen must attack wrongs in a legal way if liberties are to survive. By the blood which was shed to obtain them, by the duties which we owe to ourselves and the world, by the strongest feelings which animate the human breast, the love of liberty, self-respect and personal security, by the just pride of Americans, let us not permit these blessings to be endangered. The feelings of the community are sound: let . . . the supremacy of the law be upheld.

August 12: On Monday morning a feeling of indignation spread through the community at the sight of the devastations which had been committed the night before, and at the threats of further violence. . . .

Regrets for what is passed are idle. The town has learnt a lesson from the doings of the last few days that will never be forgotten. Feelings which should ever animate the governing power, particularly in a republic – a willingness to preserve peace by peaceful means and a reluctance to proceed to the last extremity, fatally misled the city authorities last week. These dispositions diverted them from the adoption of the only means of effecting their object. Had the force which volunteered on Saturday to keep the peace, been, as it was on Monday, organised as an armed force, not only would the designs of the violently disposed have been frustrated, but bloodshed would certainly have been prevented. Such a manifestation of power and resolution would have deterred them, and preserved the city from the horrors of the last few days.

11

An Appeal for Order

SOURCE: Baltimore *Republican,* August 10, 1835.

We would appeal to the good sense, the sound discretion, the intelligence and patriotism of every man, to exert his influence in discouraging to the utmost extent of his power any thing like the appearance or disposition to commit any disorder. The peace of society, the prosperity of the whole people, the character of the community, everything that is or should be near or dear to us as men and citizens demands it.

12

The City and the Mob

SOURCE: Baltimore *Gazette,* August 10 and 11, 1835.

August 10: In every large city there is a portion of the population fitted to be used as instruments for perpetrating lawless outrage – always ready to act when they think they can do so with a prospect of impunity – but seldom venturing to act, unless when they are countenanced either directly or indirectly by the advice or expression of opinions of a portion of the respectable part of the community. . . . Boston, Providence, New York and Philadelphia have all recently been disgraced by lawless outrages which the greater portion of the respectable citizens in each, decidedly and openly condemned – which the police in each city endeavored in vain to prevent – and which, from causes connected in some measure with the nature of the supposed grievance improperly attempted to be remedied; in some measure with the mode of trial, which is the boast of freemen – and perhaps from the difficulty of obtaining testimony – have not in any instance been adequately redressed or punished.

In each of those places a portion of the citizens believed that they had a correct object in view, but . . . amid their anxiety to correct or punish what they deemed a flagrant abuse, they appeared to forget the just and necessary rule which every good citizen and every moral and just man is bound at all times to respect – never to attempt to redress or punish one breach of the laws by committing another. In Baltimore we are, unfortunately, imitating the outrages as we have on many occasions imitated the praise-worthy acts of the inhabitants of other great cities of the union, and with similar increase of energy and effect – we say *we are,* for we believe that the outrages in our city have not yet terminated. A spirit of insubordination to the laws, and of disobediences and resistance of lawful authority has been excited and countenanced until it has attained a degree of strength too mighty to be quelled or even restrained by those who assisted to raise it, although aided by those who, by temporizing, have permitted to increase it unrestrained.

August 11: Our city will not only suffer in reputation by the recent riots, but all holders of property in the city will be severely taxed to compensate the sufferers by the lawless acts of the mob – which . . . might have been prevented with great certainty and perfect safety. Justice says, that the city, and *the* city alone, whose constituted authorities *could and ought* to have protected the property of individuals from lawless injury and did not, shall pay a full compensation to the injured.

13

Some Reflections on the Riots

SOURCE: *Niles' Weekly Register,* August 8, 15, and 22, 1835.

August 8: The state of society is awful. Brute force has superseded the law, at many places, and violence become the "*order* of the day." The time predicted seems rapidly approaching when the mob shall rule. . . .

The time was when every citizen of the United States, would "rally round the standard of the law, and unite in common efforts for the common good" – when a person, armed only with a small piece of paper, could proceed a thousand miles through the country, and bring the strongest man to answer to the law, for the law was honored. But is it so now? Alas, no!

• • • • •

Another pamphlet, of 146 pages, issued by Reverdy Johnson and John Glenn, on the affairs of the bank of Maryland, appeared on Monday last. We have not yet read it.

The feverish or fidgetty state of Baltimore may be judged from the fact, that the mayor has called a meeting of the people to "insure the preservation of the public peace."

August 15: The *ostensible* ground of the late riots in Baltimore, was in the affairs of the bank of Maryland, though we believe that other things were more at the bottom of them; together with that *general* disposition to violence that prevails at so many places. . . . We should have respected the law – even if of opinion that it shielded bad men. . . .

The ground of the rioters, (judging by their primary actions), was in the affairs of the bank of Maryland – the history of which is that of one of the most stupendous and *general* frauds ever committed – bearing especially hard upon the industrious poor; induced, by an interest, allowed even upon *running* accounts, to make deposites in it. We saw, or thought that we saw, for six months before its failure, that a grand "blow up" was probable, from an evidently forced circulation of its bills. It was the weakest bank in the city – but had more notes out than all the rest of the banks. We gave it, therefore, a "wide berth," and never held fifty dollars in its bills for 24 continuous hours. The "shop" was shut up in March 1834, and, though about seventeen months have elapsed, no satisfactory statement of its affairs has yet been laid before its creditors – being obstructed by the "law's delay," and other causes, that are not understood by the people at large. In the mean time, however, the late president of the bank, and others, have been battering one another by heavy pamphlets. . . .

On Saturday afternoon, a meeting was held at the mayor's office, at which, according to an arrangement made in the morning, six hundred men were assigned as guards to prevent the entrance of persons into the square, to be supported by a mounted force. These were supplied with badges, or strips of muslin to be worn on the left arm, and with sticks of turned poplar, or some other light wood. *They were too much for peace and not fitted for defence* – but the guards quickly repaired to the stations assigned them. . . .

On Sunday, the people, *without a head*, had nothing to do but to look on and tremble. No one felt himself safe – as every thing was given up. Anarchy prevailed. The law and its officers were away!

But Monday morning changed the aspect of things. It now appeared that the people were called upon to defend, not only their property, but also their lives – and it was manifest that there was a general, but gloomy resolution entertained to do both. Things had reverted to their *original elements – there was no law,* and a head was wanted to bring order out of confusion. This was easily found in gen. Samuel Smith.

August 22: Many reflections, on the late disasters, offer themselves. But the time is not present to publish them. And, perhaps, we shall refrain from doing it altogether. The result of the riots, however, will probably be in the establishment of a *civic guard* – strong enough to "look down" a resistance to the laws.

14

A Letter from Ebenezer L. Finley to S.C. Leakin, September 17, 1835

SOURCE: [Sheppard C.] Leakin Papers (M.S. 1349), Maryland Historical Society, Baltimore, Md.

You will recollect, that on the night of the 8th August, after having successfully repulsed a most determined and violent assault . . . by a large Detachment of the *Mob,* armed with Paving Stones and Brick Bats; – by which assault Captain Cheves was knocked down, and carried off insensible – Lieutenant Tensfield, Mr. Evan Thomas, and several of my Troop dismounted, and almost every member of it wounded: – that I . . . represented to *Jesse Hunt then Mayor* and to Judge Brice "that *unless we were furnished with arms* and *authorized to fire on the Mob;* that I could no longer be responsible for the safety of the City; that my men were knocked off their Horses, by Stones from the Mob, and severely wounded; and that unless they were armed and authorized to fire, they would no longer stand by me."

. . . I confine my queries to the acts of the Mayor, because by his Proclamation of the 9th day of August, he dis-avowed having furnished us with arms or authorized us to fire . . . in order to screen himself from the responsibility which he had assumed on the night before; he shamefully surrendered our fair city, and held up as *victims* to an *Enfuriated Mob*, the gallant few, who, *under his orders,* perilled their lives in defense of the Civil Authorities. . . .

My reason for not having addressed you before on this subject, is to be found in the fact, of my having been confined for upwards of *Five Weeks* to my room, with a Fractured Limb, and other wounds, received from the Mob.

15

A Letter from William P. Preston to Jesse Hunt, August 9, 1835

SOURCE: [William P.] Preston Papers (M.S. 978.2), Maryland Historical Society, Baltimore, Md.

From what I can gain from mixing among the crowd of last night serious and terrible movements are anticipated tonight. . . .

Apply without delay to the commanding officers at the fort – have the regulars brought into the city and a pair of cannon – distribute the artillery in such streets as may be supposed to be points of attack, namely the houses of the parties implicated in the affairs of the Bank of Maryland –

In the mean time, have notice sent to the several ministers of this City let them address their congregation in the open sts. and explain to them the inestimable blessings of social life and civil rule. . . .

There is yet virtue left among our people . . . – the respectable part of the community are panic struck – rally them and they will recover their senses and their courage. . . .

Sir believe me there are few if any creditors among the band of lawless desparadoes who are making the injuries done the creditors an excuse for plunder and blood shed . . . – they are villains who have no interest at stake in society who are the perpetrators of these horrible outrages –

I would further recommend your honor to issue proclamations without delay requiring innocent and orderly persons to remain in their houses tonight so that if it be necessary to sweep the streets with cannon charged with bullets none but the riotous may fall.

16

A Letter from Hester Wilkins to Mrs. John Glenn, August 11, 1835

SOURCE: [John] Glenn Papers (M.S. 1017), Maryland Historical Society, Baltimore, Md.

I feel very happy to be able this morning to say we are alive and all our property is safe. After you left us yesterday . . . a large concourse marched in procession to the park . . . headed by General Smith in a carriage bearing the flag of the United States. . . . They unanimously resolved to arm – some persons rose to oppose such a course but they were immediately hissed. Several thousand enlisted and at an early hour the whole city was under martial law. . . . The mob offered no violence – about 25 at eleven o'clock came up to Uncle Joseph's – beat on a painted barrel, sang and played the fife. The front parlor windows were thrown open, the girls sat at the windows, and Aunt Mary sat on the steps. They all marched off only alarming them a little. We were all very uneasy yesterday afternoon. The mob had a list of 61 names of proscribed individuals – among these were Mama's – Uncle Joseph's . . . and a large number of citizens – many of whom Dr. Baker for one moved all their furniture. . . . I feel happy to say they are overawed for the present and that many of the ringleaders and abettors of this mob have joined with the peacable to preserve tranquility. . . .

A woman brought Mama one of your cradle quilts yesterday – uninjured – and 2 of your hams and a good many of your books are at Dr. Baker's and other places.

17

A Letter from William E. Bartlett to Edward Stabler, August 12, 1835

SOURCE: [James P.] Stabler Letterbooks (M.S. 774), Maryland Historical Society, Baltimore, Md. (This letter was also published in the *Maryland Historical Magazine,* Vol. 9.)

We have seen things awfully strange in this City within a week, I tell thee. On fifth day night a considerable number of folk, good, bad, and indifferent assembled in Monument Square, before the door of Reverdy Johnson (of Bank of Maryland memory). Without much ado they dispersed, because, as they said, that was not the time they intended to operate, That time being fixed for 7th day night. On Sixth day evening the crowd again met, in numbers greater than before. Some unruly spirits now threw a few stones and broke a few glass in R. Johnson's windows. They were again advised to desist, which they did and retired by 10 or eleven o'clock, giving clear indications that they would be punctual to their engagements by the next evening. Arrangements were now made, and a few armed men surrounded the property of Johnson on 7th day evening for the purpose of protecting it. The Mob appeared, was beaten off and some three or five killed, and ten or twenty wounded. Finding themselves repulsed at Johnson's, a detachment rushed round to Glenn's (of like memory) in Charles Street. Here they made an effectual and unresisted attack, and very soon had his furniture all in the street, where it was entirely destroyed, by breaking and tareing it to pieces. The Mob now found themselves Masters, and went on unmolested in this part of the town. . . .

I do not know what Glenn's loss amounts too but when I tell thee his wines alone are said to have cost over four thousand Dollars, I am very sure thee would not pay all his losses for a sum under Twenty Thousand Dollars. The rioters remained – I mean some twenty of them picking at Glenn's House till 6 P.M. when they knocked off. Now what think thee? These twenty persons carried on their unlawful game in the presence of from 2000 to five Thousand persons, who witnessed it and not one word of objection was raised! . . .

When thee learns the true cause of all this disturbance thee will, I dare say have a different view thereof than at first sight taken.

The Bank of Maryland injured thousands. All that were connected with that institution at the time it failed, have been considered by the people at large as being enriched at their expense. The sufferers bore their loss with commendable fortitude until they supposed no lawful remedy would avail them. They then followed the example of the Vicksburg people in attempting to inflict the Lynch Law; and I suppose had they been able to catch the Obnoctious Directors of said institution, they would have been altogether satisfied to have given each of them a dress of Tar and feathers. Not finding them, they fell – as I have shown – on their property, and have doubtless distroyed one Hundred Thousand Dollars worth thereof. . . .

18

Letters from Roger B. Taney to James Mason Campbell, August 19, 1835, and March 6, 1836

SOURCE: Howard Papers (M.S. 469), Maryland Historical Society, Baltimore, Md. (The letters of Taney to Campbell, edited by Frank Gatell, were published in the *Maryland Historical Magazine*, Vol. 59.)

August 19: You will readily imagine the deep anxiety with which I have looked towards Baltimore for some days past. Fortunately we have received Baltimore and Washington papers every day and rejoice to find that the city at length recovered from its madness or terror (I do not know which prevailed) and took the measures which ought to have been taken in the first instance and which would have saved the City from the disgrace and opprobrium of the scenes through which it has passed. I grieve for my poor friend Hunt. He must have had most mistaken advisers. There ought not to have been a moments hesitation about the use of fire arms, the firm and free use of them the moment that force was attempted by the mob. The first stone thrown at those who had assembled under the orders of the Mayor should have been the signal to fire. And if this had been made known beforehand, no stone would have been thrown and there would have been no idle spectators in the way of being shot. Such a contest ought always to be treated as one in which the existence of free government is put to hazard and should be met like men who are resolved to maintain it at every sacrifice. I can imagine nothing more monstrous and abominable than to place a parcel of respectable citizens in a row with short sticks in their hands, to stand still and have their brains beaten out with brickbats and stones thrown at them by a parcel of ruffians, who I presume were for the most part hired by men behind the curtain. For it is impossible I think to doubt that this mob had been deliberately got up, and did not spring from any sudden excitement in the public mind.

March 6: I have not been at the State House since I came here. Yet I have seen a good many of the members – for every man of either party from whom I had a right to expect a call – has called to see me – except Richardson and McLean. I cannot think that these two gentlemen like Mr. Harker, mean to take up Leon Dyer as the leader of the Jackson party in Baltimore, but yet their omission of a civility which they paid me when I was here before looks rather odd.

19

A Letter from Reverdy Johnson to David M. Perine

SOURCE: [David M.] Perine Papers (M.S. 645), Maryland Historical Society, Baltimore, Md.

To David M. Perine, August 7, 1835: I find that the mob is raised in good earnest. Let me know all that has occurred – I am prevented from returning – If alone, I would be in my house tonight and die in its defense.

20

A Letter from Reverdy Johnson to the People of Baltimore

SOURCE: Baltimore *Republican,* August 15, 1835.

To the people of Baltimore, August 14, 1835: I have no fears. . . . It is impossible that with any civilized and Christian people injustice can long prevail. They may be misled for a time, but in the end they must and will be right. . . . We are now amongst you once more, and we leave not the city with life.

21

From the Diary of Benjamin Latrobe, Jr.

SOURCE: Mrs. Gamble Latrobe Collection (M.S. 1638), Maryland Historical Society, Baltimore, Md.

August 5, 1835: Found a crowd collected in Monument Square threatening to lynch Reverdy Johnson and John Glenn. The mayor walking about to encourage his constables I suppose in the keeping of order.

August 9, 1835: Left camp at 10 oclock and jogged on at a pace which brought me without adventure to Baltimore at half past 2. I found the city in great commotion. The excitement against those concerned in the failure of the bank of Maryland had ended in a mob which after assembling for 3 nights in succession without committing violence, at last broke loose and making their way into the house of John Glenn in Charles Street had turned it completely inside out hurling the furniture out of the windows and breaking it to pieces as it fell or carrying it off as lawful prize. . . . A want of harmony among the people who had no efficient leader – indeed a sentiment of sympathy with the mob against the Bank of Maryland men, paralyzed the peacable portion of the community and the work of destruction was suffered to proceed unchecked. I went down to see the demolition of Johnson's elegant house in Monument Square. The sight was as full of picturesque grandeur as it was of heart sickening horror. The magnificent furniture . . . of an elegantly provided mansion was pitched from the windows . . . and as it fell with quickly successive crashes upon the pavement below was heaped upon the pile which blazed at the base of the battle Monument with fierce and flickering lustre. . . . By this baleful light the devils incarnate laboured like industrious friends, in the destruction of the building and its contents. An immense crowd thronged the square and the streets it commanded, in whose faces lit up by the conflagration of the furniture not an expression of pity or indignation was to be seen. The rioters felt that their conduct was approved and waved as trophies in triumph from the shattered windows . . . the contents of the wardrobes which had been hurled from there. I could not stand the sight long for I felt it was every good man's duty to discountenance such outrage by at least refusing to look upon its commission. I therefore went home. My mother and my sister however persuaded me to escort them to a point from which they could see the scene. We looked at it only for a few minutes as a part of the mob came rushing towards us, on their way to another fated house, and we hurried home. I went to bed and slept as well as the confusion of sounds through the city all night, and the agitation of my own mind, would allow me. . . .

The way in which all this mischief was affected was this – some 20 or 30 individuals in the middling classes, principally butchers, who had sustained losses of varying extent, by the break up of the bank, and had sworn vengeance against all therein concerned seized upon the cause of excitement furnished by the legal and proper refusal of the trustees Moris and Gill to hand them [the bank's books] to the creditors (which cause of excitement was fomented by Evan Poultney as a screen for himself), these butchers, well might be so called, had elected as executioners of their plans of retaliation, the horde of ruffians infesting the purlieus of the town and had regularly bribed them to the business of destruction which they afterwards prosecuted while their employers stood by as spectators only in appearance but in fact as abettors prepared to sustain their employees if resisted by the citizens. . . . I however forget that I am not writing a history of these foul deeds, the recording of which belongs to the Annalist of Baltimore, who will not need any aid from my journal when he comes to publish his account of it some hundred years hence.

22

From James Gordon's Diary

SOURCE: [John M.] Gordon Papers (M.S. 404), Maryland Historical Society, Baltimore, Md.

August 17, 1835: Returning to Baltimore, I caught view of the ruins of Reverdy Johnson's house, and the military arrangement of cannon and soldiers for the night. It looked more war like than anything I have ever yet had the pleasure of seeing. . . .

Met poor Morris in the street who was too mortified to speak to me. None of the victims . . . I am sure had their sensibilities more deeply wounded.

December 22, 1835: Attended court today – the trial of the rioters still going on. Black Hawk was convicted today. I was much struck by his appearance – the great Bug Bear that struck terror into the hearts of 80,000 people was a mere youth, good natured, smart and fond of fun and I have no doubt entered into the mob merely as a frolick. One witness testified having heard him say "Now that Mr. Hunt has resigned I am mayor. I shall appoint my officers tonight and we will abolish the 10 hours system. We work now by the job and Judge Brice has given me one for this night," etc meaning to destroy his house. All in the Jack Cade style but evidently in fun as the same harangue was repeated, as a boyish bravo, before several spectators. He ought to have gone on and said in the mode of Jack, "I shall first hang up all the lawyers." He had put a curtain ring in his coat in front and a piece of gilding in his hat and these spoils of a bed chamber were as apalling at the time as the tomahawk and green scalp. Red Jacket was still more contemptible, a stupid Dutch paver. Such are the materials of a mob! Such its leaders.

23

Letter from Thomas Williams to Evan Poultney, March 11, 1836

SOURCE: The Baltimore *Republican*, March 11, 1836.

When I retired I was the owner of the small house in which I now reside, and had five thousand dollars in money. On the interest of this money I felt sure that myself and my wife (we have no children) could live comfortably for the rest of our lives. – Under this impression, seeing in the newspapers an advertisement which stated the Bank of Maryland the oldest chartered institution in the state, would receive money on deposit, giving 5 per cent for it, I concluded, inasmuch as you were its President, and the direction made up of responsible and respectable men, that I would place my money in the institution. . . . Having done so I felt comparatively happy. I drew my interest regularly, and as I lived frugally I found my income quite sufficient to my wants. Judge then how great was my pain and surprise when all at once I was informed the Bank of Maryland had stopped. The news reached me when confined to my bed by severe illness – the result of medical treatment used to save my life during the Cholera, and it nearly overcame me. To suppose that in a moment I was reduced from competence to wretchedness and poverty, almost deprived me of my reason. . . . When the Bank stopped I had in silver five half dollars – no more money in the world except what was in the Bank of Maryland. This trifle was soon gone. I then found it necessary to sell such articles of clothing as my wife and self could best dispense with. This we continued to do as long as we well could; we then commenced on our furniture, but not having been extravagant in this respect, we had little to sell; our house was soon thinned: the next means of bettering my conditions was a lessening of my expenses. It pains my heart to mention the circumstance. I had for some years supported as well as I could afford, the decrepit widow of an old sea captain, an acquaintance of mine. I could do it no longer, and she was sent to the alms-house, where she now is. Our next and last resort was the borrowing of money from my friends. This gave me great anguish. I little thought before the Bank failed that painful necessity would ever reduce me to such a measure. The honest pride of my life had been to live by the sweat of my brow, and by my own endeavours never to be bent down by pecuniary obligation. I feel that my exertions have been all in vain, and the apprehension that now in the evening of my life, I shall have to suffer the evils and sorrows of poverty, almost breaks my heart. Our condition is most forlorn. My poor wife, whom I have always been proud of seeing cheerful and comfortable, and who has ever been the source of my greatest happiness, is unhappy and literally in rags. My house is cheerless and nearly empty – my creditors for debts contracted for the merest necessity since the failure of the Bank as I can show you by my pass book, are coming on me for payment – my taxes are unpaid – and as I have not the means to pay my ground rent, my house may be sold over my head. . . . Something must be done to save us from despair. . . . My former employers, all my neighbors, and many others, will cheerfully testify that I have ever been an honest man and good citizen.

24

Trial Testimony—State of Maryland vs. David H. White, December 9, 1835

SOURCE: The Baltimore *Gazette,* December 12, 1835.

On behalf of the prosecution Mr. Weaver was first called – Witness stated, that he saw Mr. White at Mr. Hunt's house on Monday morning about 1 or 2 o'clock – in Fayette street – heard Traverser say "Mr. Hunt was one of the d . . n Bank Robbers and ought to be served no better that the rest". . . .

Mr. Ives . . . – crowd moved off to Hunt's dwelling – before Union Bank same cries as before, "pull Hunt's house down" – some person stepped forward and said the house belonged to a widow – a young man belonging to the crowd then stepped forward and said to them, "gentlemen, we have gone far enough, if we go further we shall lose the sympathies of the people" – he was a short thick set man in dark clothes, thinks he heard him called Lynch – he did not seem disposed to do any thing or molest the property, but after addressing them as before, said "good night" and went away – then Capt. White said that Hunt had cheated a widow of 50 or 350 dollars – said Hunt deserved as much as the rest – White swears a good deal – swore that Hunt deserved as much as the rest – a young man stepped up to White and said "Sir it is not so, that lady got all her money" – part of the crowd then broke off and went over to Hunt's house – mob very drunk and greatly fatigued with their night's labour – then saw White at Hunt's door – Black Hawk and others then went off well supplied with wine, they broke a bottle at Hollingsworth's corner – don't know who went off – White then at Hunt's door making use of the same language as before to some person witness does not know – party went away, leaving White with one or two others at Hunt's door, blaming him for cheating the widow . . .

Mr. Worthington was then sworn – Did not see Mr. White at all – . . . – Dyer was with them at this time – Dyer and three others stopped at the corner, said to Dyer "It's a pretty state of commotion the Town's in," he replied, "Yes, you know where Hunt's house is, take them there and destroy it" – told him I would do no such thing, &c. &c . . .

Mr. Blakely next sworn on the part of the Traverser. Witness knows Captain White – first saw him on Sunday night . . . some person said, "you had better not speak to White, he is engaged with the mob," after hearing this thought he would attend particularly to White to see if it was true and did continue in his company for 3 or 4 hours – went together to Morris's and staid there about an hour. . . .

Cross examined. . . . Witness was at Morris's an hour or more pushing through the crowd, and near the house – thinks he went in – don't know whether he went upstairs, if he did he might have been insane – drank 2 or 3 glasses of wine from a decanter broken at the Engine – was "pretty warm" – supposes because he drank – from the bottle – must have drank "pretty free" as he got "pretty warm" – . . . don't think Wilson did drink, or White – . . . Witness a carpenter by profession and has resided in Maryland for 20 years. White came from Hunt's with witness, might have been in house, didn't know – thinks he was sober – was a "little warm" might have been insane – a great many passions make a man insane besides liquor – excited to see so much property destroyed – It was foolishness. . . .

Henry Cliffe was first called on behalf of the Traverser. Witness was with Traverser on the nights of Thursday and Saturday . . . During this time saw Traverser do nothing, heard him use no language tending to excite a mob, no expressions favorable to it, and is certain he had no disposition to join it. . . .

This morning at the call of the Clerk, the Jury gave in their verdict, – *Not Guilty.*

25

Trial Testimony—State of Maryland vs. Henry Brown, December 12, 1835

SOURCE: The Baltimore *Gazette*, December 14, 1835.

Jeremiah Tittle was sworn on behalf of the State. Has known the Traverser for 25 years. Witness resides a few doors south of Mr. Morris's, but his attention was first called there by a great noise about 2 o'clock on Monday morning – went up and discovered the Traverser, said to him "Brown is this you?" he replied, "Lord yes, I have just come from the country." – Traverser was cursing about the "monied aristocracy" – witness said, Morris is an innocent man, and the "poor man's friend" – Brown replied "he did not know it, and would not have hurt him had he thought him an innocent man" – witness asked Traverser to go up with him and assist in putting the rioters out of the house – he refused – Traverser was standing near Morris's door with a basket on his arm containing 6 or 8 pounds of coffee – witness said "don't take the man's coffee" – when some person knocked the basket up, saying, "no stealing here" – a number of persons in the street and house – furniture burning in the street – saw several persons taking coffee . . . when witness conversed with him Brown spoke aloud – could be heard very well – the "d--d aristocracy," and thinks when he made these exclamations his arm was raised. . . . the mob commenced about 9 o'clock – a great many drunken people – much wine – heard them call the wine "American blood" – would say take some 'American blood' – heard Brown say nothing of this kind – is positive he said "we have done it to them" – witness stated that Brown was very drunk. . . .

It was given to the Jury, who, after an absence of some hours, returned – and the foreman informed the Court, that their verdict would be decided by the answer of Mr. Tittle to a question they desired to ask. The Foreman said they wished to know whether Brown was very drunk. The Judge informed the Jury that drunkenness would not excuse any illegal acts of the Traverser; but if they entertained any doubts of his guilt, it was their duty to acquit him at once; – it was far from the desire of the Court to see any of these men convicted, of whose guilt there could be a rational doubt; and the Law designed the punishment of those only whose guilt could be established by the clearest evidence. The Jury immediately returned a verdict of *Not Guilty*.

26

Trial Testimony—State of Maryland vs. Samuel Farr, December 14, 1835

SOURCE: The Baltimore *Gazette*, December 15, 1835.

Nicholas Brewer, deposed – . . . saw others marching two and two from the direction of the rear of Johnson's house – did not recognize any but the Traverser – Farr was at or near the head of them – heard him say "boys fall in, we are ordered to McElderry's," saw Dyer forming them, he appeared to be the leader – formed them two and two to the number of about 50 and marched off between 7 and 8 o'clock – Dyer appeared to have full command of them. Traverser did not seem to have any charge. . . . The mob at Johnson's . . . appeared particular about burning the books, would not let a book escape on any account.

Cross examined – has known Farr for many years, seen him daily . . . knew him to be an inoffensive man – did not see him do any act of violence – . . . Farr had a piece of furniture in his hand. . . .

James H. Woods, witness, stated that he was a spectator at Johnsons – . . . saw the marble portico thrown down – a clapping from a great number of people, occasional cheering while the furniture was burning – good deal of noise – saw no one interfere to stop it – undisturbed violence as far as witness could see . . . witness was also at Glenn's – saw Dyer and Wilkins and another gentleman there in the morning, Dyer was assisting them in nailing up the house, thought he was against the mob, Dyer said "he would only charge John Glenn a few hundred dollars for his services" – 4 or 5 o'clock in the morning – helping to nail up house and carrying books to Gen'l. Marriot's. . . .

Francis Hoover, deposed . . . knows the Traverser and did not see him on either of these nights – Dyer told witness at Hanover market on Monday morning, that "he had been the means of saving McElderry's house" and much more – witness doubted his authority with the mob, he then offered to bet $500 he could mob witness's house – witness thought he boasted. . . .

Mr. Worthington being sworn, testified . . . witness saw Spencer, his hand was hurt, said "his knuckles had been shot off by Hunt, and he would kill him for it" . . . – Dyer and three others stopped witness, said to Dyer that "the town was in a pretty commotion," Dyer asked "where have the boys gone to?" witness said he did not know – Dyer then told witness to go and destroy Jesse Hunt's, etc " it would be the best thing he had ever done" – . . . France put his head out of the window and told them Hunt was in the country – they asked if the furniture was in the house, he said yes – asked for a light, Spencer threw a brick bat at France's head, which struck about a foot below him, saying "you s-n of a b--h won't you give us a light" – France became frightened, said "wait and I'll come down and give you a light" – . . . a man named Osborne came up and asked witness "why don't you go to work?" – witness said "I belong to the opposite party" – he rejoined "if he had known the witness was there when they went to work, if he had not helped, he would have drubbed him – a great mind to drub him anyhow" – witness went off, afraid he might do it.

Mr. Harrison, deposed – has known Traverser for 3 years – he is a butcher, but don't know that he is acquainted with Dyer – no particular knowledge of Traverser. . . .

Mr. Brewer, called up a third time – witness was at Market on Monday or Tuesday, and heard Farr talking with others – witness mentioned to him what he had seen and heard him say in the square, when Farr acknowledged that it was so – Traverser further said that Dyer was preparing to clear himself by saying that he saved McElderry's property from the mob &c. Traverser said that Dyer should not get off in that way, that "it was his fault he got into it at all" . . .

The evidence being closed on both sides, Wm. H. Norris Esq. addressed the Jury on behalf of the prosecution. Mr. Norris felt what he said, and was listened to, by a crowded Court, for more than one hour, with the deepest attention. In a strain of impassioned eloquence he adverted to the wild and lawless spirit that recently pervaded not only this community, but which spread and is spreading itself over the whole country, threatening, if its course be not speedily arrested by the strong arm of the Law, the existence of our Republican Institutions. He appealed to the jury, as they valued the blessings of free government, a peaceful home, security for life, liberty and property, to unite in maintaining the supremacy of the laws; invoking for them, on the one hand the punishment of transgression, and on the other the respect and cheerful obedience of all, without which, all system is at an end and the foundations of all society are broken up.

The Jury without leaving the Box found the Traverser *Guilty.*

27

Trial Testimony — State of Maryland vs. James Spencer, December 15, 1835

SOURCE: The Baltimore *Gazette*, December 16, 1835.

Mr. Worthington – . . . When a proposition was made to go to Hunt's – Spencer said, "Yes, let's go up and hang him, he shot my hand off" – . . . witness saw Spencer at Hunt's door with some china cups and saucers in his hand and heard him say – "Gentlemen, who wants to go to a Tea-party, but stop I'll go and get the plates," he went and brought them and threw them all in the street – every 5 or 10 minutes Traverser was talking about Hunt. . . .

Nicholas Speaks – . . . some one threw a chair out of the window. Spencer cut it and threw it on the fire – Traverser came over to where witness was standing and said "he would kill Hunt" – said he was "a spunky fellow" – he then cut a lamp post, witness said "it shows your spunk to cut a *lamp post*". . . . Traverser appeared drunk – "not so drunk but he could cut a lamp post". . . .

Mr. Spencer was called for the Traverser – Witness is Traverser's father – his son came home Monday morning much intoxicated and went to bed – should think he did not know what he was about – very peaceable and quiet but sometimes drinks and then does not know what he is about – very little "set him so" – drink seems to deprive him of the reason he ordinarily possesses. . . .

Caleb D. Owens, deposed – Witness has known Traverser three or four years – when sober, "he is a very passive kind of man" and says nothing to any person – remarkably inoffensive – when intoxicated directly the reverse – since witness has known him, has noticed him when sober to be a quiet man – when drunk quarrelsome – and upon being further interrogated a second time witness stated, that he had seen the Traverser when intoxicated – thought him a perfect maniac. . . .

The testimony being closed on both sides, the Attorney General stated to the Jury, that drunkenness, (that being the anticipated defence) would not relieve the Traverser from his legal responsibility. . . .

The Jury in a few minutes rendered a verdict. – *Guilty.*

28

Trial Testimony – State of Maryland vs. Jesse Massy, December 18, 1835

SOURCE: The Baltimore *Gazette*, December 19, 1835.

Mr. Giddleman, deposed. – Witness has been personally acquainted with the Traverser about 12 years, were boys together – . . . crowd standing directly opposite Mr. E's house – went over to it to see what was going on – Massy was there, he appeared to be directing his conversation to those around him, witness heard him say "that he would rather have done that night than have $500; that he had helped to destroy some of the best furniture in Ellicott's house," one of the gentlemen standing by told him "he had better keep such things to himself," Traverser replied "he did not care a d--n, he had done it, did't care who knew it, and would't deny it" – witness saw nothing more of Massy after this . . . one of the mob carried off 3 or 4 sheets, said "he had lost 50 dollars by the Bank of Maryland and was only getting it" – witness went up into the garret and found there an Irishman dressing himself, had a pillow case with other articles – witness and others wanted him to surrender the goods, but he would not, and they were afraid to urge him lest he should call the mob – don't know him – about 30 years of age – pretty stout as he had on 3 or 4 suits of clothes. . . .

John Tensfield was sworn. – Witness . . . came up to help guard, and saw Massy there, – said "he had lost a drum that the guard had taken it from the mob that he had got it from a black man and if he lost the drum it would cost him seven or eight dollars" – don't know where the drum was captured or who captured it – witness again replied to the question asking the precise words used by the Traverser, "said that he had either hired or borrowed a drum, from a black man in Old Town, and if lost he should have to pay for it" – appeared to witness to be looking for the drum – said nothing more. . . .

Major Wm. Pinkney being duly sworn, deposed – witness captured a drum with a drummer, Sunday morning about 12 o'clock, carried the drummer into the square and gave him in the care of a Watchman. Heard a drum at the head of a mob, coming from Glenn's. . . . Traverser is not the man who beat the drum. . . .

The Jury . . . handed in the verdict: *guilty*.

29

Trial Testimony — State of Maryland vs. Peter Harman, December 22, 1835

SOURCE: The Baltimore *Gazette*, December 29, 1835.

Mr. Frailey, . . . deposed: – Witness has known Traverser by sight for the last 6 or 8 years – saw him on Sunday evening for the first time among the mob – witness saw him first on the portico of Johnson's house – then addressing the multitude – can't tell exactly what were the words – Traverser opened his address with: "Friends and Fellow Citizens" – witness saw him afterwards engaged pulling the oil cloth carpet off the entry – . . . Whilst Traverser was engaged, a piece of board was thrown from above, which felled him down – he was taken up after lying some time and carried into the house – saw nothing more of him afterwards – witness could not say *positively* what Traverser said, but thinks the words were, "the work of destruction goes bravely on." . . . Traverser is the same person – could tell how he was dressed – he had a brass plate on the front of his hat . . . presumes he was engaged in the mob from the brass plate of his hat and from the character of the man – did not see the Traverser place the carpet any where, for while he was engaged the portico was thrown down – the fire had been kindled at this time – did not hear him say the words: "the work of destruction goes bravely on," but judged he said so from the hat plate he had on and from the character of the man. . . .

Nicholas Speaks being sworn, deposed: – On Monday morning, after the fray as witness was going to breakfast, met Traverser, who said, "Hunt has resigned, and he be d--d if he wasn't Mayor of the city" – he said also, "I am going to appoint *my officers* now" – he said "some s-n of a b--h threw something out the window and cut his head" – that "he was going to quit the ten hour system now and go to job work" – that "Judge Brice had something for him to do" – Traverser is the same man – he was not drunk at the time – he said "he had been very hard at work and had got his head cut" – that "when he was throwing things out the window, some s-n of a b--h threw something on his head" – witness knows him by sight – has seen him with the Engines – has seen him running them. . . .

Mr. Cook sworn. Witness arrested Traverser on board of the Steamboat coming from Philadelphia – can't say how long this was after the riots – about ten days or fourteen perhaps – gave no account to witness – when witness apprehended him, he said "he expected to saw granite, but did not expect to be caught so soon". . . .

The Jury in a few minutes returned a verdict: *Guilty.*

30

Trial Testimony—State of Maryland vs. Benjamin A. Lynch, December 24, 1835

SOURCE: The Baltimore *Gazette*, January 6 and 7, 1836.

Edward Chassaing, deposed. . . . Went into the crowd, listened to their conversation, and discovered immediately that they purposed an attack on Krey's property, on account of Benzinger's part in the defence of the square. The majority were strenuous for the attack; then witness discovered Mr. Lynch in the crowd; had seen him before; he was speaking with great warmth and opposing the project and using every argument he could urge against it. . . . Finding his influence insufficient, he left them, saying that he would oppose it with all his might, that he would now go to head-quarters and use his influence there. . . . A motion to go to McElderry's being again made, Lynch cried out "Yes, by God that is the best idea;" in saying so he joined the crowd in the middle of the street, and then they appeared to form a ring in the centre of the street, as if holding a consultation: Cannot say that Lynch formed part of the ring; thinks he did not. To do Mr. Lynch justice, he did say during the course of the evening, but witness cannot say exactly when, "we have been branded by Mr. Gwynn as incendiaries, and must not give him an opportunity of substantiating his remarks by destroying the property of guiltless people;" witness does not remember the exact words, but the above is the substance.

Mr. R. Burk . . . saw Mr. Lynch there; he was talking against the conduct of the horse-guards; said they acted improperly, shooting innocent men, were d--d murderers or something to that effect. Said if he had a relation or friend injured by them he would have satisfaction. . . . A German came along with some wine, sugar, &c. from Morris's; Lynch took hold of him and asked him where he was going with it, the German replied "home." Lynch asked if he did not know he was stealing; the German said he thought it best not to let it be spoiled. Lynch told him to take it back. Some person then came by and jabbed a stick into it; the sugar jar was broken &c. Did not see Lynch after this.

George W. McCabe. . . . A proposal was made by some one to go to Captain Benzinger's; does not know who said "the property does not belong to him but his father-in-law." Lynch said "gentlemen, I oppose going there; it is hard that the father should suffer for the sins of the child," after that the party moved towards Hunt's . . . heard Mr. Lynch say from across the street, "we are the people, you are the aristocracy; we want no spectators," witness immediately turned back and left them.

Mr. Dell. . . . Old Mr. Lynch put his head out of the window; and said that the house belonged to him and not his son-in-law. Some said "go on." They got the door open and got out one or two guns and knives; by this time B. Lynch came running up, and said "my God, this is all my fault, if I had been here this would not have happened." Witness by this time had come over to the door; witness said, "Benjamin, this does not look quite so comfortable as at John Glenn's the other night;" he replied, "well, by God, the mob did right."

George Baxley. . . . Witness went to help his neighbour Lynch; while there, B. Lynch came running up and said "good god, if I had been here this should not have occurred;" when witness went up the mob had retired only one man remained. Heard B. Lynch say nothing in reference to the destruction of Glenn's property. . . .

Mr. John Lynch. . . . Mr. Lynch was proceeding to give the Traverser's declarations that the motives that induced his joining the mob were in order that he might be able to save his father's (witness's) property from destruction. – The court decided that the declaration of the Traverser could not be given in evidence, because any man might justify his participation in the mob if his own declarations as to his motives were to be received. Wm. H. Collins for the Traverser stated to the Court that it was the desire of the Traverser to show that on Sunday morning the civil authority being dissolved the father and son devised plans for the defence of the father's property, a part of which was that the son should go into the mob and control by such influence as he could gain, their proceedings. . . .

A short time, not more than a half hour after the jury had rendered a verdict of Guilty in this case, an open Barouche drawn by four greys drove down the lane and halted before the Court House door. It was presently known that the Barouche had been sent there for the purpose of conveying Mr. Lynch from the Court to Jail . . . in a sort of triumph. . . . [The Attorney General] moved the court have Mr. Lynch be arrested and given in the charge of the warden, to be conducted to prison in the usual way.

31

Memorial of Reverdy Johnson Praying Indemnity, 1836

SOURCE: Reverdy Johnson, *The Memorial of Reverdy Johnson to the Legislature of Maryland, Praying Indemnity for the Destruction of his Property in the City of Baltimore By a Mob, in August, 1835* (Annapolis, 1836).

That your memorialist is correct in stating that these outrages could readily have been avoided by proper and reasonable energy on the part of the authorities of the city, was not only demonstrated on the Monday succeeding the destruction of his property, when the mob in the pride of victory and almost in the absolute and uncontrolled possession of the town and threatening indiscriminate pillage, were instantaneously suppressed by the decided and patriotic stand assumed by General Smith. . . .

What avails it that he is told he is not . . . to be deprived of his life, liberty or property, but by the judgment of his peers or by "the law of the land," if without even the form of a trial, if not only without law, but against all law human and divine, he may be deprived of every thing he possesses, by a deluded, or hired violence, at any moment, when from any cause, no matter what, he may become an object of public prejudice or of private malice. If in such moments the civil power may slumber without responsibility, if the particular community in which the outrage may be perpetrated, may look on silent spectators of the enormity, and be safe from all liability, the boasted charter of the people's freedom, is a mere collection of unmeaning sentences, the protection it professes to guarantee to the individual citizen, is but a name; it holds but the word of promise to the ear and breaks it to the hope. Let it not be said in such cases, that the individual is entitled to redress from the immediate authors of his injuries. It is but to trifle with his misfortunes. Who were they for the most part, if not exclusively, in the particular instance? who will they ever be? The very dregs and refuse of society. Bankrupts in fortune and in fame, actuated by an inherent lust of plunder, ministering to the vindictive passions of concealed employers, or hoping to rise to comparative importance in moments of public agitation, from the obscurity to which their worthlessness would otherwise forever consign them. . . .

If the genius of good government does not invoke, in such a case, a complete indemnity, a residence under the reign of a Czar of Russia, is a thousand times to be preferred to a residence in Baltimore. Any government, no matter how despotic, is better than anarchy – any single tyrant, no matter how wicked, is better than a tyranny of the mob. Your memorialist has, however, an abiding confidence that the virtue and intelligence of his fellow citizens . . . will entertain but one opinion on the subject – that the honor and welfare of the city, and the honor and duty of the State, alike demand the indemnity.

32

Letters from "Junius"

SOURCE: The Baltimore *Republican*, 1836. (The letters of "Junius" to the Baltimore *Republican* were written specifically in opposition to John B. Morris's and Reverdy Johnson's appeals for indemnity.)

February 4, 1836: Fellow citizens, I am one of those who attribute the disturbances in our city to the iniquitous manner in which thousands of industrious and innocent persons were deprived of their property, through the medium of the Bank of Maryland; or if it will suit any man's purpose better, I state plainly, that I am clearly of opinion, that in the case referred to, fraud has produced violence, – and violence municipal disgrace. . . .

Of what avail are our natural advantages – our commercial facilities – our justly celebrated diffusion of general knowledge – or our mechanical ingenuity – if, in defiance of all these, the deserving of our community may be plundered of their property, regardless of or under colour of the laws – if society, under the distracting lash of accumulated wrongs, may at any time to suit the passions or pecuniary interests of a few individuals, be driven to acts of desperation and madness. . . . We can only be a prosperous people while our laws are fair and equal . . . – our Legislature shall *not* indemnify a few of our citizens, who owe their influence to wealth and fashion, – while hundreds whose claim is based on better grounds – sufferings unmerited, sustained by honesty – are left to drink the bitter cup of misery and grief.

February 26: The *materials* were chiefly men who for many years had sustained the characters of upright, industrious mechanics, – and the *motives* neither more nor less than an unwise – I will add unjustifiable determination, to avenge insulted justice. This however is matter of opinion. But what Mr. Johnson asserts in relation to mobs generally, cannot be matter of opinion. His doctrine that mobs must always be composed of the lower orders, and ever influenced as he suggests, is about as tenable as some other views which he has advanced with more gravity than judgment, and which in the proper place, I will prove to be perfectly absurd, if not ridiculous. – What let me ask is a mob? . . . I conceive a mob to be – a handful of villains, PLEBIANS or PATRICIANS, combined for the purpose of injuring the innocent by EVADING or VIOLATING the laws of the land. It will be seen that this definition stripped of all technicalities and plain as it is, embraces the very essense of those evils which may commonly be supposed to be the result of a mob. . . .

I am firmly convinced, that nothing so fully contributes to the destruction of the morals of a community as the triumph of contrivance and cunning. Laws become contemptible when those who are bound to obey them perceive from the example of others the possibility of evading them with impunity, because there is no corruption so poisonous in its influence, or so difficult to eradicate, as that corruption which has the perversion of law for its foundation. It is as De Lohlme has well observed, "almost incurable, because that which should operate as a *remedy* is the *source* of the evil."

March 5: The doctrine maintained in my last letter would be entirely misunderstood if it were regarded as a vindication or justification of the Mob. It merely sets forth that the *turpitude* of the acts of the mob, like other *criminal* acts, must be measured and viewed with reference to the CAUSES which produced them. It is said – "Thou shalt not do evil that good may come," and this, as a *prohibitory* command, is certainly correct; but after the act is *done*, and the supreme power is about to determine on the punishment due to a violation of the law, the *motive* of the criminal, and the *manner* of the deed, are both to be taken into consideration. For instance, an individual steals a loaf of bread. Every one will acknowledge the *crime* is positive, that the man in committing the act has violated the law, and incurred the *legal* guilt and punishment of larceny. But if, upon examination, it is proven that the theft was committed to prevent starvation, the *motive* will certainly operate in the man's favour, especially if it appear that he stole the loaf FROM ONE to whom he had a short time previously entrusted *several* loaves, but *which* owing to some unexplained cause or negligence, were not forthcoming. In such a case I am not unreasonable in saying, that although the sternness of the law would not allow a diminution of the *legal* guilt, – the *moral* guilt would be entirely obliterated.

. . . Go where you would, nothing was talked of but the Bank of Maryland – the suit in chancery – the absence of Mr. Johnson, and the possibility of his succeeding in preventing the expulsion of the Trustees. Every man cried *shame*! You could scarcely find an individual who *entirely* approved of the conduct of Mr. Johnson, and long before night the city was in a state of perfect fermentation. One over-powering sentiment of indignation seemed to influence every body. . . . There is a point before which human power cannot restrain the innate sense of natural justice. It is possible for men through the medium of their cruel and unfeeling conduct to become so utterly obnoxious to a whole community that even their rights are no longer respected. "Do unto others as you would that others should do unto you," is a sentiment more deeply seated in human nature than is commonly admitted, and whenever this great principle is openly, palpably, and unfeelingly violated, the innate sense of which I have spoken becomes offended – ungovernable wrath and indignation is the result, and seizing the rod of punishment, in defiance of human laws, it becomes at once its own avenger. It is idle to trifle, to toy, to prevaricate or to endeavour through the aid of subtle sophistry or *mongrel terms*, to set aside this doctrine. It has for its foundations the unchangeable laws of nature, and its duration will be co-equal with the race of man.

I shall not pretend to describe the scene – but if ever the desolating spirit of fury reigned triumphant, it was at the destruction of this property. The rioters appeared to be possessed by superhuman power and daring – the wildness of their conduct carrying excitement, terror, and amazement into the thousands who beheld them. . . . As a *last resort* it was determined to have recourse to *Fire Arms*. . . . And what was its effect? Did it allay the excitement, or terrify the mob? I put the question to the thousand who witnessed the scenes that followed. The answer which truth will compel them to give is – NO – they must say as I do – that where previously was seen in the countenances of men revenge and destruction, were now to be traced in characters, which could not be mistaken, *blood! blood! blood!* – And what was the result? THE ANARCHICAL DESOLATION AND MOURNFUL PARALYSIS OF REASON WHICH DESECRATED THE FOLLOWING SABBATH.

. . . No body knew where the mob was on Monday morning – in fact it had vanished. – It is true it had left behind, as terrible things commonly do, a good deal of alarm, – and Rumor as usual was amusing herself with the fears of the timid – but the mob – the genuine mob was defunct. – Public opinion which had breathed into its nostrils the breath of life, had withdrawn its vitality, and the mob was no more.

33

Symptoms of Revolution, September 25, 1835

SOURCE: Michel Chevalier, *Society, Manners, and Politics in the United States, Being a Series of Letters on North America,* © 1961 by John William Ward. Reprinted by permission of Doubleday Publishing Company, Inc.

Unfortunately, reverence for the laws seems to be disappearing among Americans . . ., and thus a door has been opened to the tyranny of a turbulent minority which calls itself the people. The appearance of this miscalled *popular justice*, administered by the hands of a few desperate or furious men who call themselves the successors of the Boston Tea Party of 1773, is a great calamity in the bosom of a country where there is no other guarantee of the public peace than a reverence for law and where the legislator, taking for granted the prevalence of order, has made no provisions against disorder. This popular justice has the greater condemnation of being for the most part grossly unjust. . . . During the outrages last month at Baltimore which lasted four days, this self-styled justice was most stupidly unjust. The mob gave out that it wished to punish those knaves who had shamefully abused the credulity of the poor in the affair of the Bank of Maryland. It is a matter of public notoriety that the bankruptcy of the bank was fraudulent; that just before it stopped payment it had offered a high rate of interest on deposits of any amount in order to attract to its counter the savings of the laboring classes; but it was also a matter of notoriety that the criminal acts of the bank were wholly the work of one Evan Poultney, who alone was, in fact, the bank. Instead of going to take vengeance for the ruin of the artisan, the widow, and the orphan on the author of it, the mob went to call to account the bankruptcy commissioners appointed by the court. . . .

In a word, the *reign of terror* has begun in the United States. Men of courage and devotion to the cause of law have no rallying point in the press; even when public authority might be disposed to support them, it proves insufficient, either through fear or concern for party interests or want of physical force. . . . Recently . . . Baltimore was given up to the genius of destruction four whole days. . . . When the most respectable citizens, those most deeply interested in the restoration of public order, held a meeting in the Exchange, the mountain in labor brought forth only a long series of *whereases* on the advantage of public order and a string of wordy resolutions which resolved nothing. Nothing, shameful to relate, but the presence of a veteran of the Revolution with the weight of eighty-four years on his head, who had retired from Congress to end his long career in repose but who felt his blood boil in his veins and mantle in his cheeks at the spectacle before him – nothing but his presence gave courage to this assembly of men in the vigor of life who were letting their city fall a prey to a handful of drunkards and depraved boys. The indignant old man started up and interrupted the reading of the resolutions. "Damn your resolutions!" he cried. "Give me a sword and thirty men and I will restore order." "What! General Smith," said one of these irresolute makers of resolutions, "would you fire upon your fellow citizens?" "Those who break the laws, drive their neighbor from his house, plunder his property, and reduce his wife and children to beggary," answered General Smith, "such fellows are not my fellow citizens." These words, which expressed the thoughts of all, but which no one dared utter, were received with a thunder of applause.

34

Mob in Baltimore

Archibald Hawkins was a witness to the riots, and his account is the best historical description of the riot.

SOURCE: Archibald Hawkins, *The Life and Times of Hon. Elijah Stansbury, an "old defender" and ex-Mayor of Baltimore. Together with Early Reminiscenses, dating from 1662, and Embracing a Period of 212 Years* (Baltimore: J. Murphy and Co., 1874).

There had been several manifestations of excitement in the public mind prior to the riot, relative to a circumstance, to which we should feel a delicacy in alluding, but for the fact that the disgraceful affair became the subject of newspaper comment. The mystery, which at that time shrouded an affair, implicating the character of a man who had held a respectable station in society, with a nefarious design upon the virtue of a young lady, *supposed* to have inconsiderately thrown herself upon his honor for protection from the attempts of another – had very unfavorably prejudiced public curiosity. Rumor had bruited a thousand lies and was still busy in the creation of her ephemeral tales, which are sought with avidity by the idle and unemployed.... Such was the state of the public mind in Baltimore during the whole of the week preceding the riot.

As food for this appetite "strange and unnatural," the ear was daily gorged with intelligence from various quarters of the total subjection of legal discipline to Lynch Law, while the press, lukewarm in its animadversions, seemed to connive at or palliate these excesses from a fatal error in opinion, that, as they had a tendency to rid the country of an obnoxious portion of society, the end justified the means....

The events of Friday evening became still more threatening of disaster. Curiosity had multiplied her votaries, and at an early hour the square was thronged to excess....

Mr. Jones appeared, but scarcely uttered a sentence, when a most discordant noise from a horn, which continued at intervals during the evening, excited a most uprorious peal of laughter. In the course of his speech, Mr. Jones took occasion to class the sufferers in a manner similar to the following:

"Fathers have suffered"——— "Yes, we have," ejaculated a boisterous auditor. "Children have suffered" ——— "Yes, we have!" from the same voice. "Orphans have suffered" ——— "Yes, we have," – and "*widows* have suffered" ——— "Yes, *we* have!" This was too much. The *widow's voice* had made a sensation, and a deafening laugh was the sympathetic reply....

[Saturday] The toils of the week were ended, and many of those who that evening received the wages of industry, as is customary at all seasons, were indulging in an extra glass. The all-absorbing topic was the anticipated tumult of the night, and almost every one expressed an intention of becoming a spectator, and doubtless, numbers of those who went, innocent of any design that would not have been justified by propriety, wrought upon by the exciting circumstances of the affray, and elated by an artificial ardor for the reckless sport, participated in the work of destruction and shared in the disgrace....

No sooner was each apartment cleared of its furniture, than the party set to work to remove the window frames which were at intervals precipitated into the flames. Several persons now made themselves very conspicuous; and one especially so, a sailor dressed character, who was generally called *"Red Jacket"* by the spectators, because he wore a red flannel shirt. This was Samuel M * * * a cooper from Franklin street. He worked without intermission, (as if bound by contract,) at a large arched window, which extended from the ceiling to the floor, and appeared marvellously interested in the *job*, and the amount of ruin which might be accomplished with his own hands. Another, a middle-aged man, (said to be a sufferer in the Bank failure,) who was assisting others in removing the copper roof from the splendid marble portico, frequently stopped to harangue the multitude on the subject of his supposed laudable exploits until he became the jest of his companions and a target for the clods of mortar which were hurled at him from above. . . .

In passing the house of Evan Poultney, the President of the Bank, he appeared at the door and assured the rioters that no resistance would be made if it was their wish to enter. No! No! we have nought to do with honest men! cried one, to which a cheer responded, and the mass moved on.

Early on Monday morning, the steps at Poultney's house were washed, and some panes of glass which had been broken in the house adjoining that of Evan T. Ellicott, repaired at the expense of the mob. . . .

BERTRAM WYATT-BROWN

New Leftists and Abolitionists: A Comparison of American Radical Styles

FROM JOHN WINTHROP'S SERMON to the Puritan travelers to the last, pious pronouncement from the White House, Americans have felt a compulsive urge to preach – to be prophets of doom and evangels of inspiration. Lately there have been so many Jeremiahs crowding into the national pulpit that there is hardly anyone left in the pews to listen. Demands for national repentance are heard on every side – from the columns of *Barron's* to the revolutionary chitchat of Stokely Carmichael on the Dick Cavett Late Show. So devoted are we to the irresistible pleasures of catechizing each other that the preaching of revolution becomes a substitute for the hard work of planning it. Dynamiting empty office buildings in New York, occupying a dean's office, razzing a Daley judge, or blowing up Rodin's Thinker outside the "establishment's" Cleveland Museum, are all sermons, not revolutionary acts. They are not preludes to truly revolutionary incidents like the storming of the Bastille, the Potemkin mutiny, or the assassination of General Trujillo. Instead, they are theatrical versions of those funda-

This essay is reprinted from *Wisconsin Magazine of History*, Vol. 53, Summer, 1970, pp. 256-268, with permission from The State Historical Society of Wisconsin. A shortened version of this paper was presented in a lecture series at Carthage College, Kenosha, Wisconsin, on February 25, 1970.

mentalist billboards throughout the South – "Prepare to Meet Thy God," "The Wages of Sin is Death."[1] Both reactionaries and radicals harken to calls for moral regeneration. Our religious impulses are not introspective; we advertise convictions as if they were toothpaste. But *self-repentance* is always in short supply in the marketplace of indignation.

"Righteousness fever" seems to strike like a recurring illness at different times in American history. Two of the most notable examples, though, are our present situation and that of the 1830s. Like conditions do not always produce similar consequences. Yet, one can discern a pattern of events that link these two periods of moral outrage, alienation, and romantic extravagance. Both belong to ages of foreign revolutions and domestic unrest. Both were preceded by a decade or so of relative stability and social calm – the post-Napoleonic era and the Eisenhower years. Men who lived through the trauma of French Revolution and Napoleonic militarism on the one hand, and the Second World War, the rise of Stalinism, and the fall of Nationalist China on the other, yearned for public order, release from the "terrors of ideological politics," and the pursuit of private, domestic interests.[2] Desperately these men – the fathers of the upcoming radicals of the next generation – tried to check the decline of what Hannah Arendt has described as "the old Roman trinity of religion, tradition, and authority."[3] Grand visions of revolutionary utopias, which only seemed to lead to totalitarian, self-defeating results wearied and frightened them.[4]

At first glance, Americans of the 1820s and 1950s seemed to have overcome their fears of ideology. Both postwar eras celebrated a national consensus about politics and social aims. After the outward menaces of foreign ideologies receded some-

[1] Robert Brustein, "Revolution as Theatre," in *New Republic*, March 14, 1970, 13-17.

[2] See Marian Morton, " 'The Terrors of Ideological Politics': Intellectuals, Liberals and Intellectual History," (unpublished Ph.D. dissertation, Case Western Reserve University, 1970); Michael P. Rogin, *The Intellectuals and McCarthy: The Radical Specter* (Cambridge and London, 1967), 1-58, 331.

[3] Hannah Arendt, *On Revolution* (New York, 1963), 113.

[4] In 1809, for instance, William Wirt confessed his own disenchantment with French experiments: "The doctrines of liberty are at an end, and so are the monarchies of Europe – all fused and melted down into one great consolidated despotism. . . . How did all America stand on tiptoe, during [Napoleon's] brilliant campaigns in Italy at the head of the army of the republic! . . . Yet see in what it has all ended! The total extinction of European liberty and the too probable prospect of an enslaved world." Quoted by William R. Taylor, *Cavalier & Yankee: The Old South and American National Character* (New York, 1963), 331.

what, Americans settled quite comfortably for a benign religious orthodoxy, stable republicanism, and social and political compromises necessary for sectional harmony. Pragmatic, low-keyed goals of economic expansion occupied their thoughts and time. Just as Charles Wilson could boast that what was good for General Motors was also good for the country, so too a businessman of 1825 could swell with pride in American manufacturing: "Poor mother earth was never so beat and exercised as now, and she must think a new race dwells on her surface."[5] Superficially, the world seemed relatively well-ordered with developing institutions, prosperity, increasingly rapid communications, and a concern for religious and social orthodoxy.

Not far below the surface, however, anxieties about the stability of society and the uncertain state of traditional values hid beneath such comforting characterizations of their times as the "era of good feelings" and "the silent generation." A conservative of 1830 grumbled: "The men of the present generation must decide the momentous question, whether this great Christian Republic shall move on in the path explored and recommended by the patriots of '76, under the healthful influence of her Bible and Sabbaths: or be thrown upon the ocean of experiment, with no other compass than that by which the leaders of the French Revolution were guided, in their bloody and disastrous course. . . ." Memories of the Bastille, the guillotine, the desecration of Notre Dame lingered like an immense shadow upon the American imagination.[6] Southerners, faced with the examples of the Gabriel, Denmark Vesey, and Nat Turner threats of massive black insurrection, could hardly forget the French Revolutionary example of Toussaint L'Ouverture and Dessalines.[7]

Against this setting in the early republic with its modern equivalent, the next generation of Americans took its cues. The upcoming zealots felt no terrors of international ideologies. The classic enemies of freedom – Jacobinism and Communism – had to be learned from textbooks and teachers, parents, and aging spokesmen. Neither Jacobinism nor Communism were to be

[5] Lewis Tappan to Benjamin Tappan, May 14, 1825, in the Benjamin Tappan MSS, Library of Congress.

[6] Reverend Joseph Claybaugh, "Discourse, Delivered at the Meeting of the First Presbytery of Ohio, in April last," in *Christian Intelligencer and Evangelical Guardian,* II: 177-178 (May, 1830); see also, for a gory reminder of French atrocities, *The Philadelphian,* February 19, 1830.

[7] William W. Freehling, *Prelude to Civil War: The Nullification Controversy in South Carolina, 1816-1836* (New York and London, 1965), 16, 50, 55, 58-60.

perfect models for the youngsters, but they at least represented points of reference by which to judge contemporary society. French and Russian (or preferably Cuban) revolutionary systems symbolized a break with the past and demonstrated the power of absolute principle to move men's hearts, even if they had little application as systems of economy or government to American needs. At the same time, the young noticed that adults did not live up to their own orthodox standards of conduct. As Barrington Moore recently observed, the present-day radicals "have been both acting upon their elders' ideals and rebelling against their betrayal, struggling to see what went wrong, and searching desperately for substitutes."[8] Slavery could not be squared with the sacred rhetoric of the Declaration of Independence; traditional American concepts of self-determination for colonial peoples were obviously betrayed in the interventions in Santo Domingo, the Cuban Bay of Pigs, and Indochina.

Cruelty, oppression, war, and institutional violence of all kinds became highly visible, monolithic, and impervious to the ameliorative plans that the older generation had devised for controlling them. Raised to believe that men were rational creatures, that society had designed safeguards to protect liberty of action, that material progress indicated divine favor, these young radicals of the 1830s and 1960s were impatient with the ancient paradox of human sin. Institutions, not the human condition, must explain the origin of evil. "Immediacy" replaced "progress" as the catchword for change: immediate withdrawal from Vietnam, immediate emancipation for the slaves. Supreme faith in human possibility took the place of institutional gradualism.

The sources for this dramatic moral transformation must be sought in two interrelated areas – the sociological and the psychological circumstances of the times. First, the sociological category:

David Brion Davis, Daniel H. Calhoun, Robert W. Doherty, and William R. Taylor have all contributed to our understanding of the underlying preoccupations of the Jacksonian era.[9] Applying the

[8] Barrington Moore, Jr., "On Rational Inquiry in Universities Today," in *New York Review of Books,* April 23, 1970, p. 31.

[9] David B. Davis, *The Slave Power Conspiracy and the Paranoid Style* (Baton Rouge, 1969) and his essay, "Some Themes of Counter-Subversion: An Analysis of Anti-Masonic, Anti-Catholic, and Anti-Mormon Literature," in *Mississippi Valley Historical*

behaviorist and literary tools of those scholars who lived through and explored the setting of the 1950s, they have made the task of drawing parallels between these periods exceedingly light. These historians have discovered that the basis for anxiety in this age of optimism lay in the economic expansion of the country and the consequent instability of old social relationships. Stanley Elkins called this process a shattering of the traditional institutions of church, elitist rule, and mercantilism. To a degree he is correct, but he failed to recognize that new institutions filled the vacuum.[10] The nation expanded beyond the older confines of city and mountain range, but it also contracted as new means of communications – steamboats, railroads, highways, telegraph, air waves, and mass printing – made the world smaller but more combustible. The very dynamism that had propelled Americans away from the ideological turmoil of continental politics in both periods so radically altered traditions and orthodoxies that glaring deficiencies developed between society's values and its practices. The very pace of change in institutional and vocational relationships – apprentice to employer, layman to minister, lawyer to client, and vice-versa – speeded this compulsive and distorting exercise. Only by reference to the eternal, unchanging absolutes which supposedly underlay a shifting social complex, one might achieve a sense of authenticity.

As a result, negative reference became a means of positive evaluation. Purists, whether they belonged to the Left or Right, discovered who they were by determining who they definitely were not. A corollary was the development of classic romantic conceptions about the Anti-Christ in a Manichean world of easily distinguishable truths and falsehoods.

Real dangers to national security subsided after the Peace of Ghent, but imagined threats of a God-denying Jacobinism, rationalistic Illuminism, Masonry, and other alien, interconnected secret poisons were alleged challenges of American liberty. Lyman Beecher and other orthodox clergy and laymen sounded the alarm of internal subversion from vague phantoms, designated loosely as "infidels," a name encompassing Catholics, Masons and pagan

---

Review, XLVII: 205-224 (September, 1960); Daniel H. Calhoun, *Professional Lives in America, Structure and Aspiration, 1750-1850* (Cambridge, 1965); Robert W. Doherty, "Status Anxiety and American Reform: Some Alternatives," in *American Quarterly*, XIX: 329-337 (Summer, 1967); Taylor, *Cavalier & Yankee.*

[10] Stanley M. Elkins, *Slavery: A Problem in American Institutional and Intellectual Life* (Chicago, 1968), 27-52.

materialists. Jacksonians used the same formula of superhuman satanism in high places to attack the eastern elite of financiers and speculators.

In this climate of general suspicion the rise of a faction that could blame most of the country's ills upon the hegemony of brutal slaveholders and their northern economic and political allies was hardly surprising. Clearly it was one of the easiest ways of distinguishing the purity of free-labor, Yankee, and traditional Christian ideals from the corruption, exploitation, and sexual license of whip-wielding southern masters. For all its humanitarian concern for the "poor slave," abolitionism carried this ingredient of self-identity through negative reference.[11]

Likewise, ideological fantasies bloomed in the 1950s and 1960s, producing such bizarre phenomena as the McCarthy Movement and Billy James Hargis's Christian Crusade. A counterpart to these visions of black manipulators was bound to appear – a mirror reflection of the fears of the Right, set obversely in Leftist terms. Focusing, like the abolitionists, upon entrenched, internal iniquity, the New Leftists denounced a new slave-power conspiracy – the "military-industrial-labor complex" and the Liberal establishment (the latter denounced by both George Wallace and present-day radicals).

Self-identification with virtue in opposition to evil cannot alone explain why abolitionists arose in the 1830s nor why radicals emerged in the 1960s. While one may question David Donald's techniques and conclusions in his essay, "Toward a Reconsideration of the Abolitionists," he remains one of the few historians before or since to grapple with the knotty problem of radical motivation. Yet, his conclusion that they were maladjusted because of a loss of status in relation to their more locally prominent New England forebears oversimplified the psychological factors involved. Likewise, Daniel Bell has exceeded the bounds of scholarly objectivity by accusing a similarly intense, well-educated elite of liberal arts majors of avenging a technocratic society in a "guttering last gasp of a romanticism soured by rancor and impotence."[12] Much more interesting and persuasive possi-

[11] Davis, *Slave Power Conspiracy and the Paranoid Style, passim.*

[12] David Donald, *Lincoln Reconsidered: Essays on the Civil War Era* (New York, 1956), 19-36; see Robert F. Berkhofer, Jr., *A Behavioral Approach to Historical Analysis* (New York, 1969), 61-67, for a discerning criticism of Donald's pioneering use of behavioral technique. Berkhofer could well be right, but the essay deserves reconsideration whatever its deficiencies. For a liberal attack on Donald's thesis, see Bertram

bilities are available for consideration than merely a man's place in some amorphous pecking order.

A more valuable approach comes from the findings of the psychologist Kenneth Keniston. Examining radicals involved in the nonviolent "Vietnam Summer" of 1967, Keniston discovered that most of them belonged to middle-class and college-trained families with Stevensonian or left-wing leanings. The centers of family life were the close-knit family unit itself and the community's affairs. Parents of young radicals took their places in P.T.A., church, civic drives, and other charitable and political activities. Turning to Donald's information about the abolitionists, we find that this breed of committed youth came from families of farmers, teachers, ministers, and storekeepers of New England. By and large, abolitionists' parents were pious Quakers, Congregationalists, Presbyterians, Unitarians, and Baptists. Keniston found that some of these faiths also appear quite prominently in the New Leftists' backgrounds, but he included Reformed Judaism. Unhelpfully Keniston presents no statistics nor any control group data.[13]

Keniston's chief point, however, is that a sense of moral uprightness dominated the young agitator's home life, a kind of rectitude that stressed social responsibility. Donald argues quite accurately along similar lines regarding abolitionists. These young men and women of both eras were usually taught to free themselves from overt biases against the less fortunate. Usually, the modern radicals' mother assumed a role of moral preceptor, not the father, according to Keniston's study. The relation between the young radical and his mother was very intimate, warm, and intense, Keniston suggested. Immediately one is reminded of the strong-willed, quietly intense, religious mothers of William Lloyd Garrison, Lewis and Arthur Tappan, Thomas Wentworth Higginson, Theodore Weld, and James G. Birney's

---

Wyatt-Brown, "Abolitionism: Its Meaning for Contemporary Reform," in *Midwest Quarterly*, VIII: 41-55 (October, 1966), an article originally written during the Martin Luther King March on Washington, summer, 1963. Daniel Bell is quoted by Kenneth Keniston, "You Have to Grow up in Scarsdale to Know How Bad Things Really Are," in *New York Times Magazine*, April 27, 1969, p. 122.

[13] Kenneth Keniston, *Young Radicals: Notes on Committed Youths* (New York, 1968), 44-51; Charles Kadushin, "Psychotherapy and the New Left," in *Columbia Forum*, XII: 22-24 (Spring, 1969), stresses Old Left over Liberal origins of radicalism, at least at Columbia. See also August Meier, "Who Are the 'True Believers'? – A Tentative Typology of the Motivations of Civil Rights Activists (1965)," in Joseph R. Gusfield (ed.), *Protest, Reform, and Revolt: A Reader in Social Movements* (New York, 1970), 473-482, suggesting a wide variety of types involved.

Aunt Doyle. According to Tilden Edelstein's excellent biography of Thomas W. Higginson, the young Higginson's father confessed "that his wife supervised the children's moral training," holding daily prayers, reading sermons aloud, and preparing them for the divine life after death.[14]

If the modern radical was a girl, Keniston surmised, she was likely to look to her father for spiritual and ethical advice. Thus, Angelina and Sarah Grimké, Elizabeth Cady Stanton, and Harriet Beecher Stowe received their moral lessons from their fathers.[15] In any case, one of the parents seemed to be the focus of childhood attention. Richard Hildreth and Elizur Wright, for example, learned spiritual duty from their schoolmastering fathers.[16] In such instances, the abolitionist sometimes spoke of a relatively cool relationship with the overshadowed parental partner. This psychological factor might lead to a feeling of neglect from the more indifferent parent. Keniston found that frequently modern radical youths with strong maternal ties complained about their fathers' absorption in business, their willingness to compromise with principle, and their conventional beliefs. It is difficult to calculate the results of Oedipal ambiguities upon the nonconformist; Keniston in other writings convincingly denies that such Freudian speculations have much validity in assessing radical motivation. Despite a "split image" of the father, radicals have a generally healthy, well-structured relationship with their parents.[17]

At once an objection springs to mind. Not all morally

[14]Keniston, *Young Radicals*, 51-60; John L. Thomas, *The Liberator: William Lloyd Garrison: A Biography* (Boston, 1963), 11-25; Bertram Wyatt-Brown, *Lewis Tappan and the Evangelical War against Slavery* (Cleveland, 1969), 5, 11-13, 25, 36; Tilden G. Edelstein, *Strange Enthusiasm: A Life of Thomas Wentworth Higginson* (New Haven, 1968), 10-11 (quotation); Betty Fladeland, *James Gillespie Birney: Slaveholder to Abolitionist* (Ithaca, 1955), 2, 5, 6, 7, 30.

[15]Gerda Lerner, *The Grimké Sisters from South Carolina: Rebels against Slavery* (Boston, 1967), 16-19, 28-29, 45-49; Robert Merideth, *The Politics of the Universe: Edward Beecher, Abolition, and Orthodoxy* (Nashville, 1968), 36n, 37; Robert E. Riegel, *American Feminists* (Lawrence and London, 1963), 45-47.

[16]Phillida E. Bunkle, "Richard Hildreth: A Biographical Study in the Applicability of the Status Thesis to an Ante-Bellum Reformer," (unpublished M.A. thesis, Smith College, 1968), 22-26, and David M. French, "The Conversion of An American Radical: Elizur Wright, Jr. and the Abolitionist Commitment," (unpublished Ph.D. dissertation, Case Western Reserve University, 1970), 25-30. I am greatly indebted to Professor French for his perceptive analysis of Wright.

[17]Keniston, *Young Radicals,* 55-60; Keniston, "The Other Side of the Oedipus Complex," in *Radical Therapist,* I: 6-7 (April-May, 1970).

concerned and strong-willed parents raise up radical-minded children today, nor did they in the early nineteenth century. Obviously some special temperament, some inner mechanism, some predisposition toward a missionary impulse must help to account for the creation of a radical frame of mind. It could be that all but one of the siblings in a family escaped the compulsion to right social wrongs and remake society. After all, Lewis and Arthur Tappan, for example, had four brothers none of whom became abolitionists; three took up less controversial causes than antislavery, while the sixth brother simply spent his life in steady drinking.[18] But even the most probing Freudian analyst has not yet reached the total, experiential depths of human diversity. When faced with this final mystery, Erik Erikson has confessed that he has to remind himself of "the remark of a co-ed who expressed the depth of the darkness in the direct way reserved to women. Her escort had just mused aloud that life was a strange thing, indeed ... But she asked quietly ... 'as compared with what?' "[19] Granted that the following remarks are more descriptive of *some* abolitionists and *some* radicals today than they are conclusive, we can say with assurance there are similar gropings toward commitment in antebellum and modern radical movements.

The intensity with which a family asserts its allegiance to conscience may be a key to the formation of radical tendencies. Many families apply high standards without arousing instincts of righteous indignation, but those who add a dimension of what Keniston calls *"specialness"* to moral imperatives may inspire a *special* response in the child. Consciously or unconsciously, they might demand of their offspring a full career of service to others, a dedication perhaps denied the father because of circumstance or denied the mother by her sexual role. Devout mothers might propose a vocation in church or healing science. One wonders how many radicals grew up midst pressures to become rabbis, Congregationalist missionaries, or teachers. Don Robertson and Marion Steele, two Long Beach sociology professors turned alienated, desert-living "hippies," for instance, were urged to become clergymen by parents of lesser achievement and social standing than that which their sons temporarily enjoyed. They did not reach a seminary but their vows of universal brotherhood,

[18] Wyatt-Brown, *Lewis Tappan*, 13, 14.

[19] Erik Erikson, *Insight and Responsibility: Lectures on the Ethical Implications of Psychoanalytic Insight* (New York, 1964), 149.

monastic poverty, and wilderness retreat from a corrupt society indicate a familiar religious impulse. As one radical, belonging to a religious household, told Keniston, "My initial thing is to get up and preach to people and expect them to follow me. That's where my impulse is, to speak out to the world."[20]

The radical youth learned that inner integrity came not from conformity to the ways of the world but to principles by which the family tried to live. The reward for superlative behavior was family and often explicitly immortal approval. "What need we care," wrote Sarah Tappan to her sons, "how little we are in the opinions of our fellow worms, if we may but shine as stars in the kingdom of heaven."[21] On a less elevated plane, sexual morality, manners, deference to elders, high marks in school, leadership and engagement in extra-curricular affairs were all goals set before the child.

Intelligent, sensitive, highly motivated, and mentally healthy, the child fulfilled his parents' aspirations. Lewis Tappan reminisced, "I had, on the whole, a happy time at school, being fond of study, ambitious to be one of the best scholars, often a favorite with the masters & a leader among the boys in our plays."[22] Family pressure was intense for Keniston's young people, too. Another example from the abolitionist past is Elizur Wright, first secretary of the American Anti-Slavery Society which the Tappans had organized in New York City. He also sought – and achieved – the exacting approval of his schoolteacher father.

At some point in adolescence, the radical-to-be suffers, Keniston points out, a severe state of depression – an identity crisis. The blow strikes young people indiscriminately, of course, but the youngster's sense of specialness, Keniston emphasizes, adds a further burden to his distress. He or she feels particularly sinful, lonely, unprepared for the battles ahead, morally inferior to others, cut loose from the aims that parents and relatives have proposed. "I did a lot of soul-searching and said to myself, 'You are very immature,' " a young radical girl recalled in an interview with Keniston.[23]

The youthful abolitionist-to-be also underwent similar doubts

[20] Keniston, *Young Radicals*, 31, 70-76; John Dreyfuss (L.A. Times-Capital Times Service), "Disillusioned Professors Defy Convention, Get Fired," in *Madison Capital Times*, February 23, 1970.

[21] Sarah Tappan to Charles Tappan, April 6, 1819, in Lewis Tappan (ed.), *Memoir of Sarah Tappan* (Boston, 1834), 73-74.

[22] "My Forefathers," p. 35, in the Lewis Tappan MSS, Library of Congress.

[23] Keniston, *Young Radicals*, 98.

involving role-confusion. Elizur Wright, Theodore Weld, Stephen S. Foster, Higginson, Joshua R. Giddings, and Charles Sumner, among others, all complained of the same melancholia – a longing for security, a moral incapacity, and often a separation from man and sometimes from God. In that more rigorously pious age, the language employed was frequently associated with the Calvinist feeling of human inability. Studies suffered; relations with others became strained. There were long walks in woods and fields, Bible reading, earnest conversations with one or two kindred spirits about the meaning of life, God's purpose, free will, holiness, mission, love.[24]

Essentially the problem was one of self-discovery, but not only inner security but also outward acceptance by the larger world, each reenforcing and interacting with the other. "Like a trapeze artist, the young person in the middle of vigorous motion must let go of his safe hold on childhood," Erik Erikson has noted, "and reach out for a firm grasp on adulthood. . . ." Self-knowledge must be reconfirmed by whatsoever recognition the community accorded its loyal youth. If that society, because of a confusion about acceptable standards and values, provides the sensitive young person with insufficient means to fulfill his need for centrality and wholeness, he may founder into a despair that goes beyond a temporary state of turmoil. Normally as Erikson said, the community offers rituals of welcome for its young.[25] Especially important for our purposes are such public testimonies as spirited professions of faith at revival meetings (most of Charles Grandison Finney's antebellum converts were under twenty-one), adult or late adolescent immersion in baptism, ordination into holy orders, a baccalaureate degree, or acceptance into or graduation from seminary or medical school.

For youths raised up to believe in their own superiority, their ability to master the normal hurdles and to search for underlying values, these visible marks of arrival at adulthood could become unsatisfying when the occupation involved as well as the ceremony

[24] French, "The Conversion of an American Radical," 51-53; Benjamin P. Thomas, *Theodore Weld: Crusader for Freedom* (New Brunswick, 1950), 3-13; "Stephen S. Foster," *Dictionary of American Biography*, (hereinafter *DAB*) VI: 558; Edelstein, *Strange Enthusiasm*, 18-34; James B. Stewart, *Joshua R. Giddings and the Tactics of Radical Politics* (Cleveland, 1970), 22-32; Bunkle, "Richard Hildreth," 32-33. Sumner suffered a depressed mental attitude while at Harvard, but did not seek religious explanations for it. See David Donald, *Charles Sumner and the Coming of the Civil War* (New York, 1960), 21.

[25] Erikson, *Insight and Responsibility*, 90.

symbolizing it was no longer integrated in the larger social context. Thus to the ordinary agonies about reaching the career or moral goal would be added doubts about its relevance. With institutions and vocations losing old functions and taking on new ones, questions about their value were not easy to answer.[26] For the radical today the issue involves the role of student. Scornfully but pertinently, a Young Socialist Alliance broadside declared: "The best student is the obedient, docile student who dutifully collects credits until he reaches the magical number when he is considered 'educated.' "[27]

The reaction of abolitionists to the changes in their most significant institution, the church, was as intense as the radicals' response to theirs – the university. The young man could no longer feel that society honored the life of divinity as much as new careers in business or the law. By the 1820s the minister was not the most learned, most respected individual in his community as he once had been. As Daniel Calhoun has shown, he was merely another atomistic entrepreneur, so to speak, seeking always the better salary and the approval of equally acquisitive, equally transient laymen. For some, this state of affairs intensified youthful feelings of inferiority and confusion about an ultimate career. Charles Turner Torrey, for instance, confided in his journal, "What shall I do, God knoweth, I do not. . . . Is it my fault that I am not as old as Methuselah? How can I help my youth? . . . But alas! The way to China [as a missionary] seems hedged up with difficulties." After attempting a few months of schoolteaching he did, however, study for the Congregationalist ministry, though frequently beset with doubts.[28] Amos Phelps, another minister-abolitionist, even broke off parish labors during a promising revival season to lecture for antislavery. He spent his short life alternating between the monotonous duties of pastoral ministry and full-time occupation in antislavery organizations. La Roy Sunderland, Samuel J. May, Joshua Leavitt, Simeon S. Jocelyn, and Orange Scott began as conventional village clergymen, but came to the conviction that the abolitionist cause was their primary responsibility. While some tried to combine the

[26] *Ibid.*, 90, 91, *passim.*

[27] "YSA Program for the Campus Revolt," Broadside [n.d.], pamphlet 68-1,247, in the State Historical Society of Wisconsin Library.

[28] Calhoun, *Professional Lives in America*, 115-171; R. Jackson Wilson, *In Search of Community: Social Philosophy in the United States, 1860-1920* (Boston, 1968), 1-21; Joseph C. Lovejoy, *Memoir of Rev. Charles T. Torrey* . . . (Boston, 1847), 29.

traditional work of the church with their social concerns for the slave, others, completely rejecting the hypocrisy and errors of their ecclesiastical brethren, unceremoniously left holy orders altogether. Stephen S. Foster, like a number of other radicals such as Elizur Wright, abandoned the career while in seminary. Foster's unhappy experience with his Union Theological Seminary career undoubtedly added a personal bitterness to his denunciation of the American church as "a brotherhood of thieves," for its failure to recognize the sinfulness of slaveholding Christians.[29] He lost his faith as well.

We should not be misled by the dogmatism of evangelical Protestantism in the era, for as Walter Houghton's *Victorian Frame of Mind* has shown, bold assertion covered hidden misgivings. The era compared itself not with the Enlightenment but with medieval times, a nostalgic, Gothic remembrance, a fantasy of faith and oneness, knightly sacrifice and bold, soaring cathedrals, in fact, a legend of certitudes and poses in which the Victorians, whether English or American, *struggled* to believe.[30] The veils of dogma were slipping away. Most of the younger, religiously motivated, gifted abolitionist leaders – Lydia Maria Child, Theodore Parker, Gerrit Smith, William Lloyd Garrison, G.W. Julian, James Birney, Elizabeth Cady Stanton, Wendell Phillips, Julia Ward Howe, Elizur Wright, Beriah Green – all deserted the evangelical faith with which they began their abolitionist careers.[31] They adopted various modes of unbelief or a vague Religion of Humanity. Nevertheless, the moral precepts and often major vestiges of their parents' and their own earlier religious faith remained, leaving them with an intense desire to create as trustworthy, righteous a world as they imagined their parents sought to sustain through outworn means.

The origins of abolitionist migration from orthodoxy must be traced to the uncertain state of that orthodoxy in their adolescence. When faced with his parents' anxieties about an acquisitive world, a community's fear of nonconformity, a national horror of revolution and sectional conflict. and a world's indifference to and doubt of divinity, the young radical-to-be was bound to have difficulty locating himself, his career, and his own

[29] "Stephen S. Foster," *DAB*, VI: 558.

[30] Walter E. Houghton, *The Victorian Frame of Mind, 1830-1870* (New Haven and London, 1957).

[31] See Wyatt-Brown, *Lewis Tappan*, 311.

set of beliefs. The society around him, entangled in cruel oppressions against all kinds of unfortunate groups, institutional hypocrisies, and empty symbols, indeed seemed "sick." In no area was the dream for American order, fidelity to principle, and that integrating force of "liberty" for all so clearly denied in actuality than in the expanding, slaveholding South.

The cold war atmosphere, national complacency, and technocratic changes of the 1950s posed similar problems for the young idealist. Both eras were ones of rapid mobility. Families not only moved into new neighborhoods, they also moved up and sometimes down the social ladder within them. This "uprootedness," as Erikson remarked, is typical of American life, but for these young persons it led to questioning of the legitimacy of the social order. Such migrations belied the family insistence upon stability and community loyalty. Surely, too, migrations of high school and college administrators and teachers, loyal to themselves and their fields of specialization alone, and not to the local "community of scholars and students" – more mobile in fact than the four-year student himself – might have similar effects upon radical youth today. As Erikson has observed, "where historical and technological developments severely encroach upon [traditional patterns of society] ... , youth feels endangered, individually and collectively, whereupon it becomes ready to support doctrines offering a total immersion in a synthetic identity (extreme nationalism, racism, or class consciousness) and a collective condemnation of a totally stereotyped enemy of the new identity." Erikson, however, was speaking chiefly about the rise of totalitarian fanaticism in Hitler's day.[32] Yet his thoughts could be applied in somewhat less volatile circumstances. Self-conscious Yankeeism in contrast to the erring South, antiracism in opposition to a racist society and antiwar in a society indifferent to organized violence also conform to Erikson's statement. Likewise, the stereotyping of enemies such as the lascivious slaveholder, the napalm-making Dow Chemical, the police "pig," was a construction of negative reference symbols for both groups of committed youth.

Each individual radical experienced a somewhat different "identity crisis" and often at widely varying times in their lives. In the cases of Lewis Tappan and Joshua Giddings, for example, psychological blows to self-confidence prior to entry into the all-absorbing, new "identity" of abolitionist crusader occurred

[32] Erikson, *Insight and Responsibility*, 93.

hard upon disasters that threatened their livelihood and their ways of viewing themselves. At the age of thirty-nine, Tappan watched helplessly while his happy world of business enterprise in Boston dissolved. In 1827, he changed his religious beliefs (from Unitarianism to Congregationalist revivalism of a kind which his mother would have approved), his occupation (manufacturer to silk merchant), and his location (from Boston to New York). Relocated emotionally and physically, he felt enabled to refind that special destiny which his mother had assured him was his for the asking (at God's pleasure and mercy).[33]

As a forty-three-year-old Ohio lawyer, Joshua Giddings experienced a similar trauma. Burdened with crushing debts in 1837, Giddings wandered alone by horseback to and then from his ancestral homestead in Connecticut, passed silently by his own house and family in Jefferson, Ohio, where he had been practicing law, and continued all the way to the prairies of Illinois, grieving for his lost sense of purpose. As James B. Stewart has so sensitively explained, Giddings entered the cause of political antislavery radicalism as a result of his personal defeats and despair.[34]

For younger men, the state of depression often occurred simultaneously with doubts about future career as undergraduate life drew to a close or during a postgraduate transitional period. The young radical-to-be knew that whatever he planned for himself could be accomplished, once he had temporarily resolved his feelings of morbid inferiority; the question was: could he reconcile desires to do good with his necessities for steady, secure employment? While trying to find the proper answer, many young Americans, whether radical or not, took up schoolteaching before entering professional work. It paid poorly, but for some, that circumstance added to its attractiveness. Charles Torrey, after leaving Yale, declared, "Perhaps I need the stern trial of poverty to compel me to learn that prudence which nothing else has, in time past, taught me." Elizur Wright was not particularly exceptional in taking up three successive jobs of obvious impermanence – schoolteaching in Massachusetts, tractarian work in Pennsylvania, and college teaching at Western Reserve in Ohio. In each case, Wright, like the modern VISTA or Peace Corps worker, was searching for that call which could command his soul, serve his

[33] Wyatt-Brown, *Lewis Tappan*, 17-55.
[34] Stewart, *Joshua R. Giddings*, 16-17, 24-33.

need to serve the world, and bring order to a fragmented, fast-changing society.[35]

It is worth noting that temporary employment as colporteur, welfare worker, teacher, or missionary among alien peoples involves a physical uprooting, a break with suburban or hometown setting, though not with contemporary society's patterns of mobility. Admittedly, the American missionary impulse can often be a force of tremendous value, but the participant may be involved in more introspective matters than his profession of moral uplift and benefaction indicates. As a tractarian agent, Elizur Wright, for instance, found himself defending his own shaky faith in evangelical religion in a debate with a whiskey-drinking, jolly Irish priest in western Pennsylvania.[36]

At this point the young person was on the threshold of his entry into the radical movement. He has decided *not* to do the ordinary tasks of life. Still relatively free of complex, inhibiting family commitments of his own, he feels the options for welldoing are fairly open. On a negative note, however, the young man or woman has become aware of his basic quarrels with ordinary social standards. He loses rapport with the authorities over him, and a process of alienation begins.

Oftentimes, as Keniston observed, a small college incident, in which the young idealist suffers a slight or receives an allegedly unjust punishment from an unfeeling bureaucracy, sparks a series of disillusioning circumstances. Stephen S. Foster, for instance, was arrested for refusing militia duty while attending Dartmouth College in the late 1830s. Later, Union Theological Seminary officials refused him accommodations for holding an antiwar prayer meeting. Foster turned away from ministerial studies, but not from the moral imperative.[37] Incidents more removed from direct personal experience may also serve as a catalyst for disenchantment. "I was really convinced Johnson would [stop the war]," a Vietnam Summer radical told Keniston. "The bombings of February, 1965, were a real shake-up for me. I went to bed for two days. It seemed to me to utterly close that door. . . ."[38]

[35]Lovejoy, *Memoir of Torrey*, 30; French, "The Conversion of an American Radical," 71-95.

[36]*Ibid.*, 90-91.

[37]"Stephen S. Foster," *DAB*, VI: 558.

[38]Keniston, *Young Radicals*, 124; see also Charles Hampden-Turner, *Radical Man: The Process of Psycho-Social Development* (Cambridge, 1970), 361-364, a study, like Keniston's, with strong sympathies for the radical viewpoint.

While abolitionists and New Leftists often spoke of these revelations as decisive moments, commitment was a process, a fact which scholars have often noted in regard to the similar experience of religious conversion. Therefore, interplay of forces within and without him propelled the recruit toward increasing identification with his new associates. One or two elder brethren function as charismatic figures and around them a community spirit begins to emerge. Having left western Pennsylvania to founder in its sins, Elizur Wright joined the staff of Western Reserve College, where Beriah Green and Charles Storrs, his faculty colleagues, encouraged his growing radicalism. Bitter that the nearby church fathers had rejected his application for ministerial license, Wright found new purpose in antislavery and he discovered in these older, reform-minded clergymen satisfactory subjects for radical emulation.[39] They provided him with examples of courage in the face of local intransigence, moral leadership, and intellectual and oratorical talents – all of which were dedicated to spreading the message of Garrisonian immediatism. Robert Moses, Mario Savio, Staughton Lynd, Tom Hayden, and many others have also provided models for action in displays of fortitude against institutional brutality and public ridicule. Theodore Weld, leader of the famous Lane Seminary Rebels, was the most notable example in abolitionist circles of this function.[40]

The new "family" of radical converts with its nucleus of "surrogate" fathers, encouraged a sublimation of self which quickly became almost a justification of the work undertaken. Antislavery gatherings radiated with that happy, soul-stirring spiritual electricity, similar to that of the successful revival or, in recent days, of a few of the rock festivals. Lydia Maria Child recalled that in the early 1830s "mortals were never more sublimely forgetful of self" than the harmonious body of abolitionists.[41] The feelings of familial trust and spirit of high honor, formerly found in their parents' households, appear to the radical as a new truth of social relations, contrasting vividly with the outer world of isolated, self-conscious, pluralistic, and selfish groups of men.

Perhaps it is natural in times of social tension for high value to

[39] Keniston, *Young Radicals*, 135-140; French, "The Conversion of an American Radical," 92-93, 96-163, 164.

[40] Thomas, *Theodore Weld*, 70-99, 117-121.

[41] Lydia Maria Child to Theodore Weld, July 10, 1880, in the Theodore Dwight Weld MSS, William L. Clements Library, Ann Arbor, Michigan.

be placed upon the harmony and sharing of good and ill of a synthetic community. Certainly Victorians seemed to make sense of their world of shifting economic and social patterns by stressing the more orthodox and sentimental elements of child, familial, and marital love. Mathew Arnold's lines: "Ah, love, let us be true to one another!/ For the world . . . hath really neither joy, nor love, nor light,/ No certitude, nor peace, nor help for pain" reflected this anxious yearning for security through sexual love that the outer world of "ignorant armies clashing in the night" made so difficult to realize. Radicals may discover in their work for the "cause" a sufficient satisfaction of their need for mutuality, but many seek more formal ties. Thus, in both antebellum and modern periods, cooperative enterprises and communitarian experiments flourished, based upon the assumed social failures of competition and upon the presumed superior character of radical inner life. Nagging doubts about the new, self-conscious style of communitarianism are not wholly dispelled, but dramatic moments that evoke a sense of solidarity make the prospects seem bright.

Essential to the continued existence of the radical unit is the process of setting its boundaries, for inclusiveness of those "reborn," so to speak, depends upon the exclusion of the unregenerate. Abolitionists, for example, turned with a fury born of disenchantment against the gradualist liberals of the colonization effort, denying them any claim to good intentions. Likewise, modern attacks upon the Old Left and Liberal generation are as harsh as those against outright reactionaries. Gradualism, history, tradition, and the institutions supporting them have to be repudiated not only to justify legitimate complaint but also to separate the radical "Elect" or saving remnant from outsiders closest to it in theory. Estrangement from the old and commitment to the new place attitudes in polar distinctions: immediatism against evolutionary progress; hope against despair; utopia against static corruption; democracy against tyranny; universal love against particularistic bigotry.

Armed with these formulations, the young radical measures all things accordingly. Disfellowship with "Christian" slaveholding sinners and dissociation of universities with war-making interests are demands that charge a universality of social sin with no allowance for discriminations. To make these breaks with alleged iniquity, it is claimed, is to lead immediately to total purity through "come-outerism." Minor discrepancies between practice and ideal assume as sinister a character as major failings. The least of sins becomes the symbol for the greatest of them. Time and again abolitionists and New Leftists seized upon insubstantial relationships and converted them into representative instances of national crime. The swift leap from the particular (Dow recruiter on campus or southern preacher in northern pulpit) to the general (militarist or proslavery society) is a necessary function of radicalism itself, but resentment of the moral arrogance implicit in the logic of totality is inevitable.

Not surprisingly then, the final seal of commitment comes hard upon signs of an uncomprehending and equally undiscriminating public reaction. Lewis Tappan and most other abolitionists were not really "root and branch" zealots until they had to face howling mobs. Silvan Tomkins has explained the psychic procedure, noting that strength of character often grows out of persecution. Again, it must be emphasized that radicals are still well within the range of normal behavior (although their perceptions of reality may, like those of their angriest opponents, seem hopelessly distorted when the fevers of emotion subside). This stage may possibly indicate maturity, yet, in a field of work in which certainty of conviction is constantly tested by the fires of popular condemnation.[42] In any case, the "call," once so vital to ministerial vocations, is now located in the "Cause," one demanding hardship, poverty, even martyrdom. For a man who has suffered anguish over his role in life, his relation to idealistic but imperfect parents, his distrust of conventional authority, and his own misgivings about his special worthiness or depravity, and his unstilled fears that community love will not change the world at large, it is most gratifying to believe that the new role promises release from all doubts – the unity of experience and ideal which conventional society could never supply.

At the same time, rejection of the prejudices and mores of middle-class culture is matched by a self-created affinity for what are deemed the hopes, life, and troubles of those groups excluded from that culture. "Revolutionary consciousness," said Gregory Calvert of SDS in 1967, "leads to the struggle for one's own freedom in unity with others who share the burden of oppres-

[42] Silvan S. Tomkins, "The Psychology of Commitment: The Constructive Role of Violence and Suffering for the Individual and for His Society," in Martin Duberman (ed.), *The Antislavery Vanguard: New Essays on the Abolitionists* (Princeton, 1965), 270-298.

sion."[43] Abolitionists urged each other to feel as if bound with those in bonds. "Purified" by the purges of repression themselves, radicals assume that persecution ennobles its victims. Empathy encourages a sense of guilt, because the white visionary cannot genuinely suffer in exactly the same fashion as "the poor slave" or ghetto black or Asian peasant. As a result, severely distorted typologies of doubtful accuracy appear in radical rhetoric – "Third World," N.L.F. fighters for freedom; humble, Christian slaves; courageous fugitives. Again, discriminations disappear so that identifications with the oppressed are imaginable.

Inevitably, this kind of cosmology renders solutions almost impossible to achieve. The absence of clear program may actually be shrewd policy, for it permits flexibility and frees the agitator to respond viscerally to circumstance. Abolitionists admitted that "immediate emancipation" was not a plan, but a doctrine. Implementations would arise, they said, to meet the demands of an aroused public. Modern radical dogma is equally negative and unstructured, in marked contrast to the 1930s Marxists' theory. Howard Zinn accurately explained: "It is the spirit, not the letter, of Marxism that the New Left upholds – not a fixed body of dogma," but rather a criticism of modern life which encompassed "a vague but exhilarating vision of the future" and stressed "an approach to life – a particular way of thinking about thinking as well as about being." The aim is "to promote action."[44] Both these modern and early national forms of radicalism are struggles of the spirit. They are not revolutionary programs at all, since they leave problems of implementing their revolutionary aims to others – by default. Revolutionary action must always be a struggle for *power*, not moral regeneration alone unless it promotes the means to that power. Conversions under the American radical rubric are bound to be limited to those with a need for this kind of spiritual satisfaction. Many may agree about the urgency for improving existing conditions, but not about the necessity for a new economic, social, and spiritual order as radicals claim. As a result, the American radical is doomed to the prophet's traditionally lonely role.

The speculations offered herein suggest that present unrest,

[43] Gregory Calvert in Massimo Teodori (ed.), *The New Left: A Documentary History* (Indianapolis, 1969), 415.

[44] Howard Zinn, "Marxism and the New Left," in Alfred F. Young (ed.), *Dissent: Explorations in the History of American Radicalism* (De Kalb, Illinois, 1968), 360.

especially on the nation's campuses, will result in no completion of the revolution *manqué* that the abolitionists began. It must be remembered that antislavery purists did not arouse a northern constituency for a holy war against slavery in the old states. Charles Beard's economic analysis may have been overly simple, but, as Eugene Genovese has explained, slavery was economically incompatible with industrial, commercial, and agricultural free labor.[45] The Civil War was a struggle for economic and political unification, analogous to that of Germany and Italy, in which southern agrarian elites capitulated to aggressive northern capitalism. The Union army and Republican party policies, not the abolitionist forces, destroyed slavery as a necessary reordering of power. The slave moved from bondage to serfdom, as he usually has throughout the history of the institution. Radical idealists were instrumental in the complex evolution of northern and southern polarity; their influence as polemical watchdogs continued through war and Reconstruction, as James McPherson has shown, but the utopian new world of racial brotherhood remained an unfulfilled dream.[46]

Like the antebellum agitators, modern radicals seek only to reach those within their cultural milieu. Although antihistorical in aims and approach, they are bound by the chains of their own past. "From the bourgeoisie," declared one radical, "you have come, and to them you shall go." [47] Efforts to collaborate with white workers and downtrodden ethnic minorities have not enjoyed much more than temporary success here and there. Garrisonians were separated from poor whites and blacks, but, as Benjamin Quarles has wisely observed, even the northern free-Negro abolitionists found it difficult to cooperate with even the most egalitarian abolitionists.[48] In that more paternalistic age, with its emphasis upon conformity of dress and decorum, abolitionists seldom felt it necessary to break with custom as a way of showing solidarity with the poor. But simulated poverty by style of hair and clothes cannot disguise the gap between the educational radical "elite"—the children of the establishment—and

[45] Eugene D. Genovese, *The Political Economy of Slavery* (New York, 1965).

[46] James M. McPherson, *The Struggle for Equality: Abolitionists and the Negro in the Civil War and Reconstruction* (Princeton, 1964).

[47] Shelley Blum, "Middle Class Professional Unions," pamphlet 68-1,258, in the State Historical Society of Wisconsin Library.

[48] Benjamin Quarles, *Black Abolitionists* (New York, 1969), 49-50, 235.

the traditional bases of revolution, the worker-peasant classes. Instead, stress is given to the "politicizing" of middle-class institutions, especially the universities and colleges, just as abolitionists sought the same moral goal for the national churches. Echoing Garrison's demands for a "true church" of "integrity and purity," Tom Hayden in equally romantic terms declared that the Columbia radicals wanted "a new and independent university standing against the mainstream of American society, or they want no university at all."[49] Such dreams have little place in the search for genuine power that must animate the true revolutionary.

We return to the original point. Americans love to preach, to clothe their personal fears and aspirations in the language of the apocalypse, to stage battles between the forces of good and evil, "to make the world safe for democracy," and, in the words of Carl Oglesby, SDS president in 1965, to "change the system that needed slaves in the first place and could 'emancipate' them only into ghettos in the second . . . to liberate for the conquest of joy . . . to go inside yourself first to rediscover the feeling of your own possible freedom, and from there to the feeling of the possible freedom of others."[50] The community of the alienated faithful – an "elect" that rejects all compromises and complicities – strenously believes in a cosmology embracing all men, all institutions, a vision impossible to achieve, but essential to proclaim if the American covenant is to survive.

It is the tragedy and also the hope of the American experience in its age-old search for meaning that radical sentiments and experimentations should arise and have their influence upon events. The climax of radical frustration is yet to come, but declension of religious zeal and yearnings for order and tranquility have always followed in the cycle of human affairs. At some point, the temple must empty, the participant – refreshed, worried, bored, touched, and exasperated – must turn home to the humdrum and familiar, remembering sadly that the dreams of youth become the broken promises of maturity.

FOR FURTHER READING

Curry, Richard O., ed. *The Abolitionists: Reformers or Fanatics?* New York: Holt, Rinehart and Winston, 1965. (Rev. ed., 1973.)

[49] Tom Hayden in Teodori (ed.), *The New Left,* 346.
[50] Carl Oglesby in *ibid.,* 450.

Davis, David B., ed. *Ante-Bellum Reform.* New York: Harper and Row, Publishers, 1967.

Dillon, Merton. *Elijah P. Lovejoy, Abolitionist Editor.* Urbana: University of Illinois Press, 1961.

Duberman, Martin B., ed. *The Abolitionist Vanguard: New Essays on the Abolitionists.* Princeton: Princeton University Press, 1965.

Horowitz, David; Lerner, Michael; and Pyes, Craig, eds. *Counterculture and Revolution.* New York: Random House, 1972.

Keniston, Kenneth. *Youth in Dissent: The Rise of a New Opposition.* New York: Harcourt Brace Jovanovich, 1971.

Lukas, J. Anthony. *Don't Shoot – We Are Your Children!* New York: Random House, 1971.

Oates, Stephen B. *To Purge This Land with Blood: A Biography of John Brown.* New York: Harper and Row, Publishers, 1970.

Thomas, John L. *The Liberator: William Lloyd Garrison, A Biography.* Boston: Little, Brown and Company, 1963.

Wyatt-Brown, Bertram. *Lewis Tappan and the Evangelical War against Slavery.* New York: Atheneum, 1971.

Zinn, Howard. *SNCC: The New Abolitionists.* Boston: Beacon Press, 1964.

Sources

1

The "Dull Chaos" of Jacksonian Society

In the antebellum period, democracy was advancing, but it exacted a price. The ideal and to some extent the reality of one (white) man being the social equal of all others led to some discomfiture, for it rendered the acquisition of wealth the sole standard of distinctiveness in an otherwise "dull chaos" of bustling atoms, to borrow D.H. Lawrence's phrase. Old receptacles of tradition – the church, the "Peaceable Kingdom" of village society, the family, statutes governing moral and social behavior, the geneological tree – lost their power to influence custom and manners. The selection which follows bears some resemblance to the complaints of David Riesman, Paul Goodman, C. Wright Mills, and others about the "other- directed" lives of quiet desperation of the gray-flannel, "silent generation" of the 1950s.

SOURCE: *American Whig Review,* I (January 1845), 95-98.

All strangers who come among us remark the excessive anxiety in the American countenance. It is not poverty, nor tyranny . . . which produces this anxiety; that is clear. It is the concentration of the faculties upon an object, which in its very nature is unattainable – the perpetual improvement of the outward condition. There are no bounds among us to the restless desire to be better off; and this is the ambition of all classes of society. That equality, that breaking down of artificial barriers which has produced this universal and restless activity in America, is destined to prevail throughout the whole earth. Commerce is to become the universal pursuit of men. But while trade is destined to free and employ the masses, it is also destined to destroy for the time much of the beauty and happiness of every land. This has been the result in our own country.

There is no necessity for the custom; but there is a necessity, weakly constituted as men are, that every individual should conform greatly to the prevailing habits of his fellows, and the expectations of the community in and with which he deals. We are all, no matter what our occupations, more or less, and all greatly, sufferers from the excessive stimulus under which every thing is done. We are all worn out with thought that does not develop our thinking faculties in a right direction, and with feeling expended upon poor and low objects.

Blessed beyond any people with the means of living, supplied to an unparalleled extent with the comforts and luxuries of life, our American homes are sombre and cheerless abodes. There is even in the air of comfort . . . something uncomfortable. They are habitations of those who do not live at home. The excessive pursuit of gain begets a secrecy of thought, a contradiction of ideas, a barrenness of interest, which renders its votary any thing but social or companionable. Conversation incessantly takes an anxious and uninteresting turn; and the fireside becomes only a narrower exchange, and the parlor a more private news-room. [In the absence of genuine warmth and cultural sharing], common suspicion of amusements has become one of the most serious evils to which our community is exposed. It makes our places of amusement low, divides the thoughtful and the careless, the grave and the gay, the old and the young, in their pleasures. And thus, too, is originated one of the greatest curses of our social state – the great want of intimacy and confidence between children and their parents, especially between fathers and sons. We are more strict in our morals in these Northern States than anywhere in the world, but it is questionable whether our morality is not of a somewhat inferior quality, and in a too narrow view. It is artificial, conventional. Our virtues are the virtues of merchants, and not of men. We have more conscience than heart, and more propriety than either.

2

The Anguish of an Antislavery Moralist: Elijah P. Lovejoy

For better or worse, America has produced more missionaries than revolutionists, more Garrisons than Lenins. The prophet, not the revolutionary, is the man to reckon with in our national experience. In a free society, even those who call themselves revolutionists become isolated and divided among themselves because of the overwhelming coerciveness, one might say, of the democratic multitude. It is a heedless leviathan more politically powerful than storm troopers, police bullies, or repressive bureaucracies; it is hardly a wonder that the radical loses faith in majoritarianism and despairs of ever raising the moral sights of the people as a whole. In the interest of space, Elijah P. Lovejoy and John Brown, both "martyrs" for black freedom from white democracy, will have to represent radical emancipationism. Divine mission, not "the pursuit of happiness," was their common aim, and in that perseverance they symbolized the courage, nonconformity, and moral vision of the abolitionist host; they also displayed the characteristic absolutism, romanticism, and personal gropings of the modern white agitator:

SOURCE: Joseph C. and Owen Lovejoy, *Memoir of the Rev. Elijah P. Lovejoy; Who Was Murdered in Defence of the Press, at Alton, Illinois, Nov. 7, 1837* (New York: John S. Taylor, 1848), pp.17-19.

Our eldest brother, Elijah Parish Lovejoy, was born at Albion, November 9th, 1802, just thirty-five years previous to the day of his burial. Three brothers preceded him to the grave; three yet live and two sisters. In childhood and youth he manifested the elements of character, which were fully developed in the trials of his last years. He was courageous, firm, and persevering.

When he had once taken a stand, he was sure to maintain it to the utmost of his power. Less than four years were numbered, when he began to exhibit his ruling passion, – an ardent desire for knowledge. At this age he read with fluency in his Bible. His letters were all learned, by his own solicitation, from his mother. He would take his book, go to her, and ask the name of a letter, and then retire to his seat, until he had marked its form, and indelibly fixed it in his memory; and then again to his mother for the name of a new letter. In the same way, he not only learned to read, but acquired much, and varied knowledge. Throughout his youth, the ends of the day saved from the axe, the plough, and the scythe, were all employed in the diligent use of books. When the small theological library of his father was exhausted, he had recourse to a public one, of a more varied character, in the vicinity. The stores of this also by weekly visits, were very soon transferred to his own mind. His memory was uncommonly retentive. While at the sabbath school, his teacher one day remarked to the class, that they might increase their lessons for the next Sabbath. In the leisure hours of the following week, he committed the 119th Psalm, and some twenty or more hymns to go with it. Poetry he drank in like water. By reading any piece of one or two pages twice, he could accurately rehearse it. The writer has heard him repeat one hundred and fifty Hymns from Watts at a single recitation. In all the exercises of the district school of which he was a member, he evinced decided superiority. One of his mates lately remarked, that it was impossible to do more than gain a place *next* the head, for he that was there could not only spell the words, but also pronounce them in their order without the book. When the school was divided by what is called "choosing sides," his name was always first heard.

Nor was he first in the school-room only. He engaged with great zest in all the sports of his early companions. Swimming was our weekly, and almost daily amusement. A very considerable portion of the bottom of the lake, we have before mentioned was visited, in a competition to see who should *dive* the greatest number of feet. Mud or clams was the only evidence admitted as proof that the effort had been successful. A depth of twelve or fifteen feet was often reached in this dangerous, exhilarating sport. Elijah being once bantered by his companions, swam the whole width of the lake, three fourths of a mile, and back again without stopping.

Under the forming hand of his assiduous mother, with a few months in each year at the district school, the first eighteen years of his life were passed. At this time he set his heart strongly upon obtaining a public education. He spent a single quarter in the Academy at Monmouth; during which he read thoroughly Virgil entire, Cicero, and Sallust. He had studied Latin but two or three weeks previous to this. His preparatory studies were continued at intervals in China Academy; and he entered a sophomore, in Waterville College, September, 1823.

3

Elijah P. Lovejoy, "The Wanderer"

Elijah, like his father, was often given to melancholy, made the more desperate by his inability to profess Christian faith in his teens, the customary point of conversion. After attending college at Waterville and graduating at the top of his class in 1826, he tried teaching school at China, Maine, but the vocation failed to meet his high ambitions for himself. Following a trek to New York City, Lovejoy headed westward by foot, and, by the shores of Lake Erie, he wrote a poem, "The Wanderer," six stanzas of which amply illustrate his state of mind as he sought identity and career.

SOURCE: Joseph C. and Owen Lovejoy, *Memoir of the Rev. Elijah P. Lovejoy; Who Was Murdered in Defence of the Press, at Alton, Illinois, Nov. 7, 1837* (New York: John S. Taylor, 1848), pp. 17-19.

The sun was set, and that dim twilight hour,
Which shrouds in gloom whate'er it looks upon,
Was o'er the world: stern desolation lay
In her own ruins; every mark was gone,
Save one tall, beetling monumental stone.

And on its rifted top the wanderer stood,
And bared his head beneath the cold night air,
And wistfully he gazed upon the flood:
It were a boon to him (so thought he there)
Beneath that tide to rest from every care.

He was a lone and solitary one,
With none to love, and pity he disdained:
His hopes were wrecked, and all his joys were gone;
But his dark eye blanched not; his pride remained:
And if he deeply felt, to none had he complained.

Take heed ye guardians of the youthful mind,
That facile grows beneath your *kindly* care:
'Tis of elastic mould, and, if confined

With too much stress, 'shoots madly from its sphere,'
Unswayed by love, and unrestrained by fear.

Oh! 'tis a fearful *blasting* sight to see
The soul in ruins, withered, rived, and wrung,
And doomed to spend its immortality
Darkling and hopeless, where despair has flung
Her curtains o'er the loves to which it fondly clung.

So thought the wanderer: so, perhaps, he *felt*:
(But this is unrevealed): now he had come
To the far woods, and there in silence knelt
On the sharp flint-stone in the rayless gloom,
And fervently he prayed to find an early tomb.

4

Elijah P. Lovejoy, "My Mother"

Lovejoy's loneliness and undefined discontent were not assuaged even when he took up newspapering in bustling St. Louis. His yearning for a return to the simplicities of adolescence in New England, two thousand miles away, appeared in his poem "My Mother," from which we excerpt two stanzas.

SOURCE: Joseph C. and Owen Lovejoy, *Memoir of the Rev. Elijah P. Lovejoy; Who Was Murdered in Defence of the Press, at Alton, Illinois, Nov. 7, 1837* (New York: John S. Taylor, 1848), p. 37.

My Mother! I am far away
From home, and love, and thee:
And stranger hands may heap the clay
That soon may cover me;

. . .

And should it be my happy lot –
After a life of care and pain,

In sadness spent, or spent in vain –
To go where sighs and sin are not;
'Twill make the half my heaven to be,
My Mother, evermore with thee!"

5

A Letter from Elijah P. Lovejoy to his Parents

Lovejoy's spiritual difficulties diminished in 1832 when at last he reconciled himself to the stern puritanism of his parents and grew more self-confident about his journalism and his ability to resist the temptations of a very unpuritan, southern culture.

SOURCE: Joseph C. and Owen Lovejoy, *Memoir of the Rev. Elijah P. Lovejoy; Who Was Murdered in Defence of the Press, at Alton, Illinois, Nov. 7, 1837* (New York: John S. Taylor, 1848), pp. 38-39.

St. Louis, January 24th, 1832.

My dear and honoured Parents:...

I have never forgotten – it has been the chief source of my consolation, that day and night you have been interceding for me at a Throne of Grace. I have never, for a moment, doubted that paternal affection ceased not to plead for mercy upon the wayward and far distant son. I knew that that love was yours, which neither time nor distance could weaken, and think you, that I should forget the many earnest and agonizing petitions which I have heard ascending from the family altar. Oh, never! I will tell you all. Last spring there was a partial revival of religion in this city. I became somewhat seriously impressed, I may say considerably so. I attended the inquiry meetings, and for some time really felt a delight in religious exercises. But gradually these feelings all left me, and I returned to the world a more hardened sinner than ever. At this time the spirit of God is manifesting itself in our city in a most wonderful manner. Its effects are such as I have never before witnessed. Meetings are held almost every evening, at which individuals of all ages and characters attend, and where the power of God to salvation is manifested, so that the blindest must see and the hardest feel. I have reason to hope that the good spirit has again visited me, inviting me to forsake the world and come to Jesus, I own that I hardly dare admit such a belief, it seems to me scarcely possible that one who has so long lived in sin, who has resisted so much light, and has so often grieved away the Holy Spirit, as I have, should be again visited with its heavenly influences. But I hope it is so.

6

The Bubble Burst

Shortly after writing the letter to his parents in January 1832 Lovejoy attended Princeton Seminary, then returned to St. Louis, where he resumed his journalism as a Presbyterian missionary. Gradually he turned his attention toward slavery and the slave trade in the river town. His blunt editorials raised pro-southern hackles, while his anti-Catholic prejudices infuriated German and Irish residents. Under threat of reprisals, he crossed the Mississippi to nearby Alton, Illinois, and continued his dual crusades, only to die, gun in hand, when a mob of "slavocrats" were about to destroy his press. Five months earlier, during the financial panic of 1837, Lovejoy penned the editorial which appears below. Though lacking the eastern sophistication of our first selection, Lovejoy's piece is a pungent criticism of American dollar-worship and its connection with slavery.

SOURCE: From Alton *Observer*, quoted in Joseph C. and Owen Lovejoy, *Memoir of the Rev. Elijah P. Lovejoy: Who Was Murdered in Defence of the Press, at Alton, Illinois, Nov. 7, 1837* (New York: John S. Taylor, 1848), pp. 188-91.

THE BUBBLE BURST

Alton, May 25th, 1837. . . . Wealth has been the god after which this nation, in the language of Scripture, has gone a whoring. . . . Our 'visions by night' have been of rail-roads, canals, bank stock, sections and quarter sections of land, and town lots. Speculation had become a perfect mania, and we had become a nation of gamblers. . . . But the bubble has burst – and all of our hopes of universal wealth are dissipated into thin air. . . . [We are a nation that] cannot be trusted with riches. . . . The love of money is an earth-born, grovelling propensity, and it debases proverbially all whom it influences. . . . How completely callous to all the dictates of conscience and humanity, and how shamelessly sordid it has rendered this nation. . . . We have seen the traffic in human beings pursued by one portion of our fellow-citizens with an unfeeling and gloatingly avaricious eagerness, which would have made the early Spanish men-hunters of Cuba blush. Husbands and wives, and parents and children have been torn asunder with an utter recklessness of feeling, that equals, to say the least, any thing of cruelty that the annals of savagedom can furnish, and all to make these victims toil and sweat unthanked and unrewarded, in order to enrich their plunderers. But worse than this, tenfold worse, and a thousandfold more alarming, we have seen Christians, not only engaging heart and soul in this horrid business, but christian ministers also, nay reverend divines, doctors of divinity . . . solemnly and officially justifying it, appealing to the Bible – to the gospel of a compassionate Redeemer – to prove it all right, and that it had the divine sanction of Heaven. And scarcely less, if indeed not greater, has been the guilt, the criminal indifference, and often the actual approval, with which these transactions have been witnessed in the free states . . . [The Lord] has come, in his Providence, and taken from us that for which we had sacrificed principle, humanity, duty, and now we find that we have 'filed our consciences' for nothing, and that our only reward is, what it deserved to be – REMORSE.

7

A Revolutionary Prophet: John Brown

John Brown was hardly a typical abolitionist, but he represented the same kind of union of religious conviction and political zealotry, romantic self-concern, and absolutism that seem so important in the Revolutionary Youth Movement II or Weatherman faction of the radical Left. The following letter is a personal reminiscence in the third person that Brown wrote to a young son of a close friend and supporter. Unintentionally, Brown reveals some of the underlying factors that may have led him to become the kind of man he was. He pictures himself as a lonely boy, unable to adjust to the death of his mother, unreconciled to her replacement by his stepmother, who was only eighteen at the time of her marriage to "Squire" Owen Brown. His search for an affection his parents were apparently unable to supply him is evident in his attachment to little toys and pets, the loss of which left him disproportionately inconsolable. Some psychologists have discovered among the cultural revolutionists and the underground extremists similar signs of personal alienation translated into political alienation. This interpretation of Brown does not question Brown's legal sanity, about which older historians debated, but it does suggest that he was a man who projected his unhappiness and personal failures into revolutionary action. Instructors and students may find this diagnosis worth debating. For a somewhat less severe approach to Brown, see *To Purge This Land in Blood* by Stephen Oates (New York, 1970), an able, sober biography.

SOURCE: Franklin B. Sanborn, *The Life and Letters of John Brown, Liberator of Kansas, and Martyr of Virginia* (Boston: Roberts Brothers, 1885), pp. 12-17.

Red Rock, Iowa. 15th, July, 1857.
Mr Henry L Stearns
My Dear Young Friend

I have not forgotten my promise to write you; but my constant care, & anxiety: have obliged me [to] put it off a long time. I do not flatter myself that I *can* write anything that will very much interest you: but have concluded to send you a short story of a certain boy of my acquaintance: & for convenience & shortness of name, I will call him John. This story will be mainly a naration of follies & errors; which it is to be hoped *you may avoid:* but there is one thing connected with it, which will be calculated to encourage any young person to persevereing effort: & that is the degree of success *in accomplishing his objects* which to a great extent marked the course of this boy throughout my entire acquaintance with him; notwithstanding his moderate capacity; & still more moderate acquirements.

John was born May 9th 1800, at Torrington, Litchfield Co. Connecticut; of poor but respectable parents: a decendant on the side of his Father of one of the company of the Mayflower who landed at Plymouth 1620. His Mother was decended from a man who came at an early period to New England from Amsterdam, in Holland. Both his Fathers and his Mothers Fathers served in the war of the revolution: His Fathers Father; died in a barn at New York while in the service, in 1776.

I cannot tell you of anything in the first Four years of Johns life worth mentioning save that at that *early age* he was tempted by Three Large Brass Pins belonging to a girl who lived in the family & *stole them.* In this he was detected by his Mother; & after having a full day to think of the wrong: received from her a thorough whipping. When he was Five years old his Father moved to Ohio; then a wilderness filled with wild beasts, & Indians. During the long journey which was performed in part or mostly with an *Ox team*; he was called on by turns to assist a boy Five years older (who had been adopted by his Father & Mother) & learned to think he could accomplish *smart things* in driving the Cows; & riding the horses. Sometimes he met with Rattle Snakes which were very large; & which some of the company generally managed to kill. After getting to Ohio in 1805 he was for some time rather afraid of the Indians, & of their Rifles: but this soon wore off: & he used to hang about them quite as much as was consistent with good manners: & learned a trifle of their talk. His Father learned to dress Deer Skins & at 6 years old John was installed a young Buck Skin. He was perhaps rather observing as he ever after remembered the entire process of Deer Skin *dressing*; so that he could at any time dress his own leather such as Squirel, Raccoon, Cat, Wolf, or Dog Skins: & also learned to make Whip Lashes: which brought him some change at times; & was of considerable service in many ways. At Six years old John began to be quite a rambler in the wild new country finding birds and Squirels, & sometimes a wild Turkeys nest. But about this period he was placed in the School of *adversity:* which my young friend was a most necessary part of his early training. You may *laugh* when you come to read about it; but these were *sore trials* to John: whose earthly treasures were very *few*, & *small.* These were the beginning of a severe but *much needed course* of dicipline which he afterward was to pass through; & which it is to be hoped has learned him before this time that the Heavenly Father sees it best to take all the little things out of his hands which he has ever placed in them. When John was in his Sixth year a poor *Indian boy* gave him a Yellow Marble the first he had ever seen. This he thought a great deal of; & kept it a good while, but at last *he lost it* beyound recovery. *It took years to heal the wound;* & I *think* he cried at times about it. About Five months after this he caught a young Squirel tearing off his tail in doing it and getting severely bitten at the same time himself. He however held on *to the little bob tail Squirrel;* & finally got him perfectly tamed, so that he almost idolized his pet. *This too he lost;* by its wandering away; or by getting killed: & for a year or Two John was *in mourning;* & looking at all Squirrels he could see to try & discover Bob tail, *if possible.* I must not neglect to tell you of a verry *bad* & *foolish* habbit to which John was somewhat addicted. I mean *telling lies:* generally to screen himself from blame; or from punishment. He could not well endure to be reproached; & I now think had he been oftener encouraged to be entirely frank; by making *frankness a kind of atonement* for some of his faults; he would not have been so often guilty of this fault; nor have been obliged to struggle *so long* in after life with *so mean* a habit.

John was *never quarrelsome;* but was *excessively* fond of the *hardest & roughest* kind of plays; & could *never get enough [of] them.* Indeed when for a short time he was sometimes sent to School the opportunity it afforded to wrestle, & Snow ball, & run, & jump, & knock off old seedy Wool hats; offered to him almost the only compensation for the confinement, & restraints of school. I need not tell you that with such feeling & but little chance of going to school *at all:* he did not become much of a schollar. He would always choose to stay at home & work hard rather than be sent to school; & during the warm season might generally be seen *barefooted, & bareheaded:* with Buckskin Breeches suspended often with one leather strap over his shoulder but sometimes with Two. To be sent off through the wilderness alone to very considerable distances was particularly his delight; & in this he was often indulged so that by the time he was Twelve years old he was sent off more than a Hundred Miles with companies of cattle; & he would have thought his character much injured had he been obliged to be helped in any such job. This was a boyish kind of feeling but characteristic however.

At Eight years old John was left a Motherless boy which loss was complete & permanent for not withstanding his Father again married to a sensible, inteligent, & on many accounts a very estimable woman: *yet he never addopted her in feeling:* but continued to pine after his own Mother for years. This opperated very unfavourably uppon him; as he was both naturally fond of females; & withall extremely diffident; & deprived him of a suitable conne[c]ting link between the different sexes; the want of which might under some circumstances have proved his ruin.

When the war broke out *with England;* his Father soon commenced furnishing the troops with beef cattle, the collecting & driving of which afforded him some opportunity for the chase (on foot) of wild steers, & other cattle through he woods. During this war he had some chance to form his own boyish judgment of *men & measures:* & to become somewhat familiarly acquainted with some who have figured before the country since that time. The effect of what he saw during the war was to so far disgust him with Military affairs that he would neither train, *or drill;* but paid fines; & got along like a Quaker untill his age finally has cleared him of Military duty.

During the war with England a circumstance occurred that in the end made him a most *determined Abolitionist:* & led him to declare, or *Swear: Eternal war* with slavery. He was staying for short time with a very gentlemanly landlord since a United States Marshall who held a slave boy near his own age very active, inteligent, & good feeling; & to whom John was under considerable obligation for numerous little acts of kindness. *The Master* made a great pet of John: brought him to table with his first company; & friends; called their attention to every little smart thing he *said or did:* & to the fact of his being more than a hundred miles from home with a company of cattle alone; while the *negro boy* (who was fully if not more than his equal) was badly clothed, poorly fed; & *lodged in cold weather*: & beaten before his eyes with Iron Shovels or any other thing that came first to hand.

This brought John to reflect on the wretched, hopeless condition, of *Fatherless & Motherless* slave *children*: for such children have neither Fathers or Mothers to protect, & provide for them. He sometimes would raise the question: *is God their Father?*

At the age of Ten years, an old friend induced him to read a little history; & offered him the free use of a good library by; which he acquired some taste for reading: which formed the principle part of his early education: & diverted him in a great measure from bad company. He by this means grew to be very fond of the company, & conversation of old & inteligent persons. He never attempted to dance in his life; nor did he ever learn to know *one* of a pack of *Cards,* from *another.* He learned nothing of Grammer; nor did he get at school so much knowlege of comm[on] Arithmetic as the Four ground rules. This will give you some general idea of the first Fifteen years of his life: during which time he became very strong & large of his age & ambitious to perform the full labour of a man; at almost any kind of hard work. By reading the lives of great, wise, & good men their sayings, & writings; he grew to a dislike of vain & frivolous *conversation* & *persons;* & was often greatly obliged by the kind manner in which older, & more intelligent persons treated him at their houses; & in conversation; which was a great relief on account of his extreme bashfulness.

He very early in life became ambitious to excel in doing anything he undertook to perform. This kind of feeling I would reccommend to all young persons both *male* & *female:* as it will certainly tend to secure admission to the company of the more intelligent; & better portion of every community. By all means endeavour to excel in some laudable pursuit.

I had like to have forgotten to tell you of one of Johns misfortunes which set rather hard on him while a young boy. He had by some means *perhaps* by gift of his Father become the owner of a little Ewe Lamb which did finely till it was about Two Thirds grown; & then sickened & died. This brought another protracted *mourning season*: not that he felt the pecuniary loss so heavily: for that was never his disposition: but so strong & earnest were his atachments.

John had been taught from earliest childhood to "fear God & keep his commandments;" & though quite skeptical he had always by turns felt much serious doubt as to his future well being; & about this time became to some extent a convert to Christianity & ever after a firm believer in the divine authenticity of the Bible. With this book he became very familiar: & possessed a most unusual memory of it[s] entire contents.

Now some of the things I have been *telling of*; were just such as I would reccommend to you: & I would like to know that you had selected those out; & adopted them as part of your own plan of life; & I wish you to have some *deffinite plan.* Many seem to have none: & others never stick to any that do they form. This was not the case with John. He followed up with *tenacity* whatever he set about so long as it answered his general purpose: & hence he rarely failed in some good degree to effect the things he undertook. This was so much the case that he *habitually expected to succeed* in his undertakings. With this feeling *should be coupled*; the consciousness that our plans are right in themselves.

During the period I have named John had acquired a kind of ownership to certain animals of some little value but as he had come to understand that the *title of minors* might be a little imperfect; he had recourse to various means in order to secure a more *independant*; & *perfect* right of property. One of those means was to exchange with his Father for something of far less value. Another was by trading with other persons for something his Father had never owned. Older persons have sometimes found difficulty with *titles*:

From Fifteen to Twenty years old, he spent most of his time working at the Tanner & Curriers trade keeping Bachelors hall; & he officiateing as Cook; & for most of the time as foreman of the establishment under his Father. During this period he found much trouble with some of the bad habits I have mentioned & with some that I have not told you of: His con[s]cience urging him forward with great power in this matter: but his close attention to *business*; & success in its management: together with the way he got along with a company of men, & boys; made him quite a favorite with the serious & more inteligent portion of older persons. This was so much the case; & secured for him so many little notices from those he esteemed; that his vanity was very much fed by it; & he came forward to manhood quite full of self conceit; & self confident: notwithstanding his *extreme* bashfulness. A younger brother used sometimes to remind him of this: & to repeat to him *this expression* which you may somewhere find; "A King against whom there is no rising up." The habit so early formed of being obeyed rendered him in after life too much disposed to speak in an imperious or dictating way. From Fifteen years & upward he felt a good deal of anxiety to learn; but could only read, & studdy a little; both for want of time; & on account of inflamation of the eyes. He however managed by the help of books to make himse[lf] tolerably well acquainted with common Arithmetic; & Surveying; which he practiced more or less after he was Twenty years old.

At a little past Twenty years led by his own inclination & *prompted also* by his Father he married a *remarkably plain*; but neat industrious & economical girl; of excellent character; earnest piety; & good practical common sence; about one year younger than himself. This woman by her mild, frank, & *more than all else*: by her very consistent conduct; acquired; & ever while she lived maintained a most powerful; and good influence over him. Her plain but kind admonitions generally had the right effect; without arousing his haughty obstinate temper. John began early in life to discover a great liking to fine Cattle, Horses, Sheep; & Swine; & as soon as circumstances would enable him he began to be a practical *Shepherd: it being* a calling for which *in early life* he had a kind of *enthusiastic longing*: together with the idea that as a business it bid fair to afford him the means of carrying out his greatest or principle object. I have now given you a kind of general idea of the early life of this boy; & if I believed it would be worth the trouble; or afford much interest to any good feeling person; I might be tempted to tell you something of his course in after life; or manhood. I do not say that I *will do it*. . . .

Your Friend
J Brown

8

John Brown as Father

John Brown's adult life was even more full of travail, mischance, and dashed hopes than his boyhood. He sired twenty children by two wives, but of these a number died under horrible circumstances – a baby by an accidental scalding, several by wasting diseases, one by murder in retribution for Brown's Pottowatomie "massacre" of proslavery partisans in the Kansas war of 1856, two by federal bullets at Harpers Ferry. Though he loved his offspring, his parental demand for obedience was excessive. John Brown, Jr., described how he was once forced to "settle" his disciplinary accounts.

SOURCE: Franklin B. Sanborn, *The Life and Letters of John Brown, Liberator of Kansas, and Martyr of Virginia* (Boston: Roberts Brothers, 1885), pp. 92-93.

We went into the upper or finishing room, and after a long and tearful talk over my faults, he again showed me my account, which exhibited a fearful footing up of *debits*. I had no credits or off-sets, and was of course bankrupt. I then paid about *one-third* of the debt, reckoned in strokes from a nicely-prepared blue-beech switch, laid on "masterly." Then, to my utter astonishment, father stripped off his shirt, and, seating himself on a block, gave me the whip and bade me "lay it on" to his bare back. I dared not refuse to obey, but at first I did not strike hard. "Harder!" he said; "harder, harder!" until he *received the balance of the account*. Small drops of blood showed on his back where the tip end of the tingling beech cut through. Thus ended the account and settlement, which was also my first practical illustration of the Doctrine of the Atonement.

9

A Letter Written in the Shadow of the Gallows

If financial debts were also to be reckoned by the same logic, then John Brown was indeed in dire need of atoning for his sins. His efforts to provide for his large brood never met with success; the family was often near destitution, owing mainly to Brown's compulsive overexpectations, lack of business sense, and ill-luck. Debts and lawsuits pursued him relentlessly. There would appear to be a psychological connection between his preoccupation to make good in the moral sense exhibited in the incident with his son and his Harpers Ferry venture – itself an atonement for an undistinguished past and a capital "investment" in future glory that would erase all "debits." His choice of language in a letter to his wife while awaiting the gallows was revealing.

SOURCE: Oswald Garrison Villard, *John Brown 1800-1859 A Biography Fifty Years After* (Boston: Houghton Mifflin, 1910), pp. 540-41.

Charlestown Jefferson Co. Va. 10th Nov. 1859.

My Dear devoted Wife

I have just learned from Mr. Hoyt of Boston that he saw you with dear kind friends in Philadelphia on your return trip you had so far made in the expectation of again seeing me in this world of "sin & sorrow." I need not tell you that I had a great desire to see you again: but that many strong objections exist in my mind against it. I have before alluded to them in what I have said in my other letters (which I hope you will soon get) & will not now repeat them; as it is exceedingly laborious for me to write at all. I am under renewed obligation to you my ever faithful & beloved wife, for heeding what may be my last but earnest request. I have before given you a very brief statement of the fall of our dear sons; & other friends. Full particulars relating to our disaster; I cannot now give: & may never give *probably*. I am greatly comforted by learning of the kindness already shown you; & allow me *humbly* to repeat the language of a far greater man & better sinner than I. "I have been young; & now am old: yet have I not seen the righteous forsaken nor his seed begging bread." I will here say that the sacrifizes *you*; & I, have been called to make in behalf of the *cause we love* the *cause of God; & of humanity*: do not seem to me as at all too great. I have been *whiped* as the saying *is*; but am sure I can recover all the lost capital occasioned by that disaster; by only hanging a few moments by the neck; & I feel quite determined to make the utmost possible out of a defeat. I am dayly & hourly striving to gather up what little I may from the wreck. I mean to write you as *much & as often* as I have Strength (or may be permitted to write.) "Be of good cheer:" in the world we must have tribulation: but the *cords* that have bound *you* as well as I; to earth: have been many of them severed already. Let us with sincere gratitude receive all that "our Father in Heaven" may send us; for "he doeth all things well." . . .

Your affectionate Husband, John Brown

10

Educational Demands

Romanticism about politics also extended to romanticism about education. The late 1960s witnessed the proliferation of "free universities" – free of all but minimal tuition, free of grades, and free of traditional themes. Socially "relevant" topics were the usual fare, but traditional schools quickly met the competition with comparable courses – with credit. Most experiments, many of them torn by internal dissensions, quickly vanished. David I. Bruck made a case for applying the "free university" concept to Harvard University. His argument reflected typical distrust of academic procedures and, to a degree, the process of study itself. Student agitations have often led to expressions of dissatisfaction with grades and instruction, and calls for reform are invariably justified in political terms. Curiously enough, some Harvard students in the rebellious 1830s accompanied a boisterous riot against academic pedantry with demands for the same goals as Bruck advocates, an end to competitive examinations and a restructuring of student-faculty relations.

SOURCE: *Harvard Crimson*, April 28, 1969. Reprinted with permission from Harvard Crimson, Inc.

The following proposes that we all refuse to write our final exams this Spring. The goal of such an exam boycott would be to attack the system of exams and grades which comprises the present academic structure. This would be done because the academic system here does not serve our interests as students and as people, but is in fact opposed to those interests. . . . When the school is considered as a center for training rather than for information, then the function of grades and exams assumes a new importance. In the conventional view, exams are no more than a technique for insuring that students learn things that they need to know, and grades encourage students to learn those things. But if schools are primarily designed as teaching models of modern economic enterprises, then grades become the hard coin of the scholastic marketplace. Students learn to sell their labor for money by selling their labor for grades. Exactly as in an office or factory, the school encourages students not to think about the intrinsic pleasure or displeasure of the work that they are required to do, but to respond solely to the easily controllable incentive system provided by the authorities.

The abolition of grades would . . . have a number of very beneficial effects. The first is that it would greatly facilitate learning. It seems reasonable to expect that students would learn a great deal more if they were able to pursue their own intellectual interests within a rational academic framework. Of course, the kind of studying that now precedes examinations would be a thing of the past, but it is unlikely that students learn very much by cramming, and it is certain that this kind of studying can only atrophy a student's capacity for thought. [Moreover] critical thought cannot flourish in a hierarchical academy whose organization faithfully mirrors the present economic organization of society. Grades can force people to study national income or genetics or Shakespeare, but they militate against the study of a new, humane society. . . . Exams are the most personally humiliating and meaningless situations that the academic system imposes on the individual student. . . . There are so many things to do in the next month that are more valuable and useful than cramming for exams.

11

Harvard Under Siege, April, 1969
Peter Kramer on the Occupation of University Hall

On April, 1969, a large contingent of students led by members of SDS occupied University Hall, removed deans and personnel, and rifled desks and files for evidence of Harvard's connections with the "imperialistic" system. Some of these letters appeared later in the columns of the *Old Mole*, a radical campus paper. Some occupied the Hall as a youthful spring prank, but others were more serious and dedicated. On April 10, President Nathan Pusey and other Harvard administrators and advisers called the Cambridge police to clear the building and restore order. A score or so of students were hurt, but no serious or permanent injuries resulted from the police action. Nevertheless, student and faculty reaction was generally one of dismay, particularly since this unprecedented use of outside police forces in Harvard Yard had been decided without prior faculty consultation. The SDS occupiers issued the following demands which displayed these characteristics typical of student activism elsewhere: (1) an identification of the particular (ROTC on campus) with the abstract (Harvard responsibility for imperialistic government policies); (2) demands for immediate amnesty, which, in a sense, required the perpetuation of *in loco parentis* paternalism and indulgence; and (3) a naive belief that the legal complexities involved in the demands were subject to easy solution through mass actions. "We have taken University Hall. Our demands are: Abolish ROTC; Replace ROTC scholarships with the equivalent Harvard scholarships. Unnegotiable, no student-Faculty committees, no handing in bursars cards [punishment for occupiers]. The Corporation [Harvard governing body] can issue a statement when they give in. The Corporation is also engaged in an attack on the people of Cambridge by kicking them out of their homes in order to transform the city into a military and research center for imperialism. We also demand that the following egregious actions be stopped: Rent rises in University owned apartments be rolled back to the level of January 1, 1968. University Road apartments not be torn down to make room for Harvard Medical School expansion. We have taken University Hall. Our movement will lose unless students who support us act now. Our strength lies in masses of students. Join Us."

A sign of the inner turmoil with which young Leftists contended as they participated in demonstrations and meetings is quite apparent in the broadside that appeared after the University Hall bust at Harvard. A mixture of local and academic issues and psychological feelings – not wider aims for social change – made up the bulk of reasons for striking (i.e., not attending classes). The broadside is evidence for Peter Kramer's skepticism: "Strike for the eight demands Strike because you hate the cops strike because your roommate was clubbed strike to seize control of your life strike to become more human strike to return Paine Hall scholarships strike because there's no poetry in your lectures strike because classes are a bore strike to smash the Corporation strike to make yourself free strike to abolish ROTC strike because they are trying to squeeze the life out of you strike."

Peter D. Kramer, a brilliant undergraduate, wrote the following piece for the *Harvard Crimson.* He showed an unusual awareness of the confusion of aims and feelings and of the impermanence and doubtful value of communitarianism in the excitement of occupying University Hall.

SOURCE: Peter D. Kramer, "I Am Frightened (Yellow); I Am Saddened (Blue)." *Harvard Crimson*, April 26, 1969, pp. 3-4. Reprinted with permission from Harvard Crimson, Inc.

I left the romantics [in University Hall] because they were happy. If I had felt that the painful jolt of the occupation might have the power to open people's lives, I could have stayed. But the enjoyment of the jolt itself, the aesthetic pleasure of rebellion, is a horrifying thought. For it is unanswerable; there is no return. The Faculty can rap on love and the Corporation [governing body of Harvard] can let the poor clip its coupons, all to no avail. Grant what concession you will, unless you turn American society upside-down and free the consciousness from the tyranny of the corporate state – and maybe not even after that – there is no answer to a man who enjoys his act of rebellion, who says isn't-it-wonderful-look-at-the-art-and-music-it's-inspiring-o-hear-people-communicate-o-dammit-I-feel-free. What do you concede to a man who has no demands? . . . True, the SDS politicos had no sense of humor. And, true, it was only when you explained the situation to yourself, not when you listened to their speeches, that their demands sounded proportional to the means they used. But the cops would probably come, so the situation would cease to be humorous, and your means would be dwarfed by the enemy's means. . . . This type of romanticism provides no plateaus where we can stop and rest. If it does not succeed entirely, it will have entirely failed; and the irate alumni will be right – we will have disrupted a great university to lengthen our spring vacation.

For this no one deserves amnesty. The CRIMSON has argued in part that those who occupied University Hall should be pardoned because they raised important issues; they pricked our political conscience. And indeed now that the Faculty says they have coped with student demands and thus rectified wrongs, they may find it difficult to punish the demonstrators.

But someone who stayed in the building for romantic goals rather than political goals is making an unfair appeal. He is asking amnesty on grounds distantly analogous to civil disobedience when he is in fact advocating a general change in life-style. The Faculty may feel guilty about its political role, but it is unfair to plead to that conscience when you want it to feel guilty about its life style in general. . . . To tell a professor that you occupied University Hall to free his life style is insulting and saddening. And, if you can't cope with the whole atmosphere of the place ("because they are trying to squeeze the life out of you") . . . you could leave. . . . My own guess is that even the most devoted romantic found the past two weeks taxing, even boring. You get nervous, you can't be alone when you walk the streets, you hear someone mention "confrontation" or "sincerity" and you want to put your hands on your ears and run and run and run. I believe it was George Orwell who said that the problem with socialism is that it takes up too many weekday nights. Well, the problem with campus disorder is that it takes up twenty-four hours a day. After a certain point, it's not enjoyable. . . .

Revolution, because it requires the concerted action of large numbers of people . . . is necessarily an institution, one which can be as stifling as a corporation. . . . My guess is also that most people voted to return to classes because they were tired of striking. I would guess, too, that the first stadium meeting might have voted to suspend the strike if God hadn't sent us such a beautiful spring day. . . . Something there was in me that was disturbed by the happiness which came before the bust. I wanted to stay; I wanted that clean feeling of opposing cops. I might very well have left for another reason; I left for this one.

12

Harvard Under Siege — SDS, Right and Left

Despite the temporary feeling of solidarity at University Hall, radicals lost little time quarreling with themselves. The Progressive Labor faction of Students for a Democratic Society offered this analysis of their allegedly less dedicated, less demanding rivals of the New Left caucus. The broadside, which appeared in the Cambridge streets sometime in April, 1969, revealed some understanding of the problem of elitism and cultural shackling among middle-class radicals.

SOURCE: Quoted by Stephen Kelman, *Push Comes to Shove: The Escalation of Student Protest* (Boston: Houghton Mifflin, 1970), pp. 138-39.

Many of us became radicals in the first place for mixed reasons: On the one hand we were angry about the war, about racism, about the countless vicious acts we saw around us. But on the other hand, we viewed America as one great wasteland, a big, monstrous, mechanized, air-conditioned desert, a place without roots or feeling. We saw the main problem, really, as: THE PEOPLE – the ways they thought and acted towards each other. We imagined a great American desert, populated by millions of similar, crass, beer-drinking grains of sand, living in a waste of identical suburban no-places. What did this imagined "great pig-sty of TV-watchers" correspond to in real life? As "middle class" students, we learned that this was the working class – the "racist, insensitive people." Viewing things from this highly self-righteous stand, we saw the people as conformist, unaesthetic, puritanical, completely incapable of understanding our sensitivities. (By comparison, the rich at least appeared sensitive.) Even some of our apparent support for Black People stemmed from considering them to be wild romantics, living totally outside society – heroically standing apart, as we ourselves wished to stand apart.

The alienation which brought us into the movement, then, was strictly a mixed bag. While involving real anger over oppression, which obviously is good, it also involved a lot of anti-worker attitudes. When white, "middle-income" students join SDS these two attitudes often are intermixed.

Actually, part of our "radicalization" involved aspiring to something like the POSITION inhabited by the rulers. *The wish was to escape (as they can) to beautiful dreams, to stick one's tongue out with impunity at the great, unthinking mass.* The right-wing of SDS plays to this bad aspect of student radicalism. They say that "alienation is a stage students go through and we must get them where they're at!"

In fact, these bad attitudes are no "stage" but an obstacle, which must be defeated in people or it will turn ours into a reactionary movement. . . .

In effect, in organizing the right-wing of SDS says to students: *You can coddle your hate-the-people escape wish, you can serve yourself. You* can join "THE MOVEMENT" and STRIKE A REVOLUTIONARY POSE, and it's alright!

13

Harvard Under Siege —A Letter from Lance Buhl

The author of the following reminiscence of events at Harvard after the seizure of University Hall was a leading figure in the effort to reconcile the various student factions and work toward responsible reforms, including the abolition of ROTC on the campus. Lance Buhl, then Master of Winthrop House and Instructor in History, chaired the famous Stadium rally in which 10,000 students participated. He is currently an Assistant Professor at Cleveland State University as well as Assistant Dean of the College of Arts and Sciences.

SOURCE: Letter, September 24, 1971, in author's possession, reprinted by permission of Lance Buhl.

The parallel between today's radicals and the abolitionists is fascinating, especially because of the religious phenomenology that links their behavior and attitudes about themselves and their worlds. Particularly interesting is the "conversion" experience, a notion that very well fits the concept of "identity crisis"; it demands of the new believer recurring professions of faith or public testimonial. There was a great deal of that kind of religious behavior observable on the Harvard campus in April, 1969. Even the act of listening to radical speakers and assenting to their remarks with punctuated phrases like "right on!" become something more than a passive act in the atmosphere of the "revival" SDS meeting. Perhaps the revival aspect helps to explain the very peculiar identification of White radicals with Blacks; certainly guilt alone does not account for it. The attempt to associate with the unself-conscious revivalistic spirit and tone of much of the Black movement may help White kids to shed some of their more natural reserve, making essentially anti-intellectual professions and yea-saying easier to indulge in.

14

Radical Violence as Rhetoric and Symbol

In late 1969 and 1970, the occupation of university buildings gave way to arson, bombings, and mass "trashing" expeditions against banks, local storekeepers, and large industrial headquarters. Though typical of the detonations elsewhere, the destruction of the Army Mathematical Research Center on the University of Wisconsin's Madison campus in August, 1970, was the most tragic. A graduate student was killed when the truck bearing the explosives blew up near the entrance to the Physics Building where the AMRC was housed. The bombers, like most members of the Weathermen Underground, are still at large. Their communiqué demonstrates the totalism of radical thinking in its most extreme form. The inclusion of a reform of parietal rules for women students among the "demands" is a rather telling example of the sense of proportion of the Wisconsin "New Years Gang."

SOURCE: *Madison Kaleidoscope, Extra* (Madison, Wisconsin), August 25, 1970.

Today (24 August) the battle cry against imperialism was raised once again, as the mathematics research center of the U.S. army was struck by revolutionary cadres of the New Years gang.

The AMRC, a think-tank of Amerikan militarism, was a fitting target for such revolutionary violence. As the major U.S. army center for solving military mathematical problems, it bears full responsibility for amerikan military genocide throughout the world. . . .

Today's (24 August) explosion was the culmination of over a year's effort to remove AMRC's ominous presence from the Wisconsin campus. Previous efforts to even negotiate were met with indifference. . . . Our actions, therefore, were deemed necessary, for with every passing day, the AMRC takes its toll in mutilated bodies.

We see our achievement as more than just the destruction of one building. We see it as part of a world-wide struggle to defeat amerikan imperialism, that monster which is responsible for the starvation and oppression of millions over the globe, that monster which is a direct outgrowth of corporate capitalism. . . .

The Vanguard of the Revolution demands the immediate release of the

Milwaukee 3, the abolition of ROTC, and the elimination of the male supremacist women's hours on the Wisconsin campus. If these demands are not met by October 30th, revolutionary measures of an intensity never before seen in this country will be taken by our cadres. Open warfare, kidnapping of important officials, and even assassination will not be ruled out. Although we have sought to prevent any physical harm to all people in the past, we cannot be responsible for the safety of pigs if our demands are not met.

Power to the People! – Marion Delgado.

Editor's Note: The detonation was supposed to occur five minutes after the phone call to the Madison Police. It exploded prematurely. The New Years Gang regrets the death of Fassnacht.

15

Black and White Radical Aims

The different aims and approach of the black radicals and the white revolutionaries underground come into stark relief in the highly logical but rather patronizing reply of the Black Panther "21" of New York to a communiqué from the followers of Bernardine Dohrn who had already declared that "freaks are revolutionaries and revolutionaries are freaks." Panthers, like most European and Asiatic revolutionaries, are puritans on matters of drugs, grass, and even alcohol.

SOURCE: Black Panther "21," "That Panther 21 Letter." *Berkeley Barb*, Vol. 12, No. 9, issue 290, March 5-11, 1971, 4-5. Reprinted with permission from *Berkeley Barb*.

This letter is . . . a response to your latest communiqué – "New Morning – Changing Weather." In it we can sense and feel your frustration and sense of isolation. We know the feeling very well, having felt it ourselves for the last 21 months. We also very keenly feel the loss of direction, the confusion and chaos that is running rampant out there. We see how the pigs are working overtime to try and fuck things up – but we also see how much of the misdirection comes from these self proclaimed "vanguard" parties themselves. How these "omnipotent" parties are throwing seeds of confusion, escapism, and have lost much of their momentum by bad tactics – in fact terrible tactics, tripping out, pseudo-machoism, arrogance, myrmydonism, dogmatism, regionalism, regimentation, and fear. ... We can see your attitudes toward the mother country "youth culture" – how it was "the forces which produced" you, "a culture that" you "were part of, a young and unformed society (nation)." We can also see "the possibilities that exist for" you "to develop the movement so that as revolutionaries" you "change and shape the cultural revolution" – You "are in a position to change it for the better." ... But we feel that most of the mother country youth culture communes smack heavily of escapism – a danger you must be aware of and guard yourselves against. ...

We understand your need to build a strong sense of community ... but you must realize that "grass and organic consciousness expanding drugs" are NOT weapons of the revolution – they may be a tool to bring you together in a sense of community but they will not bring the Amerikkkan system down. ... Then in your "youth communities" of the mother country – the emphasis is on individual freedom still, while we are dealing with group freedom still. ... We say – Right on! Use the new consciousness. BUT remember this new consciousness of love, creativity, and liberation will not stop the exploitation of the third world.

16

A Contemporary Lovejoy

Needless to say, parallels like the ones suggested in the title are artificial, for no individual is a copy of another, especially when the figures are separated by so many years of history and by so many differences in personal and environmental circumstances. Nevertheless, just as the United States has always been aggressively expansionist throughout its history, so too has its spiritual or moral life possessed a messianic character with some individuals assuming a style with its own ancestry embedded in missionary fervor. Stephen M. Bingham, a young, white civil rights lawyer and activist, is a latter-day Lovejoy in the sense that both men were romantic missionaries whose dedication to principle was so powerful that tragic consequences became almost inevitable. They both seem to conform to Keniston's typology.

On August 21, 1971, George Jackson, author of *Soledad Brother* and black revolutionary, died in a "shoot-out" with prison guards at San Quentin, California. Reportedly, Jackson had obtained a gun from Bingham shortly before, and the lawyer has been charged with murder as an accomplice in the subsequent deaths of three white guards and two white inmates. Steven V. Roberts wrote the following article for the *New York Times* about Bingham, who is still at large.

SOURCE: Steven V. Roberts, "Friends Recall Bingham: A 'Strong Social Conscience But Politically Naive,' " *The New York Times*, September 1, 1971. ©1971 by The New York Times Company. Reprinted by permission.

Los Angeles, Aug. 31 – Stephen Mitchell Bingham was arrested in Clarksdale, Miss. in 1963 while helping blacks to register to vote.

Today, he was charged with five counts of murder. Officials allege that he smuggled a gun into San Quentin prison and gave it to George Jackson. The authorities say that Jackson used the gun in an escape attempt in which he and five others were killed.

Friends and the family of Mr. Bingham, a 29-year-old Oakland lawyer, insist that he is too smart and too opposed to violence to become involved in such a plot. But they also say that he has sympathy for those who believe that racism and injustice can be eradicated only through armed revolution.

Stephen Bingham is the heir to an impressive political heritage. His grandfather, Hiram Bingham, served as a Senator from Connecticut and as Governor of the State. His father, Alfred Bingham, now a Connecticut lawyer, was an outspoken advocate of Progressivism in the nineteen-thirties. . . .

After six years at Milton Academy, Mr. Bingham entered Yale in 1960. Teachers there recall his "strong social conscience" and a limited interest in academic matters. A former woman acquaintance remembers him as "politically naive and very impressionable."

"He was easily swayed to political emotionalism without getting his facts straight," she said. "He was very concerned with getting on the inside of any group, of being in the know," she said.

When the civil rights movement emerged, Mr. Bingham wrote an article in *The Yale Daily News* urging students to go to Mississippi. "For until the black people of Mississippi and the rest of the South – and North – are free, we shall not be free," he wrote.

Mr. Bingham's father, who flew to California last week "to stand behind" his son, noted that Stephen had gone South [by] himself. "He has always shown a willingness to take risks on behalf of what he believes in," the elder Mr. Bingham told a news conference.

"He thinks I'm a square and a liberal, which is almost an epithet with him," he added. "I think he's a romantic. He inherited some of the best and some of the worst qualities of his missionary ancestors."

After graduating from Yale, Mr. Bingham entered Boalt Hall, the law school of the University of California at Berkeley. But after a year he dropped out and joined the Peace Corps with his new wife, the former Gretchen Spreckles, a member of a prominent West Coast family.

The couple spent two years in the primitive back country of Sierra Leone, in West Africa. Not long after their return, they got a divorce and Mr. Bingham returned to law school.

There, he took up the cause of farm workers who were trying to organize a union in the San Joaquin Valley. In 1968 he was arrested during a sit-in protesting the university's refusal to stop buying table grapes.

Alfred Bingham specializes in real estate and wills. When Stephen finished law school, he joined a group of young lawyers who saw their role as serving the needs of "the movement" and the poor. As a staff attorney for Berkeley Neighborhood Legal Services, he defended teen-age runaways arrested by the police. After joining a law firm in Oakland earlier this year, he helped to organize "radical caucuses" within local labor unions.

From his days in Mississippi and West Africa, Mr. Bingham retained a particular interest in black problems. Last Christmas he gave his father a copy of "Soledad Brother," a book of letters written by George Jackson, one of three black convicts accused of murdering a guard in Soledad prison. . . .

17

A Contemporary John Brown

While Bingham apparently believed that black violence was justifiable, he obviously sought other, more constructive means of helping the downtrodden. Like Lovejoy, with his preaching through the medium of the press, Bingham found radical uses for conventional instruments such as the law. A different and more disturbing kind of radical has also appeared, one that may be closer to John Brown. After interviewing a number of local underground radicals, Robert Hendin ("A Psychoanalyst Looks at Student Revolutionaries," *New York Times Magazine*, January 17, 1971) concluded that in variously manifested ways, they were victims of parental indifference, an agony which radical violence was supposed to relieve. J. Kirk Sale, an editor of the *New York*

Times Magazine, came to similar conclusions about Ted Gold, dead from a dynamite explosion in a Greenwich Village townhouse, March 6, 1970.

SOURCE: J. Kirk Sale, "Ted Gold: Education for Violence," *The Nation*, April 13, 1970. Reprinted with permission.

Theodore Gold was born in New York City on December 13, 1947, into a milieu that is by now almost predictable for contemporary activists. He was an only child. His parents were liberals of the upper-West Side Jewish variety, living in a pleasant apartment on tree-lined Ninety-third Street, comfortably well-off if not exactly rich. His father, Dr. Hyman Gold, an internist in a Health Insurance Plan clinic . . . is regarded as having an evident concern for bringing medicine to the poor. His mother, Dr. Ruth Gold, is an associate professor of education at Columbia University's Teachers College. Most sociological studies suggest that activist youth come from just this kind of background, where both parents work and dinner table ideas are likely to be at least liberal. What they don't go on to say is that when both parents are away all day and the child is raised by a black maid, as in Ted Gold's case, the resulting psychological dislocations may be as great an impetus to radicalism. In fact one might even imagine that part of the attraction of a close-knit, intimate group – as were those formed during the Columbia confrontation of 1968 and as are the Weathermen collectives and "affinity groups" – stems from family deprivation in early life. . . .

[Gold did well at Stuyvesant High, but he was not a class leader academically. An interest in liberal politics developed in these years, and during his first two years at Columbia, Gold continued his activism within institutional and acceptable lines. In the spring of 1968, however, he was aroused to a higher level of activism by the Columbia disorders. Leaving the stage to emotional orators like Mark Rudd, Gold emphasized education of the students to revolutionary ideals rather than to violence. Yet, he gradually became more attracted to Rudd's "action faction." When the Ad Hoc Faculty Committee, of which Gold was a chief student negotiator, went on record as opposed to amnesty for the rioters, Gold felt bitter and betrayed. The continued talk among radicals of "the need for courage, for 'putting your body on the line,' for shaking off 'bourgeois hangups' about violence and death, for ceasing to be 'wimps' " increased Gold's determination to use violence as retribution against liberal coerciveness.

Suspended from Columbia, Gold organized a Teachers for a Democratic Society, an efficiently run operation in his hands, but ultimately a failure. Its purpose was to radicalize high schools, but the students resented the TDS's hyper-activism.] Gold, according to some who were around him then, became more and more rigid, less and less inclined to trying to "change heads." "He had no patience for anyone not at the same level of consciousness," says one young man. . . . "He became terribly autocratic – he was *hell* to deal with." . . . [Gold joined the Weatherman group when in June, 1968, the Progressive Labor faction took over SDS, forcing out the Columbia radicals like Gold.]

The Weatherman line is complicated and has shifted over this past year to take account of different actions – and reactions. But basically the group is made up of those who feel that the only way to change this country is through violent confrontation: "The primary purpose, and the stance, of our organizing," writes Shin'ya Ono, "could not possibly be to 'turn people on,' or to have them like us, or to make them think that we are nice, but to compel them to confront the antagonistic aspects of their own life experience and consciousness by bringing the war home, and to help them make the right choice over a period of time, after initially shaking up and breaking through the thick layers of chauvinism-racism-defeatism." . . .

[Gold became a Weatherman, though a relatively moderate one, at least partly as a means of proving himself.] One young observer recalls: "Rudd continually accused people of cowardice, that was his big word then, and said how you had to get a gun, and stop being afraid, and be a man, and all that."

There is in all of this what seems to be an abiding sense of guilt, and it was probably true for Gold as for other Weathermen and those like them. To oversimplify, they tend to feel guilty about the comfortable, privileged, often very rich homes from which they come, especially when they try to take their message into the mangled, oppressed and very desperate homes of the poor. They feel guilty about what they regard as their own inescapable middle-class racism and that of the society that has showered its benefits on their parents. They feel guilty that they are, at least at the start, frightened of violence, and envy those, like the blacks and the working-class youths, who have confronted violence from infancy. They feel guilty that their brains, money or pull has kept them safe on university campuses while others are sent to Vietnam. And they feel guilty that the society which as given them and their families so much, and which they have spent the better part of their adolescence trying to change, is obdurate in its basic inequities.

[After a visit to Cuba and talks with leaders there, Gold came back convinced, as he said himself, that] revolutionary Americans are in a position to do decisive damage to the U.S. ruling class's plans to . . . expand its world rule.

Next came October 8-11 in Chicago, what the Weathermen called . . . the "Days of Rage," when they went up against the cops and found their courage not wanting. But not sufficient either – the action was too weak, too many people were arrested, too much money ($1 million) was required for bail. The Weathermen retired to their collectives, to rethink their strategy, and the next three months went through serious soul-searching. Gold apparently stayed at the Chicago collective, where most of the national leaders – Rudd, Jacobs, Bernardine Dohrn – also spent most of their time, and was an intimate part of those who planned the next strategic steps. . . . At a meeting at Flint, a critic expressed the fear that if the Third World did win a struggle with America, the American whites would suffer, since] ... there will have to be more repression than ever against white people. "Well," replied Gold, "If it will take fascism, we'll have to have facism." ... [Weathermen broke up their larger collectives and formed small "affinity groups," of which one was the $250,000 Greenwich village townhouse, owned by the father of one of the members.]

How must it have felt to be living in a house full of explosives and to be preparing actions which were certain to be dangerous? "I think the Weathermen were all prepared to die," one former Columbia student says. "They were in a way like disobedient children who wanted to be punished, and on a larger scale that's a death wish." A friend who saw Gold two weeks before the explosion reports his having said, "I've been doing a lot of exciting underground things, and I know I'm not afraid to die."

Another who knew Gold thinks it was more than just the absence of fear. "I think a desire for recognition was motivating him, I really do. He wanted to be in history – he wanted to be like Che, a tragic figure. And for tragedy you need a stage, like this historical point in time, and you need violence." And an adult around Columbia who knew Gold less well speculates: "I always felt that Ted, perhaps because of his size, or maybe his bookishness, had a kind of drive to get people to know who he was. I don't mean he wanted the limelight, not like that. But he wanted everyone to know who he was, what he was doing." Inadvertently, he did. ...

18

Counter-Culture: Revolution as New Moral Code

The links between "youth culture," as the expression goes, and revolution are not always clear, for not every "drop-out" is dedicated to violence or even to a political program. Yet, such connections exist, sometimes with confusing results, as the exchange between the Weathermen and the Panthers previously suggested. The following two documents represent an aspect of the counter-culture, which is too often romanticized by the revivalistic spirit of Woodstock. Women in the "movement," as these pieces show, found male chauvinism as imbedded in the mores of radical males as in society as a whole.

SOURCE: Unsigned, "Rat Women in Love," *Madison Kaleidoscope,* Vol. 2, no. 17, August, 1970, pp. 4-5. Reprinted with permission from Rat Collective, New York, N.Y.

RAT WOMEN IN LOVE

Fourteen women together in the country (NO MEN) pouring out our personal rages, crying and screaming and hugging and somehow it seemed so much more real than all those encounter groups. Maybe because we saw how incredibly beautiful we all were. We didn't need men to see it in ourselves and each other. We were so together practicing our karate and dancing naked in the meadow behind the house. And there were no men to say your breasts are too big or too small or your bodies are too fat or too skinny. We were so beautiful. Everyone of us. We got stoned dancing to Aretha and once again my mind was blown by how real and alive and beautiful we all were.

So the men came up to the country after most of the Collective had left. We were stunned by the contrast. Even the most well-meaning brothers who are struggling with their own sexism still carried the arrogance of power and "leadership" shit in their brains and guts. Collectivity is a concept to them, not a reality. And they f---d things up within about fifteen minutes after setting foot in the house and we (the six women who stayed on) had a long confrontation session with them and while it was exhilirating [sic] to feel each other's support and shared consciousness, it was still a drag to have to go through it all again. And I had a spillover confrontation with my man, and we went for a walk to try to heal it but couldn't. So I went up to bed, and he stayed downstairs reading underground papers. And I lay under the eaves, trying to fall asleep, thinking the thoughts I've thought a hundred times before, about sisters, about the men we love and hate and are committed to and oppressed by. Then I heard B. and her man in the next room, talking softly. I knew that she'd been going through the same pain, groping toward the same consciousness, as I had, and I thought for a minute that they were crying together on the other side of that wall. It was a few minutes before I realized that they weren't crying; they were making love. And I went through lightning-fast, acid-like changes: *Envy.* They had battled and struggled and now were at least f-----g and here was I in bed alone and my man downstairs alone and the taste of struggle still bitter in our mouths. *Guilt.* I was being too hard on my man; I was driving him into a corner, demanding too much, too fast; not being grateful enough, understanding enough, gradual enough. It was my fault that I did not have what B. had in the next room. *Contempt.* I was right – B. was too "easy." It was she who wasn't really committed, really struggling, ready to risk a moment of compromised closeness for her human freedom. *Fear.* At my own readiness to be divided from that sister, from any sister; and at the specter of aloneness more permanently; at risking everything, anything – including the familiarity of my own oppression. *Desire.* If he would only come upstairs and lie down beside me and it could be beautiful and tender and fiery and perfect and totally devoid of memories and roles and mechanics. *Despair.* Because even if he were to appear at that very moment and we were to go through all the motions, it would *not* be beautiful. but rather a charade of what we both wished desparately [sic] it might be. *Relief.* Horrifying relief, at realizing I was glad to be alone, not to have to go through that charade, not to have to settle for anything less than what I needed and desired and deserved. Relief at being able to turn over and go to sleep, unmolested, alone, and free in my bed. *Embarassment.* Omi god, what had I been doing, anyway, listening in on people f-----g? It just isn't done, by my mother's standards or even our own "hip, radical" ones. Am I turning into some sort of sickie? The certainty that I would (1) never be able to tell B. about the experience, let alone (2) share all those feelings in the context of the awkward situation with other sisters. Which I have done, a sign that I'm beginning to really trust the sisterhood.

And then, just as I dozed toward an exhausted sleep, one last minute flash of something unexpected, sharp. *Anguish.* Because my man and I had been out in a country meadow earlier that night, lying silent under a mandala of stars we never even glimpse in the city, breathing warm air heavy with the smell of earth and honeysuckle and wild roses, watching the summer moon tip the buttercups all silver and feeling the dew settle on our hair. And we had not spoken. Had not touched. Because his confusion and my pain grew between us in that meadow, and because I could no longer "make it right," reach over as I have done a thousand times before and say it didn't matter. We don't get out into the country and lie in a night-summer meadow much – hardly ever. We live in a poisoned air city and are justly paranoid and tight and tired and rushed and fighting the System and we may be dead soon. And it wasn't *right,* goddam it, to have had my moment in that meadow, just the way it could have been in some other world, society, culture, dream. Because I'm only here once and I'll die and never, never have that moment. Because I can't settle for anything less, anymore. Because Because [sic] I may never be the free, laughing, brain-awake, sex-alive whole woman I'm struggling to be, and I may never live with the true brother I'm struggling to love still – but unless I go all the way and throw every risk to the winds of my commitment in that struggle, unless I settle less and less for nothing other than total ecstasy of freedom, than I am dead. Not in a superficial way, like being killed, but in the more profound way: dead, like that part of myself I left behind in that redneck country farmer's summer meadow, where I lie on wet grass forever, not understanding, and waiting for a love that will not happen.

PAUL BUHLE

Debsian Socialism and the "New Immigrant" Worker

SOCIALISTS AND COMMUNISTS in the United States during the twentieth century have keenly felt their organizational weakness and distance from the working class, relative to their political counterparts abroad. Political activists have formally accepted the strategic relation of party and class delineated in the *Communist Manifesto* of Marx and Engels:

> The Communists do not form a separate party opposed to other working class parties.
>
> They have no interests separate and apart from those of the proletariat as a whole.
>
> They do not set up any sectarian principles of their own by which to shape and mould the proletarian movement.
>
> The Communists are distinguished from the other working class parties by this only: 1. In the national struggles of the proletarians of the different countries, they point out and bring to the front the common interests of the entire proletariat, independently of all nationality. 2. In the various stages of development which the struggle of the working class against the bourgeoisie has to pass through, they always and everywhere represent the interests of the movement as a whole.[1]

[1] *Communist Manifesto* (New York, 1961), pp. 33-34. On the general character of the problem of Socialism and internationalism, see Horace Davis, *Nationalism and Socialism* (New York, 1967), especially Chapters 3, 7, and 8.

Yet Socialists and Communists, who generally found this mandate theoretically unimpeachable, could not follow its dictates in practice. Confined to narrow sectors of the working class in directly political activities, Marxists have been able to adopt only one side of Marx and Engels's proposition: either they established "sectarian principles of their own" in a pure but impotent gesture, or they bent their activities to the needs and interests of those sectors most readily accessible to radicalism, thereby violating the spirit of Socialism even while agitating for its arrival.

Most important for Debsian Socialists concerned with the working class was the dilemma posed by the interlinking of ethnic and class strata during the birth of modern industry. Objectively, the "Old Immigration" (from northern and western Europe) dominated the Aristocracy of Labor: skilled workers proud of their craft and often politically active. The "New Immigrants" from eastern and southern Europe, often illiterate and unable to speak English, bound to the Catholic Church, largely indifferent to Socialist political notions, provided the majority of recruits for labor's mass within the new factories. From the beginning of their movement, most Socialists had been naturally inclined toward the "real American worker" and away from the newer immigrant. But the changes within industry and the sporadic strikes of new workers in 1909-1913 destroyed Socialist indifference. In the meantime, certain individuals within the Socialist Party articulated the cause of the unorganized and unskilled as the very basis of future Socialist theory and activity.[2]

By 1912, the Socialist movement as a whole had resolved to follow strategic lines of moderation, stressing election efforts and agitation within the American Federation of Labor, at the expense of support for industrial organizing and specific concentration upon the unskilled worker. But Socialist political failures, the coming of World War I, the development of intense political repression, and events in Europe which radicalized the new immigrant communities all transformed the demographic character

[2] I will be concerned in this essay with the situation of the unskilled "old immigrant" and the so-called "native American worker" only insofar as their consideration is necessary for the subject. "American" workers sometimes, especially in Western factories, played roles similar to the new immigrant workers, but Socialists were primarily concerned with the native workers' role in extractive industries, lumbering, agriculture, and sea-related work. New immigrant workers, on the other hand, were singled out here because their presence characterized the new, mass-production industries. Similarly, for the purposes of this essay, I have not considered black workers or women workers as such, or in relation to the Socialist Party.

of the party. The Socialist movement fell victim to factional dismemberment and dissolution in 1919, just when it most nearly represented the forces of the industrial working class. Yet in the course of Socialist successes and limitations could be traced a fundamental shift in class relations and the dramatic inability of an avowedly Marxist movement in the United States to consciously exemplify the class solidarity which it fervently proclaimed.

The relationships of Debsian Socialists with various segments of the working class were shaped by several decades of intensive industrial development and changes in class formations, from the largely agrarian economy of an earlier period to the urban capitalism of the new era. The transition between periods created a widespread sense of disaffection among various sectors of the population, but no major insurrection nor even the basis for a revolutionary political movement on the European scale. Indeed, the hostility of workers toward the new modern wage-slavery was expressed in a characteristic American fashion with sporadic militance involving considerable violence while lacking any but the most limited political implications. Trade unions were formed on a national scale and were ambivalent toward the mass struggles. Throughout, a small band of Socialists wandered in the valley of the lost, sometimes preaching sectarian messages heard only by themselves, sometimes engaging in union organization work which did not necessarily permit widespread Socialist proselytization. True to Marx's conception, Socialist activity was a response to class activity, but to the Socialists' dismay the uneven and confusing character of the class struggle was replicated and even magnified within the Socialist movement itself.

In the last quarter of the nineteenth century, three general waves of mass strikes involved millions of workers. For the most part, these workers responded to the effects of a massive change at the heart of production, from simple manufacture – the amalgamation of craftsmen under one roof – to modern industrial production. In 1877, wage reductions for railroad workers resulted in a nationwide surge of discontent, bringing violent resistance to employers and militia in Pittsburgh, Chicago, and elsewhere, and the seizure of city government in St. Louis. In 1885-87, a partially successful railroad strike encouraged a widespread movement for the eight-hour day, with parades and rioting climaxing in the Haymarket Square riot in Chicago on May 4, 1886, and in 1892-94 depressed conditions created wage reductions and promoted solidarity, from the Homestead strike to the strike of coal and silver miners to the American Railway Union actions against the Great Northern and finally against Pullman. In all these, Socialists had played some role, but in none were they a leading element; the spontaneous and unorganized character of the movements permitted only brief, if sometimes important, radical political interventions.[3] Only the Pullman strike, with the terrific defeat it inflicted upon the working class movement, encouraged an indigenous sentiment toward the formation of a large-scale political Socialist movement. Symbolically, the strike's leader, Eugene Debs, was converted to Socialism while in prison for violating an injunction. Within a decade Debs was to rise as the archetype of the revolutionary internationalist worker Marxism idealized and to become the leading individual figure of the American movement – so much so that an entire period (roughly 1900-1920) has gained its designation from him.

Meanwhile, the few thousand active Socialists, mostly German-American immigrants, worked largely within existing trade union structures. As the character of the preindustrial, reformist unionism was replaced with the exclusiveness of the American Federation of Labor, Socialists' adherence to the principle of internationalism suffered serious practical blows.

In Europe, Marx's own First International showed a discontinuity between theory and practice. Established primarily among British handicraft workers who sought through its influence to prevent European competition, the International could not withstand the effects of the continental mass revolts (especially the Paris Commune) upon the conservative sensibilities of British union leaders. Strangled with internecine fights, the International's headquarters was moved to Manhattan. There, in the ultimate metropolitan testing ground for true internationalism, the American Section Number One sought to appeal to masses of

[3]For the general character of mass strike movements, I have relied heavily upon a prospective book, the manuscript for which was kindly loaned me by the author: Jeremy Brecher, *Strike!* (San Francisco, 1972); for the nineteenth century descriptions, consult Chapters 1 through 3.

Paul Sweezy offers some suggestive remarks on the proletariat's transformation from handicraft- to manufacturing- and at last to industrial workers in "Marx and the Proletariat," *Monthly Review* XIX (December, 1967), 25-42. Sweezy hypothesizes that once the working class has passed from manufacturing to industrialism proper, a certain element of their revolutionary character is vitiated – a provocative notion given the disappearance of mass rioting, on the late nineteenth century scale, in the twentieth century. See fn.[59] for further exploration of this problem.

Irish, German, and older stock American workers. Significantly, the American Section failed utterly to expand its actual political base to native-born workers but was able through trade union work and contacts to play an influential role in several unions and in the National Labor Union.[4]

The National Labor Union was less a modern union federation than a quasi-political amalgam of handicraft and manufacturing workers' groups. Reformist and internationalist, the NLU during its short existence in the 1860s declared for free immigration (naturally enough, since the economy was developing rapidly) but appealed for the prevention of purposefully imported strikebreakers and contract laborers. Most important in the long run, the NLU took an ambiguous position toward Chinese laborers; even among radical-minded workers, the international solidarity of workingmen stopped short of "Coolie Labor." Through this geographical and political back door, exclusionism and the specific rejection of internationalism entered into modern labor and Socialist movements of the United States.

With the disappearance of the First International early in the 1870s, Socialist tendencies underwent several stages of evolution, resulting in the formation of a Socialist Labor Party in 1877. Like their predecessors, Socialists involved with labor worked within existing movements, the Knights of Labor (formed in 1869) and the American Federation of Labor (formed in 1881). The Knights reflected both the past and future of American workers: reformist and agrarian-minded like the NLU, they proclaimed a naive solidarity which included all workers (except the Chinese, about whom they too equivocated). Like the NLU, the Knights expected their following to appear largely among the recent immigrants attracted by developing industry, and therefore stood for unrestricted immigration from Europe, save contract labor and strikebreakers. In practice, Knights leadership could not bear the implications of its position, and drew back in timidity at the forces unleashed by the railroad strike of 1885-86 and the direct actions of mobs. Within a few years the Knights had gained, and then lost, over a half-million workers with the flow and ebb of confidence in the possibility of unionization for the unorganized.

[4] Charles Leinenweber, "Immigration and the Decline of Internationalism in the American Working Class Movement, 1864-1919," (unpublished Ph.D. dissertation, Berkeley, California, 1969), Chapters 1 and 2. This dissertation contains an extremely important critique, only one portion of which has been published: "The American Socialist Party and New Immigrants," *Science & Society* XXXII (Winter, 1968), 1-25.

By 1890 the organization had virtually disappeared and was dealt the deathblow by the withdrawal of disappointed Socialists in 1894. The AFL, on the other hand, built slowly but successfully.

The development of AFL policy on internationalism marked a new phase for labor and its Socialist contingent. Emanating almost exclusively from the skilled trades and squeezed between mechanization and the expansion of the unskilled work force through immigration, the AFL resolved to practice control of the labor market for the benefit of the minority. In the AFL's first few years, this meant little more than a continuation of the opposition to contract and "Coolie" labor. During the depression of the 1890s, however, impetus for stronger measures emerged. In 1893, the AFL in convention adopted a position on Chinese laborers more severe than the Chinese Exclusion Act (and maintained this position in 1894-95, although it had also passed a Socialist platform for "collective ownership" of the means of production). In 1898, the AFL under the leadership of Gompers established a permanent opposition to unrestricted immigration from Europe, providing a number of formulae finally resolved in the quota system. No matter that, as Socialist scholar Isaac Hourwich later pointed out in great detail, the effect of immigration had not been to bring down the wages of skilled workers. The AFL leadership and a voting majority of its affiliates believed with increasing fervency in the undesirability of unskilled "New Immigrants" from eastern and southern Europe. Some Socialist-led unions and many Socialist workers continued to protest against this position, but few, in relative terms, found in this exclusionism sufficient reason to affiliate with the dual or revolutionary unions established by radicals.[5]

The Socialists' policies were further shaped by the strength they developed within particular unions. John Laslett has analyzed six leading examples of Socialist union strength: the Brewery Workers' Union, the International Ladies Garment Workers' Union, the International Association of Machinists, the Boot and Shoe Workers' Union, the United Mine Workers, and the Western Federation of Miners. In the first two cases, ethnic factors clearly predominated. The Brewery laborers brought German-American Socialism across the Atlantic and reinforced its implications with a form of industrial unionism granting equal pay to all employees.

[5] Leinenweber, "Immigration," Chapters 3 through 5.

The Garment Workers were unskilled, largely Jewish, workers recently emigrated from Russia, uniquely intellectual and political in their Marxism among American radical workers. In the machinists' and shoe workers' trades, the degradation of skill promoted a sense of grievance which Socialists could explain and utilize. In the mining camps, the inclusiveness of labor, the frequent isolation from the larger community, and the sheer necessity to combine for livable conditions, along with a number of other factors, promoted violent resistance and some political radicalism. Interestingly, Socialist strength even by the 1890s was disproportionately great among the first industrial unions. But, more important for our analysis, all these Socialist-oriented unions save the miners related their Socialism to increasingly archaic conditions.[6]

Judging primarily from short-term results, Socialist leaders sought by the 1890s to gather the lessons of union activity for a radical political strategy. In general, there were two lines of reasoning. Victor Berger and other Socialists influential in the AFL concluded that the best road to influence among workers was a mutual tolerance and even noninterference between trade union and party, linked to political agitation for Socialist principles within the unions' given activity. DeLeon and the partisans of the Industrial Workers of the World attempted, instead, to construct revolutionary unions of workers outside the AFL. For both strategies, the climax of hopefulness arrived around 1912, when the promise of Socialist support in the AFL and the mass organization of industrial workers in the IWW were at their respective heights. For both the promise was shortly to be denied.

Daniel DeLeon, fiery leader of the Socialist Labor Party, had concluded at the onset of the depression of the 1890s that capitalism was approaching its downfall and Socialists had to prepare themselves for revolutionary activity. Thus DeLeon was impatient at the compromises necessary for Socialists to work within unions, and above all fearful of the Socialist movement's domination by timid, self-satisfied skilled workers and middle-class political elements. After tactical defeats in the Knights and the AFL in 1895, DeLeon led a withdrawal of several thousand workers from both into the Socialist Trades and Labor Alliance. Proclaimed as a movement to organize new unions, it succeeded in

[6] John Laslett, *Labor and the Left* (New York, 1970), Chapters 2 through 7.

little more than conducting Socialist propaganda and disorganizing competing AFL affiliates. By 1905, reduced to a shell, it folded into the Industrial Workers of the World.[7]

Other Socialists drew different conclusions. Entrenched unionists in the SLP and their political allies seceded from the SLP rather than withdrawing from the AFL, denouncing dual-unionism as a curse. At last, DeLeon's policy resulted in a rupture that left the SLP a sect. Meanwhile, the collapse of the American Railway Union strike in 1894 left Debs with a body of men who sought to move their economic grievance to the political field. After an abortive utopian colonization experiment, Debs' organization merged with the dissident SLPs and other unaffiliated radical elements to form the Socialist Party in 1901.[8]

These splits and reorganizations did not in fact resolve the class question which challenged the very existence of Socialism. DeLeon and his followers, along with the most incendiary elements in the Socialist Party, were advocates of abstract internationalism. For them questions of class sectors did not exist, since "worker" was already a universal category; one had only to appeal to this worker's class-consciousness sufficiently to make him understand the meaning and solution of his existence. For Socialists with influence in organizations and among constituencies, these questions were necessarily concrete and not to be evaded. For the time being it was enough for all sides to appeal to some aspect of doctrine: the DeLeonites, Debs, and others to the inherent internationalism of the working class; and Victor Berger, AFL functionaries, and others to the inevitable evolution of Socialism and the necessity of adapting to existing conditions. Both sides were in fact quite naive about Marxist doctrine, but this was of little matter since Marx and Engels had left no firm answers to such questions. Ultimately, however, the capacity of all Socialists would be tested for the application of doctrine and acquired knowledge to unprecedented conditions.

As Socialism was reorganized into a unified movement (save for the minuscule SLP), a party trade union policy was necessarily

[7] The most incisive single treatment of DeLeon in the 1890s remains Louis C. Fraina, "Daniel DeLeon," *New Review* II (June, 1914), 390-99. See also Don M. McKee, "Daniel DeLeon" (unpublished Ph.D. thesis, Columbia, 1955); and Paul Buhle, "Daniel DeLeon, American Socialist: The First Ten Years, 1886-1896," (unpublished BA thesis, University of Illinois, 1966).

[8] See Howard Quint, *The Forging of American Socialism* (Indianapolis, 1966), Chapter 10.

devised. The position of the Socialists was ultimately a form of theoretical abstention: Socialists were not to interfere in the trade union movement as outsiders but were to work within it as loyal members. Simultaneously, it was presumed, unions would not interfere in Socialist affairs but would have a fraternal attitude. Such was the interlinkage that the German Social Democratic Party and radical trade unions had toward each other: the Germans called it rather grandly the "twin pillars of Socialism" while American socialist Victor Berger preferred a more modest version, "the two-armed labor movement."[9] Unfortunately for this strategy, the AFL as a body was demonstrably not Socialist. Indeed, after the turn of the century Gompers increasingly attacked Socialists publicly and joined with other conciliatory labor leaders and leading capitalists in the National Civic Federation, an open expression of class harmony. The AFL Socialists responded in the only way they could, on the one hand criticizing Gompers' "pure and simple" craft unionism and on the other hand upholding the AFL as such. By 1912, the Socialists gained their maximum strength within the AFL, due in part to the adhesion of the Brewery Workers and the Western Federation of Miners to the organization. Max Hayes, Socialist candidate for the presidency, received one-third of the votes; Socialists captured major and minor posts in a variety of unions including Gompers' own Cigar-Makers; and the AFL Convention of the following year even made slight concessions to the necessity for labor political action. On the other side of the ledger, the virulent antiforeignism and racism (directed particularly at the Chinese) became increasingly strident, especially with the rise of militant strikes of immigrant workers after 1909. With World War I, all hopes for Socialist takeover of the Federation were washed away. Protected to a degree by Washington, AFL unions lost all interest in dealing with the now-impotent Socialists.[10]

Individual Socialist strongholds fared no better. In the IAM and the Shoe Workers, radicalism disappeared first, a victim of the industries' stabilization. In the garment trades, Jewish workers had another cycle to turn in the assimilation process before the New

[9] Leinenweber, "Immigration," 163. A fuller description of Milwaukee Socialist thought is contained in Paul Buhle, "Introduction to the *Social Democratic Herald,*" to be published in Joseph Conlin, ed., *American Radicalism,* 1890-1960 (Westport, Connecticut, 1973).

[10] Leinenweber, "Immigration," Chapter 5; Marc Karson, *American Labor Unions and Politics, 1900-1918* (Boston, 1965), 130-31.

Deal evoked their political loyalty, but prohibition along with other pressures destroyed the older immigrant ties in the Brewery Workers. Only in the minefields did Socialists and other radicals maintain long run strength, and then not so much within national unions as within individual locals. Perhaps the difficulties and relative isolation of the miners' lives obstructed that assimilationist process which absorbed other layers of workers.[11]

Up to the time of World War I, AFL-oriented Socialists had no difficulty in explaining away the Federation's limitations. In several places, most notably Milwaukee, the AFL was run by Socialists and provided the basic support for the Socialist movement. In the view of Victor Berger ("architect of victory" in local elections in Milwaukee) and other old-line Socialists, the skilled workers were indeed the backbone of the work force, the "real American workers." The "Marxist" views held throughout most of the Socialist Party, Left to Right, could be held to justify Berger's view: capitalism was monopolizing business, undercutting workers' living conditions, ruining the old middle class, and leading to a situation where workers would be open to Socialist education. Until 1912, major party structures seemed to point in this direction: Bryan's Democratic Party represented the petite bourgeoisie's last gasp, the Republican Party the arrogant demands of the plutocracy, and the Socialist Party the future voice of the worker. When conditions were ripe, Berger assumed, the educated and "Americanized" workers would respond first, leading the others (including the New Immigrants) along behind, as indeed happened in Milwaukee municipal elections.[12]

The weakness of this analysis was the central problem of the Socialist Party. By 1911, Socialist leaders granted that they had failed to attract precisely that working class "family man" they had most fervently sought. The party had tripled in size from diverse other elements: the "brain workers," as intellectuals were euphemistically called; the tenant farmers and farm workers of the Southwest; small town and countryside members drawn from Populist ranks by such forces as the *Appeal to Reason*; and a growing number of unskilled, footloose workers. Especially from 1910 onward, Socialists won an increasing number of local elections by appealing beyond the ranks of the faithful, but they

[11] Laslett, 295-300.

[12] My description relies heavily upon an unpublished manuscript by Mari Jo Buhle, "Debsian Socialists and Progressivism."

were not attracting or retaining skilled workers, except in certain areas (notably Milwaukee and Reading), or among certain ethnic groups.[13] The appearance of the Progressive Party in 1912 brought home the threat to the Socialist Party's very existence: how could Socialism distinguish itself from this new force without abandoning the cautious program of reformism that attracted so much of its following? For Berger and others, the Progressive campaign and the apparent reinvigoration of the reformist middle classes were an illusion to be vanquished by recession.[14] In the meantime, older skilled working class groups and middle class sectors within the party generally agreed on the more immediate threat, the radical workers indifferent to law and order, represented by the IWW and Socialist leader "Big Bill" Haywood.

The Industrial Workers of the World had been created in 1904-05 by a coalition of radical labor and political forces which had renounced hopes for revolutionizing the AFL. Inclusive as the AFL was exclusive, the IWW set itself to the task of organizing the other 95 per cent not represented by the AFL, including all races, nationalities, and women. The very style of the IWW, an insistence upon government from the shop floor upward to politics and from the masses of workers up to the educated and currently powerful sectors, was a standing threat to the social system. As William Preston has said, through "pursuing these aims, the IWW aroused intense opposition from all those – left, right, and center – who had implicitly accepted a definition of the American way imposed and diffused by the business elite."[15] Whatever their real success, the "Wobblies" posed a specter of total transformation which, when linked concretely with the most miserable and ill-treated sectors of the population, necessarily evoked terrible fears of

[13] When several notable Socialists suggested the possibility of forming a labor party, a debate raged over the Socialists' political problems generally. See comments by conservative Socialists John Spargo and William Ghent in the "Comment and Discussion" of the *New York Call,* November 18 and November 19, 1909, respectively; and the communication by Left-Socialist William English Walling to the "Letters" column on December 11, 1909.

[14] See two articles by Left-Socialist Frank Bohn on Progressivism: "The Socialist Party and the Government of Cities," *International Socialist Review* XII (November, 1911), 275-78; and "The Middle Class and Progressivism," *New Review II* (February, 1914), 70-82.

[15] William Preston, "Shall This Be All? U.S. Historians versus William D. Haywood, et al.," *Labor History* XII (Summer, 1971), 439. Preston points to the inadequacy of historical discussions, past and present, on the IWW as an organ of class expression; my own consideration of generally the same historical works is contained in "New Perspectives on the Wobblies," *Monthly Review* XX (June, 1970), 44-53.

repayment for exploitation, potentially the revolutionary circumstances that Lenin called "festivals of the oppressed."[16]

Contrary to sanguine expectations, the IWW floundered and underwent two important splits in its first years. Most painful was the departure of the Western Federation of Miners, the only large and financially stable affiliate the IWW ever possessed. After several years of intensive agitation in the West, Wobbly leaders turned toward the East and, inevitably, the immigrant workers. In 1907-1908, Wobblies led a strike in Bridgeport, Connecticut, which welded together native American workers and unskilled Hungarians. That same year, Wobblies organized five thousand silk workers of varying nationalities in Paterson, New Bedford, Lawrence, and other cities, holding a convention in 1908 to establish the first IWW industrial union. In 1909, Wobblies made their first intervention into a major strike of the unskilled immigrant workers. A spontaneous strike at the Pressed Car Steel Company in McKees' Rocks, Pennsylvania, first brought miserably exploited eastern European workers and slightly better paid native Americans together, then split them apart with a proferred settlement which favored skilled (i.e., "American") laborers. Immigrant workers rejected this settlement, threatening violence to stop the importation of scabs. Into this situation the IWW leapt, bringing organizers to speak in English and nine other languages. After a minor riot that left six dead, a second "compromise settlement," unfavorable to the immigrants, was accepted by the strikers. Pressed Steel drew the logical conclusions, used skilled native workers to break the remnants of the strike, and conferred new favors upon the minority.[17]

Nonetheless, Wobblies and friendly Socialists began to feel a new dawn was breaking. Despite repeated IWW organizational failures for two more years, agitation and unrest proliferated among immigrant workers in heavy industry. Where possible, the Socialist political organization was adapted to those efforts. "If the political organization has not attracted the proper quota to its standard in the past," wrote the Socialist Fred Merrick in 1911, "it is . . . because they think we are following some kind of utopian, Sunday school program. Let it become clear to the Pittsburgh worker that the party wants to protect the worker while he organizes in a militant manner . . . and is not seeking to

[16] V.I. Lenin, *Two Tactics of Social-Democracy in the Democratic Revolution* (New York, 1963), 95.

[17] Melvyn Dubofsky, *We Shall Be All* (Chicago, 1969), 199-209.

advance another group of politicians," and the Socialists would enjoy an "avalanche" of support.[18] A year later in Pittsburgh, Wobbly leader William Trautmann wrote for the *International Socialist Review*:

> [T]he capitalists are very much alarmed. They attribute all . . . evil things to Socialist propaganda, and this is true as far as the agitation among the hundreds of thousands of aliens go. The North Slavish and South Slavish nationalities, and the Italians as well as the Hungarians, form a veritable hotbed of revolutionary possibilities. They are ready to demand much. . . . No longer has the labor aristocrat, represented in his craft union and his walking delegate, the whip hand over the formerly despised working man.[19]

One event more than any other solidified the fears of respectable America and agitated the hopes of industrial revolutionaries who sought to create a new Socialist movement within the old party – the Lawrence strike.

Lawrence, Massachusetts, was the archetypal setting for the American Industrial Dream gone sour in mouths of the dispossessed immigrants. Established as a model town in 1845, it had developed by 1912 into a haven of cheap labor for the woolen mills from recently arrived immigrants, their wives, and their children. Living conditions were deplorable, and were further threatened by a reduction in wages for women and children commensurate to the reduction of hours (to fifty-four hours per week) by state statute. The AFL had shown little interest in organizing the "foreigners," and although the IWW had had little previous success until August of the previous year, the Wobblies assumed control of the mass, spontaneous walkout sparked by Polish women on January 12. The IWW leadership of the strike has already become legend – "Big Bill" Haywood, the "Rebel Girl" Elizabeth Gurley Flynn, poet Arturo Giovanitti, and Joe Ettor. Famous also was the response of the workers, most specifically a women's banner calling for "Bread and Roses Too." Beneath the understandable glitter of American radical history, however, lies the reality of bitter division between native American, skilled workers and their foreign, unskilled counterparts (including women and children).[20] A young reporter for the SLP's *Daily People*, Louis Fraina, saw that:

[18] Fred H. Merrick, " 'Justice' in Pittsburgh," *International Socialist Review XII* (September, 1911), 163.

[19] William E. Trautmann, "Over a Volcano," *International Socialist Review* XIII (September, 1912), 221.

[20] Dubofsky, Chapter 10.

The situation here, and the spirit of the meetings, strengthens the belief that the non-skilled worker is the revolutionary force in capitalist society. The skilled workers are wavering; the non-skilled are solid to a man [sic]. It is this non-skilled mass, produced by the machine process, that must be moulded into shape, and out of it to make the new, Socialist world.[21]

The next day he concluded, "Would that all the proletariat of America were 'foreigners.'!"[22] The *International Socialist Review*, voice of Wobbly sympathizers within the Socialist Party, hailed the strike as:

... one of the most inspiring struggles the American workers have ever known. Separated by many different languages, customs and religions, the men and women, the boys and girls of Lawrence have joined hands to fight. ... This is your fight and my fight. An injury to one worker is an injury to all workers. We cannot save ourselves without freeing the whole working class. Now is the time to show the men and women at Lawrence that Socialism means something today as well as the abolition of wage slavery tomorrow.[23]

The key to the Socialists' optimism was their own successful intervention in the conflict. As the strike wound on, the Socialist *New York Call* spearheaded the drive for thousands of dollars of strike funds and for something more dramatic, the mass removal of children from the strike scene to Socialist homes in New York City and elsewhere. Led by a recent convert to Socialism, Margaret Sanger, this move both aided and greatly dramatized the struggle. Meanwhile conservative Socialist Victor Berger, by now a Congressman from Wisconsin, demanded and obtained a Congressional investigation, further publicizing the situation.[24] At last, two months after the strike had begun, a settlement was reached. In the *ISR*, the editors hailed the victory as but "one engagement" in the "Big Fight." As the editors added, "winning tactics have been discovered and have already received the virtual endorsement of the Socialist Party of America. Industrial Unionism is no longer an untried theory. Henceforth its progress will be swift and sure."[25]

Regretfully for Socialism and for the immigrant workers,

[21] "Strikers' Foes Decry Children Movement," *Daily People*, February 17, 1912.

[22] "Terrorizing the Textile Strikers," *Daily People*, February 18, 1912.

[23] Mary Marcy, "Battle for Bread at Lawrence," *International Socialist Review* XII (March, 1912), 542.

[24] Dubofsky, 250-52.

[25] Leslie H. Marcy and Frederick Sumner Boyd, "One Big Union Wins," and "Editorial: Victory at Lawrence," *International Socialist Review* XII (April, 1912), 630 and 679 respectively.

victory was by no means so imminent. By initiating and exploiting nationality differences between workers, by causing a temporary "depression" which threw thousands of workers out of jobs, and by playing upon the IWW's lack of tenacity as a job-conscious organization, the mill owners ultimately limited the IWW's long-term strength to marginality. At the same time, it became painfully clear that the Socialist Party could not capitalize on the very situation of open class struggle which underlay their Marxian program. Although the Socialist Party had at one time considerable success among segments of skilled workers in Massachusetts, its strength by the time of the Lawrence strike was minimal. Still linked to the state's craft unionist leaders, rank-and-file Socialists contributed money but very little else. James Carey, former shoeworker and leader of the Massachusetts party, spoke from the platform in Lawrence about the woolen trust and the necessity for workers to vote Socialist. The Socialist state vote in 1912 actually dropped, and the party polled only 6 per cent of the ballots in Lawrence. In reality, the Lawrence strikers were poor material for political Socialism: only 15 per cent of the eligible men were citizens, and of the rest many were Irish Catholics generally hostile to Socialism. Thus, political Socialism could not elicit a fundamental class response from the most downtrodden workers, and the forces were never joined.[26]

After Lawrence, the IWW's luck failed. The next year in Paterson, New Jersey, Wobblies came to lead a silk workers' strike which manifested great support temporarily, but could not withstand the familiar divisions within the work force and the dwindling of Socialist backing. As a Jewish worker told John Reed, "English peoples not go on picket line. Mericans no lika fight!" In such a situation, Socialists could no longer confidently throw full support into campaigns that drained energy and finances. Over 1912-1913, Wobblies led a walkout of foreign and native rubber workers at Akron, and workers at Studebaker in Detroit. Both were unsuccessful.[27]

The result of the Wobblies' failure was central to the whole future of the Socialist Party. So long as the Lawrence strike and the unrest of immigrant workers pointed toward an immediate realignment of class forces, the IWW and pro-IWW members of the Socialist movement could hail the opening of an industrial

[26] Henry F. Bedford, *Socialism and the Workers in Massachusetts, 1866-1912* (Amherst, 1968), 244-63.

[27] Dubofsky, Chapter 11.

orientation *within* political Socialism. Left-Socialists noted with real pride the role Victor Berger had played in the Lawrence strike, and asserted that they could work enthusiastically with more moderate forces for the election of local and national Socialists, while differing as to the precise importance that successful election campaigns would have. As Haywood wrote in 1911, all Socialists believed in using the ballot, but:

There are those – and I am one of them – who refuse to have the ballot interpreted for them . . . I know . . . that when workers are brought together in a great organization, they are not going to cease to vote. That is when workers will *begin* to vote for directors to operate the industries in which they are all employed.[28]

In the absence of that industrial success, Socialist factions were bound to collide. The moderate Socialists had growing fears about the violence and seemingly anarchistic actions of the unskilled workers. Haywood brought these fears to the surface and provided the moderates with a means of attack in a speech to Manhattan Socialists during the Lawrence strike. Summing up his experiences with the lawlessness of the class struggle in his mining experiences and the persecutions he had suffered at the hands of the law, he said:

. . . We know the class struggle in the West. And realizing, having contended with all the bitter things that we have been called upon to drink to the dregs, do you blame me when I say that *I despise the law* (tremendous applause and shouts of "No!") and I am not a law-abiding citizen. (Applause.) And more than that, no Socialist can be a law-abiding citizen. (Applause.) When we come together and are of a common mind, and the purpose of our minds is to overthrow the capitalist system, we become conspirators against the United States government. And certainly it is our purpose to abolish this government (applause) and to establish in its place an industrial democracy. (Applause.) Now, we haven't any hesitation in saying that is our aim and purpose. Am I correct? (Tremendous applause.) . . .

Well then, it isn't only the men of the West who understand the class struggle. You understand it here just as well as we do there. . . .[29]

Obviously, it was indeed the purpose of the Socialist movement to abolish capitalism. But moderate Socialists insisted upon separating that ultimate aim from the tactics of participating in

[28] William D. Haywood, "The General Strike," *International Socialist Review* XI (May, 1911), 684.

[29] "Socialism, the Hope of the Working Class," *International Socialist Review* XII (February, 1912), 466.

civil society within the laws provided by democratic capitalism. In 1912, there was more reason than ever for believing Socialists could win by these rules: an unprecedented number of electoral victories including 1200 local officials (and of that number, seventy-nine mayors), a presidential vote of nearly a million, or 6 per cent of the national ballot, a momentous rise of party membership to over 100,000 and an advance in the party press to new heights of circulation, and a power within the AFL unknown since the 1890s. With such successes on the one side, and doubtful Wobbly efforts on the other, the moderates' campaign was pressed home. At the 1912 convention, a clause had been inserted into the party constitution specifying recall for any member of the National Executive Committee advocating sabotage. Inevitably, Haywood raised the subject again, was recalled, and had his recall ratified by national party referendum.[30] Haywood withdrew from the party in disgust and, although accurate estimates are difficult to make, perhaps 10 to 15 per cent of the party's militants withdrew with him.[31]

Contemporaneously, the party pushed to a conclusion its attitudes toward recent immigrants and immigration. In 1907, when the International Socialist Congress at Stuttgart had voted against any restriction of immigration, Morris Hillquit of the American delegation vainly argued that – as he expressed it later – some "races and nations" were too backward for assimilation into the modern labor movement. In 1908 an ambiguous resolution was presented to the American Socialist convention, asserting the right of workers to "protect themselves against injury to their interests, caused by the competition of imported foreign laborers," referring possibly only to contract labor. The resolution was passed, but larger questions were deferred and a Committee on Immigration established with a majority of outspoken exclusionists. A struggle at the 1910 convention again resulted in an ambiguous resolution written by Morris Hillquit, which argued:

> The Socialist party of the United States favors all legislative measures tending to prevent the immigration of strikebreakers and contract laborers, and the mass importation of workers from foreign countries, brought about by the employing classes for the purpose of weakening the organization of American labor, and of lowering the standard of life of American Workers.
>
> The Party is opposed to the exclusion of any immigrants on account of

[30] For a defense of Socialist Party attitudes toward Haywood, see James Weinstein, *Decline of Socialism in America, 1912-1925* (New York, 1967), 27-33.

[31] For the strength of the Socialist Party at the time, see *Ibid.*

their race or nationality, and demands that the United States be at all times maintained as a free asylum for all men and women persecuted by the governments of their countries on account of their politics, religion or race.[32]

In 1912, the party endorsed an anti-Asiatic report and a minority report agreeing with the Stuttgart resolution. The campaign book for the 1912 election, taken in part from the works of moderate Robert Hunter, argued the evils of immigration and the "likelihood of race annihilation and the possible degeneration of even the succeeding American type."[33]

Such was the party's official attitude, supported most fervently by Socialists linked to constituencies of skilled, AFL workers, and by moderate reformers who shared the Progressives' fears of "race suicide." Against the inertia of the victorious Right within the party, the Left could only offer a minority of votes and a mighty indignation. No one expressed this indignation better than Debs himself, mistrusted by party moderates while lionized by workers inside and outside the party. In 1910, Debs had written a "letter" to delegates to the upcoming convention saying in part:

The alleged advantages that would come to the Socialist movement because of such heartless exclusion would all be swept away a thousand times by the sacrifice of a cardinal principle of the international socialist movement, for well might the good faith of such a movement be questioned if it placed itself upon record as barring its doors against the very races most in need of relief, and extinguishing their hopes and leaving them in dark despair at the very time their ears were first attuned to the international call and their hearts were beginning to throb responsible to the solidarity of the oppressed of all lands and all climes beneath the skies. . . .

Let those desert us who will because we refuse to shut the international door in the faces of their own brethren; we will be none the weaker but all the stronger for their going, for they evidently have no clear conception of the international solidarity, are wholly lacking in the revolutionary spirit, and have no proper place in the Socialist movement while they entertain such aristocratic notions of their own assumed superiority.[34]

Such appeals, even from Debs, were of no avail since the moderate forces felt the very basis of their strength threatened. Indeed, Victor Berger, Max Hayes, and others had personally taken such extreme positions on race and immigration that they must have viewed the final resolution as a merely acceptable compromise.[35]

[32]Quoted from Leinenweber, "Immigration," 172.

[33]*Ibid.*, 176.

[34]"A Letter from Debs on Immigration," *International Socialist Review* XI (July, 1910), 16-17.

[35]For examples of flagrant racism, see Victor Berger, "We Will Stand by the Real

Yet moderate Socialists were destined to be deprived of the fruits of their factional victories. After 1912, crises external and internal beset the party; trade union support which had reached its peak that year began to decline. The effects of the Progressive movement and the legislative promises of the Wilson administration cut into reformist support; and there was a general slump in Socialist activism, indicating an uncertainty and vague discouragement about the future. The onslaught of World War I hastened the process of internal decay among the older Socialist forces. Severe repression in the Midwest and Southwest along with a growingly rapid deterioration of Socialist strength in AFL unions greatly reduced the "real American" membership.[36]

Concurrently, the party had already begun to gather those internal forces which were crucial to its future, the foreign-language workers. As early as 1904, foreign-language groups unaffiliated with the Socialist movement sought a relationship between the party and themselves. After a series of mechanisms were tried, the party convention of 1910 passed a constitutional amendment establishing autonomous status for foreign-language "federations." Already by 1912, seven groups had affiliated, contributing 13 per cent of the party's membership.

The events in Europe and the entry of America into the war radicalized eastern and southern Europeans in the United States. By 1915, the foreign-language federations provided a third of the party's shrunken membership of 80,000, and its own press began to overtake the "American" counterpart.[37] The militant Socialist position against the war brought further working class support, notably among new immigrants in some metropolitan areas. The Socialist candidate for mayor of New York in 1918, Morris Hillquit, received 21.7 per cent of the vote despite vicious "Hun-baiting" from the major parties.[38] By 1919, the party had

---

American Proletariat," *Social Democratic Herald,* October 12, 1907; and Ernest Untermann, "The Endless March," *New York Call,* May 12, 1912.

[36] There remains no adequate account of the decline of Socialist Party activities immediately following 1912, and the "slump" that nearly all Socialists felt. Weinstein, in attacking Communist (and other) historical retrospects on the decline after 1912, calls the party's activity a "leveling off." But the difficulties were in fact pervasive. For another reflection on the dampened perspectives, see Mari Jo Buhle, "Women and the Socialist Party 1901-1914," in Edith Hoshino Altbach, ed., *From Feminism to Liberation* (Cambridge, 1971), 65-86.

[37] Leinenweber, "Immigration," 205-210.

[38] Kolko, "Decline of American Radicalism," *Studies On the Left* VI (September-October, 1966), 9-26. For Kolko, the period of severe government repression begins significantly just when the Socialist Party poses a genuine class threat to American institutions.

nearly regained its size of 1912. As Gabriel Kolko has pointed out, however, this new party was predominantly one of foreign workers: from 13 per cent seven years before, the percentage of members in the language federations had jumped to 52 per cent of its 109,000 enrolled. The old leadership temporarily made game efforts to adapt. Even Victor Berger denounced the pro-war AFL and offered a contribution to IWW defense funds. The forces of moderate Socialists were, however, for the moment anyway, exhausted, and the future apparently lay with the Left.[39]

With the change of conditions, moderate Socialist theories had fallen to the ground. The best that could be claimed was a return to normal after the war, and with government repression on the one hand and new ranks of immigrant Socialists on the other, this perspective seemed increasingly unrealistic. Revolutionary thought, meanwhile, had undergone great changes since pre-1910 days. Before the rise of unskilled workers' strikes from 1909 onward, the Left generally had little to explain its position but a declamatory rhetoric of abstract internationalism, support for the IWW, and a catalog of the Socialist moderates' sins.[40] Lacking a stable base such as the Right had in the skilled workers, Leftists could only insist that a day of revolution was approaching for which Socialists had to prepare. The militance of immigrant workers in the East and migrant workers in the West rooted Left hopes in a real constituency, and broadened Left theory from abstraction to concrete analysis.

The conceptualization of mass activity by the unskilled workers had begun outside the ranks of the Socialist party, among a few early industrial unionists and above all Daniel DeLeon. His attempt to create an alternative to the AFL in the 1890s, through the Socialist Trade and Labor Alliance, had been merely a political effort to incorporate union activity into the Left on a daily basis. By 1905, however, DeLeon had drawn on the experience of his own failures along with the insights of certain American unionists and the theories of the Italian syndicalist theorist, Antonio Labriola, to synthesize a broader interpretation. Now he announced industrial unionism was the very basis of all revolutionary

[39] Note James Weinstein's valuable summary of Socialist Party voting patterns, in *Decline of Socialism in America,* 154-59 and tables 4 and 5 on 173-76. Unfortunately, the centrality of the war issue makes true support for Socialist principles difficult to determine.

[40] See Ira Kipnis, *American Socialist Movement, 1897-1912* (New York, 1952), 176, for a commentary on Socialist Left-wing editor Herman Titus, a representative of the pre-1910 Left.

activity, for through revolutionary unions the workers would be prepared socially and politically to seize control of society. Politics remained necessary for the sake of education and to provide a legal umbrella for union activity. But the specifically political conceptions of doctrinaire Socialism in the nineteenth century, evoking visions of mass political parties leading workers to the barricades, were outdated and now obstructive.[41]

DeLeon failed to develop his ideas further, and after his expulsion from the IWW in 1908 his following dwindled. But his reformulation of the very meaning of Socialist politics and radical unionism was continued and broadened by others. Most prominent among his theoretical successors was Austin Lewis, a lawyer and veteran of the Socialist movement from the final decades of the nineteenth century. Lewis' writing was not prolific, a handful of articles and two short books, yet it broke through the previous limitations of Marxist theory in the United States to German-style exegesis or simple propaganda. Most significantly for us, it did so precisely through a critique of unskilled workers.

Lewis' analysis began with the situation of the skilled workers. Once central to production, they had dominated the Socialist movement at its formation and imbued it with their sense of craft, which was in fact conceived as a kind of property. They disdained unskilled workers as a kind of "lumpen-proletariat," outside the sphere of labor toward which Socialists oriented themselves, because outside of organized labor. Yet the revolutionization of production had outwitted even the Socialists who constantly expounded their understanding of history. Skill began to lose "its commanding influence" in the large factory where the key element became instead "the discipline and coordination of the mass of workers." The operation of modern markets for producing and selling mass consumption needs intensified this development which appeared almost as a "conspiracy to dethrone the skilled craftsman . . . as the determining and necessary factor in the production process." Against this objective development, the craft union leaders had no adequate protection; they could broaden their unions for industrial control but their narrow-minded suspicion and contempt for unskilled workers rendered their "minds incapable of grasping" even the possibility.[42] In civil

[41] See DeLeon's pronouncement on the IWW convention, *The Preamble to the I.W.W.,* later reprinted as *The Socialist Reconstruction of Society* (New York, 1956), a widely read document especially before DeLeon's expulsion from the IWW's ranks.

[42] "Mechanics of Solidarity, II," *New Review* III (December 15, 1915), 357.

society, craft unionists could command considerable and indeed sometimes growing influence. In California, where Lewis lived, the "avenues to political preferment are crowded from the organized labor bodies."[43] Skilled craftsmen became congressmen, mayors, supervisors, and a variety of minor officials in that fluid environment. By World War I, the AFL could gain favors from the government, including the Adamson Act, and a variety of reforms in such areas as California where a Progressive administration gained power. Yet these gains did not at all indicate the growing power of the working class. To the contrary, they denoted the bourgeoisification of privileged sectors of the work force and, by and large, solidarity of these layers with the government and business against the interests of the unskilled workers.[44]

In the short run, this development had had a doleful effect upon the American Socialist movement. With the maturation of Socialism in the 1890s and finally in the birth of the Socialist Party, the skilled workers' groups together with the discontented forces of the small bourgeoisie (the dying old middle class, farmers, small town elements all "thoroughly whipped" by modern industrialism) dominated the new movement against the element of unskilled workers who could promise few votes and little stability. Even at this point, Lewis claimed, the unskilled were becoming recognized, if only through the abuse heaped on the movement of poor, unorganized and migratory workers by orthodox Socialist politicals.[45] As their activities grew and developed, unskilled workers began to gain more influence among Socialists. "Without industrial action," Lewis commented, the "Socialist Party would be a somewhat uninteresting symptom of trade union and petty-bourgeois discontent," as evidenced by the hodgepodge of Socialist election promises.[46] After McKees' Rocks, the rank-and-file of trade unions, including some Socialists, began to recognize the reality of their own situation and the potential of the unorganized. Yet buoyed by election returns, the moderate Socialists continued and even expanded their campaign against revolutionary elements. Whole groups of militant Socialists and thousands of individuals had joined and left the Socialist Party even before the recall of Haywood. It was "pathetic," noted Lewis,

[43] "Potential Solidarity," *Ibid.*, III (October 1, 1915), 254.
[44] "The Way That Failed," *International Socialist Review* XVII (June, 1917), 738.
[45] "Mechanics of Solidarity," *New Review* III (December 1, 1915), 332-35.
[46] Austin Lewis, *The Militant Proletariat* (Chicago, 1911), 179, 183.

> . . . to see the type of men who are being driven out of the Socialist party. Young and vigorous workmen, full of ambition for the cause of the proletariat, enthusiastic and generous, refuse to be herded along a path which leads to disillusion and makes only for the advantage of misleaders. . . . Their places are taken by the smooth bourgeois, mealy-mouthed anemic ethicists and political adventurers. It is a poor exchange and we are all the poorer thereby. The men should have stayed since they could do no better; they should have stayed and helped the rest of us.

Yet the Socialist Party lived, and by its very existence drew revolutionary forces toward itself. "In spite of all of its present vileness, its double dealing and . . . belly-crawling . . . to labor organized on safe, sane and conservative lines," the party would be forced along the path toward militancy by the economic actions of the unskilled workers.[47]

The only future for the workers' movement and for the Socialist movement, Lewis concluded, lay in the mass struggles of the unskilled. Capitalists, Socialists, and labor leaders had been themselves "completely taken by surprise" by the first wave of mass strikes after 1909. The implications were enormous: "a portion of the working class had at last arrived at the place where mass action was their natural and spontaneous expression; and that portion of the proletariat which had hitherto been considered incapable of organization had consciously striven for a new and effective form of organization which transcended all its predecessors in scope and potential.[48] Why, Lewis asked, had it emerged in such a unique form? The answer lay in the *psychology* of mass production, and Lewis utilized insights gleaned from the works of Thorstein Veblen to analyze this psychology. It was not agitators but rather the "very environment of factory life" which produced the new movement. The machine industry:

> . . . rules the mass of unskilled proletarians. It drives them to work together in unison. It forces them to keep time with the industrial machine and in so doing teaches them the goose step of industrial organization, for organization by the employer is the first step to the self-organization of the employed. . . . Preaching cannot put the idea into the mind of the worker. Facts themselves force him to revolt. Facts also teach him the method of revolt. This method more and more takes the form of spontaneous mass action. This is the reflex upon the mind of workers who have nothing in common and never had anything in common except the fact of common environment, a common objection to the machine industry.[49]

[47] "A Positive Platform," *International Socialist Review* XII (April, 1912), 664.
[48] "Mechanics of Solidarity, II," 358.
[49] "Organization of the Unskilled," *New Review* I (December, 1913), 961.

The necessity of solidarity, moreover, imparted to the Socialist movement that élan that it had so sadly lacked. Lewis pointed to the Labor Day parade of Mexican unskilled workers in Los Angeles in 1910: while the skilled crafts displayed their union signs and emblems, the Mexicans could find no other symbol than a simple placard bearing the phrase, "Workers of the World Unite."[50]

From this understanding of the nature and potential of the unskilled work force, Left writers sought to create an essentially new theory of Marxism for the United States. In abandoning the comfort of the skilled-worker constituency in theory and practice, they attempted to fulfill in fact the tasks which Frederick Engels had set out as necessary guidelines for an American revolutionary movement in 1886:

> There is no better road to theoretical clearness of comprehension than to learn by one's own mistakes. . . . And for a whole large class, there is no other road, especially for a nation so eminently practical and so contemptuous of theory as the Americans. The great thing is to get the working class to move *as a class*; that once obtained, they will soon find the right direction, and all who resist . . . will be left out in the cold. . . .[51]

Thus the unskilled workers would of necessity rise in a variety of ways, fail, and rise again with new understanding and confidence in their capabilities as a class. The strategy for their activity was called by the Left "Mass Action," a term delineated and popularized by the Dutch Left-Socialist (and noted astronomer) Anton Pannekoek. Against those moderate Socialists, or anarchists, who pictured the distinction between daily agitation and the day of the revolution as the great rupture in civil life, Pannekoek insisted that Mass Action was a *process* of revolution whereby strikes turned into demonstrations and demonstrations into factory seizures over a period of years. For Pannekoek, the

[50] "Basis of Solidarity," *New Review* III (August 15, 1915), 186. As in Europe, the upsweep of unorganized workers inspired a general expression of fervor which, Left Socialists hoped, would itself be a spur to activity. As Robert Rives LaMonte wrote in a widely reprinted article: "Socialist writers from Ferdinand Lassalle to Miss Vida Scudder have always insisted upon the spiritual rebirth effected by a vivid sense of class consciousness and class responsibility. But the Old Socialism, which has made its powerful appeals to class emotions only at infrequently recurring elections, could not make this spiritual awakening of the toiling masses an actuality. The New Socialism, with its call to the workers to fight the Class War daily in the shops, is day by day effecting the moral rebirth of the workers." – "The New Socialism," *International Socialist Review* XIII (September, 1912), 216.

[51] Frederick Engels to Florence (Kelley) Winchevsky, December 28, 1886, printed in *Marx and Engels' Letters to Americans* (New York, 1953), 166-67.

decisive factor was not the theories and activities of the parties, but the instincts developed in the daily lives of the masses:

> Liberal theoreticians may, from the heights of their wisdom, look down with contempt upon the instinct of the masses. Marxian theoreticians, who know how class conditions determine opinions, recognize in this instinct the class feeling, the mighty power which, springing forward from the economic position of the proletariat, impels and leads the masses forward in the great social struggle.[52]

According to the American Left theorist, Louis C. Fraina, this Mass Action based upon class instinct would not abolish politics but rather would push revolutionary politics to the fore. With the power of the state used against strikers, Socialists in office or running for positions would become tribunes of the people's rights in battle. While revealing the "futility of parliamentarism in itself," the interventionist role of the state demonstrated the very existence of the state as a vital stake in politics.[53]

After the fall of the Paris Commune, Marx had drawn the lesson that the levers of the state could not simply be used by the working class, but would have to be smashed and replaced by new forms. Fraina and the Left now repudiated the view of the American moderates like Berger that the machinery of government could be utilized and expanded into Socialism. The system of capitalism, Fraina held, had begun its merger with the state. Externally, the system mirrored imperialism, and internally a self-avowed Progressivism linking the ruling interests of the society with those of the middle classes and upper layers of skilled workers. While the old reformism of the middle classes, Populism, had long been crushed, the new middle class initiative of Roosevelt's "New Nationalism" was an ominous bench mark in American political life:

> ... [a] clear and consistent formulation of the requirements of the new era of controlled industry and collectivist Capitalism. It called for the extension

[52] Anton Pannekoek, "Revolutionary Instinct of the Masses," *New York Call*, October 27, 1912. In August 1 of the same year a series of debates between Pannekoek and Karl Kautsky was begun – translated from the German theoretical organ *Neue Zeit* – which the *Call* editor described as "the most notable contribution to Socialist thought that we have had in a long time." See Editorial, "A Notable Series," in August 15 issue; and "Mass Action and Revolution" in August 15, September 1, and September 8 issues of the *Call*.

[53] Louis C. Fraina, *Revolutionary Socialism* (New York, 1918), 191. For a fuller analysis of Fraina's views and their importance, see Paul Buhle, "Louis C. Fraina-Lewis Corey, 1892-1953," (unpublished Master's thesis, University of Connecticut, 1967).

of the functions of the Federal government, regulation equally of capital and labor, the Strong Man policy of administrative centralization of the powers of the state, and the necessity of coordination and unifying all the forces of the capitalist class through the national administrative control of industry. . . .[54]

Certainly, Fraina conceded, the new forces of rationalization were progressive "within limits that are rigidly defined": the cessation of the anarchy of production, development of welfare services, and so forth. But in their implications for the world, and ultimately for the American people, the same forces were "compellingly reactionary."[55]

By the time of Fraina's major theoretical contributions in 1918-19, Socialists had good cause to complain of American capitalism's reactionary nature. Wartime repression had brought mass arrests of Wobblies, vigilante attacks on radicals of all kinds, and suppression of the major Socialist publications. Simultaneously, there opened a strike wave which seemed to vindicate the Left's expectation.

In 1919, mass labor stoppages occurred on a level unknown since the 1890s. Strikes had in fact continued through the war, at one point shutting down the most important munitions center of the country and involving thousands of workers in solidarity demonstration for various actions. In Seattle a general strike ensued, temporarily closing all the city's business. Concurrently, a pattern of strikes developed in most major industrial areas, including new textile strikes in Lawrence and Paterson and a violent and protracted national coal strike. Most important for Fraina and his cohorts, however, was the Great Steel Strike. During the war the introduction of technological rationalization had brought the procedures of time-and-motion studies and a generalized company effort to increase the rate of exploitation. Meanwhile sporadic strikes had broken out, and rioting in Youngstown had followed an explosion in a plant. The AFL, made confident by wartime stabilization, initiated an organizing committee headed by William Z. Foster, later head of the American Communist Party. Despite AFL timidity, a strike ensued in 1919 at the insistence of the unions' thousands of new members. These largely immigrant workers were at the core of the 350,000 strikers whose activities paralyzed much of the industry. Despite heroic

[54] Fraina, p. 66.
[55] *Ibid.*, 65.

efforts, repression quelled any mass social movement from developing in support of the strike, and workers divided into no less than twenty-four AFL affiliates lacked the solidarity and support to win. Finally the strike was defeated, a monument to the lost hopes of 1919.[56]

This defeat symbolized both the inability of labor to achieve industrial organization and the failure of the Left to transcend its old social basis. As the productive organization of the textile mills had marked one stage of modern production, the technological innovations of the postwar steel mills marked the next. Against the combined powers of capital and state, both the IWW and AFL had thrown their best efforts and had failed. Industrial organization on a widespread basis was to await another generation.

The Socialist movement also fell on evil times. The Russian Revolution had set into motion forces across the world for the formation of new revolutionary Communist parties. Despite the antiwar position of the Socialist Party and the common support given by Socialists to the Revolution, the Bolsheviks' declaration of a new stage of revolutionism prevented international solidarity. The National Executive Committee, reacting prematurely and undemocratically to the specter of competition, refused to recognize a newly elected and more radical NEC, summarily expelling a full two-thirds of the party's membership including all of the major foreign-language federations. A small minority of the expelled members joined one or another of the two competing Communist parties, while most disappeared from the radical movement entirely. Wrecked, the Socialist movement never regained any significant strength, while the Communist movement remained trivial for over a decade.[57]

The understanding of the Socialist moderates, as we have seen, was at least a decade out of date in 1919. The theories of the Left were, at best, ahead of their time. Before the excitement of the Russian Revolution, Fraina had warned that immediate insurrection in the United States was not to be expected, that because of the expansion of imperialism, American capitalism had yet another "cycle" to complete.[58] With the outbreak of events in Russia and in Europe, the Left threw caution to the winds while

[56] Brecher, Chapter 4; George Rawick, "Working Class Self-Activity," *Radical America* II (March-April, 1969), 23.

[57] Weinstein, Chapters 4 to 6.

[58] Louis Fraina, "The Future of Socialism," *New Review* III (January, 1915), 14.

only the moderates stressed the remoteness in time of the revolutionary Moment. In a larger sense their comprehension of "State Capitalism" uniting domestic reforms and repression with imperialist policy abroad was prescient; but it was with a dour satisfaction that Socialists could recognize their vindication.

The false expectations of Left Socialists were based, as those of moderates had been earlier, in the supposed emergence of a universal proletarian, the worker stripped of all his loyalties save that to his class. Clearly enough, the skilled worker was not that universal figure, and the Socialists who adapted their theories to his interests ultimately gloried in his respectability and restraint. The unskilled worker and especially the immigrant worker were harder to characterize, for the vast bulk of American society (including reform wings in the Socialist and suffragist movements) misunderstood and distrusted the Italian, Bohemian, Pole, and Slavonian as if they were identical. In effect, Austin Lewis, Louis Fraina, and others merely reversed the stereotypes and, looking at the workers' role within industry, asserted a social solidarity which in fact existed only sporadically and in certain situations. The evolution of the universal proletarian (if it is ever to be reached) had very far yet to go, especially in a society where female and minority group workers continued to suffer special disadvantages.

In the long view, the Socialist problem with the immigrant worker was for that time and place insoluble. Even at best, the language federations were inadequate devices for introducing European workers into the American class struggle. The federations' leadership continued to look primarily to events in their old homelands. Consequently neither moderates nor revolutionaries could devise a means for integrating the rank-and-file federation member into American work. In the 1920s, the Communist Party simply forced an Americanization of the most disciplined cadres (driving thousands from Communist ranks), later reinstating language groups for the Popular Front policies of the 1930s. No policy, however brilliant and diligently applied, could achieve what was a social and personal transformation. For the foreign-born radical worker to become an American, in fact, was for him to join the consensual modes of the larger society (as most of the radicals' children did) and relinquish those very traits that had made him distinctively radical. Only when those larger social modes themselves began to give way, perhaps in the ensuing collapse of the state capitalism that Fraina described, could radical action be performed by masses of people unimpeachably "American."[59]

FOR FURTHER READING

Brecher, Jeremy. *Strike!* San Francisco: Straight Arrow Books, 1972.

Davis, Horace. *Nationalism and Socialism.* New York: Monthly Review Press, 1967.

Draper, Theodore. *Roots of American Communism.* New York: Viking Press, 1967.

Fraina, Louis C. *Revolutionary Socialism.* New York: Communist Publishing Association, 1918.

Haywood, William D. *Bill Haywood's Book.* New York: International Publishers, 1929.

Kipnis, Ira. *The American Socialist Movement, 1897-1912.* New York: Columbia University Press, 1952.

Laslett, John H.M. *Labor and the Left: A Study of Socialist and Radical Influences in the American Labor Movement, 1881-1924.* New York: Basic Books, 1970.

Lewis, Austin. *The Militant Proletariat.* Chicago: Charles H. Kerr Co., 1911.

Pannekoek, Anton. *Workers' Councils.* Cambridge, Massachusetts: Root and Branch, 1971.

Weinstein, James. *The Decline of Socialism in America, 1912-1925.* New York: Monthly Review Press, 1967.

[59]There is no intent here to imply that working class activity loses its importance or its progressive character after the period of cultural assimilation, but rather the thrust it poses lies culturally within the system even while activity (such as the sit-down strikes of the 1930s) implies the expropriation of society's physical machinery by its operatives. Only at the end of the process of social integration, when imperial and internal decay reinforce one another, does the class tension over the control of industry show (along with and indeed inseparable from the other tensions of society) a renewed revolutionary possibility. On the political implications of these notions, see Paul Buhle, "Marxism in the United States: 39 Propositions," *Radical America* V (November-December, 1971).

Sources

1

The Battle for Bread at Lawrence

The following is the excerpted text from a report by Mary E. Marcy, an associate editor of the *International Socialist Review.* Most interesting, perhaps, is the text of the lecture by William D. Haywood, a simple and clear exposition of internationalism repeated in substance at every major Wobbly-led strike of the period.

SOURCE: "The Battle for Bread at Lawrence," *International Socialist Review,* XIII (March, 1912), pp. 535-43.

The primary cause of the strike, a cut of 22 cents in the weekly wage was, after the arrival of Joseph J. Ettor, organizer for the Industrial Workers of the World, merged into a series of demands. These demands included a 15 per cent increase in wages, the abolition of the bonus and premium system and double pay for overtime work.

With the accession of Ettor a new spirit of militancy began to permeate the strikers. Too late the mill owners offer to grant the original demand. But the new spirit of solidarity among the men and women, bringing with it a sense of their own power, welded them together in a determination to secure more of their product – to improve their condition. . . .

Haywood Arrives

January 24 Haywood reached Lawrence to help carry on the strike. We quote from the *Evening Tribune,* Lawrence:

William D. Haywood arrived in Lawrence at 11:50 o'clock from New York City Wednesday morning and over 10,000 strikers turned out together with three bands and two drum corps, to greet him at the North Station with a tremendous ovation.

Long before the time when he was scheduled to arrive the strikers assembled at the depot in eager anticipation of the coming of the famous labor organizer. Even at 9 o'clock there was a large crowd awaiting his arrival.

Before 10 o'clock the number of strikers at the station had been greatly increased. The sidewalks on Essex street were filled to their greatest capacities. Common street was crowded all morning also with strikers wending their way to the Boston & Maine station. About 10:30 o'clock the Franco-Belgian band arrived, having marched from the Franco-Belgian hall on Mason street. This band was followed by about 200 of the Franco-Belgian element of the strikers. The band stopped in front of the postoffice and played several selections.

The number of strikers was being continually augmented and the crowd seemed to be growing restless. About 11 o'clock a parade of about a thousand strikers came up Essex street. In this parade were the Umberto and the Bellini bands and St. Joseph's drum corps. When this contingent arrived there was great cheering. The bands played almost continuously and there was a great deal of noise. Every time that the cab train came in sight the crowd would commence cheering and the bands would play with renewed vigor.

Shortly after 11:30 o'clock a large parade came up Common street and joined forces with the strikers already at the station. At the head of this parade there was a sign painted on cardboard in large black letters, "All in One." There were many American flags carried by the strikers.

Finally the time for the arrival of Mr. Haywood came and when the train came in sight there was a great demonstration. When the train was approaching the crowd kept pushing up near the tracks and it looked as if someone would be run over.

When the strikers caught sight of Haywood they went almost insane with delight and cheered incessantly while the bands and drum corps boomed out stirring selections. The scene was certainly a wild one. As Mr. Haywood came out of the car he took off his hat and waved it to the crowd. The strikers surrounded Haywood and then the parade started down Common street. Haywood was near the head of the parade and was surrounded by thousands of howling and cheering strikers. The parade was over 10,000 strong. The bands played and excitement of the highest pitch prevailed.

In the afternoon a monster mass meeting was held on the commons.

When Haywood was introduced there was such an enthusiastic demonstration that it was many moments before he could make himself heard. He said in part:

"Sister and Brother workers: There are times in every man's life when he feels that words cannot express his feelings. That is the way that I feel now when I look out into this sea of faces. The ovation that was given to me this morning was certainly marvelous and I deeply appreciate it. Mr. Ettor has told you of my history with the I.W.W. My dream in life is to see all workers united in one big union. You should carry this idea into effect because without it you will be forced back into the mills and have even worse conditions, not only in the textile works, but all workers. It behooves you to stick together and fight this present strike to a finish. You will win out if you are loyal to yourself. I saw in one of the papers that Lawrence was afraid of my coming. It is not Lawrence that fears my coming, it is the bosses and the superintendents and the owners of the mills that fear me. This is a familiar scene to me, to see soldiers guarding mills, as I have often been in just such strikes before, but I have never, in all my experience, seen a strike defeated by soldiers. It is necessary to keep a tight rein on yourselves. If we can prevail on other workers who handle your goods to help you out by going on strike we will tie up the railroads, put the city in darkness and starve the soldiers out. The only way to make such a condition possible is to have one big union. In London once when there was a strike everything was stopped and it became necessary for the officers of the soldiers to ask permission to carry food to the horses who were starving. In France they stopped the railroads and won a strike in three days. Soon I hope to see the workers so organized that when the mills in Lawrence go on strike, for instance, the mills in every city will go on strike. In this way you will lock the bosses out for once and for all. You have been ground down terribly in these mills. I can see that by your faces. Let me urge you on in this strike. I came here to say that the working class all over the country will help you out. In a few days I am going to the west and in every city that I go to I will say to the unions: 'Help the strikers in Lawrence by sending provisions and money.' Don't let the bosses fool you. This international question will never be solved unless you solve it yourselves. Stand heart to heart, mind to mind, and hand to hand with all your fellow workers and you will win out.

"All you people come from other nations and you all come to America with the expectation of improving your conditions. You expected to find a land of the free, but you found we of America were but economic slaves as you were in your own home. I come to extend to you tonight the hand of brotherhood with no thought of nationality. There is no foreigner here except the capitalist and he will not be a foreigner long for we will make a worker of him. Do not let them divide you by sex, color, creed or nationality, for as you stand today you are invincible. . . .

"You can't weave cloth with bayonets. The blue cloth that you have woven has gone to clothe those soldiers, but it will wear out. United in this organization we will never weave any more for them; let them go naked.

"Don't let this be a single handed struggle. Join hands with the others. Let us build up a new organization in which every man contributes his part toward the welfare of others. Let us enforce a regime in which no man can make anything for profit.

"The only way to win is to unite with all other textile workers. No one branch can get along without the other. The woolsorter is necessary, no matter how stinking his job may be. You are textile workers but you don't seem to realize what an important factor you as textile workers are to society. You are the men and women who clothe the world. You make the clothes for the working class and the robes for the rich. The continuance of civilization is in many cases due to your efforts. You are more important to society than any judge on the supreme bench, than any judge, lawyer, politician or capitalist or any man who does not work for an honest living. Those who do nothing are always looked up to as the prominent citizens of a city.

"It is an inspiration to see you all together in one great cause. I hope to see the boundary line between all nations broken down and one great nation of the working class. There are only two nations in the world today; the working class on one side and the capitalists on the other. We of the working class must stand together."

The wonderful solidarity displayed by the strikers has surprised everybody. There are more languages spoken in the confines of Lawrence than in any other district of its size in the world. But in spite of these barriers, the strike was an almost spontaneous one and seventeen races, differing widely in speech and custom, rose in a concerted protest. Lacking anything like a substantial organization at the outset, they have clung together in furthering a common cause without dissension. Too much credit cannot be given Comrades Joseph Ettor and Wm. D. Haywood in the splendid work of organization and education they have carried on in Lawrence. Says the *Outlook* for February 10:

"Haywood does not want unions of weavers, unions of spinners, unions of loom-fixers, unions of wool-sorters, but he wants one comprehensive union of all textile workers, which in time will take over the textile factories, as the steel workers will take over the steel mills and the railway workers the railways. Haywood interprets the class conflict literally as a war which is always on, which becomes daily more bitter and uncompromising, which can end only with the conquest of a capitalistic society by proletarians or wage-workers, organized industry by industry.

"Haywood places no trust in trade agreements, which, according to his theory, lead merely to social peace and 'put the workers to sleep.' Let the employer lock out his men when he pleases, and let the workmen strike when they please. He is opposed to arbitration, conciliation, compromise; to sliding scales, profit-sharing, welfare work; to everything, in short, which may weaken the revolutionary force of the workers. He does not ask for the closed shop or the official recognition of the union, for he has no intention of recognizing the employer. What he desires is not a treaty of industrial peace between the two high contracting parties, but merely the creation of a proletarian impulse which will eventually revolutionize society. Haywood is a man who believes in men not as you and I believe in them, but fervently, uncompromisingly, with an obstinate faith in the universal good will and constancy of the workers, worthy of a great religious leader. That is what makes him supremely dangerous."

Governor Foss, himself one of the mill owners, and Mayor Scanlon have never before met "strike leaders" like Ettor and Haywood. This is probably their first experience with representatives of labor who cannot be "reached" in some way. More than one attempt was made to come to an "understanding" with Ettor. It was even shown how he could persuade the strikers to accept a few of their demands, call off the strike and make himself the most popular labor leader in the country with the mill companies, but in preference, the *Boston Herald* says:

"He is to be found at almost any hour in some long low-ceiled hall talking earnestly to row upon row of set faces which strangely contrast the racial peculiarities of many quarters of the earth."

Talking, talking, always talking on One Big Union. It was agreed by the mill owners long before Haywood's arrival that he was the worst possible man they could have opposing them. . . .

Mr. Haywood was asked what his idea was relative to a committee coming to Lawrence to investigate conditions here, and later to investigate conditions throughout the state.

Haywood replied: "I have no hope in a legislative investigation, as I think it will result in nothing. The workers here have broken loose and other cities are soon going to break loose, too. It is immaterial to me, however, whether or not there is a legislative investigation.

"We have no hope in the two political parties which you represent, but I have no doubt that if the legislative committee comes here the strikers will give them all the information they want, and will furnish guides to bring you through the homes of the workers.

"If you gentlemen desire to improve conditions here, you could do well by withdrawing the militia and urge upon the legislature, favorable action on the bill for $10,000 for the Lawrence strikers, or double that amount.

"I have no question that the strikers here could improve conditions in the mills themselves, because they have the labor power.

"It is a vital matter, however, and I am glad to see that it has aroused the politicians, and it is high time that they saw it was someone else other than the 'upper ten' who were responsible for the prosperity of good old Massachusetts. Good will result if you go about the investigation honestly." . . .

On February 2, Ettor was arrested on a charge of complicity in the murder of Anna La Pizza, an Italian woman who was shot during a street meeting in Lawrence, January 30. Several business men in Lawrence proved that Ettor was not present at the time of the shooting but he was refused bail. Every one recognized this as another move on the part of the mill owners to cripple the strike.

The strikers were denied the privilege of congregating to hold meetings. Col. Sweetser is reported as saying:

"I will allow no mass meetings. I will allow no parades. We are going to look for trouble – legitimate trouble from now on. We are not looking for peace now."

On January 30 John Rami, an 18-year-old Syrian striker, was bayoneted by a member of a squad of Massachusetts militia. The boy was stuck through the back like a pig as he ran with seven companions before an unprovoked charge of the state soldiers. He died a few hours afterward in the Lawrence hospital. Many other strikers were injured by the soldiers.

But in spite of these disasters and the threat of Col. Sweetser, Elizabeth Gurley Flynn gathered together 12,000 strikers and marched with them down to hold a meeting on the commons. The soldiers faced them with bayonets, but yielded before the determined crowd of men and women.

At present a reign of terror has the entire city of Lawrence in its grip. Fourteen hundred soldiers have converted the streets into an armed camp. The classic doors of one of our oldest colleges have been thrown open to permit the youth of "our best families" to join the militia and "insolent, well-fed Harvard men parade up and down, their rifles loaded with ball cartridge, their bayonets glittering, keen and hungry for the blood of the strikers who are fighting the resources of the entire state to secure a wage that will enable them to live in comparative sufficiency and decency." (*New York Call.*)

Wm. E. Trautmann and James P. Thompson, organizers for the I.W.W., have joined Haywood in Lawrence, to help in the work of organization. Telegrams have been sent to the Switchmens' Unions and other railroad organizations asking them to refuse to handle the goods of the woolen companies, and Haywood has been called to Fall River and New Bedford where the workers are taking up plans for a state-wide strike in the textile mills.

Plans were laid for sending the children of the strikers to New York to be cared for during the fight and in response to the enthusiastic appeal of the *New York Call,* over 1,000 men and women offered to care for children until the strike was over.

The Lawrence strike is one of the most inspiring struggles the American workers have ever known. Separated by many different languages, customs and religions, the men and women, the boys and girls of Lawrence have joined hands to fight as one man against the common enemy – the woolen companies.

The strikers are accustomed to hunger and cold; hardships for themselves they can hope to endure, now that comrades in other cities have offered to feed and care for the children so that they may struggle on unhindered by the cries of the little ones for bread. . . .

In response to a motion by Comrade Haywood, the members of the National Executive Committee of the Socialist party have issued a call for funds to aid the strikers. The Socialists at Lawrence have set the wheels revolving by a movement to recall Mayor Scanlon. Socialist locals in Massachusetts and in every state in the union are holding meetings and selling literature and collecting donations to send to Lawrence.

On Sunday, Feb. 11th, at the Grand Central Station, New York City, 5,000 comrades met a carload of little strikers from Lawrence. The police, delegated to "preserve order" were swept aside and the children were caught up and swung shoulder high by strong working-class arms. At the Labor Temple warm food and clothes awaited them after which the comrades who were to care for them took the children home. Philadelphia has offered to care for 250 children. The tocsin of class solidarity has sounded throughout the land. Now is the time to show your colors.

This is your fight and my fight. An injury to one worker is an injury to all workers. We cannot save ourselves without freeing the whole working class. Now is the time to show the men and women at Lawrence that Socialism means something today as well as the abolition of wage slavery tomorrow.

2

The Socialist Party and Immigration

The following selection provides most of the Majority Report of the Socialist Party Committee on Immigration at the 1912 National Convention, and statements by the two leading antagonists on the party's official position. Ernest Untermann was the most profound scholar of Marxist exegesis in the American Socialist movement, translator of two volumes of Marx's *Capital,* author of philosophical texts published in the German Social-Democratic movement, and mentor of such American party notables as Jack London. John Spargo was the party's leading popularist, author of *The Bitter Cry of Children* and a series of other works, including a sentimental biography of Marx. Yet both were also practical activists, and deeply concerned from personal experience with the problem. Equally significant, the Socialist Left could provide no major articulation of an internationalist position; thus it was left to Spargo, a moderate by any standards and advocate of restricted immigration, to argue out the realities of the new immigration's effect upon the labor movement.

SOURCE: *National Congress of the Socialist Party, Chicago, May 15 to 21, 1910* (Chicago: Socialist Party, 1910), pp. 75-77, 84-85, 93-97.

REPORT OF COMMITTEE ON IMMIGRATION

[Majority Report]

The Socialist party aims to realize a system of society in which economic class distinctions, the foundation of all other class distinctions shall no longer exist, and in which all human beings without regard to nationality or race shall have equal opportunities as members of the industrial army of the world.

In the struggle for the realization of our social ideals it is the duty of the Socialist party to combat vigorously all those tendencies of the capitalist system which weaken the working classes of the different countries in their struggle for emacipation, and to promote and accelerate all those tendencies which increase their power of resistance, raise their standard of living and facilitate the organization and propaganda of the most militant and intelligent portions of the working class.

We recognize, however, that our present decaying capitalistic system generates many contradictory phases and antagonisms which at times compel the Socialist movement in its efforts to conform its acts to the present and immediate interests of the working class, to come into apparent conflict with its ultimate ideals. This, however, is an unavoidable condition of the general law of social progress. We work toward our ultimate ideals through and despite these apparent contradictions. We recognize with Marx that the progress of working class emancipation does not proceed uniformly and by identical methods in all countries, but that the working class of each nation will have first to settle matters with its own ruling class before absolute international working class solidarity can be realized.

The general question of Immigration and Emigration with its multitude of conflicting elements falls clearly into the category of contradictions referred to above. In a conflict between ultimate ideals and immediate class interests, the law of self-government asserts itself above all ultimate ideals. The Socialist Party in its present activities cannot outrun the general development of the working class, but must keep step with it. We agree with the statement of the *Communist Manifesto* that the Socialists "fight for the immediate aims, for the enforcement of the immediate interests of the working class," and that precisely "in the movement of the present we also represent and take care of the future" of our movement.

In advocating the policy of restricted immigration, or even the exclusion of specific races, we are not necessarily in contradiction with the essential principles of solidarity of the working class. On the contrary, we are convinced that this policy may, under some conditions, and especially under present conditions in the United States, be the most effective means of promoting the ultimate realization of international and inter-racial solidarity.

We agree with the conclusions of the International Congress at Stuttgart to the effect that "Immigration and Emigration of workingmen are phenomena as inseparable from the substance of capitalism as unemployment, overproduction and under-consumption of the working man, and that they are frequently one of the means to reduce the share of the working men in the product of labor, and that they at times assume abnormal dimensions through political, religious and national persecution."

Also we thoroughly endorse the statement of the same body that "it is the duty of organized working men to protect themselves against the lowering of the standard of life which frequently results from the mass import of unorganized working men."

We believe that this statement applies with peculiar force to conditions in the United States. If it be admitted that the working class of each nation has first to settle matters with its own ruling class; if it be furthermore admitted that by defending the immediate interests of the working class we are taking care of the ultimate ideals of the future; and if it be finally admitted that the principle of national autonomy prevents the International Congresses of the Socialist Party from laying down specific rules for the carrying out of the general principles recognized as valid by all Socialists: then we may well cede the right of the International Congress to declare that it "sees no proper solution of these difficulties in the exclusion of definite races and nations from immigration," and nevertheless deny that an opposite policy is necessarily "in conflict with the principle of proletarian solidarity."

For this reason we are convinced that we are fully justified in endorsing every demand and position taken by the International Congress in its resolution on Immigration, with the exception of those passages which refer to specific restriction or to the exclusion of definite races or nations.

We do not believe that such measures are necessarily "fruitless and reactionary" as stated by the International Congress, but on the contrary are convinced that any measures which do not conform to the immediate interests of the working class in the United States are fruitless and reactionary.

Such a measure or measures would place the Socialist Party in opposition to the most militant and intelligent portion of the organized workers of the United States, those whose assistance is indispensable to the purpose of elevating the Socialist Party to political power.

We have no special recommendations to make that would enlarge upon the general position on Immigration and Emigration taken by the International Congress in its Stuttgart resolutions. But the present conditions compel us to make an important exception in the matter of exclusion of immigrants from specific and definite nations. This exception refers altogether to the mass immigration of Chinese, Japanese, Coreans and Hindus to the United States. We advocate the unconditional exclusion of these races, not as races *per se* – not as peoples with definite physiological characteristics – but for the evident reason that these peoples occupy definite portions of the earth in which they are so far behind the general modern development of industry, psychologically as well as economically, that they constitute a drawback, an obstacle and menace to the progress of the most aggressive, militant and intelligent elements of our working class population. . . .

Just as emphatically as we insist on the exclusion of the races named above, so we on the other hand insist that our position shall not be construed as applicable to those immigrants of other races and nations who have behind them a long history of faithful service in the struggle of the working class and which contain most valuable revolutionary elements much needed here in our common conflict with the exploiting classes. . . .

Ernest Untermann, *Chairman*.
Victor Berger,
Joshua Wanhope.

[Discussion]

[Ernest Untermann]

The Socialist Party finds itself continually confronted by the fact that the realization of the ultimate ideals of our movement is obstructed and defeated by the very class for whom we are fighting this struggle. Whenever any occasion shall arise in which the Socialist Party has to decide whether it wants to emphasise some ultimate ideal or whether it wants to take part in the present struggle and defend its own citizens, then the law of self-preservation will always enforce itself and the present needs of the situation will imperatively demand attention.

It has been said that the position of the committee is a violation of the principle of international solidarity. Look closely at that claim and you will find that it is a very specious one and really does not deserve attention. But because so many comrades attribute great weight to it, let me point out to you that the very men who are the originators of that claim have continually violated it themselves. I have only to refer to the attitude taken by the Socialists in Europe on other problems of their own in which there has come a conflict between ultimate ideals and present realities.

Don't you remember when Hervé of France demanded from the Stuttgart Congress that they should adopt an uncompromising declaration against any kind of war, that then he was quickly reminded by the German Socialists themselves that there were two kinds of war, a defensive war and an aggressive war, and that if at any time the Socialists of Germany should find themselves confronted by a war of aggression, they would take up arms and they would follow the call to arms of Emperor William and stand shoulder to shoulder with the aristocrats and capitalists against the working men of any other country attempting to invade their country? They did not think that was a violation of the principle of international solidarity. . . .

Again, when in Germany itself the question of immigration from Poland came up and the so-called "Sachsengänger" were emigrating from Poland and Eastern Russia into Germany for the sake of getting jobs during harvest time, a great hue and cry went up from the German Socialists against that sort of emigration. They did not think that the insertion of a demand for the exclusion of the Sachsengänger was a violation of the principle of international solidarity.

But when it comes to Asiatic exclusion – oh, that is a horse of another color. It is supposed to be a violation of the principle of international solidarity. If we do the same that they did, if we refuse to be crowded out, if we refuse voluntarily to abdicate, if we refuse to give our places to outsiders and get off the earth, then that is a violation of the principle of international solidarity. Marx said, "Workingmen, unite," but he did not mean that they should all come to the United States. The principle of international solidarity may very well be maintained in another way. You know, I am a foreign born citizen myself, and I may look inconsistent upon this platform when I advocate exclusion. But, my friends, if I had been told at home that it is better for the revolutionary Socialist to stay at home and suffer than to come to the United States and make other people suffer, I would have stayed at home and worked for the revolutionary movement at home. But because I was told that the young men should go out in the world and find their fortune abroad, because I was told that there was plenty of room here in the United States, I came here, and then when I entered into the competition with my comrades here, I found out by long experience that living conditions in the United States were no better and the opportunities for further development no better than they were in Europe. If I thought I could do better in Europe I would go there. Now I am not going back to Europe, but I have become an American; I am a cosmopolitan; I have no home anywhere, no matter where, and I am going to stay in the United States and see if I can live here. . . .

[John Spargo]

Let me at the very beginning . . . refer to some of the statements and arguments and theories advanced by Comrade Untermann in his defense of the position of the majority. And since he began by quoting from the news of the day, I too may begin by quoting from the news of the day, from page 10 of the same paper from which he quoted at page 12. There I find that five regiments of American militiamen are sent into Hannibal, Missouri, to defend what? American scabs against foreign strikers! (Applause.) I suggest to you that the same manufacturers who are urging the free importation of foreign laborers may, if that kind of thing continues, arrive at a position where they will say that they prefer to have the docile American working man rather than the revolutionary immigrant. In point of fact, that is the position that is being arrived at, and by no inconsiderable body of employers of labor in this country. When the McKeesport strike occurred and they felt somewhat of the temper of these alien workers with whom they had to deal, it was very evident to any one who took the slightest trouble to sense the feeling of the middle class, the employing class, in that great center that they were beginning to feel that they wanted to get the foreigner out rather than to get him in, and anybody today, who knows our great eastern industrial centers, must know that there is coming over the minds of the capitalist class of America a consciousness that the revolutionary temper is by no means the exclusive proprietary possession of those whose forefathers came over and landed at

Plymouth Rock, but that there is good fighting material among our alien proletariat. (Great applause.) . . .

Now we are told that, due to the mass of Asiatic immigration into a certain section of the country, we have a non-political Industrial Workers of the World organization; that Asiatic labor is one of the causes – the most important cause – of this tendency away from political action, and in the direction of reaction and anarchism; and yet, Comrade Untermann, the Industrial Workers of the World was not born in the west. It was born in the middle west, right in this city of Chicago, where there is relatively no Asiatic labor at all. And the one battle of that same movement in this country has found its field not in the west with your Asiatic labor, but in the east against your alien European labor. And I call Comrade Untermann's attention to the fact that if you take any number of the trades, the more important groups in our labor organizations, you will find this thing to be true in this country. . . .

You come to us to-day and you ask us to take this action against Asiatic labor upon this ground: the ground that the Asiatic worker, when he comes in, begins to tear down the standard of living; and that his competition by his working for low wages is a serious menace to the workers of this country. You tell us it is not because of his race that you want to exclude the Jap, but simply because he is an economic competitor who lowers the standard of living, working for lower wages and making the immediate struggle of the working classes harder. And I reply to you that I perfectly acquiesce in the principle that, if ever the time comes when there is such a serious menace to the worker's standard of living, at that time, no matter how regretfully, we should have to say: "We must protect that which we have." I should be sorry to see our old international watchword go by the board; I should be sorry to see the international spirit taken out of our movement, and crossed or embittered at any point by any kind of race line, or any suggestion of race prejudice, but if the worst came to the worst I should be in the position of one of two men on a raft adrift at sea. Comrades, as long as there was enough for both it was all right, but when it came to the last drink or the last crust, then both would fight like dogs for that last drink and that last crust. What you ask us to do if we have to do it, is an evil thing, and can only be justified as the lesser of two evils. Now, if you want to exclude the Jap because he lowers the standard of living or if you want to exclude him because he works for lower wages, why, I ask you, pick out the Jap? Those phenomena are not peculiar to the Jap. They are true of the Englishman when he comes first. It was true of the Irishman when he came in large numbers. It was true of the German; and it is true today of the Russian Jew. It is true today of the immigrant from Southern Europe. It is true to-day of the Italian. It is true of the Greek. The immigration of these men is one of our big problems in the east. But I say to you that you cannot take that position. You cannot exclude the Japanese today on the economic ground and be just and fair. I say to this congress – there is a small number of Japanese workers coming into this country, the number is relatively insignificant. No evidence, that anybody has been able to gather, warrants the suggestion that the Jap lowers the standard of living any more than the Englishman did when he came, the Irishman, the German, the Jew or the Italian. Now this is what I found. I found there was a consensus of opinion that the Jap, when he came to the Pacific slope, was like the Jew when he comes to the Ghettos of our eastern cities. And by the way I do not think I can congratulate that majority for its frankness in that report. There are certain compliments handed out to the Jew to placate him, to satisfy him for the moment, that won't fit the facts in the case. The Ghetto represents quite as bad a social condition as any Jap or any other Asiatic laborer is likely to produce. Now, what did I find? I found there is a consensus of opinion that the Jap temporarily lowered wages, and I know – not as a matter of theory at all, Comrade Untermann, but as a matter of pretty practical knowledge – that that is what immigrants coming into a country generally do. I worked in the city of New York for far lower than the prevailing wages. I worked in the city of New York for seven dollars and fifty cents a week. Why? Because I stood in the bread line. Because I stood in line waiting for a job to sweep the snow from the streets of the city of New York. And if I was willing to sweep that snow I was willing to take whatever I could get in order to plant my feet firmly on American soil. I say to you that is true of the great bulk of our mass immigration. We have to face this fact; America is not a race. America is a nation made up of an amalgamation of all the nations of the world, and just as in our civic life we have got to take all these nationalities and blend them into a common citizenship of as high a type as we can attain, so we must blend together all the varied elements that come to our shores, and not until we have exhausted every other means open to us, shall we be justified in saying to any race: "You cannot come inside." And I say to you that we have not yet exhausted every means open to us. Our great labor organizations have largely neglected the foreign immigrants, and especially the Asiatic immigrant. Our own party has largely neglected the foreign immigrant, and made no efficient efforts to get him into the ranks of the organized proletariat of this country. What do I find? I find that Jap, like most other people, as soon as he gets a start, and gets his grip on the life of the nation, then he is ready to organize, ready to fight to protect his interests. Then he is ready to make demands. You cannot frighten me by telling me that some Japs were brought in to break a strike somewhere, where European laborers were on strike. I know that is true; but for every instance of that kind that you bring I shall bring another instance of European or American workers going in to take the place of Japs and Chinamen on strike. . . .

I took the trouble some time after I had been elected to this committee and had gathered together a great volume of statistical data – I took the trouble to see what I could make out of that data, to give it the form of a graphic chart. I took the map of the United States of America, and on that map I painted over certain localities colors to represent certain kinds of industries, where certain kinds of labor were employed. And then I began an investigation on my own account to find out just what the actual experience of the labor organizations of those various callings had been, and this is what I found: I found that in the East, beginning in the anthracite regions and following the coal miner all along his trail, this was the cry: "Every other worker we can assimilate, but we can not assimilate the Sicilian. We ought to be protected against the Sicilian. The Sicilian ought to be excluded." That was the coal miners' cry. He cared not at all for the Jap. Then I went to the cigar makers and I said, "What is your experience?" and they said: "In the early eighties our fear was the Chinaman; and we sent train loads of men across this continent with the cry, 'The Chinese must go.' We instructed our men to boycott the Chinese laundries, Chinese restaurants, Chinese servants of all kinds. We fought the Chinamen and their exclusion took place. And not until then did we begin to try to organize the Chinamen. And then we found that the Chinamen were easily organized, were good fighters, and maintained high wages. But as soon as the Chinamen were out of the way we were frightened by the Jap peril. The Japs went into the cigar business and began to cut our prices. Now, we said, we have the yellow peril once more. But soon the Japanese did not cut our prices any more. You cannot buy a cheap Japanese made cigar in any of the eastern states. But you can find in San Francisco a cheap cigar, made by cheap European labor. So," said the cigar maker, "we soon found that the Japs did not really menace our organization. But the Belgians came along. We cannot assimilate the Belgian; we cannot fight the Belgian; the Belgian is the enemy of the cigar makers' union to-day." And every official will tell you that they fear the Belgians and not the Jap, and I tell you the same thing is true going down the lines of all the trades. I spoke to one man prominent in the Garment Makers' union. I asked him: "What is the situation in your trade? Why is it that the organization in Rochester has gone down? Why have you the trouble in Cleveland? Why isn't your union holding its own?" They said, "Our trouble is with the Russian Jew, and with the Italian, and they make it impossible for us to carry on our organization." And what was the meaning of all this? It simply means that when I got my chart completed and looked it over, I found that everywhere there were local conditions that seemed to justify an expression of hostility against a race or races as such and I say to you here in all sincerity: You must face this fact, that, if in response to the request of the workers of the Pacific slope you agree here to-day to exclude the Jap, to-morrow in response to an equally strong demand from the miners in the East, and from the garment makers and the cigar makers you will have to exclude the Sicilian, you will have to exclude the Russian Jew, and will have to exclude the Italian.

There is no middle way at this hour. If you are frank, members of the majority of this committee, if you are frank in making your report, then the shoe is on the wrong foot. If you propose to exclude a race because of its economic competition with the workers already here, don't begin with the least significant, or with the least important. Don't begin with that race which, less than any other, is given to pulling down the standard of living; begin with those that are more important; and that you won't do. Instead of that you throw bouquets at them and tell them what splendid revolutionary material they make.

Comrades, I should be the last man, I think, to try to ignore the experience of our comrades of the west. I have seen the Jap in the west. I have seen him work. I have felt something of his meaning there as an industrial and socialistic phenomenon. But I cannot blind my eyes to the fact that if to-day you vote Asiatic exclusion, next time you will be voting Italian exclusion, or Hebrew exclusion, or some other kind of exclusion, and I cannot blind myself to the fact that this is a relatively – relatively, I say – small and insignificant part of our present immigration problem. Our present immigration problem is by no means a problem of specially dangerous competition from any race or races as such. Our immigration problem lies in this very surely: Our proletariat in America, as I state in my report, is becoming a foreign and an alien proletariat. You have in Pittsburg a very graphic illustration of what I mean. There are men, not brought from Japan, not from China, but from southern Europe mainly accepting a low standard, never reached by any organization of the workers, either economic or political, in any degree at all. They too are aliens. They too are without votes. They too will constitute a peril. And if you want to know what I think to be the most important aspect of the immigration problem at this hour, it is for the organized workers of America in the Socialist Party and in their trades unions to go out and say to these workers: we must break down this barrier, and you must become part of our organization. You must become part of this great world struggle.

Go down to Gary, Indiana; and while you are talking about the menace to our civilization from the Asiatic, there is a menace, a real menace at the very doors of this great city. They are not a menace because they are Croatians, they are not a menace because they are Roumanians, they are not a menace because they belong to any particular nationality: they are a menace because the organized workers of this country fail to do their duty, fail to recognize the situation.

3

Socialists and the Language Federations

The following excerpt from the discussion of Foreign Speaking Organizations at the Socialist Convention of 1912 indicates the mutual irritation of the "American" and "new immigrant" Socialists concerning the appropriate modes of collaboration. To this date, historians have revealed little about the internal workings of the federations, or their real influence in the party.

Clearly enough, however, there were no simple political

boundaries for discerning attitudes; Charles E. Ruthenberg, whose comments are published here, was to become the leading functionary in a Communist Party of the 1920s primarily based upon language groups; and the Finnish Federation, represented by the delegate from Michigan, was a center both of the cooperative movement (ordinarily considered a moderate form of activity) and of the bloc of foreign-language groups oriented towards Bolshevism in 1919.

SOURCE: *Socialist Party National Proceedings, 1912* (Chicago: Socialist Party, 1912), pp. 86, 87, 89.

[Delegate C.E. Ruthenberg]

We find, and it has been told to me by men who are in touch with the foreign organizations, that they are now circulating in this country literature for the separation of the church and state. They are circulating literature against feudalistic organizations in society, and all this is due to the fact that we permit them to separate themselves from our own organization and do not require them, through contact with the organized party in this country, to keep in touch with the organizations and institutions of our own country. I believe that we must force them in some way to come in touch with the locals in our counties or cities and the way to do that is to oblige them to buy their due stamps from the county organization. . . . At the last congress certain resolutions were adopted, and the comrades thought they had solved the problem of the foreign-speaking organizations. They increased the number of national translators at the headquarters. Organizations have been formed in the different states, entirely independent of the local and state organizations; no connection whatever with them. In fact, there is one in the city of Portland, affiliated with the national organization, paying dues to the national organization, which was all the time under the impression that they were part of the Socialist Labor Party! They were affiliated with the national organization and did not even know the name of that organization.

And this is exactly the condition you are going to bring about by maintaining these independent organizations, having no connection whatever with the state and local organizations. It is all very well to put in a provision that these foreign-speaking branches shall be an independent part of the national organization, but the only way to make them a part of the organization is to bring them into connection with the local and state organizations. Of course, the difficulty arises that the state and local organizations have rules of their own, and it will be necessary to provide rules under which both can work without interfering with each other, according to our interpretation of state autonomy. If you want to make it possible for the foreign-speaking branches to maintain their activity as organizations, if you want them to get into the work of the Party in the United States, and to cease from lines of propaganda which have no bearing upon the situation in this country, you must bring them into closer connection with the local or the state organizations.

[Del Aaltonen of Michigan]

I happen to be a member of a foreign-speaking organization, viz., the Finnish. In 1910 at the congress at Chicago, provision was made for the organization of these foreign-speaking federations within the American Socialist Party. At that time there was only one or two comparatively small organizations affiliated with the American Socialist Party. Now we have six or seven, and five or six more that are ready to come in. Our Finnish organization has probably made more progress than all the rest of the organizations together, since its organization. In 1910 our membership numbered about 6,000. Now we number 12,000; and last year the 217 Finnish locals in the American Socialist Party have transacted about $200,000 worth of business. This shows that this plan laid down last Congress is not practical. This shows that it does not bring the foreign workingmen in America into touch with the Socialist movement. You cannot compel him to do anything. If you could compel the Finlanders to do anything, then the Russians would have been able to compel us to do something which they have been trying to do for hundreds of years. There is nothing that can compel people who know their rights to do anything.

All these foreign-speaking comrades have joined in this plan read by our secretary on the platform. All of us have agreed with him. The view we have taken in this matter is not to give these foreign-speaking branches any distinct national organization. That is the only proposition.

The proposition is to organize them, because I am one of those who believe in organization and nothing else. Organization is the only thing that will emancipate the laboring class. According to the last census there are about 18,000,000 foreign-born people in America. What are you going to do with them?

There have been comrades on the floor of this Convention who have said that in some localities, viz., in New York and in Cleveland, Ohio, as I understood, the foreign comrades in those localities have absolutely nothing to do with the local organizations. This is no fault of theirs. It is the fault of the American socialists, because they don't do anything in order to get in touch with them. There is not a single Finnish organization in the entire country that is not affiliated with the local and county organizations, that have been requested to do so; but in many cases the American comrades seem to have the idea that these comrades are a different sort of people, having nothing to do with the American people.

4

Revolutionary Socialism

In this selection, Louis Fraina provides an outline of the theoretical contribution he sought to make to the nascent Communist movement, then still a tendency within the Socialist Party. As Fraina was to disappear from American Communism, so his insights were ultimately denied and obliterated as the Communist Party came to maturity in the United States. In Fraina's system, Imperialism united wide sectors of the population through expansion of the national State, forcing the proletariat to take on the entire edifice, with Barbarism as the potential cost of working class defeat. For the later Communists, on the contrary, the "progressive" strata extended all the way to Franklin D. Roosevelt, permitting radicals to work in trans-class coalitions for the ultimate and inevitable arrival of Socialism. Only on the question of Industrial Unionism might Fraina and the later Communists agree, and here, too, he was by far the more prophetic: Industrialism was for him a mere *form,* a boon to workers' practical unity but particularistic and nonrevolutionary in content when divorced from the social and political context of class struggle.

Generations later, New Left writers were to unknowingly reconstruct many aspects of Fraina's outline, with a similar urgency and theoretical schematism. Only the future could show whether these latter insights would also be lost in the collapse of another phase of American radicalism, or whether they could be developed beyond the limits of their political origins.

SOURCE: *Revolutionary Socialism* (New York: The Communist Press, 1918), pp. 48-51, 84-85, 86-88, 132-36, 186-88, 193-97, 207-9.

The character of strength and danger inherent in Imperialism flows from precisely this circumstance, that it seduces hitherto liberal and oppositional elements, organizes them into the social and psychological army of Imperialism. By means of innumerable visible and invisible threads of interest and dependency, finance-capital bends to its will and purpose the whole of capitalist society. It reigns supreme. Imperialism accomplishes that which never prevailed hitherto, the complete domination of capitalist autocracy in its most revolting form; and it manages, moreover, at least temporarily, to scatter the opposition to chaff, – except the potential opposition of the revolutionary industrial proletariat.

Imperialism accomplishes another determining thing: it brings the "labor movement" into its service. At this stage, Imperialism becomes specially interested in the psychology and action of the working class. In the struggles of Imperialism, a national Capitalism must present a united front. The unity of capitalist interests becomes imperative, as any material division of energy through unbridled rivalry of interests weakens the economic, political and military power of the nation. The unity of the various layers of the capitalist class has been secured partly through compromise, largely through their subordination to and dependence upon monopolistic finance-capital. But this unity is incomplete unless it includes the workers. Industrial regularity and efficiency are indispensable in the international competition of Imperialism, equally during peace and war, and a discontented class of workers becomes exceedingly unpleasant and perhaps dangerous. Monopolistic finance-capital secures support for its imperialistic adventures among the other layers of the capitalist class by a "distribution" of the profits of Imperialism; and this policy is extended to groups of skilled labor, their support being secured by means of higher wages, steady employment, better hours and conditions of work generally, and legislative measures conferring status upon skilled labor. The tendency is to create a homogeneity of interests, which is largely, if temporarily, successful. Skilled labor, sensing its importance and opportunity, makes the attempt through its unions to secure even larger concessions, and establish for itself a place in the governing system of the nation. It rejects the general class struggle against Capitalism, and acts as a caste the psychology and action of which are determined by the aspiration to absorb itself in the ruling system of things. The general process creates a reactionary mass whose interests are promoted by the more intense exploitation of the proletariat of average, unskilled labor, the overwhelming mass of the workers, and by imperialistic adventures.

The governmental form of expression of this development is State Capitalism. The unity of class and group interests must be and is maintained and conserved by the authority of the state. The end of economic individualism is symbolized by governmental control of industry and conditions of labor; the state, moreover, acts directly to intensify the concentration of industry and "regulate" the revolts of labor.

In becoming a movement of general social reform, Socialism expressed the interests of the aristocracy of skilled labor and the lower layers of the petty bourgeoisie, and of the new middle class in its earlier stages of development. Practically every revolt, every aspiration of a middle class being destroyed by concentrated industry was echoed in Socialist propaganda and activity. The demand of this class for government ownership of industry became the *leit-motiv* of Socialist propaganda, and Socialism in practice was a movement for government ownership and the extension of the functions of the state generally. Compromise after compromise was struck with the fundamentals of Socialism in order to placate and secure the support of non-revolutionary and non-proletarian groups.

Moreoever, Socialism adopted the policy of the pacific "penetration" of Socialism into Capitalism, realizing the Socialist community by the extension of capitalist collectivism. The practice of the movement based itself upon the development of Capitalism, instead of upon the revolutionary development of the proletariat. It was a policy that expressed the trend toward State Capitalism and emphasized the trend. Where the Socialist movement was large, as in Germany, it practically absorbed the national liberal forces of social reform; where small, Socialism became an integral part of the national liberal reform movement. Capitalism, not the proletariat, was to bring Socialism, – this was the actual policy of the movement, in spite of utterances and a theoretical system to the contrary.

The task of the proletariat was conceived as decisively the immediate improvement of its material welfare, but this process of improvement was determined almost exclusively by the proposals of skilled labor and the small bourgeoisie. The transformation of Socialist tactics was general; the revolutionary struggle for the overthrow of Capitalism was displaced by the policy of "modifying" Capitalism and softening of class antagonisms. The Socialist theory of Marxism maintained itself, although not in any sense expressing the actual basis of the movement; against it washed the tides of revisionism, which desired an adaptation of theory in accord with the bourgeois practices of the movement, and the tides of revolutionary thought, which desired to have the movement adapt its practice to the requirements of Imperialism and the new revolutionary epoch into which the proletariat had emerged.

The apparent futility of theoretical controversy among the Socialist intellectuals was a consequence of considering differences in tactics as theoretical problems, instead of as essentially problems in practice, in the actual relations of classes and the expression of class interests. The doctrinaire Socialist, the pseudo-Marxist, conceives Socialism as a sort of super-science, unaffected by the conditions which affect bourgeois science. The illusion has an apparently materialistic basis. The doctrinaire Socialist assumes that there are no divisions within the proletariat, its interests being *one;* and that, accordingly, Socialist theory possesses a unity of thought impervious to reactionary influences. But the assumption is not valid. The immediate interests of the working class are *not* one – although they are, ultimately; it *is* split by divisions – between the skilled and the unskilled; and Socialist theory is not only susceptible of reactionary interpretation, but *was used* for reactionary purposes.

This circumstance of power is determinant. The unskilled proletariat is the typical product of modern Capitalism and controls the basic industries. This proletarian class controls equally the destiny of Capitalism and of skilled labor. The mining industry and the steel industry are dominated by the unskilled; and, except in a few cases, as for example the locomotive engineers, this is equally true of the railway industry and of transportation generally.

What are the characteristics of the proletariat of average unskilled labor? The unskilled proletariat is the industrial proletariat of standardized machine industry. An unskilled proletarian is not necessarily and always simply a worker who has no skill. The Mexican peon, the "coolie" of China, may have no skill or craft, but he is not an unskilled proletarian in the sociological sense. The unskilled proletariat is a *machine proletariat.* As Capitalism develops, the industrial process is standardized, the labor specialized. The perfection of machinery expropriates the skilled worker of his skill, as such, makes him simply a machine-minder, or drives him into minor industries where technological development lags; individual skill becomes of no importance except for a small group, and what slight aptitude may be necessary can be acquired in a few days or weeks. The worker becomes an appendage of the machine; it is no longer a skilled worker that uses the machine, but the machine uses an unskilled worker. Labor becomes average labor, standardized and specialized as an automatic factor in the machine process. The machine subjects the worker to its process; the procedure becomes mechanical, the organization systematic and standardized; standardization eliminates skill, craftsmanship, intelligence and individuality; the worker no longer has the skill of a craft: he has simply labor power, hands and muscle, and the eyes that direct these hands and muscle. A new skilled labor is created, the very small minority of engineers, superintendents, and technicians generally. The efficiency movement climaxes this development; its exponents are concerned not in the skill of the workers, but *in the regularity and standardization of their movements.* The proletariat becomes in fact a machine proletariat.

The machine process dominates not a single factory or industry, but the whole of industry, integrating and standardizing the industrial system. Industry correlates itself, and if it ceases functioning at one point, the whole system feels the shock. The concentration of capital and the machine process operate jointly to unify the industrial system, in which common labor controls the working activity. Thus, while the machine process strips the worker of all skill, it simultaneously creates and places in his hands an immense power, the power of at any moment dislocating the process of production through the mass action of any considerable group of proletarians. The strikes of the unskilled unconsciously but inevitably assume the large proportions of mass revolts, including scores of thousands of workers, where the strikes of the crafts seldom did; it is easy to replace a few thousand workers at their jobs, but it is much more difficult to replace twenty or one hundred thousand. The proletariat instinctively adjusts itself to this fact.

The machine process makes a homogeneous mass out of the heterogeneous racial and religious elements; the machine process subjects the diversity of these workers to a common discipline, a common suffering, a common ideology. "By and large," says Veblen, "the technology of the machine process is a technology of action by contact." *Action by contact!* This technological fact permeates the consciousness of the unskilled workers, subtly inculcates them with the ideal of solidarity of action. The outstanding fact in the revolts of the unskilled is that they exhibit a remarkable degree of solidarity and assume revolutionary proportions and expression. The great industrial revolts of the past twenty years in this country have been revolts of the unskilled, revolts that coalesced around revolutionary organizations and activity. While the skilled were bargaining, the unskilled were fighting. Moreover, the strikes of the unskilled have been remarkably free from violence, while the craft unions have repeatedly indulged in that individual and secret violence which is characteristic of groups beaten in the social struggle. The machine process impresses upon the minds of the unskilled the value of force, of control of the industrial process, of solidarity in action; and these circumstances inevitably discourage sporadic acts of individual violence. It is the great fact and hope of the machine proletariat that, during the great strikes of the unskilled, in which men and women speaking dozens of languages participated, there was no violence on their part, no hysteria of despair, but there was determination, solidarity, the aggressive spirit of the revolution in action. The proletarian revolution is not fostered by violence, but it makes use of industrial power and organized force.

But the machine process does not simply organize the proletariat through the mechanism of production itself; it simultaneously creates a new ideology among the workers. The skilled worker thinks in terms of craft, of the individual and his property; the unskilled proletariat thinks in terms of the mass, of power, and of the *control of the machine process.* The skilled cling to craft strikes, the unskilled turn to mass action. All the facts, all the indications prove that the action of the unskilled industrial proletariat inevitably proceeds along general and revolutionary lines, that it *is* a revolutionary class.

● ● ● ● ●

Industrial unionism becomes an expression of, and develops real strength and influence among, the unskilled workers, in whom common conditions of labor, absence of craft distinctions and the discipline of machine industry develop the necessity and potentiality of the industrial form of organization. The power of this proletariat lies in its mass and numbers, in its lack of artificial distinctions of skill and craft. Being a product of the massing of workers in a particular industry, the unskilled strike *en masse,* act through mass action; being united and disciplined by concentrated industry and its machine process, the unskilled proletariat organizes its unions industrially, in accord with the facts of industry, in accord with the conditions of its work and existence. Industrial unionism in form is an expression of the integration of industry and the proletariat by the mechanism of capitalist production itself, and it becomes peculiarly the unionism of the revolutionary proletariat. All groups of workers in an industry are organized and unified into one union, cast in the mold of the industry in which they work, artificial differences of occupational divisions being swept aside. Strikes become general and acquire political significance, action becomes the action of the mass, the integrated action of an integrated proletariat. Where the craft unions initiated the strike of a single group of workers in an industry, the industrial union initiates a strike of *all the workers.* The ideology of solidarity becomes the practice of solidarity.

Industrial unionism, as the expression of unskilled workers impelled by objective conditions to subjectively accept class action, acquires a revolutionary concept, consciousness and activity. Instead of the craft union motto of "A fair day's pay for a fair day's work," industrial unionism inscribes upon its banners the revolutionary motto, "Abolition of the wages system." The ultimate purpose of industrial unionism is the organization of all the workers in accord with the facts of production, constructing in this way the structure of the new society within the old, as a necessary phase in the overthrow of Capitalism and the establishment of a new society which shall function through the industrially organized producers. Not the state, but the industrial union is the instrument of revolution, – equally the might for the revolutionary act and the norm of the new society. Industrial unionism is not simply a means, a more effective means than any previously used, to carry on the every-day struggle against the employing class: it is Socialism in action and Socialism in the making.

• • • • •

Industrial unionism, in itself, and even if it recognizes and accepts the Socialist parliamentary struggle, has its own limitations. Industrial unionism, in its dogmatic expression, assumes a general organization of the proletariat before Socialism can be established, the construction of a general industrial organization that may seize and operate industry. In terms of infinity, it may be conceivable that some day, somehow, the majority of the proletariat, or an overwhelming minority, may become organized into industrial unions under Capitalism. In terms of actual practice, this is inconceivable. The proletariat of unskilled labor, which alone may accept industrial unionism, is a class difficult to organize; its conditions of labor discourage organization and make it move and act under the impulse of mass action. The conditions of Capitalism, its violent upheavals and stress of struggle, exclude the probability of an all-inclusive proletarian organization; moreover, should we hesitate to act until this general organization materializes, Capitalism may turn in on itself and establish a new form of slavery. In its dogmatic expression, industrial unionism has much in common with the parliamentary Socialist conception of the peaceful "growing into" Socialism; it evades the dynamic problems of the Revolution, substituting theory for reality and formula for action. It is fantastic as a general proposition, it is particularly fantastic considering the period of violent upheavals and struggle into which the world is now emerging, to consider that the proletariat under Capitalism can through industrialism organize the structure of the new society. The structure of industrialism, the form of the new communist society, can be organized only during the transition period from Capitalism to Socialism acting through the dictatorship of the proletariat; all that can be done in the meanwhile is to develop a measure of industrial organization and its ideology of the industrial state, which may constitute the starting point for a proletarian dictatorship in its task of introducing the industrial state of communist Socialism.

The supremacy of the proletariat is determined by its action, and not by its organization. The proletariat acts even where there is no organization, through mass action; organization is a means to action, and not a substitute for action. The function of an organization, in the revolutionary sense, is that it may serve as the centre for action of the unorganized proletarian masses, rally and integrate the general mass action of the proletariat, organizing and directing it for the conquest of power. Socialism hastens the overthrow of Capitalism through revolutionary action. In this sense, parliamentarism and industrial unionism become integral phases of mass action.

Mass action is not a *form* of action as much as it is a *process and synthesis* of action. It is the unity of all forms of proletarian action, a means of throwing the proletariat, organized and unorganized, in a general struggle against Capitalism and the capitalist state. It is the sharp, definite expression of the revolt of the workers under the impact of the antagonisms and repressions of Capitalism, of the recurring crises and revolutionary situations produced by the violent era of Imperialism. Mass action is the instinctive action of the proletariat, gradually developing more conscious and organized forms and definite purposes. It is extra-parliamentary in method, although political in purpose and result, may develop into and be itself developed by the parliamentary struggle.

Organizations, political and economic, have a tendency to become conservative; a tendency emphasized, moreover, by the fact that they largely represent the more favored groups of workers. These organizations must be swept out of their conservatism by the elemental impact of mass action, functioning through organized and unorganized workers acting instinctively under the pressure of events and in disregard of bureaucratic discipline. The great expressions of mass action in recent years, the New Zealand General Strike, the Lawrence strike, the great strike of the British miners under which capitalist society reeled on the verge of collapse, – all were mass actions organized and carried through in spite of the passive and active hostility of the dominant Socialist and labor organizations. Under the impulse of mass action, the industrial proletariat senses its own power and acquires the force to act equally against Capitalism and the conservatism of organizations. Indeed, a vital feature of mass action is precisely that it places in the hands of the proletariat the power to overcome the fetters of these organizations, to act in spite of their conservatism, and through proletarian mass action emphasize antagonisms between workers and capitalists, and conquer power. A determining phase of the proletarian revolution in Russia was its acting against the dominant Socialist organization, sweeping these aside through its mass action before it could seize social supremacy. And the great strikes and demonstrations in Germany and Austria during February, 1918, potentially revolutionary in character, were a form of mass action that broke loose against the open opposition of the dominant Socialist and union organizations, and that were crushed by this opposition. *Mass action is the proletariat itself in action,* dispensing with bureaucrats and intellectuals acting through its own initiative; and it is precisely this circumstance that horrifies the soul of petty bourgeois Socialism. The masses are to act upon their own initiative and the impulse of their own struggles; it is the function of the revolutionary Socialist to provide the program and the course for this elemental action, to adapt himself to the new proletarian modes of struggle.

• • • • •

There is no alternative for the proletariat: either war and again war, or the Social Revolution.

The world war has brought Capitalism to the verge of collapse. It has compelled the state to lay a dictatorial hand upon the process of production, and the nation to negate its own basis by striving to break through the limits of the nation. It has compelled industrial necessity to subordinate itself to the overwhelming fact of military necessity. The debts of the belligerent nations are colossal, and they will fetter the nations, constitute a crucial problem in the days to come. The war has weakened Capitalism while it has strengthened a fictitious domination of the capitalist class. Contradications and antagonisms have been multiplied. War has become the normal occupation of Capitalism, and the transition to peace will shake Capitalism to its foundations, posing new and more acute problems for solution. Industry will have to adjust itself to a peace basis, and it will be a herculean task; the proletariat will have to adjust itself to the new conditions, new struggles and new problems, and the experiences of war are not calculated to make it submissive.

The proletariat will find upon the conclusion of peace that all its sacrifices have availed it naught, and that the old system of exploitation persists in intensified form. Capitalism will equally find that war has availed it naught: its old economic problems will not have been solved and new problems have been created. Will Capitalism answer with a feverish era of industrial expansion? But war debts will weigh upon the nation, and an era of expansion will simply hasten the new crisis and a new war. There is a point where Capitalism comes up against an impasse in the industrial process. The forces of production inexorably generate new contradictions and crises. Capitalism verges on collapse.

The fatalist uses these facts, and they *are* facts, as an argument for an inevitable collapse of Capitalism and an equally inevitable coming of Socialism. The argument is as futile as it is fatalistic. The world war, in which millions of workers have sacrificed and died in the cause of Imperialism, is a warning of an alternative. The fatalist attitude in practice allows Capitalism to dispose of things in its own brutal way. And instead of a coming of Socialism, the world may see the coming of a new barbarism, the "common ruin of the contending classes." If war becomes the normal state of society, if the proletariat as the modern revolutionary class has not the initiative and the energy to assume control of society, then instead of a new society we shall have a new era of rapine and conquest. Europe rending itself, Europe and America rending each other, and the two rending Asia, or Asia rending them all. A collapse of Capitalism, in one form or another, is inevitable; but the coming of Socialism is not equally inevitable. It may become a collapse of all civilization.

BARBARA WELTER

The Feminization of American Religion: 1800-1860

THE RELATIONSHIPS among nineteenth-century reform movements in the United States, their overlapping of personnel, and their disparity and similarity in motivations and results are popular themes in social history.[1] In the women's movement, which concentrated on obtaining suffrage but had more specific and more diffuse goals as well, almost all of the leaders and most of the followers were active in other reforms. Indeed, the abolitionist, temperance, and peace societies depended on their women members to lick envelopes, raise money through fairs, and influence their husbands and fathers to join in the good work. Although sometimes frustrated and even betrayed by these other reform movements, the woman's movement on the whole benefitted from the organizational experience, political knowledge, and momentum generated by other reforms. At the same time American

[1] Martin Duberman has done this very effectively in his introduction to *The Anti-Slavery Vanguard: New Essays on the Abolitionists* (Princeton, 1965) and his biography of James Russell Lowell (Boston, 1966). Alice Felt Tyler, *Freedom's Ferment: Phases of American Social History to 1860* (Minneapolis, 1944) and Arthur M. Schlesinger, Sr., *The American as Reformer* (Cambridge, 1951) attempt a synthesis of the reform movements of the nineteenth century. A contemporary account of the nature of the reformer by Ralph Waldo Emerson, "Man the Reformer," in Ralph Waldo Emerson, *Nature, Addresses, and Lectures,* ed. Edward Waldo Emerson (Boston, 1903) is the first and perhaps the best attempt at this kind of social history.

religion, particularly American Protestantism, was changing rapidly and fundamentally. Although not overtly tied to the woman's movement, these religious changes may have had more effect on the basic problems posed by women than anything which happened within the women's organizations or in related reform groups. Because of the nature of the changes and the importance of their results to women's role, American religion might be said to have been "feminized." The term is used here, like the term "radicalization," to connote a series of consciousness-raising and existential, as well as experiential, factors which resulted in a new awareness of changed conditions and new roles to fit these new conditions.

For the historian to attempt an analysis of the relationships between institutions and movements at a given point in time is a fascinating exercise in social history. It may well be an exercise in futility, however, because he lacks sufficient knowledge of the society he studies, or because the theories of change and social dynamics are applicable only to the present, or at least not to the particular segment of the past which he explores. The hazards of the sociological vocabulary, the limited number of sources (or the overwhelming magnitude of sources in some areas), and the difference between sociological and historical logistics and time are significant barriers.[2] Within these limitations this article proposes to discuss the process of "feminization," to apply this definition to religion in America in the first half of the nineteenth century, and to explore the results of a "feminized" religion.

In some ways the allocation of institutions or activities to one sex or another is a continuation of the division of labor by sex which has gone on since the cave dwellers. At certain times survival required that the strongest members of society specialize in a given activity. Once the basic needs of survival were met, other activities, not of current critical importance, could be engaged in. These more expendable institutions became the property of the weaker members of society which, in western

[2] For example, Max Weber, *The Theory of Social and Economic Organization*, translated by A.M. Henderson (Glencoe, Ill., 1957); Robert Merton, *Social Theory and Social Structure*, Rev. Ed. (Glencoe, Ill., 1960); Talcott Parsons, *Structure and Process in Modern Society* (Glencoe, Illinois, 1960); Richard H. Tawney, *Religion and the Rise of Capitalism* (New York, 1922); W. Seward Salisbury, *Religion in American Culture* (Homewood, Ill., 1964); Hadley Cantril, *The Psychology of Social Movements* (New York, 1941); Cyclone Covey, *The American Pilgrimage* (Stillwater, Oklahoma, 1960); and David O. Moberg, *The Church as a Social Institution: The Sociology of American Religion* (Englewood Cliffs, N.J., 1962).

civilization, generally meant women.[3] In the period following the American Revolution, political and economic activities were critically important and therefore more "masculine," that is, more competitive, more aggressive, more responsive to shows of force and strength. Religion, along with the family and popular taste, was not very important, and so became the property of the ladies. Thus it entered a process of change whereby it became more domesticated, more emotional, more soft and accommodating – in a word, more "feminine."

In this way the traditional religious values could be maintained in a society whose primary concerns made humility, submission, and meekness incompatible with success because they were identified with weakness. At the same time American Protestantism changed in ways which made it more useful to American society, particularly to the women who increasingly made up the congregations of American churches. Feminization, then, can be defined and studied through its results – a more genteel, less rigid institution – and through its members – the increased prominence of women in religious organizations and the way in which new or revised religions catered to this membership.

American churches had regarded it as their solemn duty to lead in building a godly culture, and the "city on the hill" which symbolized American aspirations had clusters of church steeples as its tallest structures.[4] In the nineteenth century the skyscraper would replace the steeple as a symbol of the American dream, and the ministers of God fought against this displacement. Politics captured the zeal and the time once reserved to religion, and the pulpits thundered against those men who mistakenly served power itself and not the Source of Power. The women's magazines and books of advice also warned against politics as a destroyer of the home. Cautionary tales equated the man who squandered his energy in political arguments with the man who drank or gambled; both were done at the expense of the home and religion.[5] Women

[3] See especially Robert Briffault, *The Mothers: The Matriarchal Theory of Social Origins* (New York, 1931) and Johann Jakob Bachsfen, *Myth, Religion and Mother Right,* translated by Ralph Manheim (Princeton, New Jersey, 1967).

[4] For basic histories of American religion see Winthrop Hudson, *American Protestantism* (Chicago, 1961); W.W. Sweet, *The Story of Religions in America* (New York, 1930); W.L. Sperry, *Religion in America* (New York, 1946); T.C. Hall, *The Religious Background of American Culture* (Boston, 1930); J.W. Smith and A.L. Jamison, eds., *Religion in American Life* (Princeton, 1961); and E.S. Bates, *American Faith: Political and Economic Foundations* (New York, 1940).

[5] For example, Eliza W. Farnham, *Woman and Her Era,* 2 vols. (New York, 1964),

and ministers were allies against this usurper, from which they were both excluded. Women were forbidden to go into politics because it would sully them; the church was excluded for similar reasons. Increasingly, in a political world, women and the church stood out as anti-political forces, as they did in an increasingly materialistic society, dominated by a new species, Economic Man. For women and the church were excluded from the pursuit of wealth just as much as they were kept out of the statehouse, and for the same rhetorical reasons. Both women and the church were to be above the counting house, she on her pedestal, the church in its sanctuary. Wealth was to be given them as consumers and as reflections of its makers.[6]

Democracy, the novel by Henry Adams, gives a fascinating insight into what happens when a woman ventures near the source of power, politics, and Washington. In venturing so near the sun she burns her wings and, limping badly, heads for home.[7] Human nature as defined by the church and human nature as defined by the state seemed totally different in the eighteenth century when the idea of original sin conflicted with the Jeffersonian hopes for perfectability through democracy. During the nineteenth century the churches moved toward the eighteenth-century premise of progress and salvation. Democracy, on the other hand, seems to have reverted to a more cynical or perhaps realistic view of human nature, closer to the Calvinist tradition. Women, however, precisely because they were above and beyond politics and even beyond producing wealth, much less pursuing it, could maintain the values of an earlier age. If women had not existed, the age would have had to invent them, in order to maintain the rhetoric of eighteenth-century democracy. As the religious view of man became less harsh, it meshed nicely with the hopes of Jefferson and Jackson.

The hierarchy, ministers, and theologians of most religions

---

and Charlotte Perkins Stetson Gilman, *His Religion and Hers: A Study of the Faith of Our Fathers and the Work of Our Mothers* (New York and London, 1923).

[6] A classic account is in Thorstein Veblen, *The Theory of the Leisure Class* (New York, 1919). In nineteenth-century tariff policy, women are urged to consume only goods manufactured at home. In his report on manufactures in 1790, Alexander Hamilton urged the adoption of manufacturing as a means of providing employment for women, an argument approved of by the nineteenth-century economist Matthew Carey. However, the use of women as cheap labor paid scarcely any lip service to these rhetorical rationalizations, and Veblen's theory of women as consumers and symbols of prosperity increasingly applied only to the middle classes.

[7] Henry Adams, *Democracy: An American Novel* (New York, 1882).

remained male. There were almost no ordained female ministers – Antoinette Brown Blackwell was an exception and not too happy a one – and few evangelical or volunteer female ministers.[8] When Orestes Brownson growled about a "female religion" he was referring largely to the prominent role which women played in congregations and revivals. However, he was also sniping at the tame minister, whom he caricatured with such scorn as a domesticated pet of spinsters and widows, fit only to balance teacups and mouth platitudes. Brownson's solution, to join the Church of Rome, undoubtedly was motivated by a number of personal and ideological reasons. Not the least of these, however, in the light of his contempt for feminine and weak Protestantism, was the patriarchal structure of the Catholic Church.[9]

Besides their prominence during services, women increasingly handled the voluntary societies which carried out the social office of the churches, by teaching Sunday school, distributing tracts, and working for missions. This was only the external sign of the internal change by which the church grew softer and the religious life less rigorous. Children could be baptized much earlier. The idea of infant damnation, which Theodore Parker rightly said would never have been accepted had women been in charge of

[8] The best brief sketch of Antoinette Brown Blackwell is by Barbara M. Solomon in *Notable American Women: 1607-1950*, 3 vols., Vol. I (Cambridge, Mass., 1970), 158-60, hereafter referred to as NAW. Other biographies are Laura Kerr, *Lady in the Pulpit* (New York, 1951) and Elinor Rice Hays, *Those Extraordinary Blackwells* (New York, 1967). Mrs. Blackwell became increasingly dissatisfied with pastoral work and the Congregational Church and by 1854, after one year's service, resigned her pulpit to do volunteer work among the poor and mentally disturbed. In later life, after her family was raised, she returned to the ministry, where she campaigned for woman suffrage. Mrs. Blackwell was a philosopher rather than a theologian and, like her sister-in-law Elizabeth, was more concerned with the application of her profession to women's life than in achieving distinction in her own field.

[9] *The Works of Orestes A. Brownson, Collected and Arranged by Henry F. Brownson*, 20 vols. (New York, 1966) give a complete picture of Brownson's views on women. Briefly, he was opposed to the "woman worship" of his age, and horrified at the woman's movement because it preached interference with marriage and procreation. "Of course we hold that the woman was made for the man, not the man for the woman, and that the husband is the head of the wife, even as Christ is the head of the Church. . . ." (Vol. XVIII, p. 386) He saw the weakening of American family life as the greatest crisis of the age, and the women's movement, in its stress on individual rights, hastened the dissolution of the family as a social unit and contributed to the disastrous trend of isolation. (Vol. XVIII, 388.) Moreover, the woman's movement was yet another indication of the increasing "spirit of insubordination" in society and like other such movements required "no self-sacrifice or submission of one's will." (Vol. XVIII, 416.) He was convinced that its leaders were not only opposed to the Christian family, "but to Christianity itself." (Vol. XVIII, 414.)

theology, quietly died around the middle of the century.[10] These changes were of great benefit to women's peace of mind. Now, if a diary recorded the loss of a child, at least the loss was only a temporary one. Women had found the prospect of parting forever from a beloved child, because there had been no baptism or sign of salvation, almost unbearable. The guilt with which these women so often reproached themselves at least need not concern eternal suffering, and the difference mattered to a believer.

The increasing softness and flexibility in the American churches were reflected in their role in social stratification as well as in their theology. The highly touted classless society of the Revolution was becoming increasingly stratified and self-conscious. The churches represented all different stages in the transition from wilderness to social nicety. The revivals had to fight not only hardness of heart but the lack of social prestige they entailed. Anglo-Catholicism had stood for a softer life both materially and spiritually since at least the time of the Glorious Revolution. It was also to a degree partially identified with higher social and economic status. The Episcopal Church and the Presbyterian Church were increasingly the churches of the well-to-do, and they offered their members a higher social status to correspond with their wealth. Women used their membership in a more prominent church as an important means of establishing a pecking order within the community.[11]

The male principle was rarely challenged by Trinitarians or Unitarians – whether three or one, God was male (and probably white). However, during the first half of the nineteenth century two ideas gained popularity which showed an appreciation for the values of femaleness – the first was the idea of the Father-Mother God and the second was the concept of the female Saviour. The assignation to God of typically female virtues was nothing new.

[10] Quoted in Henry Steele Commager, *Theodore Parker* (Boston, 1936), 150 and in Theodore Parker, *A Discourse of Matters Pertaining to Religion* (Boston, 1842), 201. The issue of infant damnation led several Congregational ministers into the more permissive theology of Unitarianism, including Sheba Smith and Antoinette Brown Blackwell. Barbara M. Cross, *Horace Bushnell: Minister to a Changing America* (Chicago, 1958) deals with one minister's solution to the tensions of change. Unitarian theology is covered fully in E.M. Wilbur, *History of Unitarianism*, 2 vols. (Cambridge, Mass., 1945-1952.)

[11] E. Digby Baltzell, *The Protestant Establishment: Aristocracy and Caste in America* (New York, 1964); Henry F. May, *Protestant Churches and Industrial America* (New York, 1949); Louis Wright, *Culture on the Moving Frontier* (Bloomington, Indiana, 1955), and David O. Moberg, *Church As a Social Institution* (Englewood Cliffs, N.J., 1962).

Presumably a God who was defined as perfect would have all known virtues, whether or not he had a beard. The Shakers went farther, however, and insisted that God had a dual nature, part male and part female.[12] Theodore Parker used the same theme, in pointing out the need for female virtues, particularly the lack of materialism, and finding these virtues in a Godhead which embodied all the symbols of mother's mercy along with father's justice.[13] Joseph Smith consoled his daughter with the thought that in heaven she would meet not only her own mother, who had just died, but she would also "become acquainted with your eternal Mother, the wife of your Father in Heaven." Mormon teaching posited a dual Parenthood within the Godhead, a Father and a Mother, equally divine.[14]

This duality of God the Father with a Mother God almost necessitated the idea of a female counterpart of Christ. Hawthorne in *The Scarlet Letter* has Hester muse on the coming of a female saviour. She reflects that because of her sin she is no longer worthy to be chosen.[15] The female saviour is an interesting amalgam of nineteenth-century adventism, the need for a Protestant counterpart to the cult of the Virgin, and the elevation of pure womanhood to an almost supernatural level. If the world had failed its first test and was plunging into an era of godlessness and vice, as many were convinced, then a second coming seemed necessary. Since the failure of the world also represented a failure of male laws and male values, a second chance, in order to effect

[12] *Testimony of the Life, Character, Revelations and Doctrines of Our Ever Blessed Mother, Ann Lee and the Elders With Her; Through whom the word of eternal life was opened on this day of Christ's Second Appearing; Collected from living witnesses, by order of the ministry, in union with the Church* (Hancock, Massachusetts, 1816). A basic history of the Shakers is Marguerite Melcher, *The Shaker Adventure* (Princeton, 1941).

[13] Theodore Parker, "A Sermon of the Public Function of Woman," Preached at the Music Hall, March 27, 1953 (Boston, 1853) and in many other sermons.

[14] Susa Young Gates, *History of the Young Ladies' Mutual Improvement Association of the Church of Jesus Christ of Latter Day Saints* (Salt Lake City, 1911), 16ff. Eliza R. Snow Smith, wife of both Joseph Smith and Brigham Young, wrote a hymn on this theme, "O My Father," in *Poems, Religious, Historical and Political* (Salt Lake City, 1877), 173.

[15] Nathaniel Hawthorne, *The Scarlet Letter* (Boston, 1850), "Earlier in life, Hester had vainly imagined that she herself might be the destined prophetess, but had long since recognized the impossibility that any mission of divine and mysterious truth should be confided to a woman stained with sin, bowed down with shame, or even burdened with a life-long sorrow. The angel and apostle of the coming revelation must be a woman indeed, but lofty, pure, and beautiful; and wise, moreover, not through dusky grief, but the ethereal medium of joy; and showing how sacred love should make us happy, by the truest test of a life successful to such an end." (240) This new saviour will reveal "a new Truth" to re-order the relations between men and women.

change, should produce a different and higher set of laws and values.[16] The role was typecast for the True Woman, as the Shakers and the Mystical Feminists (and later the Christian Scientists) were quick to point out.

The changes in interpretation of Christ which made him the greatest of humans and stressed his divinity in the sense that all men are divine were also interpreted as feminine. The new Christ was the exemplar of meekness and humility, the sacrificial victim.[17] Woman too was the archetypal victim, in literary and religious symbolism. If Christ was interpreted as a human dominated by love, sacrificing himself for others, asking nothing but giving everything and forgiving his enemies in the bargain, he was playing the same role as the true woman in a number of typical nineteenth-century melodramatic scenarios. As every reader of popular fiction knew in the early nineteenth century, woman was never more truly feminine than when, on her deathbed, the innocent victim of male lust or greed, she forgave her cruel father, profligate husband, or avaricious landlord. A special identification with suffering and innocence was shared by both women and the crucified Christ. "She was a great sufferer," intoned one minister at a lady's funeral, "and she loved her crosses."[18]

The minister who interpreted this feminized Christ to his congregation spoke in language which they understood. By 1820 sermons were being preached on the "godless society" which spent its time and money on politics and the pursuit of wealth, and appeared in church "only at weddings and funerals."[19] Observers

[16]This idea is set out most clearly in Eliza W. Farnham, *Woman and Her Era,* 2 vols. (New York, 1964).

[17]A history of the major theological and social changes in Christianity could be written in which the primary sources were biographies of Christ. A perceptive treatment of this subject is Edith Hamilton, *Witness to the Truth: Christ and His Interpreters* (New York, 1948). Another sort of survey is *Christ In Poetry,* an anthology compiled and edited by Thomas Curtis Clark and Hazel Davis Clark (New York, 1952). Two popular nineteenth-century biographies were Lyman Abbott, *Jesus of Nazareth: His Life and Teachings* (New York, 1869) and Frederic William Farrar, *The Life of Christ* (New York, 1874). A sample of the "Sunday School" biography is Caroline Wells Dall, *Nazareth* (Washington, D.C., 1903). Mrs. Dall saw the mission of the Saviour as the revelation of "the universal Fatherhood of God, the common brotherhood of man" and the repudiation of the "old dogma of a corrupt nature by showing how Godlike a human life could be," 24.

[18]C.A. Bartol, "The Image Passing Before Us: A Sermon After the Decease of Elizabeth Howard Bartol" (Boston, 1883).

[19]Theodore Parker had several sermons on this subject, including "A Sermon of Merchants" (November 22, 1846); "A Sermon on the Moral Condition of Boston"

of the American scene noted frequently that American congregations were composed primarily of women and that ministers spoke to their special needs. Mrs. Trollope cast her cold eye over the flounce-filled pews and remarked that "it is only from the clergy that the women of America receive that sort of attention which is so dearly valued by every female heart throughout the world . . . I never saw, or read, of any country where religion had so strong a hold upon the women, or a slighter hold upon the men."[20] One reason for this prominence was, she felt, that only the clergy listened to women, all other ranks of man's society and interests were closed to them.

The hymns of this period also reflect the increasing stress on Christ's love and God's mercy. The singer is called upon to consider Christ his friend and helper. (To some degree, if the period before the Civil War is seen as one of feminization for Protestantism, the period following it might be termed a period of juvenilization, for increasingly the child as the hope and redeemer of his parents and society is stressed.) Woman's active role in the writing of hymns used in the Methodist, Presbyterian, Episcopal and Congregational hymnals at this time is very small. They contributed almost no music but did quite a few translations, particularly from the German. They were represented best in the lyrics to children's hymns.[21] It is perhaps significant that a hymn

---

(February 11, 1849); "A Sermon on the Spiritual Condition of Boston" (February 18, 1849); and "A Sermon of the Moral Dangers Incident to Prosperity" (November 5, 1854).

[20] Frances Trollope, *Domestic Manners of the Americans* (New York, 1949; original edition 1832), 75. This American phenomenon (which has parallels in most Western countries) of women forming the majorities of church congregations, has been explained in various ways. The way most favored by the nineteenth century involved the natural predeliction of women for good and therefore for religion. One twentieth-century writer believes that church-going is accounted for largely by a "psychology of Bereavement." The Puritans were bereft of England, the nineteenth-century woman was bereft of her children (or her personhood), and so forth. Therefore insofar as the individual American was pleased with himself, self-confident, and victorious over nature or property he had, presumably, increasingly less need for church – Cyclone Covey, *The American Pilgrimage,* 44-69. Another sociological explanation believes that women are "conditioned to react in terms of altruism and cooperation rather than of egocentrism and competition," and therefore are prime candidates for submission to external authority in both worlds – W. Seward Salisbury, *Religion in American Culture,* 88. Other explanations stress the supposed attraction of children to authority figures of the opposite sex. God is the father, ergo Oedipus aeternus. Woman's supposed innate masochism might, it could be argued, produce more guilt feelings than are produced in males, and religion is supposed to remove feelings of guilt. In any case, whether psychological or cultural, the historic fact of female-dominated churches and male-dominated clergy remains.

[21] Hymn books consulted were: Baron Stow and S.F. Smith, *The Psalmist: a new*

which became extremely popular at weddings had words written by a woman. "O Perfect Love" exhorts the young couple to emulate the perfect love of Christ in their own marriage:

> O perfect life, be thou their full assurance
> Of tender charity and steadfast faith,
> Of patient hope, and quiet, brave endurance,
> With childlike trust that fears nor pain nor death.

This was a pattern for domestic bliss much favored by women and the church, since it required the practice of those virtues they both cherished so highly – and which were found increasingly in only one partner of marriage. The implication is one which was made more explicit in the women's magazines: the burden of a marriage falls on the wife; no matter how hard her bed, it is her duty to lie on it. Marriage, and life itself, were at best endurance contests and should be entered in a spirit of passive acceptance and trust.

Another great favorite, "Nearer My God, to Thee," written by Sarah Adams in 1841, carried the same message: "E'en though it be a cross, that raiseth me; Still all my song would be, Nearer, My God, to thee, nearer to thee."[22] The hymns of the Cary sisters, Phoebe and Alice, repeated this theme with variations: "No

---

collection of hymns for the use of the Baptist Church (Boston, 1843); *Psalms and Hymns Adapted to Social, Private and Public Worship in the Presbyterian Church in the United States of America: Approved and authorized by the General Assembly* (Philadelphia, 1843); *Hymns of the Protestant Episcopal Church in the United States of America: Set Forth in the General Convention of Said Church in the Year of Our Lord, 1789, 1808, 1826* (Philadelphia, 1827); *Collection of Hymns for Public and Private Worship: Approved by the General Synod of the Evangelical Lutheran Church* (Columbus, Ohio, second edition, 1855); Abiel A. Livermore, ed., *Christian Hymns for Public and Private Worship* (Boston, 1846); Samuel Longfellow and Samuel Johnson, *A Book of Hymns for Public and Private Devotion* (Cambridge, 1846) (Unitarian); *Plymouth Collection of Hymns and Tunes; for the use of Christian Congregations* (New York, 1855); *Hymnal of the Presbyterian Church: Ordered by the General Assembly* (Philadelphia, 1866); *The Hymnal: Published by the Authority of the General Assembly of the Presbyterian Church in the United States of America* (Philadelphia, 1895); *Hymns of the Faith with Psalms* (Boston, 1887) (Congregational); *The Baptist Hymn and Tune Book* (Philadelphia, 1871); *Hymns: Approved by the General Synod of the Lutheran Church in the United States* (Philadelphia, 1871, revised from the edition of 1852); *Hymns for Church and Home* (New York, 1860) (Episcopal); and *Hymnal: According to the Use of the Protestant Episcopal Church in the United States of America printed under the authority of the General Convention* (Oxford, 1892; original edition 1872).

[22] "O Perfect Love" was written by Charlotte Elliott, a pious English invalid, who also wrote the popular revival hymn "Just As I Am" – Harvey B. Marks, *The Rise and Growth of English Hymnody* (New York, London and Edinburgh, 1937), 127. Sarah Adams, perhaps the most famous of the nineteenth-century hymn writers, had the dubious distinction of seeing her most popular hymn, "Nearer, My God to Thee," identified with imperialism and patriotism. It was reputedly quoted by McKinley on his deathbed, was Theodore Roosevelt's favorite hymn, and was sung by the gallant men on

Trouble Too Great But I Bring It to Jesus," and "To Suffer for Jesus Is My Greatest Joy," for example.[23] Another favorite stressed the total dependence of the singer on Jesus: "I Need Thee Every Hour."[24] The lyrics to this lend themselves all too well to the *double entendre* as those of us forced to sing it in Sunday Schools remember to our shame, but in fairness to our interpretations it is true that the imagery in many of these hymns seems very physical. In the desire to stress the warmth and humanity of Christ, he becomes a very cozy person; the singer is urged to press against him, to nestle into him, to hold his hand, and so forth. A love letter to Christ was the only kind of love letter a nice woman was allowed to publish, and sublimation was as yet an unused word. If Julia Ward Howe had called her book of love lyrics a book of hymns even Hawthorne (who thought her husband should have whipped her for the book) would have approved.

The ultimate in such expressions of total absorption in Christ and a yielding up of an unworthy body and soul to his embrace is the widely-sung "Just As I Am, Without One Plea."

> Just as I am, without one plea,
> But that thy blood was shed for me,
> And that thou bidd'st me come to thee,
> O Lamb of God, I come, I come.
>
> Just as I am, though tossed about
> With many a conflict, many a doubt;
> Fightings and fears within, without,
> O Lamb of God, I come, I come.
>
> Just as I am, poor, wretched, blind;
> Sight, riches, healing of the mind,
> Yea, all I need, in thee to find,
> O Lamb of God, I come, I come . . .
>
> Just as I am: thy love unknown
> Has broken every barrier down;
> Now to be thine, yea, thine alone,
> O Lamb of God, I come, I come.[25]

---

the sinking *Titanic* – Louis F. Benson, *The English Hymn: Its Development and Use in Worship* (Richmond, Virginia, 1962; original edition, 1915), 272.

[23] Mary Clemmer, ed. *The Poetical Works of Alice and Phoebe Cary: With a Memorial of Their Lives* (New York, 1876), 172; Alice Cary, *Ballads, Lyrics and Poems* (New York, 1866), 276.

[24] "I Need Thee Every Hour" was written by Mrs. Annie S. Hawks, and was considered a particularly appropriate hymn for Women's Circles and Mothers' Meetings – Edward S. Ninde, *The Story of the American Hymn* (New York, 1921), 150.

[25] Charlotte Elliott in Marks, *Rise and Growth of English Hymnody,* 128.

Since so many of women's problems were presumably physical and thus, like the weather, beyond help, it behooved them to endure what they could not cure. The "natural" disasters of childbirth, illness, death, loss of security through recurrent financial crises – all made "thy will be done" the very special female prayer, especially since submission was considered the highest of female virtues. In their hymns women expressed this theme of their lives, as a kind of reinforcement through repetition. However the woman who wanted a more active role in religion than enduring, or even than teaching Sunday school, had several possibilities open to her at this time. She could become a missionary, she could practice an old religion in a new setting, or she could join a new religion which gave women a more active role.

The Christianizing of the West, indeed the domesticating of the West, was probably the most important religious, cultural, and political event of the first half of the nineteenth century.[26] So long as the West was unhampered by the appurtenances of civilization, including women with their need for lace curtains, for coffee cups and Bibles and neighbors within chatting distance – it was an unknown and possibly dangerous phenomenon. All the Protestant religions and Catholicism as well considered it their special duty to bring God and women westward as soon as possible. Law, order, and consumers were enhanced by the presence of churches and women. Missionary work appealed to women as a way to have an adventure in a good cause, although the Mission Boards which passed on applications were firm in ruling out "adventuring" as a satisfactory motive. Missions to far off China or Burma were usually denied to the single woman, but the determined girl could quickly find a husband in other zealous souls determined on the same career. The majority of American

[26] The Christianizing of the West is seen as a central theme in virtually all standard accounts of the American religious experience. T. Scott Miyakawa, *Protestants and Pioneers: Individualism and Conformity on the American Frontier* (Chicago and London, 1944) applies Frederick Jackson Turner's frontier thesis to the religious life of the West, and agrees with Turner that in this, as in other areas, the frontier "either drastically altered or rejected the older cultural traditions," 226. Nineteenth-century witnesses to the propagation of the faith included the travel accounts of Robert Baird, *Religion in America: or, an Account of the Origins, Progress, Relation to the State and Present Condition of the Evangelical Churches in the United States* (New York, 1844); Caroline Kirkland, *The Evening Book: Or, Fireside Talk on Morals and Manners, with Sketches of Western Life* (New York, 1852); Harriet Martineau, *Retrospect of Western Travel,* 3 volumes (London, 1838); and *Society in America,* 3 volumes (London, 1837), as well as the critical Mrs. Trollope.

missionaries in the period before the Civil War stayed within the continent, taking the Christianizing of the Indians as their special challenge and duty.[27]

Mary Augusta Gray reflected on the interior dialogue with which she came to her missionary vocation:

> Ever since the day when I gave myself up to Jesus, it had been my daily prayer, "Lord, what wilt thou have me do?" and when the question, "Will you go to Oregon as one of a little band of self-denying missionaries and teach these poor Indians of their Saviour?" was suddenly proposed to me, I felt that it was the call of the Lord and I could not do otherwise.[28]

The missionaries to China usually went with a sense of doom and impending martyrdom, and the heroic exploits of such women as Ann Hasseltine Judson were fodder for this belief. Mrs. Judson had died, as she knew she would, far from home but near to Jesus, and thus her story became one much favored in children's biographical literature.[29] However even the home missions carried the same possibility for martyrdom, as the fate of Narcissa and Marcus Whitman proved.[30] There is no question but that the aspiring missionary was aware of this possibility and that he

[27] Robert F. Berkhofer, Jr., *Salvation and the Savage: An Analysis of Protestant Missions and American Indian Response, 1787-1862* (Lexington, Kentucky, 1965) and R. Pierce Beaver, *Church, State, and the American Indians: Two and a Half Centuries of Partnership in Missions Between Protestant Churches and Government* (St. Louis, 1966).

[28] Mrs. Owens, ed., "Diaries of Pioneer Women of Clatsop County," *Oregon Pioneers Association,* Vol. XXIV (1896), 89-94.

[29] Adoniram Judson, a baptist missionary, brought three wives to join him in his labors in Burma: Ann Hasseltine (1789-1826), followed by Sarah Hall Boardman (1803-1845) and Emily Chubbuck (1817-1854) who returned to the United States after her husband's death in 1850. The combined trials of these three women culminating in their early deaths were considered excellent propaganda for the Mission Boards – James D. Knowles, *Memoir of Mrs. Ann H. Judson, Late Missionary to Burma* (New York, 1829); Arabella W. Stuart, *The Lives of Mrs. Ann H. Judson and Mrs. Sarah B. Judson, with a Biographical Sketch of Mrs. Emily C. Judson* (New York, 1851); Gordon L. Hall, *Golden Boats from Burma* (New York, 1961); Emily Forester [Judson], *Memoir of Sarah B. Judson* (New York, 1848); Walter N. Wyeth, *Sarah B. Judson* (Boston, 1889); Asahel Clark Kendrick, *The Life and Letters of Mrs. Emily C. Judson* (New York, 1860). Another popular missionary heroine was Harriet Atwood Newell (1793-1812), who was the first American to die on a foreign mission – NAW, Vol. II, Mary Sumner Benson, "Harriet Atwood Newell," 619-620; Harriet Newell, *The Life and Writings of Mrs. Harriet Newell* (Boston, 1831).

[30] The Whitmans were married in 1836 and almost immediately embarked for Oregon. Narcissa survived the hazards of frontier life, the loss of her daughter by drowning, increasing blindness and constant harassment by Indians and rival religious groups only to die with her husband in a massacre at Waiilatpu in 1847 – Clifford M. Drury, *First White Women over the Rockies,* 3 volumes (New York, 1963-66); Jeanette Eaton, *Narcissa Whitman* (New York, 1941); Opal Sweazea Allen, *Narcissa Whitman* (New York, 1959); and the *Proceedings* of the Oregon Pioneers Association, *passim.*

welcomed it. Part of the reason for this is perhaps the theology of the period which taught that the death of a martyr assured heaven. The desire for death in the service of the Lord seems in the cases of some missionary women to be their strongest motive.

Eliza Spalding, a Connecticut girl who had been converted at an early age, found that distributing tracts and doing visiting among the poor was not enough for her. She asked divine guidance about her future and received the impulse to go to Oregon. When her husband tried to dissuade her she replied: "I like the command just as it stands, 'Go ye into all the world,' with no exception for poor health. The dangers in the way and the weakness of my body are his; duty is mine." Mrs. Spalding survived the trip, leaving the following diary entry:

> Oh, that I had a crust of bread from my mother's swill pail. I cannot sit on that horse in the burning sun any longer. I cannot live much longer. Go on, and save yourself and carry the Book to the Indians. I shall never see them. My work is done. But bless God that He has brought me thus far. Tell my mother that I am not sorry I came.

Her husband wrote to the Mission Board: "Never send another white woman over these mountains, if you have any regard for human life," but of course they did, for the women clamored to come to the Indians and to death, if need be.[31]

Although the West has been seen as a fertile ground for democratic innovations, this was not necessarily true for women's role. Simply because of the lack of numbers, most western churches gave women the freedom to participate in church services, and the West was the natural breeding place for such women evangelists as Carry A. Nation and Aimee Semple MacPherson. However there was still pressure to conform to the traditional female role within religion, as Narcissa Whitman wrote shortly before her death:

> In all the prayer meetings of this mission the brethren only pray. I believe all the sisters would be willing to pray if their husbands would let them. We are so few in number, it seems as if they would wish it, but many prefer the more dignified way. My husband has no objection to my praying, but if my sisters do not, he thinks it quite as well for me not to.[32]

[31] Eliza Spalding, whose health continued to decline with each year in the West, died of tuberculosis in 1851 at the age of forty-three – Clifford M. Drury, *The First White Women over the Rockies,* I, 173-233; "Diary of Mrs. E.H. Spalding," Oregon Pioneers Association, Vol. XXIV (1896), 106-110.

[32] T.E. Elliott, ed., Narcissa Prentiss Whitman, "The Coming of the White Woman,

In the West, but especially in the East, the spirit of revival was strong during this period. The language, like that of the hymns, was sexual in its imagery and urged the penitent to "stop struggling and allow yourself to be swept up in His love." Obviously this kind of imagery had a familiar ring to women, for it was in similar language that they were encouraged to submit to their husbands. Whether in the divine or human order, woman was constantly urged to be swept away by a torrent of energy, not to rely on her own strength which was useless, to sink into the arms of Jesus, to become absorbed and assimilated by the Divine Will – in other words, to relax and enjoy it. The fantasies of rape were nourished by this language and by the kind of physical sensations which a woman expected to receive and did receive in the course of conversion. "A trembling of the limbs," "a thrill from my toes to my head," "wave after wave of feeling," are examples of female reaction to the experience of "divine penetration."[33]

Mrs. Maggie N. Van Cott, who called herself the first lady licensed to preach in the Methodist Episcopal Church in the United States, told in her autobiography of receiving the "great blessing of fullness" as a result of which she was "perfectly emptied of self and filled with the Spirit of God." In showing her the way, God had announced "I am a jealous God; thou shalt have no other Gods before me," which she interpreted to mean that her Master wanted her complete devotion.[34]

Ellen G. White had a similar vision in which she was shown a steep frail staircase, at the top of which was Jesus. As she fell

---

1836," as told in the *Letters and Journal of Narcissa Prentiss Whitman* (Portland, 1937), 108.

[33] Histories of revivalism in the United States are numerous. One of the best is Timothy L. Smith, *Revivalism and Social Reform in Mid-Nineteenth Century America* (New York and Nashville, 1957). An interesting psychological study is Sidney George Dimond, *The Psychology of the Methodist Revival: An Empirical and Descriptive Study* (London, 1926). Other sources are Paulus Scharpff, *History of Evangelism: Three Hundred Years of Evangelism in Germany, Great Britain, and the United States of America,* translated by Helga Bender Henry (Grand Rapids, Michigan, 1966); F.G. Beardsley, *A History of American Revivals* (The Tract Society, n.p., 1912); Bernard A. Weisberger, *They Gathered At the River: The Story of the Great Revivals and Their Impact Upon Religion in America* (Boston and Toronto, 1958); C.A. Johnson, *The Frontier Camp Meeting* (Dallas, Texas, 1955); and Whitney R. Cross, *The Burned-over District: The Social and Intellectual History of Enthusiastic Religion in Western New York, 1800-1850* (Ithaca, New York, 1950). The most famous nineteenth-century account of revivals was by the man who made them, Charles G. Finney, *Lectures on Revival* (Boston, 1836).

[34] Mrs. Maggie N. Van Cott, *The Harvest and the Reaper: Reminiscences of Revival Work* (New York, c.1883), 49, 67-9.

prostrate, her guide gave her a green cord "coiled up closely," which she could uncoil to reach Him. From that time "my entire being was offered to the service of my Master."[35]

Particularly interesting are those first-person accounts which discuss these experiences and then go on to say how little her husband understands her and how he tries to interfere with this wholehearted commitment to Christ. "Oh, the bliss of that moment, when my soul was enabled to cast all her care upon Jesus and feel that *her* will was lost in the will of God," rhapsodized Myra Smith at 4:14 a.m. one Sunday. Soon after she wrote: " . . . I find sweet comfort in doing the will of God instead of my own . . . I feel that God calls me to labor in a more special manner than he usually does females . . . I am not understood by my husband and children but I don't murmur, or blame them for it. I know they can't tell why I seem at times lost to everything around me."[36] Richard Hofstadter points out that revivalism was one of the manifestations of a pervasive anti-intellectualism in mid-nineteenth-century America.[37] However it can be further annotated by means of the popular custom of dividing qualities into male and female categories. By this nomenclature all the intuitive and emotional qualities are most natural to women, all the cerebral and intellectual policies of linear thought the prerogative of men. When in terms of religion a more intuitive, heartfelt approach was urged it was tantamount to asking for a more feminine religious style.[38]

Although at the intellectual and, therefore, presumably "masculine" end of the scale, Transcendentalism might also be considered representative of certain feminine standards. One hanger-on to Transcendental circles and ardent feminist, Caroline Dall, saw Anne Hutchinson as the first Transcendentalist and, by extension, the first feminist in the American colonies.[39] Her argument was that antinomianism was an open door to the exercise of individual

[35] Ellen G. White, *Life Sketches* (Mountain View, California, 1915; first edition, 1860), 32-34.

[36] MS Diary of Myra S. Smith, June 19, 1859, Elizabeth and Arthur Schlesinger Library, Radcliffe College, Cambridge, Massachusetts.

[37] Richard Hofstadter, *Anti-Intellectualism in America* (New York, 1963).

[38] Barbara Welter, "Anti-Intellectualism and the American Woman: 1800-1860," *Mid-America,* Vol. 48 (October, 1966), 258-70.

[39] Caroline Dall, "Transcendentalism in New England: A Lecture Given before the Society for Philosophical Enquiry, Washington, D.C., May 7, 1895," in *The Journal of Speculative Philosophy,* Vol. XXIII, No. 1 (1897), 1-38. C. Gregg Singer, *A Theological Interpretation of American History* (Nutley, New Jersey, 1964) saw Transcendentalism as a direct repudiation of Puritanism, because it glorified man instead of God.

rights, by either sex or by any group. If God, not the ordained clergy, picks His spokesmen, then women are as likely as any to be among the chosen, for as any popular novel or sermon would have it, women are more religious, more noble, more spiritual than men – so all the more likely to be a vehicle for God's message. Besides, if one adheres to the principle of autonomous conversion, then there is no way to second-guess the Almighty; any soul may receive Him, no sex barred. In the Quaker religion the Inner Light was expected to be equally indiscriminate in the choice of vessels to illuminate, and the Society of Friends practiced theoretical religious equality from its beginnings.

The Transcendentalists accepted a similar definition of equality before God. All souls were equally divine, without regard to sex or race. As Nathaniel Frothingham points out, Transcendentalism was a part of the Woman's Rights Movement in the most profound sense in that it posited her as an innate equal, whose potential had been hampered by society. Ralph Waldo Emerson went through a number of phases in the formulation of his own position on women. His theoretical approach, contained in a number of essays, was sometimes at variance with the way in which he actually coped with his Aunt Mary, his two wives, and the irritatingly untheoretical presence of Margaret Fuller. In an essay, "Woman," Emerson tried to analyze the religious style of females. He concluded that ". . . the omnipotence of Eve is in humility." This, he continued, was the direct opposite of male style, which was to stress the necessity and potency of the male to the object loved. Religion perforce requires humility, since God does not depend on human strength. Women also, according to Emerson, possess to a high degree that "power of divination" or sympathy which the German Romantics prized so highly. They have "a religious height which men do not attain" because of their "sequestration from affairs and from the injury to the moral sense which affairs often inflict. . . ." It was therefore not surprising that "in every remarkable religious development in the world, women have taken a leading part."[40]

The idea of a regenerated reconstituted society was important to most members of the Hedge Club, and they looked optimistically towards an America in which man would leave behind his

[40]Octavius Brooks Frothingham, *Recollections and Impressions, 1822-1890* (New York and London, 1891), 136. Ralph Waldo Emerson, *The Complete Writings of Ralph Waldo Emerson* (New York, 1929, 1st edition 1875), "Woman," 1178-84.

chains and emerge closer to nature and nature's God. The concept of ideal manhood and of ideal womanhood was often discussed at these meetings, and, of course, in Margaret Fuller's Conversations.[41] Womanhood was believed to be, in principle, a higher, nobler state than manhood, since it was less directly related to the body and was more involved with the spirit; women had less to transcend in their progress. "I trust more and more every opportunity will be offered to women to train and use their gifts, until the world finds out what womanhood is," wrote William Henry Channing. "My hope for society turns upon this; the regeneration of the future will come from the exalting influence of woman."[42] Most of these Transcendentalists were unconvinced about woman's role in politics, but they were totally convinced that she represented the highest and best parts of man.

Margaret Fuller contributed another important idea to the feminization of religion in her stress on the importance of the will. As historians such as John William Ward have pointed out, this belief in the power of the American will was typical of Jacksonian America. Like other aspects of the so-called American character, however, it did not necessarily hold true for all groups within the society. (David Riesman, for example, has reconsidered some of his statements about American character because of the remoteness of the female half of the population from his producer economy.)[43] For Margaret Fuller the will was the instrument to power for women even more than for men, and she set out to convince her world of this fact. Woman traditionally was urged to negate her will, or at least to yield it up to her father, her husband, and her God. Margaret Fuller told her to actively pursue her goals, to "elect" her destiny. Miss Fuller possessed Emerson's "spark of divinity" by which she was able to convince the young girls and wives who flocked to her that they too were divine and could go out and accomplish great (but unnamed) things. This preaching to women of their worth before God and man was sound Transcendental doctrine, but the stress on female worth, on transcendent

[41] Caroline Dall, in her voluminous diaries and notes, recorded many impressions of these conversations besides the ones she published – Caroline Healy Dall MSS, Massachusetts Historical Society and Radcliffe Women's Archives.

[42] Octavius Brooks Frothingham, *Memoir of William Henry Channing* (Boston and New York, 1886), 296.

[43] David Riesman, Introduction to Jessie Bernard, *Academic Women* (New York, 1966). The late David Potter also reconsidered his assessment of the American character in his essay, "American Women and the American Character" in John A. Hague, ed., *American Character and Culture* (De Land, Florida, 1964), 65-84.

womanhood, was a personal interpretation of Margaret Fuller. She gloried in her role of Sibyl, and relished all references to her as Delphic and/or Oracular.[44] The cult of the will, as Donald Myers writes, found its triumph in Christian Science, also the religion of a woman, in which even death bows to positive thought.[45] Margaret Fuller's intent and fervid preoccupation with the making-over of the self presented a considerable threat to the men in her circle. For if sex itself, as well as health, family, education, income, all counted for nothing – what standards remained? It was perhaps the vicious circle of antinomianism after all; a religion open to the vagaries of God's choice or the boundaries of the human will is a religion without class lines and certainly without sex discrimination.

The Transcendentalists sought concrete expression of their philosophy in the community of Brook Farm, and the setting up of ideal communal societies was one way in which nineteenth-century religion expressed its dissatisfaction with past religious styles and its hope for the future. The equal rights of Transcendentalism were much in evidence at Brook Farm. One participant in that noble experiment recalled hearing a lecture on women's rights during his time in residence. The young lady speaker:

> . . . was much put out, after orating awhile, to note that her glowing periods were falling on dull ears. Our womenfolk had all the rights of our men-folk. They had an equal voice in our public affairs, voted for our offices, filled responsible positions, and stood in exactly the same footing as their brethren. If women were not so well off in the outer world, they had only to join our community or to form others like it.[46]

In the constitution of Brook Farm, as in many other communal societies, there are promises to the women members that they would be liberated from the tyranny of men and of the stove, and given greater freedom to develop their own identities. Charles Nordhoff, writing on the influence of women in utopian communities in 1875, found that women's participation in discussions gave them "contentment of mind, as well as enlarged views and

[44] See in particular Margaret Fuller (Ossoli), *Woman in the Nineteenth Century* (New York, 1845), *Life Without and Life Within,* edited by A.B. Fuller (Boston, 1859) and Caroline W. Healey (Dall), *Margaret and Her Friends: Or, the Conversations with Margaret Fuller Upon the Mythology of the Greeks and Its Expression in Art* (Boston, 1896).

[45] Donald Meyer, *The Positive Thinkers* (Garden City, New York, 1965).

[46] John Van Der Zee Sears, *My Friends at Brook Farm* (New York, 1918), 89.

pleasure in self-denial." Women in communal life found stability, which they needed and wanted, and many small comforts provided by the men for which "the migrating farmer's wife sighs in vain." The simplicity of dress typical of many groups was "a saving of time and trouble and vexation of spirit." Their greatest contribution to communal society was their "conservative spirit," which operated in the aggregate as it had in family life. Nordhoff concluded that women expressed the basic excuse for being of the communist society, for her "influence is always toward a higher life."[47]

When the commune moved from the planning stages to the land itself, somehow or other, women ended up in the kitchen or the laundry. Men might serve on these committees, but the overriding principle of the division of labor mandated their presence outdoors. In the communal societies whose records I studied, there is no record of any complaint on the part of the women, nor was there any recorded instance of women challenging their husbands on a given vote. There seems also to be no pattern of a woman's bloc.[48] But the actual role of women is less important than the way in which the changed pattern of social life was supposed to bring true equality to both sexes and liberate man from his own tyranny at the same time woman was freed from the conventional bonds of family life.

The Fourierist philosophy, which, so far as recorded sources tell, was never completely followed in the United States, provided for a good deal of sexual freedom within a definition of human nature which relied on "natural affinities." Parts of the human race were exempted from monogamy because they had "natural affinities" towards several members of the opposite sex. The fact that women, as well as men, might be expected to have these preferences was regarded as "peculiarly French," and not relevant to the American Phalanx.[49]

[47] Charles Nordhoff, *The Communist Societies of the United States* (New York, 1912; original edition 1875), 412.

[48] New Harmony (Indiana), Yellow Springs Community (Ohio), Brook Farm (Massachusetts), North American Phalanx (New Jersey), Ceresco (Wisconsin), Northampton Association (Massachusetts), Fruitlands (Massachusetts), Oneida (New York) and Modern Times (New York).

[49] John Thomas Codman, *Brook Farm: Historic and Personal Memoirs* (Boston, 1894), 111, and articles in *The Dial* and *The Harbinger,* throughout their publication, translating and commenting on Fourier. Fourier's ideas on the role of women in the new society can be found in Francois Marie Charles Fourier, *Theory of Social Organization* (New York, 1876).

Within the Americanized version of Fourierism there was much "wholesome intercourse" between the sexes. The opportunity to work and study and talk together was rare enough for middle-class American youth, and the Phalanxes gave them much more freedom than most families allowed. The great charm of the communal life, one remembered fondly long after the community itself was a thing of the past, "was in the free and natural intercourse for which it gave opportunity, and in the working of the elective affinities."[50] The young women who participated in these experiments were emboldened to pursue lives as teachers or reformers after they left the Phalanx. The Transcendental idea of the infinite worth of the individual and his ability to work out his destiny was greatly appealing to these young women. Even if women continued to do woman's work and find their greatest individual destiny in monogamous marriage, there was a statement of equality and of alternatives on the record.

The experiment at Oneida, conducted by John Humphrey Noyes as an example of his Perfectionist religion, was a particularly interesting application of new religion to women. One of the avowed purposes of the Oneida Community was to give women "extended rights" within "an extended family." The way in which Noyes defined these rights was sharply criticized by his contemporaries and has not received very sympathetic treatment from historians. In many ways he really was, as he claimed to be, "Woman's best friend." Noyes believed that the search for complete perfection began with control over one's own body. For women this was a complicated phenomenon, involving not only the marital rights but the right to choose whether she wished to have children. Noyes spoke very cogently about the trauma of the nineteenth-century woman, who bore her children with such pain and hope, and saw them die as infants.[51] In a society which defined woman as valuable largely in relation to her ability to bear children, it was logical that women thought of their own worth in those terms. When a child died it was an affirmation of personal guilt and possibly sin. What have I done, the bereaved mother asked her God, that I should be punished? Pages of women's diaries are filled with personal recriminations. For months she

[50] Amelia Russell, "Home Life of the Brook Farm Association," *The Atlantic Monthly*, Vol. 42 (October, 1878, pp. 457-66) and (November, 1878, pp. 556-63), 561.

[51] Robert Allerton Parker, *A Yankee Saint: John Humphrey Noyes and the Oneida Community* (New York, 1935), is an excellent biography with many quotations from Noyes' writings.

flagellated herself with the remedies she might have used, the errors of judgment she could have avoided, the ways in which she might have offended a jealous God. Noyes proposed to define her worth in different terms: she was a loving companion and "yoke-fellow" on the road to perfection. Childbearing was only part of her duty, to be engaged in sparingly and under controlled conditions, and to be separated from sex.[52] In terms of woman's self-image this proposal was one of the most radical of the century.

The form of birth control used by Noyes, which he called "male continence," consisted in "self-control" which prolonged intercourse but stopped the act short of ejaculation. Interestingly enough, this insistence on control was only for the man; there was no limit to the amount of pleasure a woman was allowed to get from the act. Moreover, sexual intercourse was accepted as a good in itself, completely outside the propagation of the species, and as an important means of self-expression for both sexes. Noyes went so far in identifying the sex act with perfectionism as to assert that sexual intercourse was practiced in heaven. This insistence on the joys of sex was rare enough, but, couched in terms of a conjugal relation which promised equal rights of choice and no penalty of childbearing on the woman, it was extraordinary. Perfectionism stressed the "giving, not the claiming," the act of loving, rather than the social and economic benefits of marriage.[53] In these ways, it acceded to the feminine spirit and role. The nineteenth-century belief that "love is a game, nothing more to a man/ But love to a woman is life or death," that "love is woman's whole existence," was applied by Noyes to both sexes. "We should pray, give us this day our daily love, for what is love but the bread of the heart. We need love as much as we need food and clothing, and God knows it. . . ."[54] In the popular jargon of phrenology, Noyes separated "amativeness" from both "union for life" and "procreativeness." In the phrenological manuals, amativeness was considered to be particularly well developed in men; the other two qualities, along with "philoprogenitiveness" to be peculiarly suited to female skulls.[55] Noyes stressed love for both sexes and freedom

[52] *Ibid.*, 67.

[53] *Ibid.*, 182-3.

[54] *Ibid.*, 183.

[55] Phrenology was a nineteenth-century mixture of science, religion, and cultural reinforcement; both conservatives and liberals used its terminology, sometimes seriously, sometimes with tongue in cheek. Among the most popular phrenological manuals were

of choice for both, which gave to women the continuation of her preoccupation with love plus the right to a repetitive use of her loving. Marriage at Oneida was a working out of the feminine rhetoric of love on a sequential basis.

Although Mormonism was treated as a great foe of women's rights, and even its female proponents agreed that it placed the male in a dominant role, it had certain components which made it part of the overall movement towards "feminization." Like Perfectionism it claimed to be acting in the name of a better life for women. "No prophet or reformer of ancient or modern times has surpassed, nay, has equalled, the Prophet Joseph Smith in the breadth and scope of the opportunities which he accorded womanhood," wrote a dutiful and satisfied daughter of both the Prophet and Zion.[56] Mormonism required its followers to accept the words of their spiritual Father without murmur, and to obey the precepts of authority. The important concept of the Mormon priesthood is one which excludes women (as well as blacks by some interpretations). However, Joseph Smith, when the women of his group asked him for a written constitution for their Relief Society, told them he would give them "something better for them than a written constitution . . . I will organize the sisters under the priesthood after a pattern of the priesthood . . . The Church was never perfectly organized until the women were thus organized."[57]

Thus the women of the Church of Jesus Christ of the Latter Day Saints claimed that they were admitted as "co-workers and partners" in the important work of attaining salvation. They were in the priesthood only when taken by their husbands and only with their husband could they enter into a special heaven. Their consent was required for plural marriage, which became their passport – again, only with their husbands – to the highest stages of celestial bliss. And yet, patriarchal as it was, women were not ignored by this new religion. Indeed, they were given explicit and critical directions for salvation. No man could get to heaven alone, by any combination of faith or good works; he had to come

---

Jessie A. Fowler, *A Manual of Mental Science* (London and New York, 1897); G. Spurzheim, *Outlines of Phrenology* (Boston, 1832); and Lorenzo N. Fowler, *Marriage* (New York, 1847).

[56] Susa Young Gates, *History of the Young Ladies' Mutual Improvement Association*, 2.

[57] *History of the Relief Society of the Church of Jesus Christ of Latter Day Saints* (Salt Lake City, 1966), 18.

bringing his family with him. Women could legitimately claim that Mormonism recognized their importance more than any other religion because it tied them to their husbands for all time and eternity. Motherhood was stressed in Utah even more than in the rest of American society, but it was the importance of producing souls not bodies that counted. Since every woman, in theory, could be united to the man of her choice, she could go to heaven with her love, not her forced compromise. Recognizing the fact that society gave women status only as a married woman and as a mother, the Mormons gave each woman the opportunity to have that coveted status in this life and in the next. What is surprising is not the formulation of Celestial Marriage, but the fervor with which Mormon women defended it as important to their ideas of themselves as valuable and valid persons.[58]

Like the Church of the Latter Day Saints, Roman Catholicism during this pre-Civil War period had both masculine and feminine manifestations. The patriarchal system of authority, which so pleased Orestes Brownson, has already been mentioned. The diatribes against Rome which were prevalent in the 1830s and 1840s stressed this authoritarian and anti-democratic aspect of the Church. In other words, Catholics were not allowed to exercise their masculine prerogatives of intellectual autonomy and independent judgment. When a modest number of conversions to Roman Catholicism occurred during the last days of Brook Farm, some observers found the cause to be the discouragement and disappointment which the failure of that experiment created in its members. Most of the converts were female, and disparaging statements were made about the need to abandon the heritage of the New England Protestant (masculine) Church to find solace in a more soothing, structured (feminine) religion.[59]

The letters of the converted Fourierists do nothing to deny that they found the Church of Rome more suitable to their needs, but

[58]For example, see the testimony of Joseph Smith's wives in Don Cecil Corbett, *Mary Fielding Smith: Daughter of Britain; Portrait of Courage* (Salt Lake City, 1966), and the women in Edward W. Tullidge, *The Women of Mormonism* (New York, 1877). Tullidge quotes Eliza Snow Smith as saying that the Mormon Church "is the oracle of the grandest emancipation of womanhood and motherhood," 194. Mrs. Hannah T. King, in 1870, proposed a resolution opposing the federal bill outlawing polygamy which ended with an acknowledgment of the Church of the Latter Day Saints "as the only reliable safeguard of female virtue and innocence; and the only sure protection against the fearful sin of prostitution . . .", 385. There is also a considerable literature of anti-Mormonism, in which the Mormons are portrayed as despoilers of female virtue and degenerates of the worst sort, very much in the Maria Monk tradition.

[59]Octavius Brooks Frothingham, *George Ripley* (Boston, 1882), 236-7.

their emphasis is not on feminine dependence but on womanly warmth. Sophia Ripley wrote to a sympathetic friend that she found "the coldness of heart in Protestantism and my own coldness of heart in particular" to be repugnant. After her conversion she saw herself clearly for the first time: "I saw that all through life my ties with others were those of the intellect and imagination, and not human heart ties; that I do not love anyone. I never did, with the heart, and of course never could have been worthy in any relation." Catholicism united her for the first time with humanity, and that chill intellectual pride which New Englanders wore like Lady Eleanor's mantle at last melted away. "I saw above all that my faith in the Church was only a reunion of my intellect with God," and not a union of hearts. To her mentor Bishop Hughes she poured out her fears that "this terrible deathlike coldness" had produced a "heart of stone" which even the love of Christ could not melt. He reassured her that if she had been born in the Church perhaps her nature would have been softened, but she must offer to God not the heart she coveted but the heart she had: "Oh God, take this poor cold heart of mine, and make of it what thou wilt . . . This heart of yours is a cross which you must bear to the end if needs be."[60] Catholicism, then, at least to some of its members, incorporated the love and warmth so characteristic of women and so necessary to them.

Like Mormonism, Roman Catholicism was also regarded as a religion for the many, not the few. This sense of religion as a means of keeping down intellectual arrogance and spiritual pride is one which accords with a subtle but important aspect of female definition during this period. In Hawthorne's stories and novels the woman is the symbol of the earth, the tie with domestic detail and bodily warmth which prevents man from soaring too high or sinking too low.[61] Louis Auchincloss has called women "guardians and caretakers" because of their role in preserving literary and cultural traditions.[62] Inasmuch as religion is concerned they might as well be termed "Translators and Vulgarizers." In the Transcendental novel, *Margaret,* Sylvester Judd says of woman: "She

[60] MSS Letters of Sophia Dana Ripley and Charlotte Dana, Dana Papers, Massachusetts Historical Society, Boston, Massachusetts; March, 1848.

[61] For example, Ellen in *Fanshawe,* Phoebe in *The House of the Seven Gables,* and Annie in "The Artist of the Beautiful" all represent the principle of the common humanity of the ordinary man rather than the singular arrogance of the individual.

[62] Louis Auchincloss, *Pioneers and Caretakers: A Study of Nine American Women Novelists* (Minneapolis, 1965).

translates nature to man and man to himself."[63] Women, in religion, as in popular taste, take the bold and bitter and make it bland. One critic of American conformity blames the low standards of American culture on the fact that women are the audience and arbiters. "Averse to facing the darker brutal sides of existence, its uncertainty and irrationality, they prefer the comforting assurance that life is just bitter enough to bring out the flavor of its sugared harmonies."[64] Women in the first half of the nineteenth century took Christianity and molded it to their image and likeness.

"The curse of our age is its femininity," complained Orestes Brownson. "Its lack, not of barbarism, but of virility."[65] These changes, which annoyed Brownson as much in literature as in religion, made women as well as men conscious of their virtues. Womanhood and virtue became almost synonymous. Although the values of the nineteenth century have predominated during the twentieth century, it becomes increasingly more clear that they are not the only values and that the so-called feminine virtues may assume more than rhetorical significance. The giving over of religion to women, in its content and in its membership, provided a repository for these female values during the period when the business of building a nation did not immediately require them. In order to do this, it was necessary first to assign certain virtues to women and, then, to institutionalize these virtues. The family, popular culture, and religion were the vehicles by which feminine virtues were translated into values.

Religion carried with it the need for self-awareness, if only for the examination of conscience. Organizational experience could be obtained in many reform groups, but only religion brought with it the heightened sense of who you were and where you were going. Women in religion were encouraged to be introspective. What they found out would be useful in their drive towards independence. The constant identification of woman with virtue and with religion reenforced her own belief in her power to overcome obstacles, since she had her own superior nature and God's own Church, whichever it might be, behind her. Religion in its emphasis on the brotherhood of man developed in women a

[63] Sylvester Judd, *Margaret: A Tale of the Real and Ideal* (Boston, 1882; first edition, 1851), 378-9.

[64] Morris Raphael Cohen, *American Thought: A Critical Sketch* (New York, 1962; original edition, 1954), 41.

[65] Orestes Brownson, *Works,* "Literature, Love and Marriage," Vol. XIV, 421.

conscious sense of sisterhood, a quality absolutely essential for any kind of meaningful woman's movement. The equality of man before God expressed so effectively in the Declaration of Independence had little impact on women's lives. However the equality of religious experience was something they could personally experience, and no man could deny it to them.

FOR FURTHER READING

Most of the books which helped in reaching the conclusions of this article are found in the text of the footnotes. It is difficult to single out any books which were particularly pertinent, since few sources treat religion and women together; however, the following are some standard works in both these fields:

Sweet, W.W. *The Story of Religion in America.* New York: Harper and Row, 1939.

Sperry, W.L. *Religion in America.* New York: Macmillan, 1946.

Hudson, W.S. *American Protestantism.* Chicago: University of Chicago Press, 1961.

Ellis, J.T. *American Catholicism.* Chicago: University of Chicago Press, 1956.

Smith, T.L. *Revivalism and Social Reform in Mid-nineteenth Century America.* Nashville, Tenn.: Abingdon Press, 1957.

Cross, W.R. *The Burned-over District.* Ithaca, N.Y.: Cornell University Press, 1950.

Tyler, A.F. *Freedom's Ferment.* Minneapolis: University of Minnesota Press, 1944.

Irwin, I.H. *Angels and Amazons.* Garden City, N.Y.: Doubleday, 1934.

Flexner, Eleanor. *Century of Struggle.* Cambridge, Mass.: Harvard University Press, 1959.

Lutz, Alma. *Created Equal: A Biography of Elizabeth Cady Stanton.* New York: John Day, 1940.

O'Neill, W.L. *Everyone Was Brave.* Chicago: Quadrangle Books, 1969.

Sinclair, A.A. *The Emancipation of American Women.* New York: Harper and Row, 1966.

Scott, A.F. *The Southern Lady.* Chicago and London: University of Chicago Press, 1970.

Calhoun, A.W. *A Social History of the American Family,* 3 vols. Cleveland: Case Western Reserve University Press, 1917-19.

Sweet's book is a great classic in the field, filled with information and useful for theological and pastoral controversies. Sperry's book is less objective but has more insights, for better or for worse, into the social as well as the religious consequences of religious change. Hudson's book, although very brief, gives a succinct summary of the major religious bodies which made up the Protestant church in the United States over the past three hundred years. The history of Catholicism by Ellis is somewhat dated, in that the aftermath of Vatican II is not discussed. However, the chapters on the nineteenth century are accurate and informative, although without much discussion of the social or intellectual relationship of the Roman Church to the rest of the country. Smith's book is very well documented and is a real social history of the period, as is Cross's work on New York. Together they form an excellent background for the revival mood and movement. Tyler's book covers much ground quickly, but says a great deal, and is particularly good on the woman's movement. Irwin concentrates on the personalities and Flexner on the institutions in woman's long struggle for her rights. The Lutz biography of perhaps the single most important woman in the American woman's movement is adequate but not inspiring, and makes no effort to relate Stanton's life to her times. The Sinclair book is a popular survey of the woman's movement, but highly readable and based on many primary sources. The books by O'Neill and Scott are among the very best to come out of the renewed interest in women's history; both are excellent, exceptionally well researched, and perceptive, as well as sympathetic, to the ladies with whom they deal. The Calhoun trilogy is a marvelously Victorian piece of research and prejudice, into which you can dip interminably, like an old Sears Roebuck Catalogue, accepting or rejecting the information as you choose.

Sources

1

The Shakers

SOURCE: John Humphrey Noyes, *History of American Socialism* (New York: Hillary House Publishers, Ltd., 1961), pp. 601-607. Reprinted with permission.

UNION MEETINGS

"The two Elders and the two Eldresses held their meetings in the Elders' room. The three Deacons and the three Deaconesses met in one of their rooms. The rest of the family, in groups of from six to eight brothers and sisters, met in other rooms. At these meetings it was customary for the seats to be arranged in two rows about four feet apart. The sisters sat in one row, and the brothers in the other, facing each other. The meetings were rather dull, as the members had nothing to converse about save the family affairs;

for those who troubled themselves about the things of the world, were not considered good Shakers. It was expected that in coming there we should leave the 'world' behind us. The principal subject of conversation was eating and drinking. One brother sometimes eulogized a sister whom he thought to be the best cook, and who could make the best 'Johnny-cake.' At one meeting that I attended, there was a lively conversation about what we had for dinner; and by this means, it might be said, we enjoyed our dinner twice over.

"I have thus given the routine for one day; and each week-day throughout the year was the same. The only variation was in the evening. Besides these union meetings, every alternate evening was devoted to dancing. Sundays also had a routine of their own, which I will not detail.

"During the time I was with the Shakers, I never heard one of them read the Bible or pray in public. Each one was permitted to pray or let it alone as he pleased, and I believe there was very little praying among them. Believing as they did that all 'worldly things' should be left in the 'world' behind them, they did not even read the ordinary literature of the day. Newspapers were only for the use of the Elders and Deacons. The routine I have described was continually going on; and it was their boast that they were then the same in their habits and manners as they were sixty years before. The furniture of the dwellings was of the same old-fashioned kind that the early Dutch settlers used; and every thing about them and their dwellings, I was taught, was originally designed in heaven, and the designs transmitted to them by angels. The plan of their buildings, the style of their furniture, the pattern of their coats and pants, and the cut of their hair, is all regulated according to communications received from heaven by Mother Ann. I was gravely told by the first Elder, that the inhabitants of the other world were Shakers, and that they lived in Community the same as we did, but that they were more perfect.

THE DANCING MEETINGS

"At half-past seven P.M. on the dancing days, all the members retired to their separate rooms, where they sat in solemn silence, just gazing at the stove, until the silver tones of a small tea-bell gave the signal for them to assemble in the large hall. Thither they proceeded in perfect order and solemn silence. Each had on thin dancing-shoes; and on entering the door of the hall they walked on tip-toe, and took up their positions as follows: the brothers formed a rank on the right, and the sisters on the left, facing each other, about five feet apart. After all were in their proper places the chief Elder stepped into the center of the space, and gave an exhortation for about five minutes, concluding with an invitation to them all to 'go forth, old men, young men and maidens, and worship God with all their might in the dance.'

Accordingly they 'went forth,' the men stripping off their coats and remaining in their shirtsleeves. First they formed a procession and marched around the room at double-quick time, while four brothers and four sisters stood in the center singing for them. After marching in this manner until they got a little warm, they commenced dancing, and continued it until they were all pretty well tired. During the dance the sisters kept on one side, and the brothers on the other, and not a word was spoken by any of them. After they appeared to have had enough of this exercise, the Elder gave the signal to stop, when immediately each one took his or her place in an oblong circle formed around the room, and all waited to see if any one had received a 'gift,' that is, an inspiration to do something odd. Then two of the sisters would commence whirling round like a top, with their eyes shut; and continued this motion for about fifteen minutes; when they suddenly stopped and resumed their places, as steady as if they had never stirred. During the 'whirl' the members stood round like statues, looking on in solemn silence.

A MESSAGE FROM MOTHER ANN

"On some occasions when a sister had stopped her whirling, she would say, 'I have a communication to make;' when the head Eldress would step to her side and receive the communication, and then make known the nature of it to the company. The first message I heard was as follows: 'Mother Ann has sent two angels to inform us that a tribe of Indians has been round here two days, and want the brothers and sisters to take them in. They are outside the building there, looking in at the windows.' I shall never forget how I looked round at the windows, expecting to see the yellow faces, when this announcement was made; but I believe some of the old folks who eyed me, bit their lips and smiled. It caused no alarm to the rest, but the first Elder exhorted the brothers 'to take in the poor spirits and assist them to get salvation.' He afterward repeated more of what the angels had said, viz., 'that the Indians were a savage tribe who had all died before Columbus discovered America, and had been wandering about ever since. Mother Ann wanted them to be received into the meeting to-morrow night.' After this we dispersed to our separate bed-rooms, with the hope of having a future entertainment from the Indians.

INDIAN ORGIES

"The next dancing night we again assembled in the same manner as before, and went through the marching and dancing as usual; after which the hall doors were opened, and the Elder invited the Indians to come in. The doors were soon shut again, and one of the sisters (the same who received the original communication) informed us that she saw Indians all around and among the brothers and sisters. The Elder then urged upon the members the duty of 'taking them in.' Whereupon eight or nine sisters became possessed of the spirits of Indian squaws, and about six of the brethren became Indians. Then ensued a regular pow-wow, with whooping and yelling and strange antics, such as would require a Dickens to describe. The sisters and brothers squatted down on the floor together, Indian fashion, and the Elders and Eldresses endeavored to keep them asunder, telling the men they must be separated from the squaws, and otherwise instructing them in the rules of Shakerism. Some of the Indians then wanted some 'succotash,' which was soon brought them from the kitchen in two wooden dishes, and placed on the floor; when they commenced eating it with their fingers. These performances continued till about ten o'clock; then the chief Elder requested the Indians to go away, telling them they would find some one waiting to conduct them to the Shakers in the heavenly world. At this announcement the possessed men and women became themselves again, and all retired to rest.

"The above was the first exhibition of the kind that I witnessed, but it was a very trifling affair to what I afterward saw. To enable you to understand these scenes, I must give you as near as I can, the ideas the Shakers have of the other world. As I gathered from conversations with the Elder, and from his teaching and preaching at the meetings, it is as follows: Heaven is a Shaker Community on a very large scale. Every thing in it is spiritual. Jesus Christ is the head Elder, and Mother Ann the head Eldress. The buildings are large and splendid, being all of white marble. There are large orchards with all kinds of fruit. There are also very large gardens laid out in splendid style, with beautiful rivers flowing through them; but all is spiritual. Outside of this heaven the spirits of the departed wander about on the surface of the earth (which is the Shaker hell), till they are converted to Shakerism. Spirits are sent out from the aforesaid heaven on missionary tours, to preach to the wandering ones until they profess the faith, and then they are admitted into the heavenly Community.

SPIRITUAL PRESENTS

"At one of the meetings, after a due amount of marching and dancing, by which all the members had got pretty well excited, two or three sisters commenced whirling, which they continued to do for some time, and then stopped suddenly and revealed to us that Mother Ann was present at the meeting, and that she had brought a dozen baskets of spiritual fruit for her children; upon which the Elder invited all to go forth to the baskets in the center of the floor, and help themselves. Accordingly they all stepped forth and went through the various motions of taking fruit and eating it. You will wonder if I helped myself to the fruit, like the rest. No; I had not faith enough to see the baskets or the fruit; and you may think, perhaps, that I laughed at the scene; but in truth, I was so affected by the general gravity and the solemn faces I saw around me, that it was impossible for me to laugh.

"Other things as well as fruit were sometimes sent as presents, such as spiritual golden spectacles. These heavenly ornaments came in the same way as the fruit, and just as much could be seen of them. The first presents of this kind that were received during my residence there, came as follows: A sister whirled for some time; then stopped and informed the Eldress as usual that Mother Ann had sent a messenger with presents for some of her most faithful children. She then went through the action of handling the articles to the Eldress, at the same time mentioning what they were, and for whom. As near as I can remember, there was a pair of golden spectacles, a large eye-glass with a chain, and a casket of love for the Elder to distribute. The Eldress went through the act of putting the spectacles and chain upon the individuals they were intended for: and the Elder in like manner opened the casket and threw out the love by handsful, while all the members stretched out their hands to receive, and then pressed them to their bosoms."

2

A White Woman in the West

SOURCE: L.A. Kibbe, ed., "More Letters of Narcissa and Marcus Whitman," *Oregon Historical Quarterly,* Vol. XLVII, no. 1, March, 1946, pp. 29-33. Reprinted with permission of the Oregon Historical Society.

Tonight the water is again nearly to its winter height & threatens to overflow our garden & plantation & the streams are all swimming deep to the poor travelers. Today Brother Spalding went to Walla Walla to pay Mr. Pambrun a visit & tomorrow returns & Mr. P. & Mr. Ermatinger are expected to return with him. So you see I am not beyond the reach of visitors, if I am west of the Rocky M. Yes, & probably our house always will be a house of entertainment both for sick & well people. The boy sent from Vancouver in the spring to receive medical aid, seems to be recovering quite fast. Brother S. leaves for Clearwater Thursday, & then probably I shall be alone for a season, or without seeing company; but that is not the worst of it; he has so managed as to entice my better half to go with him & assist in building him a house.

When during his absence the cares and responsibility of this whole establishment on poor, febble me; & now do you not think it would be very sustaining to my heart to have you here to step in & put your shoulders too [?] especially attend to the worshipping part? Think of me 100 miles separated from my husband or one praying friend, surrounded with savages & crushed to the earth because there is so much to be done for these benighted minds. Sister Spaulding is often left just so. Husband has made a loud & bitter cry to the Board & Brother Augustus [?] W. & Levi Gray Esq. [?] Wheeler for labourers & ploughs & hoes to save these starving multitudes from an untimely grave. If you wish to know what his heart is you must obtain these letters & read them. & then I hope you will make up your mind to tell us when you are a coming to help in this glorious work. Our prospects both in temporal & spiritual things are very encouraging & I wish I could tell you more about us but cannot.

Our little daughter comes to her mother every now & then to be cheered with a smile or a kiss & to be taken up to rest for a few moments & then away she goes running about the room or out of doors, diverting herself with objects that attract her attention. A refreshing comfort she is to her parents in their solitary situation. While at Brother L last winter we had the inexpressible consolation of giving her away to God in that everlasting covenant of Baptism, so wisely provided for, to sustain a parent's heart in the laborious yet pleasing task of training a child for the Lord. I send you a small lock of her hair, which I beg you will accept, and let it remind you of your new relation west of the Rocky Mountains.

Now Dear Brother & Sister, farewell. If you cannot come to help us here, pray for us & make a business of it so we may feel the influence of your prayers on our own souls & see it on those around us. With love to all, & hoping to hear from you some day & of the prosperity of Zion, of an increasing missionary spirit in her wall that shall compel her to go forth into all the world & preach the gospel to every creature.

I am your affectionate sister
Narcissa Whitman

3

Mrs. Spalding's Diary

SOURCE: T.C. Elliot, ed., "The Coming of the White Women, 1836," *Letters and Journal of Narcissa Prentiss Whitman*

(Portland: Oregon Historical Society, 1937), pp. 12 and 24. Reprinted with permission of the Oregon Historical Society.

DIARY OF MRS. SPALDING

June 15th Fort Wm.* We are camped near the Fort, and shall probably remain here several days, as the Co. are to leave their waggons at this and make arrangements to transport their goods the remainder of the journey, on mules. It is very pleasant to fix my eyes, once more, upon a few buildings, several weeks have passed, since we have seen a building.

June 19th 1836 Fort Wm. Today is the sabbath, and the first we have spent in quietness and rest, since the 8th of May. This morning an elderly man (an Englishman) came to our camp, wishing to obtain a testament. Said he had seen but one, for four years – had once indulged a hope that he was a christian; but for several years had not enjoyed religious privileges – had been associated with ungodly men – neglected religious duties, and now feared he had no interest in the Saviour. I gave him a bible, which he received with great joy and thankfulness. Mr. S. in compliance with the request of the chief men of this expedition, met with the people under the shade of a few trees near our camp for religious service. A large assembly met, and were very attentive while Mr. S. made a few remarks upon the parable of the prodigal son. . . .

June 23rd . . . Our ride today has not been so fatigueing or lengthy as yesterday. Rode from nine o'clock A M until 1 o'clock P M in the same direction, south west as yesterday. Felt a calm and peaceful state of mind all day. Had sweet communion with him who delights to dwell with the humble & contrite in heart. Especial in the morning. I had a freedom in prayer for my beloved Parents. Earnestly desired that God would bless them in their declining years, & smoth their passage to the tomb; that in the absence of their early comforts, he would fill their souls with his more immediate presance, so that they may never have cause to regret the sacrifice they have made for his Name Sake. Father, accept the sacrifice & may they prove a blessing to the world.

24th Sab Eve. Our route today has been a very mountainous one. Came about eight miles. Painful as it is for me to journey on the Holy Sabbath, I have enjoyed notwithstanding a melting sense of the presence of that Being who has promised to be "with his deciples always." Found it good to rest my soul on this today. Although I can truly say "my soul thirsts yea even faints for the courts of my God," the word of his saints below; the privation has been made good to me by a rich supply from the fountain head God, the

*More generally known as Fort Laramie.

Father, Son & Holy Ghost. O blessed blessed privaledge, that such a sinner *as I* may have access to a mercy seat through such a Saviour as Jesus Christ. It is good to feel that he is all I want, & all my righteousness, & if I had a thousand lives I would give them all to him. I long to be more like him, to possess more of his meek Spirit.

4

A Female Missionary

SOURCE: Emily C. Judson, *Memoir of Sarah B. Judson of the American Mission in Burmah* (New York: Sheldon & Co., 1868), 18-23.

CHAPTER II
A New Life

"Till David touches his sacred lyre,
In silence lay the unbreathing wire;
But when he swept its chords along,
Even angels stooped to hear the song.
So sleeps the soul till Thou, oh Lord!
Shall deign to touch its lifeless chord –
Till waked by Thee, its breath shall rise,
In music, worthy of the skies."

Moore.

Of Sarah's early religious impressions I have learned but little, except that they were like those of most thoughtful children, sometimes strong, but always evanescent. Now she would appear excessively alarmed at the thought of death, and now seem utterly forgetful of her mortality; at one moment we find her distressed and tearful, and in the next all happiness, as though the earth were one vast flower, and she a butterfly, moulded expressly to sip its sweets. But this could not continue, and at the age of sixteen there came a change – a spirit-birth. The "lifeless chord" was touched at last, and angels bent to hear the music. It was a melody which angels could appreciate; but it may yet find an echo in many a human bosom.

"I have this day," (June 4, 1820,) "in the presence of the world, the holy angels, and the omniscient God, publicly manifested my determination to forsake the objects of earth, and live, henceforth, for Heaven. What have I done? Do I realize the importance of the step I have taken? Oh, my Saviour! I am weak, and the heart of man is deceitful; but I do hope in thy mercy. Thou didst die even for the chief of sinners, and I know thou wilt pardon all who come to thee believing. Take me, dear Saviour, all sinful, unworthy as I am – do with me what thou wilt, but oh! preserve me from wounding thy precious cause!

"I have to-day wept tears of pity, I can almost say anguish, at the stupidity of sinners. Inhabitants of a Christian country, the word of God in their hands; the mild, compassionate Saviour waiting to receive them; the Spirit striving, and yet they bent upon their own destruction. But have I not more reason to be astonished and weep at my own coldness – I who have *felt* that Jesus bled and died, even for *my* sins; *I wander* from the way of life! 'Turn me, oh God, and I shall be turned, draw me, and I shall run after thee.'

"To-day I had a long and serious conversation with my beloved sister Harriet. Sweet child! she wept when I told her of her dangerous state. I reminded her of the shortness of time, the certainty of death, the value of the soul, and the terrors of the Day of Judgment; and she appeared greatly distressed. But alas! I have reason to fear that her emotions were of a different nature from those I would fain excite. I know that she loves me tenderly, and apprehensions of an eternal separation cannot fail to give her pain. Oh! that the Holy Spirit might convince her, and convince my other sisters, and brothers, of the importance of seeking an interest in the Saviour."

Behold the little missionary! her youthful feet tremblingly leaving their first impressions on the path of life, seizing upon the work nearest her, laboring and praying in the family circle – the true charity which "begins at home," and ends with the boundaries of the universe. But even then she did not think of home *merely;* and we may well believe that the shadow of her future life was, at that early period, flung back upon her spirit.

"It is my ardent desire," she writes to a friend, "that the glorious work of reformation may extend, 'till every knee shall bow' to the living God. For this expected, this promised era, let us pray earnestly, unceasingly, and with faith. How can I be so inactive, when I know that thousands are perishing in this land of grace; and millions, in other lands, are, at this very moment, kneeling before senseless idols."

But to return to the journal: a single sheet of paper folded as a little book, and the last that she ever kept. In less than a month after her baptism, she says: "While I have this day had the privilege of worshipping the true God in solemnity, I have been pained by thinking of those who have never heard the sound of the gospel. When will the time come that the poor heathen, now bowing to idols, shall own the living and true God? Dear Saviour, haste to spread the knowledge of thy dying love to earth's remotest bounds!"

"I have just completed the perusal of the life of Samuel J. Mills; and never shall I forget the emotions of my heart, while following thus the footsteps of this devoted missionary. I have almost caught his spirit, and been ready to exclaim: Oh! that I, too, could suffer privations, hardships, and discouragements, and even find a watery grave, for the sake of bearing the news of salvation to the poor heathen! Then, I have checked myself in the wild, unreasonable wish. Sinners perishing all around me, and I, an ignorant, weak, faithless creature, almost panting to tell the far *heathen* of Christ! Surely, this is wrong. I will no longer indulge the vain, foolish wish, but endeavour to be useful in the position Providence has placed me. I can pray for deluded idolaters, and for those who labour among them; and this is a privilege indeed."

Ah, meek, true-hearted one! Such prayers as thine, through Him who never turns away from humble prayers, are the strength of many a human hand; and God grant that their pure incense may ever circle round the lone missionary of the Cross, and buoy up his spirit in the midst of toil, and privations, and the bitter, biting ingratitude of those who cannot understand the good it brings. Blessings on thy sweet, beautiful girlhood! – or blessings rather on its memories; for no blessings of ours can reach thee now, bright, sainted spirit that thou art! But the warmth, the humility, the deep devotedness, the whole graceful symmetry of thy lovely character – may it never be lost upon thy fair countrywomen!

With one more extract, the little journal must be closed. "When, dear Redeemer, when shall I be 'free from this body of sin and death?' I long to sit forever at thy feet, and gaze upon thy face. But, perhaps, before this happiness is mine, many a sorrowful, sinful day must be passed in this deceitful world. If so, I must not be impatient. Heaven is the place that I most desire; and should I *ever* be welcomed to its bliss, I shall be entirely satisfied. I ask only a heart to serve God, and labour for Him; and then, after living many years in this world, if I be admitted to the joys of heaven, sweet will be my rest."

Another glimpse of the manner in which Sarah, young as she was, commenced her "new life," may be gained, through the following to a friend. It is given as an apology for having neglected letter-writing. "I am deeply engaged in my studies, and my other avocations are numerous and imperious. Besides, I have been for six weeks past employed with a gentleman, upon the evidences of the soul's immortality, independent of the Scriptures. You may well believe that this subject has engrossed a large portion of my thoughts; and we have not yet finished the discussion."

5

Transcendent Woman

SOURCE: Ralph Waldo Emerson, "Woman," in *Miscellanies* (Boston, New York, and Cambridge: Harvard University Press, 1893), pp. 344-47 and 351.

We may ask, to be sure, – Why need you vote? If new power is here, of a character which solves old tough questions, which puts me and all the rest in the wrong, tries and condemns our religion, customs, laws, and opens new careers to our young receptive men and women, you can well leave voting to the old dead people. Those whom you teach, and those whom you half teach, will fast enough make themselves considered and strong with their new insight, and votes will follow from all the dull.

The objection to their voting is the same as is urged, in the lobbies of legislatures, against clergymen who take an active part in politics; – that if they are good clergymen they are unacquainted with the expediencies of politics, and if they become good politicians they are worse clergymen. So of women, that they cannot enter this arena without being contaminated and unsexed.

• • • • •

But the starry crown of woman is in the power of her affection and sentiment, and the infinite enlargements to which they lead. Beautiful is the passion of love, painter and adorner of youth and early life: but who suspects, in its blushes and tremors, what tragedies, heroisms and immortalities are beyond it? The passion, with all its grace and poetry, is profane to that which follows it. All these affections are only introductory to that which is beyond, and to that which is sublime.

We men have no right to say it, but the omnipotence of Eve is in humility. The instincts of mankind have drawn the Virgin Mother –

> "Created beings all in lowliness
> Surpassing, as in height above them all."

This is the Divine Person whom Dante and Milton saw in vision. This is the victory of Griselda, her supreme humility. And it is when love has reached this height that all our pretty rhetoric begins to have meaning. When we see that, it adds to the soul a new soul, it is honey in the mouth, music in the ear and balsam in the heart.

> "Far have I clambered in my mind,
> But nought so great as Love I find.
> What is thy tent, where dost thou dwell?
>
> 'My mansion is humility,
> Heaven's vastest capability.'
>
> The further it doth downward tend,
> The higher up it doth ascend."

The first thing men think of, when they love, is to exhibit their usefulness and advantages to the object of their affection. Women make light of these, asking only love. They wish it to be an exchange of nobleness.

There is much in their nature, much in their social position which gives them a certain power of divination. And women know, at first sight, the characters of those with whom they converse. There is much that tends to give them a religious height which men do not attain. Their sequestration from affairs and from the injury to the moral sense which affairs often inflict, aids this. And in every remarkable religious development in the world, women have taken a leading part. It is very curious that in the East, where Woman occupies, nationally, a lower sphere, where the laws resist the education and emancipation of women, – in the Mohammedan faith, Woman yet occupies the same leading position, as a prophetess, that she has among the ancient Greeks, or among the Hebrews, or among the Saxons. This power, this religious character, is everywhere to be remarked in them.

The action of society is progressive. In barbarous society the position of women is always low – in the Eastern nations lower than in the West. "When a daughter is born," says the Shiking, the old Sacred Book of China, "she sleeps on the ground, she is clothed with a wrapper, she plays with a tile; she is incapable of evil or of good." And something like that position, in all low society, is the position of woman; because, as before remarked, she is herself its civilizer. With the advancements of society the position and influence of woman bring her strength or her faults into light. In modern times, three or four conspicuous instrumentalities may be marked. After the deification of Woman in the Catholic Church, in the sixteenth or seventeenth century, – when her religious nature gave her, of course, new importance, – the Quakers have the honor of having first established, in their discipline, the equality in the sexes. It is even more perfect in the later sect of the Shakers, wherein no business is broached or counselled without the intervention of one elder and one elderess.

A second epoch for Woman was in France, – entirely civil; the change of sentiment from a rude to a polite character, in the age of Louis XIV., – commonly dated from the building of the Hôtel de Rambouillet. I think another important step was made by the doctrine of Swedenborg, a sublime genius who gave a scientific exposition of the part played severally by man and woman in the world, and showed the difference of sex to run through nature and through thought. Of all Christian sects this is at this moment the most vital and aggressive.

Another step was the effect of the action of the age in the antagonism to Slavery. It was easy to enlist Woman in this; it was impossible not to enlist her. But that Cause turned out to be a great scholar. He was a terrible metaphysician. He was a jurist, a poet, a divine. Was never a University of Oxford or Göttingen that made such students. It took a man from the plough and made him acute, eloquent, and wise, to the silencing of the doctors. There was nothing it did not pry into, no right it did not explore, no wrong it did not expose. And it has, among its other effects, given Woman a feeling of public duty and an added self-respect.

One truth leads in another by the hand; one right is an accession of strength to take more. And the times are marked by the new attitude of Woman; urging, by argument and by association, her rights of all kinds, – in short, to one-half of the world; – as the right to education, to avenues of employment, to equal rights of property, to equal rights in marriage, to the exercise of the professions and of suffrage.

6

Women as Souls

SOURCE: Sarah Margaret Fuller Ossoli, *Woman in the Nineteenth Century and Kindred Papers Relating to the Sphere, Condition and Duties of Women*, Arthur B. Fuller, ed. (Boston: J.P. Jowett & Co.; New York: Sheldon, Lamport & Co., 1855), pp. 335-37.

EDUCATE MEN AND WOMEN AS SOULS

Had Christendom but been true to its standard, while accommodating its modes of operation to the calls of successive times, Woman would now have not only equal *power* with Man, – for of that omnipotent nature will never suffer her to be defrauded, – but a *chartered* power, too fully recognized to be abused. Indeed, all that is wanting is, that Man should prove his own freedom by making her free. Let him abandon conventional restriction, as a vestige of that Oriental barbarity which confined Woman to a seraglio. Let him trust her entirely, and give her every privilege already acquired for himself, – elective franchise, tenure of property, liberty to speak in public assemblies, &c.

Nature has pointed out her ordinary sphere by the circumstances of her physical existence. She cannot wander far. If here and there the gods send their missives through women as through men, let them speak without remonstrance. In no age have men been able wholly to hinder them. A Deborah must always be a spiritual mother in Israel. A Corinna may be excluded from the Olympic games, yet all men will hear her song, and a Pindar sit at her feet. It is Man's fault that there ever were Aspasias and Ninons. These exquisite forms were intended for the shrines of virtue.

Neither need men fear to lose their domestic deities. Woman is born for love, and it is impossible to turn her from seeking it. Men should deserve her love as an inheritance, rather than seize and guard it like a prey. Were they noble, they would strive rather not to be loved too much, and to turn her from idolatry to the true, the only Love. Then, children of one Father, they could not err nor misconceive one another.

Society is now so complex, that it is no longer possible to educate Woman merely as Woman; the tasks which come to her hand are so various, and so large a proportion of women are thrown entirely upon their own resources. I admit that this is not their state of perfect development; but it seems as if Heaven, having so long issued its edict in poetry and religion without securing intelligent obedience, now commanded the world in prose to take a high and rational view. The lesson reads to me thus: –

Sex, like rank, wealth, beauty, or talent, is but an accident of birth. As you would not educate a soul to be an aristocrat, so do not to be a woman. A general regard to her usual sphere is dictated in the economy of nature. you need never enforce these provisions rigorously. Achilles had long plied the distaff as a princess; yet, at first sight of a sword, he seized it. So with Woman; one hour of love would teach her more of her proper relations than all your formulas and conventions. Express your views, men, of what you *seek* in women; thus best do you give them laws. Learn, women, what you should *demand* of men; thus only can they become themselves. Turn both from the contemplation of what is merely phenomenal in your existence, to your permanent life as souls. Man, do not prescribe how the Divine shall display itself in Woman. Woman, do not expect to see all of God in Man. Fellow-pilgrims and helpmeets are ye, Apollo and Diana, twins of one heavenly birth, both beneficient, and both armed. Man, fear not to yield to Woman's hand both the quiver and the lyre; for if her urn be filled with light, she will use both to the glory of God. There is but one doctrine for ye both, and that is the doctrine of the SOUL.

7

What Has Christianity Done for Women?

SOURCE: Elizabeth Cady Stanton, *Eighty Years and More – 1815-1897: Reminiscences of Elizabeth Cady Stanton* (London: T. Fisher Unwin, 1898), pp. 380-83.

Miss Anthony left in December, 1884, for Washington, and I went to work on an article for the *North American Review*, entitled, "What has Christianity done for Women?" I took the ground that woman was not indebted to any form of religion for the liberty she now enjoys, but that, on the contrary, the religious element in her nature had always been perverted for her complete subjection. Bishop Spaulding, in the same issue of the *Review*, took the opposite ground, but I did not feel that he answered my points.

In January, 1885, my niece Mrs. Baldwin and I went to Washington to attend the Annual Convention of the National Woman Suffrage Association. It was held in the Unitarian church on the 20th, 21st, and 22d days of that month, and went off with great success, as did the usual reception given by Mrs. Spofford at the Riggs House. This dear friend, one of our most ardent coadjutors, always made the annual convention a time for many social enjoyments. The main feature in this convention was the attempt to pass the following resolutions:

"WHEREAS, The dogmas incorporated in religious creeds derived from Judaism, teaching that woman was an after-thought in the creation, her sex a misfortune, marriage a condition of subordination, and maternity a curse, are contrary to the law of God (as revealed in nature), and to the precepts of Christ, and,

"WHEREAS, These dogmas are an insidious poison, sapping the vitality of our civilization, blighting woman, and, through her, paralyzing humanity; therefore be it

"*Resolved*, That we call on the Christian ministry, as leaders of thought, to teach and enforce the fundamental idea of creation, that man was made in the image of God, male and female, and given equal rights over the earth, but none over each other. And, furthermore, we ask their recognition of the scriptural declaration that, in the Christian religion, there is neither male nor female, bond nor free, but all are one in Christ Jesus."

As chairman of the committee I presented a series of resolutions, impeaching the Christian theology – as well as all other forms of religion, for their degrading teachings in regard to woman – which the majority of the committee thought too strong and pointed, and, after much deliberation, they substituted the above, handing over to the Jews what I had laid at the door of the Christians. They thought they had so sugar-coated my ideas that the resolutions would pass without discussion. But some Jews in the convention promptly repudiated this impression of their faith and precipitated the very discussion I desired, but which our more politic friends would fain have avoided.

From the time of the decade meeting in Rochester, in 1878, Matilda Joslyn Gage, Edward M. Davis, and I had sedulously labored to rouse women to a realization of their degraded position in the Church, and presented resolutions at every annual convention for that purpose. But they were either suppressed or so amended as to be meaningless. The resolutions of the annual convention of 1885, tame as they are, got into print and roused the ire of the clergy, and upon the following Sunday, Dr. Patton of Howard University preached a sermon on "Woman and Skepticism," in which he unequivocally took the ground that freedom for woman led to skepticism and immorality. He illustrated his position by pointing to Hypatia, Mary Wollstonecraft, Frances Wright, George Eliot, Harriet Martineau, Mme. Roland, Frances Power Cobbe, and Victoria Woodhull. He made a grave mistake in the last names mentioned, as Mrs. Woodhull was a devout believer in the Christian religion, and surely anyone conversant with Miss Cobbe's writings would never accuse her of skepticism. His sermon was received with intense indignation, even by the women of his own congregation. When he found what a whirlwind he had started, he tried to shift his position and explain away much that he had said. We asked him to let us have the sermon for publication, that we might not do him injustice. But as he contradicted himself flatly in trying to restate his discourse, and refused to let us see his sermon, those who heard him were disgusted with his sophistry and tergiversation.

However, our labors in this direction are having an effect. Women are now making their attacks on the Church all along the line. They are demanding their right to be ordained as ministers, elders, deacons, and to be received as delegates in all the ecclesiastical convocations. At last they ask of the Church just what they have asked of the State for the last half century – perfect equality – and the clergy, as a body, are quite as hostile to their demands as the statesmen.

8

The Spirit of Woman

SOURCE: Eliza W. Farnham, *Woman and Her Era*, Vol. II. (New York: A.J. Davis & Co., 1864), pp. 392-95.

Well, what is spiritual development? How can I tell you? Will you tell me what gravitation is? What is the inner-life? Will you tell me what Chemical Affinity is? Gravitation draws the lesser to the greater, you inform me. Yes, and spiritual development draws the lesser toward the greater life – the poor, thin, lean souls, to the great, rich, strong ones, and these to the Great Soul. Still your question remains unanswered, and mine also. Chemical affinity draws atoms together, and binds them there, till a stronger one dissolves their union. Yes, and spiritual development draws human souls together. They are attracted and cohere in proportion as this experience has descended into them – the savages least of all, the barbarians less, Men more – Women most. Still our questions stand.

Shall I presume to answer what seems so nearly unanswerable? If I do, it is with a humility which I hope may exempt the almost inevitable failure from harsh criticism, and in the hope of receiving as well as giving a little help.

"We acknowledge spiritual faculties," says some impatient reader, "and spiritual development means, of course, their unfolding into activity in the life. That is all. So that we become religious, or moral, or good, or affectionate, where before we were the opposite of these. Nothing is more easily stated." Pardon me. Spiritual development does mean these surely, or something like them, but it also means more. These are features of spiritual development, but they are not *it.* Forehead, nose and mouth do not make a face. They are indispensable to it; but the face is not complete because they are there. There are good people who are scarcely more spiritual than their maternal cows, or patient oxen. There are moral people who have no more of the odor of spirituality about them, than the cabbage has of the rose. There are affectionate people, but there are also affectionate quadrupeds – dogs for instance, whose attachments outlive those of many human friends. Nay, there are religious persons – church-members of years' standing, of stainless records, who have no more spirituality than lamp-posts.

Spirituality means something more than these. It includes them as parts of its completeness; where it is they must be; but it is the higher element – the event, which reduces them all, and causes each individual trait to be forgotten in its own universal sufficiency. It is the development of the spiritual faculties, but it is also the establishment of the one sovereignty whose reign over the life is Order, and Harmony, and Peace. It is the alliance of the being with the Divine, and sympathy and practical unity with His Purposes; the opening of communication between the Great Fountain and the little spring whose sealed margin its flowing current has passed, but will now feed with the eternal waters. It is the rising of a sun upon the soul, which is not to be clouded, or clouded only for moments, that vanish away as the shadow of an April vapor from the landscape – the shadow less felt than the enhanced brightness and warmth following it.

The spiritual is the Creative power in the soul of Man or Woman. It is this by virtue of its oneness with the Great Artist and Creator. It never lacks resource – is not daunted by any array of circumstances – for is not the Infinite its all-sufficing support: knows no despair, sees no failure; knows that failure is impossible, because its aims are one with the Divine aims, which cannot fail. Its object is growth, real growth into the character of the Divine, whether for self or another – not the furtherance of a creed, a system, a belief, a form, a ritual, but the opening of the inner faculties to the reception and love of absolute Truth; the inspiration of all the powers to serve humanity in the pure spirit of actual Love, of which Truth is the body; and of this effort it knows that success is the unfailing result, as growth from germination, maturity from bloom.

This is perhaps the broadest manifest distinction to be taken between spiritual development and action and those of any other branch of our natural tree. The passions have their objects, but often fail in the effort to grasp them; the affections strive for what they desire, but the most earnest and persistent striving does not always win: the intellect defines its aims, and moves toward them, giving all its power, subtilety, stratagem and skill to their achievement; not unfrequently to find itself foiled at the last step. And when failure comes, these currents regurgitate upon their centers, and create bitterness, confusion, discord and despair in those desolate places. It is disappointment, the blight against which the human soul utters its most articulate and universal cry of complaint.

But the spiritual nature knows no such experience. Its aim is expansion, and the simplest form of pure earnest desire secures that. "Ask, and it *shall* be given; seek, and ye *shall* find. Knock, and it *shall* be opened unto you." Truer language could not be employed to describe the privileges of the spiritually developed. What shall be given? Not meat and raiment, even to the most deserving; martyrs have perished by the road-side, lacking them. What shall the seeker find? Not riches, power or ease, however he may merit them; the noblest have so seldom enjoyed these, that their possession has, through all the ages, been reckoned almost a reproach even to the good – a proof of some moral defect in the soul – presumptive testimony to some complicity with the unwholesome powers, to whose magazine of resources they are assumed to belong. They are not the current certificates of saintliness. What door shall be opened? Not those of worldly privilege, comfort or advancement. These "open but to golden keys." You knock there in vain, do you *but* knock. No hand but your own will open to you.

But of all that may be asked or sought by the spirit for its help, growth, and more perfect action, nothing is uncertain as to its coming; nothing will be withheld. The universe is its storehouse, which the more it is drawn upon, is filled the more for its service; and its great portal of privilege will swing back to the humblest hand that presses for admission there. When the spirit acts sovereignly, it employs the whole nature harmoniously. Sense, passion, affection, intellect, have all and each their sufficient work; when the spirit is satisfied, they too are filled and content. Its perfect sovereignty is – not in their extinction; for it is cherishing, never destructive toward anything that exists – but in their cheerful abdication in its favor. They forget themselves. Hunger and thirst, cold and nakedness are impossible as experiences in this life. They may be incidents in its career – threads in the fair web it is weaving day by day, but not the web itself.

9

The Worship of Mary

SOURCE: Orestes A. Brown, *The Works of Orestes A. Brown*, Vol. XIII (New York: AMS Press, 1966), pp. 82-85. Reprinted by permission.

There are two ways in which the love and service of Mary will contribute to redeem society and restore Christian purity, – the one the natural influence of such love and service on the heart of her worshippers, and the other the graces which in requital she obtains from her Son and bestows upon her clients. Mary is the mother of chaste love. The nature of love is always to unite the heart to the object loved, to become one with it, and as far as possible to become it. Love always makes us like the beloved, and we always become like the object we really and sincerely worship. If we may say, Like worshippers, like gods, we may with equal truth say, Like gods, like worshippers. The love of Mary tends naturally, from the nature of all love, to unite us to her by a virtue kindred to her own. We cannot love her, dwell constantly on her merits, on her excellences, her glories, without being constantly led to imitate her virtues, to love and strive after her perfect purity, her deep humility, her profound submission, and her unreserved obedience. Her love checks all lawlessness of the affections, all turbulence of the passions, all perturbation of the senses, fills the heart with sweet peace and a serene joy, restores to the soul its self-command, and maintains perfect order and tranquillity within. Something of this effect is produced whenever we love any truly virtuous person. Our novelists have marked it, and on the strength of it seek to reform the wild and graceless youth by inspiring in his heart a sincere love for a pure and virtuous woman; and the most dissolute are restrained, their turbulence is calmed, their impure desires are repressed, in the presence of true virtue. If this is so when the beloved is but an ordinary mortal, how much more when the beloved, the one with whom we commune, and whose virtues we reverence and long to possess, is Mary, the mother of God, the simplest and lowliest of handmaidens, but surpassing in true beauty, loveliness, and worth all the other creatures of God!

When the type of female dignity and excellence admired is that of an Aspasia, a Lamia, a Phryne, a Ninon de l'Enclos, society is not only already corrupt, but is continually becoming more corrupt. So when the type of female worth and excellence, the ideal of woman, is Mary, society is not only in some degree virtuous, but must be continually rising to sublimer excellence, to more heroic sanctity. The advantage of having Mary always before the minds and hearts of our daughters, as their model in humility, purity, sweetness, and obedience, in simplicity, modesty, and love, is not easily estimated. Trained up in the love and imitation of her virtues, they are trained to be wives and mothers, or holy virgins, spouses of Jesus Christ, sisters of the afflicted, and mothers of the poor. The sentimentalists of the day tell us that it is woman's mission to redeem society from its present corruption, and we believe it, though not in their sense, or for their reasons. Woman has generally retained more of Catholic faith and morality than has in these evil times been retained by the other sex, and is more open to good impressions, or rather, offers fewer obstacles to the operations of grace. During the worst times in France, when religion was abolished, when the churches were desecrated, the clergy massacred, and the profane rites of the impure Venus were revived, the great majority of the women of France retained their faith, and cherished the worship of the Virgin. We have no sympathy with those who make woman an idol, and clamor for what they call "woman's rights," but we honor woman, and depend on her, under God, to preserve and diffuse Catholic morality in the family, and if in the family, then in the state. There is always hope for society as long as woman remains believing and chaste, and nothing will contribute so much to her remaining so, as having the Blessed Virgin presented to her from the first dawn of her affections as her mother, her queen, her sweet lady, her type of womanhood, a model which it must be the unremitting labor of her life to copy.

Undoubtedly the worship of Mary is restricted to Catholics, and to those Catholics not undeserving of the name; but this is no objection to our general conclusion. We are too apt to forget that the church is in the world, and that it is through her that society is redeemed, – too apt to forget that the quiet and unobtrusive virtues of Catholics, living in the midst of a hostile world, are always powerful in their operations on that world; and that the world is converted, not by the direct efforts which we make to convert it, but by the efforts we make to live ourselves as good Catholics, and to save our own souls. The little handful of sincere and devout Catholics, the little family of sincere and earnest clients of Mary, seeking to imitate her virtues in their own little community, are as leaven hidden in three measures of meal. Virtue goes forth from them, diffuses itself on all sides, till the whole is leavened. No matter how small the number, the fact that even some keep alive in the community the love and veneration of Mary, the true ideal of womanhood, the true patroness of the Christian family, the mother of chaste love, adorned with all the virtues, and to whom the Holy Ghost says, "Thou art all beautiful, my dove," must have a redeeming effect on the whole community, and sooner or later must banish impurity, and revive the love of holy purity and reverence for Catholic morality.

For, in the second place, the worship of Mary is profitable, not only by the subjective effect it has upon her lovers, but also by the blessings she obtains for them, and, at their solicitation, for others. In these later times we have almost lost sight of religion in its objective character. The world has ceased to believe in the Real Presence; it denies the whole sacramental character of Christianity, and laughs at us when we speak of any sacrament as having any virtue not derived from the faith and virtue of the recipient. The whole non-Catholic world makes religion a purely subjective affair, and deduces all its truth from the mind, and all its efficacy from the heart, that accepts and cherishes it, so that even in religion, which is a binding of man anew to God, man is every thing, and God is nothing. At bottom that world is atheistical, at best Epicurean. It either denies God altogether, or excludes him from all care of the world he has created. It has no understanding of his providence, no belief in his abiding presence with his creatures, or his free and tender providence in their behalf. Faith it assumes is profitable only in its subjective operations, prayer only in its natural effect on the mind and heart of him who prays, and love only in its natural effect on the affections of the lover. This cold and atheistical philosophy is the enlightenment, the progress, of our age. But we who are Christians know that it is false; we know that God is very near unto every one of us, is ever free to help us, and that there is nothing that he will not do for them that love him truly, sincerely, and confide in him, and in him only.

Mary is the channel through which her divine Son dispenses all his graces and blessings to us, and he loves and delights to load with his favors all who love and honor her. Thus to love and serve her is the way to secure his favor, and to obtain those graces which we need to resist the workings of concupiscence, and to maintain the purity of our souls, and of our bodies, which are the temple of God. She says, "I love them that love me," and we cannot doubt that she will favor with her always successful intercession those whom she loves. She will obtain grace for us to keep ourselves chaste, and will in requital of our love to her obtain graces even for those without, that they may be brought in and healed of their wounds and putrefying sores. So that under either point of view the love and worship of Mary, the mother of God, a mother yet a virgin, always a virgin, virgin most pure, most holy, most humble, most amiable, most loving, most merciful, most faithful, most powerful, cannot fail to enable us to overcome the terrible impurity of our age, and to attain to the virtues now most needed for our own individual salvation, and for the safety of society.

In this view of the case, we must feel that nothing is more important than the cultivation of the love and worship of Mary. She is our life, our sweetness, our hope, and we must suffer no sneers of those without, no profane babblings about "Mariolatry," to move us, or in the least deter us from giving our hearts to Mary. We must fly to her protection as the child flies to its mother, and seek our safety and our consolation in her love, in her maternal embrace. We are safe only as we repose our heads upon her bosom, and draw nourishment from her breasts. The world lieth in wickedness, festering in moral corruption, and it is a shame to name the vices and iniquity which everywhere abound. Hardly has childhood blossomed into youth, before it withers into old age. We have no youth, we have only infancy and worn-out manhood. What is to become of us? Our help is in thee, sweet Mother, and we fly to thy protection, and, O, protect us, thy children, and save us from the evil communications of this world, lost to virtue, and enslaved to the enemy of our souls!

10

His and Hers Religion

SOURCE: Charlotte Perkins Stetson Gilman, *His Religion and Hers: A Study of the Faith of our Fathers and the Work of our Mothers*, 1923, pp. 276-81. Courtesy of Appleton-Century-Crofts, Educational Division, Meredith Corporation.

It has been possible for the minds of men to "believe" in Jesus and keep on fighting just the same. Women, so believing, became submissive and obedient. Christianity has been an invaluable religion for women and slaves, as Nietzsche has so violently shown, but this does not carry the reproach he intended. The women and the slaves were higher human types by far than that apotheosis of the male, the "great blond beast" he so extolled.

There is one general hope before the lazy, the weak, the irresponsible, in regard to the coming change of view: namely, that it *is* coming. But whether our own children and grandchildren will be benefited much, depends on us, now; on our immediate conduct. There are two lines of action before us, both indispensable; one in our separate minds, the other in our united conduct. The change in our minds is not altogether easy. After the main position is accepted, there follows a moving of mental furniture as extensive as can well be imagined.

Before those who wish to preach the life-based religion three wide fields are open. There are the "doctrines," large, reliable, provable truths, bringing boundless hope as well as peace and comfort. There are the explanations, applying these truths to show us what has made our troubles in the past and will make our joy in the future. And there is the great new province of social research, now beginning to be studied, that we may learn how most safely, surely, and rapidly to help the world.

Are there in such teaching any disadvantages?

Women are only half the world. What have men to fear, to fight, in such reversal of what they have long held dear?

Nothing, unless a man should fear and fight his mother; there is no one else coming. It is the mother who is rising, whose deep, sweet current of uplifting love is to pour forward into service. The limitation of her love ana service to the home has given us our kitchen-economics, our nursery-ethics, our parlor-manners. Her powers freed from those limits, will lift the world. Our general sentiment about the mother, our underlying worship of the mother will at last be justified when she steps forward into the larger motherhood of the world, her world as much as man's.

The man does lose sex supremacy. It never belonged to him. His period of mastership has been marked too blackly with the crimes and diseases of that usurpation, to be regretted. But he does not lose his race supremacy, a far higher thing. It will be generations yet before women can cease to depend on men for service, help, and teaching in all the thousand lines of world-service. Men have made the world, men are the world, in this sense, with room for all the pride they need. That honest pride in real human accomplishment ought to enable them to bear dissociation of their achievements from their sex.

Why should men dread to face a world more human and less sexual? Will not the wide and steady increase of human happiness, human beauty, human power, and human love make up to them for the kind of world behind us? Are men, in truth, so satisfied with the kind of women they have made? Do they not already know well the blessing of that human affection we call friendship, "passing the love of women"?

It is true that life looks dull to them without its struggling and fighting; but when the morbid impulse which produces it is no longer felt, the warfare will not be missed. Moreover, if fighting must be had, there is room for all the furious energy of every man alive in resisting the relentless grip of the "Dead Hand," the huge, heavy, driving pressure of the past.

Our natural impulses are good, and need no harsh suppression, but our unnatural impulses, the wrong habits of ages, urging us to all manner of evil conduct – these are enemies indeed. Whoso ruleth his ancestors' spirit is greater than he that taketh a city.

The highest chivalry ever taught is needed now to reach the hand of patient helpfulness to the half-grown woman creature as she strives toward humanness. The virtues dearest to men – truth, courage, justice – must be taught to women. There is before us no overturning, no attempt at a new domination of women over men. The woman, acknowledging her backwardness, has to face exertion quite outside her old experience, in the long upward road. She has to grow, to reach his height; man has to wait and help her on. It is not a contest between them, but a recognition of a common hope, a common power, a common duty.

Men are going to lose a servant, a victim, a vampire, a "horse-leech's daughter, crying, 'Give! Give'!" They will gain a woman more worth loving than they have ever known.

If we can assume any large group of people as affected strongly by this new attitude in religion, or scattered small groups here and there, what conduct should be urged upon them? In what respects would it differ from that now practised by progressive thinkers in any religion?

In many respects it would not differ. Every legitimate step toward race-improvement already started could be pushed forward with new hope and new vigor. The world about us is sprouting like a garden in the spring, with all manner of undertakings which tend to help us on. But these, at present, are jumbled without proportion or relation, earnest persons pushing their favored benefit or reform beside or against others, with small knowledge of what it is they are trying to improve.

Charity, that social osmosis by which withheld nutrition has forced its way through diseased tissues of the body politic, still diverts simple minds from such change in industrial relationship as would make all charity needless. And religion, straddling between its old belief that poverty was almost a virtue and its new perception that it is almost a crime, both helps and hinders.

To clarify and relate these efforts we must seek the aid of social experts, as men employ business experts to advise industrial improvements. Sociology is a new study; we have so recently become conscious of our large relationship that it is too soon to look for an established science. But earnest students will find no great difficulty in ascertaining enough general facts, enough proven processes, to begin on.

No one needs special knowledge to see the basic needs of mere physical humanity, as good air, good food, good housing, good clothing, good education, and good employment.